PRAISE FOR *October Men*

"*October Men,* like all Roger Kahn's books, flows like a river after spring rain. The steady mixture of history, humor, and drama makes it a fast read, but the depth of historical research and psychological analysis of character should give it a place in every baseball fan's permanent collection." —*The Dallas Morning News*

"Kahn, as always, captures the personalities of this wild group with a grittiness that you don't find in today's environment of tight-lipped, highly controlled management of team news.... Kahn's best moments, though, remain the volatile collisions, especially the Martin meltdown that led to his firing." —*Chicago Tribune*

"*October Men* seems effortlessly written, like all of Mr. Kahn's books.... A compelling story." —*The Wall Street Journal*

"Good news for fans of the game, and of words."
—*The Washington Post*

"Both insightful and compelling...With crisp, smart writing, he makes the case that the team was a less-than-harmonic convergence." —*Chicago Sun-Times*

"Yankee-haters—and there are plenty of them out there—might long since have had enough of this sort of folklore. But a quarter century seems about right for such a skilled historian and raconteur to look back and put one of the great group of pinstriped characters in proper perspective." —*The Toronto Star*

"Unforgettable... [*October Men*] stands out among recent serious baseball writing." —*Weekly Standard*

OCTOBER MEN

▼

NONFICTION

The Head Game: Baseball Seen from the Pitcher's Mound, 2000

A Flame of Pure Fire: Jack Dempsey and the Roaring '20s, 1999

Memories of Summer, 1997

The Era, 1993

Games We Used to Play, 1992

Joe and Marilyn, 1986

Good Enough to Dream, 1985

A Season in the Sun, 1977

How the Weather Was, 1973

The Boys of Summer, 1972

The Battle for Morningside Heights, 1970

The Passionate People, 1968

Inside Big League Baseball (juvenile), 1962

FICTION

The Seventh Game, 1982

But Not to Keep, 1978

EDITED

The World of John Lardner, 1961

The Mutual Baseball Almanac, 1954, 1955, 1956

ROGER KAHN

OCTOBER MEN

REGGIE JACKSON, GEORGE STEINBRENNER, BILLY MARTIN, AND THE YANKEES' MIRACULOUS FINISH IN 1978

▼

A HARVEST BOOK
HARCOURT, INC.

Orlando   Austin   New York   San Diego   Toronto   London

www.HarcourtBooks.com

Library of Congress Cataloging-in-Publication Data
Kahn, Roger.
October men: Reggie Jackson, George Steinbrenner, Billy Martin,
and the Yankees' miraculous finish in 1978/by Roger Kahn.
p.   cm.
Includes index.
ISBN 0-15-100628-8   ISBN 0-15-602971-5 (pbk.)
1. New York Yankees (Baseball team) 2. Jackson, Reggie.
3. Steinbrenner, George M. (George Michael), 1930–. Martin, Billy, 1928–89
I. Title: Reggie Jackson, George Steinbrenner, Billy Martin, and
the Yankees' miraculous finish in 1978.   II. Title.
GV875.N4K36   2003
796.357'09747'1—dc21   2003000536

Text set in Minion
Designed by Linda Lockowitz

Printed in the United States of America

First Harvest edition 2004
A C E G I K J H F D B

To Katy with love...

... and to the memory of unforgettable friends:
Joe Black, Woodie Broun, Ed Fitzgerald, Otto Friedrich,
Ring Lardner, Jr., and Harold Rosenthal

CONTENTS

▼

Prologue • *1*

CHAPTER ONE • A Holiday for Some • 18

CHAPTER TWO • The New York Red Sox
(and Other Curiosities) • 32

CHAPTER THREE • Steinbrenner Unbound • 62

CHAPTER FOUR • Manumission • 77

CHAPTER FIVE • The Dark Prince • 92

CHAPTER SIX • R. Martinez J. • 113

CHAPTER SEVEN • The Doughnut as a Whole • 141

CHAPTER EIGHT • The Gathering Storm • 169

CHAPTER NINE • A Bickering Spring • 196

CHAPTER TEN • Thirty Billion Calories on the Field • 215

CHAPTER ELEVEN • The New York Choirboys • 237

CHAPTER TWELVE • Ten Days that Shook the Bronx • 265

CHAPTER THIRTEEN • Resurrection • 304

CHAPTER FOURTEEN • The Game • 333

Epilogue: Finis Coronet Opus • 350

An Informal Bibliography • 365

Acknowledgments • 369

Index • 371

▲

SOME LINES
ON THE AUTHOR'S TRADE

A few months later I became a baseball writer,
that luckiest of men, paid to see every day what others
have to pay to see occasionally. Living in the finest hotels,
packed with steak and wine, spending the springs in Florida,
Arizona, California, Havana, allowed, nay required,
to talk continually with the nation's idols,
is he not the favorite of the gods?

—HEYWOOD HALE BROUN,
A Studied Madness

▼

OCTOBER MEN

▼

W HOEVER FIRST PROCLAIMED the mantra, "There is no 'I' in Team," was a better speller than a thinker. I will concede that high-bounding egos get in the way of team performance when the sport is husband-and-wife mixed doubles. But major-league baseball, the underlying subject of the next 350 or so pages, is a big-time, big-money, big-ego business. Across decades, the numbers have changed. The egos are pretty much constant.

The New York Yankees of the late 1970s, specifically the championship teams of '77 and '78, would certainly hold the record, if such records were kept, for the greatest number of clashing egos on a single ball club. As it happened, many of the principal players, Reggie Jackson, Bucky Dent, and the late Billy Martin, came from broken homes. The late captain, Thurman Munson, would not speak to his father for many years. Remembering Psych 101, or simply looking about, we know that families in conflict do not always produce tranquil offspring. Add powerful and willful owner George Steinbrenner, a media that can well be described as hyperactive, and some subtle and some not-so-subtle racism, and what you find in that big ball yard in the Bronx is *double, double, toil and trouble.* Still, conflict is the stuff of drama. With the 1978 Yankees, you also find a time that many believed, and many still believe a quarter century later, was *the* Yankee season nonpareil.

Coming as I do from a home in which history was the defining religion, I don't think this Yankee band sprang suddenly to life full grown on the trampled soil and potholed pavement of 161st Street. Teams, like almost everything else, flow out of history. Before we plunge head first or even topless into the boiling torrents of tumultuous seasons, it seems in order to pause and consider some of what went before. Warmup time. A precautionary deep breath. Batting practice. Whatever. There is this to be said for the literary device called a prologue: It worked for Chaucer.

THE FIRST ENTIRELY professional team, the Cincinnati Red Stockings of 1869, won 56 of 57 games and played a set in California, seven years before the annihilation of George Armstrong Custer's misguided legion. I sometimes ask others how on earth a professional baseball team could have proceeded through the prairie, mountains, desert, and extended stretches of Indian country that lay between Cincinnati and Sacramento almost a century and a half ago. My favorite response remains the tentative guess of one usually assured uptown lady. "Pony Express?" she asked with dazzling innocence. Actually 1869 was the year of the Golden Spike. Like so many ensuing generations of ball players, the Red Stockings (and their bats and balls and uniforms) traveled by train, on the way to their implausible winning percentage of .982.

In 1884, the Providence Grays, the equivalent of a contemporary "small-market franchise," beat out the wealthier Boston Beaneaters for the National League pennant, then won what can fairly be called the first World Series by defeating the New York Metropolitans of the American Association in three straight games. Providence fans who traveled to New York City for the final two carried brooms and cheered their team with bleats of "Sweep, Sweep, Sweep." Including the Series, Charles "Ol' Hoss" Radbourn of the Grays won sixty-two or sixty-three games—records differ—in that single season. Afterwards he was proclaimed "the Prince of Twirlers." Syphilis killed him in 1897 when he was forty-two and a sorrowing newspaper man wrote: "In [Radbourn's] prime his name was used as frequently as was the President's." That is a good farewell notice, though not a great one. During Radbourn's prime, the principal occupant of the White House was a one-term machine politician, Chester A. Arthur.

I have an enduring weakness for the New York Giants of 1905, as did its storied manager, John Joseph McGraw. All at once that season came the flowering of the first great New York team, displaying McGraw-style baseball—the sporting equivalent of war—and the aloof triumphs of the restrained cowlicked collegian Christy Mathewson. McGraw managed the Giants for three decades, through nine World Series, into the Depression summer of 1932. More than once he told his friend, the newspaper columnist Frank Graham, that of all the ball clubs he had played for, managed, and watched, the Giants of '05 were the greatest "without the slightest goddamn question." McGraw cited team speed, which he had emphasized with an aggressive bunting, running game, and Mathewson's pitching: thirty-one victories and thirty-two complete games in thirty-seven starts, three shutouts in six days during a World Series rout of Connie Mack's Philadelphia Athletics. Graham later added his own words: "On the ball field McGraw's Giants, except for Mathewson, slid with spikes high, threw knockdown fast balls, and screamed in profane, cocked-fist, brawling rage. McGraw's 1905 Giants were not playing cricket."

"The attitude of National League umpires," a McGraw champion named Arthur James wrote in the New York *Evening Mail*, "is that baseball is a step-sister to parlor tennis and a foster-brother to drop the handkerchief.... But baseball is played by real men with real tempers and real enthusiasm. No proper citizen has a wish to see the national game put on a pink-tea basis." Off the field McGraw was a reasonably proper citizen who liked such classic New York restaurants as Rector's, enjoyed night life along the Great White Way, and took his winter vacations in lush, fashionable Havana, where he once organized a handicap race matching a sprinter, a horse, and a motorcyclist. He was a complex, rough-hewn, home-grown American boulevardier. "But in 1905," Graham told me, "John's anger dominated him and that produced interesting results. His rages intimidated the weaker clubs and terrorized most of the umpires." Aside from, or within, all the ranting, McGraw was the first great practitioner of percentage baseball, playing a right-handed lineup against left-handed pitching, knowing which base to steal, when to squeeze, and all the rest. After McGraw's rousing 1905 season, baseball was never again as simple as it had been before. Almost a century later aspects of John McGraw's baseball survive in the tactical game practiced by such modern masters as Joe Torre and Bobby Cox. His furious approach also survives in its fashion whenever an emotional manager, say Lou Piniella, plucks second base out of the earth and shot-puts it at an umpire's bridgework. Casey Stengel played under McGraw and became a disciple. In turn Billy Martin, who played for Stengel years afterward, became a McGraw disciple once removed.

New England's long (some would say interminable) *liebestod* with the Red Sox has led to general neglect of the old Braves, a team whose clean lineage has been disturbed by successive moves to Milwaukee and Atlanta. Uniquely in major-league history, the 1914 Boston Braves moved from last place on July 4 to a pennant, winning 68 of their last 87 games, a victory pace of .782. A tall Southerner named George Stallings managed this club, wearing civilian clothes in the dugout, a practice also favored by Connie Mack, who seldom mouthed anything more heated during games than, "Good grief, look at that play." Civvies or not, Stallings was a firebrand, whose curses, one historian reports, "turned the air blue in the vicinity of the Braves dugout." He played platoon baseball, alternating starters in five positions from day to day.

Stallings got splendid work from a three-man pitching rotation (Bill James, Dick Rudolph, and George Tyler), but in October, Mack's Athletics were prohibitively favored to win their second consecutive World Series. Three Philadelphia starters, "Gettysburg Eddie" Plank, Charles "Chief" Bender, and Herb Pennock, called variously "the Squire, or Knight of Kennett Square," have since been elected to the Hall of Fame, along with second baseman Eddie Collins and third baseman Frank "Home Run" Baker, stars in Mack's renowned "$100,000 infield. " (One hundred thousand dollars was a phenomenal value then for the contracts and bodies of four ball players.)

Long afterward Raymond "Rube" Bressler, who won ten games as a Philadelphia rookie, told Lawrence Ritter that the 1914 Athletics "were one of the greatest teams ever assembled, if not *the* greatest. [But in the World Series] overconfidence did us in. We thought it would be a pushover... Also Connie sent Chief Bender and Eddie Plank home to Philadelphia a week before the Series to rest up, and they lost that fine edge. Their control was off." The Braves won four straight games and sportswriters acclaimed them as "the Miracle Braves." Perhaps in pique, but also to swell his bank account, Mack broke up his team by selling Collins, shortstop Jack Barry, Pennock, and Baker, among others. The Athletics then finished last for seven consecutive seasons and did not win another pennant for fifteen years.

"I don't care for the way the Red Sox play baseball," Robert Frost told me, one clear September afternoon in 1960. "They play too much in the manner of Boston gentlemen." We were standing outside Frost's cabin on the shoulder of a steep Vermont hill.

"How do you like your baseball played?" I said.

Frost was eighty-five. He said, "Spike 'em as you go around the bases." His green eyes twinkled. "Do you happen to know, did Lefty Rudolph ever pitch in a World Series?"

"Yes, sir. 1914."

Frost smiled and clapped me on the shoulder, and that is how I learned that the 1914 Miracle Boston Braves were the favorite team of a great ball fan and greater poet.

The Yankees, the core—I am resisting the temptation to say nuclear core—of this book, now are commonly called a dynasty, as in Ming or Bourbon or Plantagenet. The editors of *Forbes* magazine pronounced in the spring of 2001 that the Yankees were the most valuable of baseball franchises. *Forbes* thinkers set Yankee worth at $635 million, more than twice what Rupert Murdoch paid for the Los Angeles Dodgers two years earlier. The Bronx franchise has developed a cachet as impressive in its way as Mercedes or Chateau Lafite. But the Yankee origins, far from golden, were plain as infield dirt. Not until twenty years after the franchise came to New York did the Yankees become a significant urban fixture, akin to the Sixth Avenue El. During those early decades, broadly 1903 to 1923, New York was Giant country, a position some recidivists continued to embrace clear up until the season of 1958, when the Giants set up shop in San Francisco. Even as that ardent columnist Jimmy Cannon was thinking up tabloid odes to Joe DiMaggio and Yogi Berra, he told me in a Hell's Kitchen growl: "The Giants were the *real* New York team. The Yankees are strictly for tourists."

The Yankees finally were able to win their first two pennants, in 1921 and 1922, but the Giants still outclassed them in the World Series. As a team, the 1921 Yankees batted an even .300 during the regular season, impressive but not as remarkable as it sounds. The 1921 Detroit Tigers, managed by Ty Cobb, batted a collective .316. They finished sixth. (Manager Cobb also played center field and batted .389. His right fielder, Harry Heilmann, hit .394.) During an era when winning teams routinely posted collective season batting averages of .280 or more, McGraw's pitchers kept the Yankee team below .210 in two successive World Series.

In what was probably the biggest of all baseball deals up to that time, the Yankees had acquired Babe Ruth from the Boston Red Sox for $135,000 and perhaps $250,000 more in collateral payments on January 3, 1920, a date that for New Englanders still lives in infamy. Next season, 1921, Ruth startled the cosmos by hitting fifty-nine home runs. To put this in a peer setting, that year Ruth hit more homers than five American League *teams.* But in the eight games of the 1921 World Series at the old Polo Grounds, Giant pitchers held Ruth to a single homer and struck him out no fewer than eight times. The Sultan of Swat was striking out once a day. In the Series of '22, Ruth hit no homers at all and batted .118. Had fierce and wily John McGraw seen a crippling weakness in Ruth's free-swinging style? Did World Series pressure turn the big man's bat to jello? Was Ruth merely an overrated, overpriced cask of lard, topped by a half gallon of Prohibition ale? One sunlit October afternoon at the Polo Grounds in 1923 provided answers.

It was the first Series game and the Giants and Yankees were tied 4 to 4 when Casey Stengel, McGraw's centerfielder, walloped an inside-the-park home run off Bullet Joe Bush. Damon Runyon wrote:

This is the way old "Casey" Stengel ran yesterday afternoon running his home run.

This is the way old "Casey" Stengel ran running his home run home in a Giant victory by a score of 5 to 4 in the first game of the World's Series of 1923

This is the way old "Casey" ran, running his home run home, when two were out in the ninth inning and the score was tied and the ball was still bounding inside the Yankee yard.

This is the way—

His mouth wide open.

His warped old legs bending beneath him at every stride.

His arms flying back and forth like those of a man swim-ming with a crawl stroke.

His flanks heaving, his head far back....

Runyon's "Old Casey Stengel" was a graybeard of thirty-three. Final score: Giants 5, Yankees 4. Excluding a tie, this was the eighth consecutive World Series game that McGraw's Giants had won from the Yankees.

This time is sometimes remembered as the dawning of the Golden Age of Sport. A charismatic reformed hobo, Jack Dempsey, the Manassa Mauler, had become the heavyweight box-ing champion in 1919, and, soon after, he was the most famous athlete in the world. Patrician Bill Tilden dominated tennis with spin shots, finesse, and a cannonball serve not seen before. Coinci-dentally, or not so coincidentally, this time was also the dawning of the golden age of sportswriting. On October 11, the day after Sten-gel's inelegant, effective sprint around the bases, Heywood Broun of the *New York World* asked John McGraw a reasonable question. "In a tight spot and with the game on the line, will you pitch to Babe Ruth or intentionally walk him?"

McGraw's Irish eyes narrowed. "Why shouldn't we pitch to Ruth? I've said it before and I'll say it again. We pitch to better hit-ters than Ruth in the National League."

Broun later wrote, "Ere the sun had set on McGraw's rash and presumptuous words, the Babe had flashed across the sky fiery portents which should have been sufficient to strike terror and conviction into the hearts of all infidels. But John McGraw clung to his heresy with courage worthy of a better cause." In the fourth inning of the second game Ruth poled a home run that sailed clear over the roof of the upper deck in right field. ("A pop fly," Broun wrote, "with a brand new gland.") In the fifth, Ruth pulled a fierce line drive that carried into the lower deck, his second homer. In the ninth, Ruth hit the longest drive of the day, some 480 feet into center field, but the ball traveled so high that the redoubtable Casey Stengel, still running hard, was able to make the catch. The Yankees won the game, 4 to 2, and won the Series 4 games to 2. After that no one, not even McGraw, could argue that the bunt was as effective as the home run. As Broun put it, playing nicely off the New Testament: "The Ruth is mighty and shall prevail."

The Brooklyn Dodgers of 1947 did not win the World Series, a wild, somewhat messy and gloriously exciting affair. The '47 Yankees, a team of DiMaggio, Henrich, Rizzuto, Berra, were the winners in seven games. That was the Yankees' eleventh World Series victory, all gained, of course, in the quarter century after 1922. But in 1947 something special that was happening in the Brooklyn club began to work profound changes on America and indeed the world. Branch Rickey brought a fiery black American to play first base for Brooklyn, and Jackie Robinson had a good, though hardly a great, year. He batted .297, with twelve home runs. He stole twenty-nine bases, a total that led the National League but was second best in the majors. He stole two more in October against the Yankees but was far from a deciding factor in the Series, in which he hit only .259 with no home runs. Carl Furillo, the Dodger outfielder, batted .353. Pee Wee Reese, the Dodger shortstop, hit .304. Reese stole three bases.

Having set down these few numbers, I have not told the story of the team. Robinson was the first black allowed to play major-league ball since 1884, when one Moses Fleetwood Walker caught forty-one games for a Toledo club that finished eighth in the big-league American Association. Branch Rickey, president of the Dodgers, gifted, crafty, and both eloquent and grandiloquent, traced his decision to integrate the majors clear back to 1903 when he was a student/coach at Ohio Wesleyan College in Delaware, Ohio. On a trip to play Notre Dame, Rickey and his first baseman, a black predental student named Charles Thomas, crashed into a whites-only policy at the Hotel Oliver in South Bend, Indiana. Young Rickey thundered and threatened until the hotel allowed Thomas to spend the night on a cot in Rickey's room. Rickey told me years afterward: "In the room Charles Thomas began to weep. His shoulders heaved, and he rubbed one great hand over the other muttering, 'Black skin. Black skin. If I could only make it white.' He was trying literally to claw the black skin off his white bones." Right then, Rickey said, he resolved that "somehow, someday I was going to open up our game to Negroes."

His chance finally came in Brooklyn after Governor Thomas E. Dewey of New York signed the Ives–Quinn Law on March 12, 1945. Ives–Quinn was crafted with the specific purpose of outlawing the anti-Jewish admissions quotas practiced by New York State medical schools. But the legislators' broad language made it a crime to limit jobs or economic opportunities in *any* field—welding, surgery, modeling, baseball—on the grounds of race, religion, or color. "Having that law on my side after I signed Robinson," Rickey told me through cumulonimbus puffs of cigar smoke, "was a comfort during some very dark days."

Some owners threatened to throw Rickey out of baseball. "Try that," he said, "and you'll be arrested as soon as you set foot in New York State." At least seven St. Louis Cardinals attempted to organize a general strike against Robinson. "If you strike," Ford C. Frick, the president of the National League, told them, "you will be suspended. You will find the friends you think you have in the press box will not support you. You will be outcasts. I don't care if it wrecks the National League for five years. This is the United States of America and one citizen has as much right to play as another."

When the Dodgers came to the old border town of Cincinnati on their first trip west that year, the fans at Crosley Field began to jeer Robinson. Harold "Pee Wee" Reese had grown up in the seg-

regated city of Louisville, 105 miles down the Ohio River valley. A
number of Reese's boyhood friends were among those taunting
Robinson. During infield practice, some of the Cincinnati ball
players swelled the nasty noise. "Jungle Bunny." "Snowflake." And
much worse. There Robinson stood, one solitary black man,
catching hell. Reese raised a hand and stopped the infield practice.
Then he walked from shortstop to first base and put his arm
around the shoulders of Jackie Robinson. He stood there and
looked into the dugout and into the stands, stared into the torrents
of hate, a slim white Southerner who wore number 1 and just happened to have an arm draped in friendship around a black man
who wore number 42. Reese did not say a word. The deed was beyond words. "After Pee Wee came over like that," Jackie said years
afterward, "I never felt alone on a baseball field again." *Black and
white together*, in the refrain from the famous civil-rights song. I
think it is reasonable to suggest that without Jackie Robinson,
Martin Luther King would have lived out his days delivering eloquent sermons in an obscure Baptist church in Georgia.

It no longer matters very much, to me at least, that this Brooklyn Dodger team could not defeat the Yankees in October. For the
record, the Yankee ball players did *not* unduly needle Robinson.
Joe DiMaggio specifically avoided at least one nasty confrontation,
when Robinson, covering first awkwardly, blocked DiMaggio's
path. "I could have stepped on his heel," DiMaggio said. "Play
hard. That was my way. But if I did, it could have been a fight and
then it would have been the niggers against the dagos, and I didn't
want that. I didn't want that at all." DiMaggio himself had en-
dured elements of bigotry, notably when *Life* magazine published
a profile in which the writer expressed surprise that DiMaggio's
breath did not smell of garlic and "he does not slick back his hair
with olive oil."

In his popular *Summer of '49*, David Halberstam writes that
Robinson "humiliated [Yogi Berra] by stealing it seemed at will

and he [Berra] did not seem to want to catch anymore." As statistician Bill James points out in *The Baseball Book, 1991*, Robinson stole only one base while Berra was catching during the 1947 World Series. James comments, "Welcome to the world of 1949, where memory is truth." As James suggests, substituting memory for reporting is hardly reliable, and the practice becomes particularly unfortunate in highly promoted books. The gaffes therein tend to pollute the stream of history. But my point here is more baseball-specific. Robinson's mere presence in the Series of 1947 was a greater factor than was his base running, or for that matter, his bat. Joe DiMaggio understood that and accepted him as a fellow ball player.

DISCLOSURE BY A young *Wall Street Journal* reporter named Joshua Harris Prager that the 1951 New York Giants used a fairly complicated system to steal visiting catchers' signs produced, at least publicly, a reaction that echoes Claude Rains' famous one-liner in *Casablanca*. People said they were "shocked... *shocked.*" But like Rains, who played a charming, corrupt French police captain, baseball insiders were not shocked at all. In *Pitching in a Pinch*, published in 1912, Christy Mathewson tells of a sign-stealing setup in Philadelphia. Someone sat in a building behind center field peering through binoculars, with one hand on a Western Union buzzer. A wire ran under outfield and infield to the third-base coaches' box where another buzzer was buried just below the surface of the ground. By keeping one foot over the concealed buzzer, the third-base coach got a signal—one buzz or two—which he then relayed to the batter. One buzz was a fast ball. Two buzzes signaled a curve. But calamity struck on a day of scattered showers. "There was a big puddle in the coaching box that day," Arlie Latham, the Senators' third baseman at the time, told Mathewson. "I noticed the Philadelphia coach stood with his foot in the puddle, even though the water was up to his shoelaces." After a bit,

Washington players dug in the dirt and unearthed the buzzer. The game stopped. The players began pulling, and they kept pulling. The wire ran more than 350 feet to a center-field clubhouse. Latham told Mathewson, "All the newspapers laughed." This was more than one hundred years ago.

"The first time I came to bat at Cleveland in 1949," Al Rosen, the old slugging third baseman, told me, "[Manager Lou] Boudreau calls me up to pinch hit. He says, 'See that scoreboard out there? See where it says, RUNS, HITS, ERRORS? If you see a hand come sticking out of there, it's a breaking ball.' I walk up, it's the first pitch, and I see the hand. Here comes the curve. I hit a screamer. Double. I really pounded it. I'm standing on second base, and I say, 'Is this the way it always is up here?'" In 1950, his first full season with Cleveland, Rosen hit thirty-seven home runs, then a record for a rookie. But sign stealing or no, the Indians finished no better than fourth.

Television cameras today easily pick up catchers' signs, which is why television monitors are barred from big-league dugouts. But they have proliferated in the so-called luxury boxes, many of which are owned by the home team. Stick a smart scout in a private box among the monitors, and you are sign stealing twenty-first-century style. If I've thought this up by myself, and I have, it is just possible that ten (or a hundred) baseball men have long since come up with the same idea.

Bobby Thomson, the Royal Scots Express—he was born in Glasgow—is uncomfortable with the recent noise about sign stealing. He says, in effect, that sometimes he took tips; but on October 3, 1951, when he hit his famous home run off Ralph Branca—called and re-called, after Longfellow, "the shot heard 'round the world"—he did not. Mostly Thomson was a believer in uncomplicated batting: See the ball, hit the ball.

Thomson remembers the '51 Giants with pellucid clarity. The team started slowly. He was playing center field. Things picked up, but not immediately, when Willie Mays came up from Minneapolis, took over center, and Thomson moved to third base. On August 11, the Giants were thirteen games behind a mighty Brooklyn Dodger team, peopled with such Hall of Famers as Reese, Robinson, Duke Snider, and Roy Campanella. From that day until the end of the regular season, the Giants won thirty-nine of their last forty-seven games, a winning percentage of .830, accomplished under unrelenting pressure.

Thomson told me that down the stretch, Leo Durocher, managing the Giants and a former manager of Brooklyn, preached a repetitive sermon of hatred. The Dodgers were not only the Giants' great rivals, they were terrible people, Durocher said day after day. "They're the kind of guys who, if you take your eyes off them at a party, they start groping your wife's tits. Those guys are bastards."

"Did you really believe that stuff?" I asked Thomson.

He looked quizzical. "Sort of sounds ridiculous now, doesn't it?" he said. "But two things. Leo said not every Dodger was a bad guy. Gil Hodges was okay. That, I guess, made it a little more believable. Then Leo said this day after day. If you hear something often enough, you do begin to believe it."

So the Giants, Al Dark, Monte Irvin, Sal Maglie, began on some level to despise the Dodgers. The teams finished tied and split the first two of a best-of-three playoff.

Thomson remembers saying good-bye to his mother in the house on Flagg Street in the New Dorp section of Staten Island where he had grown up, on the morning of a memorable game. He mounted his blue Mercury and drove to the ferry. He remembers thinking, "If I can just get three for four and maybe a hundred 'ribbies' [runs batted in] then the old Jints will be all right." The thinking comforted him. He had been hitting well. Three for four seemed a reasonable goal. But at the ballpark, the game proved very difficult. Thomson singled down the left-field line in the second inning and running with his head down almost reached second base before noticing that Whitey Lockman, who had singled, was stopping there. Thomson was tagged out in a rundown, an embarrassing end to a threat.

Thomson doubled off Don Newcombe in the fifth inning, but there was no follow-up. His long fly to center scored the Giants' first run in the seventh inning. But he misplayed two ground balls after that, and when the eighth inning was done, the Dodgers led, 4 to 1. In the last of the ninth, Dark singled to right, Don Mueller singled to right, and Whitey Lockman doubled to left. The Giants got a second run, but Mueller tore his ankle sliding into third. Play suspended for several minutes while he writhed.

Charlie Dressen, the Dodger manager, replaced Don Newcombe with Branca, who started Thomson with a hip-high fast ball toward the inside corner. "Should have swung at that," Thomson told himself, backing out of the box. Reese and Robinson exchanged glances that said, "If he throws another pitch that good, we're cooked." In sports-page patois, he did and they were. Instead of throwing a breaking ball away—Branca had a fine curve—the pitcher tried a fast ball up and in. "It had nothing but Ralph's hand on the ball," Reese told me. "Good location. No zip." Thomson lined a home run into the left-field seats. The Giants won the ball game, 5 to 4, and with that game they won the pennant. For seconds that seemed to some like minutes, the crowd sat silent. Then came a roar. It was a roar matched all across the country, wherever people sat at radios or television sets; a sound of delight, horror, but mostly shock. This Giant team had come from thirteen games back and won the pennant.

Ralph Branca walked to the clubhouse and collapsed in tears. Bobby Thomson appeared live on the Perry Como show and received a check for five hundred dollars. Driving home to New Dorp, he said, three thoughts repeated through his mind. *The old Jints had won. He had pushed his runs-batted-in total up to 101. He had gone out there and gotten his three for four.* Six hours after the homer, he pulled the blue Mercury into the driveway. His older brother Jim, a fireman, came out to greet him.

"Do you know what you've done?" Jim Thomson said.

"Yep. I got my three for four."

Jim stared hard. Only then, Bobby Thomson told me, did he begin to understand that this day's home run would be something that people would talk about for all the rest of his days.

This was, of course, a classic pennant race, matching two extraordinary rivals and coming down to what some said was the single greatest baseball game ever played. It happened once. Rejoice. It would never happen again...

Then came the New York Yankees of 1978. Considering this band of brigands now, a quarter century after their great triumphs, one is struck by the remarkable changes wrought across twenty-five years. Recent successful Yankee teams have above all practiced restraint, a concept inimical to Billy Martin and Reggie Jackson. These days the working media, and particularly the press, are kept at a distance. Many outbursts—some are inevitable across a pennant race—go unreported. The long-ago intimacy of Pullman travel, where ball players and sportswriters shared private sleeping cars and diners, is history, like the Twentieth Century Limited. The modern Yankees travel in chartered jets from which the media are, quite simply, barred. Good sportswriting, Red Smith liked to say, "lets you smell the cabbage cooking in the kitchen." For good or ill, before Yankee clubhouse doors are opened to the journalists of today, the joint has been deodorized.

This transformation invites a consideration of Yankee history in snapshots taken twenty-five years apart. In 1928, when Prohibition reigned, Babe Ruth was hitting fifty-four home runs and attempting to drink New York City dry of bootleg ale. The press enjoyed Ruth, accepted large gifts from the Yankees, and reported only the big man's homers. In 1953 the Yankees fielded an all-white team and dumped a promising black first baseman, Vic Power, from their minor-league organization because they heard that back home in Arecibo, Puerto Rico, Power had been running with a fair-skinned blonde. He had indeed. He introduced me to her after they were married. Power batted .284 across twelve major-league seasons, all spent with other teams. The elephant in the Yankee living room in '53 was racism. Nobody, least of all those reporters Casey Stengel grandly called "my writers," ever mentioned that fact in print, any more than they mentioned Stengel's drinking (profoundly amiable) or Mantle's drinking (less congenial) and Mantle's womanizing (nothing short of hysterical). Although the earlier methods were different, and cruder than those employed today—sometimes involving graft—the Yankees managed news in 1928 and 1953 as successfully as the Yankees manage news and news people today. Remarkably and uniquely, 1978 comes down to us as the year in which Yankee news management failed completely, and a very rugged Yankee baseball team did not. The result lets us see through a crack in the prism the way things truly were.

That championship season began, of course, in April. It is unoriginal but pleasing to remark in a prologue, "Whan that Aprille with his shoures soote..."

▼

CHAPTER ONE

A HOLIDAY FOR SOME

O N THE EARLY EVENING of October 1, 1978, after six months of roistering with an intensity unmatched in the long history of hyperkinetic, high-proof roistering that so enriches the annals of American baseball, the New York Yankees found themselves tied for first place. The team had won 99 of 162 games, a commendable winning percentage of .611, but so had their traditional rivals, the Boston Red Sox. Autumn had taken hold along the eastern seaboard, bringing bright clear skies and quickening winds. The regular season of '78 was history. Still, in a sense, the teams found themselves just where they had been some six months earlier on Opening Day, April 8—tied, toe to toe, and glowering. As nature is said to abhor a vacuum, baseball abhors a tie, so now the Yankees were going to have to fly to Boston and meet the Red Sox yet again in a single-game playoff on October 2. As more than one sportswriter pointed out, the entire season for the two teams was coming down to one game. The regular season had ended and it had not ended. (In an interesting theory advanced by the author W. P. Kinsella, a ball game can stretch from the first inning clear to infinity. Uniquely among team sports, baseball proceeds outside of time. There is no clock.)

By every reasonable standard, the 1978 Yankees should have been terminally exhausted. Their opening-day manager, Alfred Manuel "Billy" Martin, had been drinking so heavily that his personality, none too tranquil when he was sober, had erupted with repeated explosions of anger, hatred, and paranoia, until he had finally gotten himself "resigned" back in July. While his great predecessor, Casey Stengel, mellowed with drink, booze turned Martin into a human Gatling gun. "You always wanted to be around Billy for the first drink," suggests Gene Michael, then the Yankees first-base coach. "You never wanted to be around him for the last one."

I knew Martin when he was a young infielder for Stengel's Yankees. He was a winning ball player who could be fine, if somewhat raucous, fun. But he also had an unpleasant, combative side. During spring training in 1953 he turned to the late Ben Epstein, a genial reporter for Hearst's tabloid *Daily Mirror*, and said, "I hear you used to be a wrestler."

"Yeah," Epstein said. Years earlier he had earned a living in his home state of Arkansas by wrestling as "Pat Rollo, the Undefeated Middleweight Champion of Bulgaria." Standing in the marble lobby of the Hotel Soreno, Martin said, "I'll show you some holds." Epstein said fine, although Martin was twenty-five years younger than he. "How's this?" Martin said, hoisting Epstein and starting an airplane-propeller twist. "Off," Epstein said, no longer quite so genial. Martin dropped Epstein to the lobby floor, believing that he was terminating the episode. But Epstein rallied, applied one of his Bulgarian flips, and left his opponent helpless. With Allie Reynolds and a few other Yankees watching, Epstein applied a Bulgarian twist. Martin cried out in pain. Epstein said, "Had enough?"

"Okay," Martin shouted. "Anything you want. Lemme loose." Epstein told me some time afterward, "I remember two things about the match. First, the only thing that got damaged was my watch, and Reynolds fixed it for me right away. Second, when I

said 'Had enough?' that was the first time Pat Rollo, the Undefeated Middleweight Champion of Bulgaria, had ever spoken in
English." This episode foreshadowed the more visceral confrontation of July 1978 when Martin, talking while intoxicated, threw
down another challenge quite beyond his strength and pretty
much forced his boss to fire him.

The boss—George Michael Steinbrenner III of Bay Village,
Ohio; Tampa, Florida; and the South Bronx—is said to be the only
owner in baseball who walks into his clubhouse humming the
theme from *Patton*. He is famously a hard-fisted businessman who
shouts and rants and cultivates a climate of creative terrorism. As
I write these lines, Steinbrenner is a vigorous, vastly wealthy character just past seventy who speaks to the press infrequently, ignores
rumors he has undergone a face-lift, and employs a high-powered
New York public relations firm to protect his image. Back in 1978,
he was available to the press and public more or less on whim.

When the late Ed Linn began work on a book about Steinbrenner and his team, George telephoned me and made a troubling request. Would I arrange for him to see the manuscript
before publication so he could "check it out for accuracy"? Steinbrenner knew that Linn had collaborated on books with Bill
Veeck, then running the Chicago White Sox, and the two—Steinbrenner and Veeck—regarded each other with loathing. Steinbrenner's deep concern, it seemed to me, was that Linn would
write the book with a hatchet sharpened by Veeck. Linn was a
friend of mine. I certainly liked (and like) Steinbrenner. What to
do? I simply relayed George's request to Linn, who was working in
his cluttered basement office on Long Island. Linn thought for a
while, then called me back and said, "Fine. Tell him he can read
every passage in the book that isn't about him."

The role of telephonic go-between enlivened my life for several
weeks, but failed to produce anything approaching accord. Aside

from the Veeck element, Steinbrenner had serious grounds for concern. He didn't know Linn and had brushed off several interview requests more casually than he might have with better advice. His background, which Linn intended to explore, contained more than one disquieting episode. Within six months of the day Steinbrenner acquired control of the Yankees (January 3, 1973), he had pleaded guilty to two felony charges, for essentially making illegal contributions to Richard Nixon's 1972 presidential campaign. With great intensity and in fine detail, Steinbrenner explained to me afterward that he considered himself an independent Democrat and that he had been victimized by Nixon and Nixon's henchmen. (We will consider that story at length later on.) Working on his own from other sources, Linn categorically rejected Steinbrenner's explanation. His book portrays Steinbrenner as an arrogant, law-breaking manipulator. In Linn's version only a shrewd lawyer and a plea bargain saved Steinbrenner from a prison sentence and probable expulsion from baseball. Such accusations—they were around before Linn wrote them—cut deeply. "Owning the Yankees is just unique," George remarked to me once with distinct tenderness. "I've had lots of offers to sell. No way. Owning the Yankees is like owning the *Mona Lisa.*"

The Steinbrenner of 1978 was relatively new to both baseball and New York City, and he still was close to the humiliating felony rap, which among other things cost him his right to vote. (President Reagan restored that with a pardon.) Back then he was decidedly more frantic than the seasoned, confident, mostly triumphant, sometimes guarded swashbuckler one encounters today. He wanted very much to become a sporting presence, a social presence, and a power beyond baseball in the business world. He ran with Bill Fugazy, the limousine king; wined Barbara Walters, the television queen; and huddled with Lee Iacocca, the commandant at Chrysler. After one lunch at the 21 Club, on 52nd Street, Steinbrenner and

Walters made a bet: Which of the two would be recognized by more passersby as they walked the quarter block from the gates of the elegant restaurant to Fifth Avenue? (My understanding is that nobody recognized either.)

Operating his baseball team in the South Bronx and surfing the fast life in Manhattan, the kid from Bay Village reached back toward his Ohio roots that, beneath the charm and bluster and bravado, he seemed to need for security, as the savage wrestler Antaeus in Greek mythology needed the earth for strength. Steinbrenner lured Al Rosen away from an executive position at Las Vegas' most prominent hotel and hired him as club president. Rosen, a man of great personal strength and high intelligence, had been a slugging third baseman for the Cleveland Indians, twice leading the American League in home runs and winning the Most Valuable Player Award in 1953. But he had not before held a front-office baseball job. "What I remember about Rosen," says Moss Klein, a solid reporter who covered the Yankees for the *Newark Star–Ledger,* "is that he was the one person in the ruling group who, however crazy things got, always told the truth. It was as if Rosen didn't know how to tell a lie."

The day after Martin resigned in July, Steinbrenner and Rosen had replaced him with bulbous-nosed Bob Lemon, who for nine years, 1948 through 1956, had been the ace of a fabled Cleveland pitching staff. Lemon won twenty games seven times for the Indians and was inducted into the Baseball Hall of Fame in 1976. He is remembered for his gifts, for his nose, and for a candid comment he uttered more than once: "When I lost a ball game, I never took it home with me. Along the way I stopped at a few bars and left it there." Lemon started 1978 managing a lethargic Chicago White Sox team. Seventy-four games into the season, he was fired by, of all people, Steinbrenner's baseball antagonist, Bill Veeck. (Veeck replaced Lemon with Larry Doby, only the second African American to manage in the major leagues.)

Steinbrenner, Rosen, Martin, and Lemon: This, then, was the foursome chained together at various times within the Yankee command post, a baseball equivalent of Fort Apache, the Bronx. Four very gifted, very assertive men. Each possessed star power, and when they clashed, significant portions of the cosmos seemed to shake. That is one view, anyway, and the popular one. A dissenting opinion goes like this: After Martin vaporized, all you really had were three tough guys from Cleveland trying to make it in New York.

WHEN THE YANKEES awakened on the morning of October 1, they were riding a six-game winning streak and holding on to first place by one game. All they had to do to secure the division championship and complete what could well be the greatest comeback in the annals was thump a journeyman lefthander named Rick Waits, whom they had already beaten three times, and defeat a Cleveland team that was festering in sixth place, thirty games behind them. The Yankees led with an ace, Jim "Catfish" Hunter, and he yielded five runs in the first two innings. "The fabled money pitcher," Moss Klein wrote, "went bankrupt in a big game." Cleveland defeated the Yankees, 9 to 2. Meanwhile, 202.7 miles northeast at Fenway Park, the Red Sox won their eighth straight, beating the last-place Toronto Blue Jays, 5 to 0. The Yankee lead, so damnably hard to gain, was history.

The Metropolitan New York media people—radio reporters, blow-dried television interviewers, and the sportswriters from the suburbs—made their familiar trudging march toward the Yankee clubhouse, a place without windows or natural light, remote from the brightness of the playing field, buried among the catacombs far below the vaulting three-tiered grandstand. For a time the clubhouse door stayed shut. Out of media range, Ron Guidry walked into Bob Lemon's office. "Tomorrow," he said. "I want the ball." Guidry had won twenty-four. He had pitched consecutive two-hit shutouts against the Red Sox in September. "You got it," Lemon said.

After the clubhouse door opened, most Yankees ducked the reporters. With a championship on the line, they had lost to a journeyman pitcher and a bad ball club. Was there anything left to say, any words worth uttering except expletives? Well, maybe a few. Not many on this Yankee gang understood the magical possibilities of silence.

"There are games when you can tell right away you either have it or you don't," babbled the swift, quirky centerfielder, Mickey Rivers. "We didn't have it. The Indians wanted to win and maybe we just thought we couldn't lose." Rivers spoke in a mumble, superimposed on a thick Miami drawl. He was a popular and effective ball player, a passionate horse player, and usually broke. Rivers' full name was and is John Milton Rivers. He may well be the only person named for John Milton who has never heard of John Milton.

"We got beat," Reggie Jackson said, "and it wasn't just another game. We knew the Red Sox were winning. We knew what was happening. Now we got to get them tomorrow."

"I'm hoping for six or seven strong innings from Guidry," Bob Lemon said. "Then I can go to [Rich] Gossage."

Guidry, slim, graceful, contained, and nicknamed "Lou'siana Lightnin'," would be working with three days' rest instead of his customary four. At 5-foot-11 and 155 pounds, Ronald Ames Guidry exemplified the lilting word *lithe*. "Too small for a pitcher," some scouts had said. "Too skinny." Now at twenty-eight Ron Guidry threw 95-mile-an-hour fast balls and broke off great sliders that rammed right-handed hitters in the bat handle. By 1978, "Gator" Guidry had become the best pitcher on earth.

The media of Metropolitan New York was then as now a disquieting beast. Some reporters were solid; other were frantic. One locked himself into a toilet stall in the Yankee clubhouse bathroom earlier so that he could overhear ball players' conversations and take notes without being detected. Graig Nettles discovered the man and threatened violence until Al Rosen intervened. Further complicating the scene was the late-season entry of female reporters into the dressing rooms, armed by a recent court order that cited equal employment opportunity. Sparky Lyle celebrated this milestone of liberation by affixing a long white sock, a "sani," to his penis, creating at least a fleeting impression of exceptional length. With stealth newspapermen hiding in the bathroom and aggressive newspaperwomen trying to look nonchalant as they stood among naked athletes, some embarrassed, some clowning, the historic ball players' sanctuary, the clubhouse, was no longer what it once had been.

To the joy of many, including Bob Lemon, New York's three major newspapers, the *Times,* the *Daily News,* and the *Post,* had shut down on August 18 when a mechanical group, the pressmen, went out on strike, and others, including the reporters' union, walked out "in sympathy." Talking about a late-season Yankee hot streak, Lemon said later he didn't believe it could have happened if the ball players had been forced to deal with all the reporters and columnists who covered the team for the big three of New York newspapers.

Guidry usually dealt with reporters by offering one of three answers: He smiles slightly as he recalls, "I'd tell them yes, maybe, or no." After a while, he says, the reporters tired of these answers and stopped coming around. But he has always been a stand-up character and on the eve of the play-off Guidry let his reserve drop a bit and answered questions. "No, I'm not worried about being tired. Am I sure? I won't know for sure until I start pitching, but I think I'll be okay."

"I'm ready," Gossage said. Bob Lemon had not thrown him

into today's game, which the Yankees had lost almost from the start. "I've got to be ready. There's no tomorrow after tomorrow."

The clubhouse was mostly quiet; some thought it was like a soldiers' camp on the night before a battle. But this was Yankeetown, 1978, and there were always wars within the wars. Cliff Johnson, a huge (6 foot 4 and 230 pounds) backup catcher and pinch hitter, looked over at Jackson jabbering at a scribbling half moon of reporters from suburban and out-of-town newspapers. "What's he talking about?" Johnson began. "What the hell is there to say? Does Jackson ever shut up? Shit. That guy just never stops talking." Before the biggest game of the year the protagonists were not Henry V's "little band of brothers" gathered at Agincourt. No, not at all.

The charter flight from LaGuardia to Logan Airport was uneventful—less than forty minutes in the air—and the ball players checked into the Sheraton Hotel, not far from Back Bay, in an area dominated by the Prudential Tower, then the tallest building in Boston. Toward nine o'clock they scattered into their rooms and into a welcome and forgiving privacy.

RICHARD "GOOSE" GOSSAGE, a strapping righthander out of Colorado Springs, had left the Pittsburgh Pirates as a free agent after the 1977 season and signed a six-year contract with the Yankees on November 23. The terms: $2.75 million, about $460,000 a year. Today it may appear that batboys make that sort of money, but in those days free-agent baseball was just emerging from long decades of feudalism, and the Gossage contract was front-page news. Albert "Sparky" Lyle, whose relief pitching won him a Cy Young Award in 1977, was working for the Yankees under a feudal-era contract: $140,000 a year. Now here came Gossage, riding off a nice but not a great year with a team that missed the play-offs, joining the World Champion Yankees for more than three times Lyle's salary. Gossage was in fact drawing the highest salary any team had ever paid to a reliever. Questions bubbled to the surface. Was Gossage worth that much? Was President Jimmy Carter worth that much? Was anyone? Wouldn't this high-rolling—and to some observers, reckless—spending set off explosions in the Yankee clubhouse, particularly around the locker occupied by the opinionated, extroverted Sparky Lyle?

At a press conference called to introduce Gossage to New York, he certainly simplified things. "This deal," he said, "is what the Yankees need to make a dynasty." Gossage thinks now, without being certain, that either his agent, Jerry Kapstein, or George Steinbrenner put him up to making the dynasty remark on the theory that brashness would dazzle the New York media. He is a well-spoken and confident man, who says, "My style was never to boast. My style was to let my pitching boast for me." Now in the play-off game, his pitching would have to speak for him, for his team, for the whole season.

"When we got to the hotel," Gossage says. "I went up in the elevator with Lou Piniella. He told me he was turning in to get some sleep. I thought I'd do the same. But when I lay down I started tossing. I was going to pitch the last two or three innings. And now I'm in my hotel room. And I can't sleep. I just felt too nervous and excited." At length Gossage decided, as so many pitchers before him, to regain his composure in a saloon. A surprise was waiting for him when he got there.

RON GUIDRY is by habit a late retirer. In his words, "I go to bed last most of the time." But he stayed in his room at the Sheraton, and he says he slept well. "I didn't get a lot of hours of sleep, but I did sleep fairly deep. I was up early. I had breakfast by myself, and I went to the park early. Didn't wait for the team bus. I took a cab." Guidry had thought about his mental preparation; he knew what he wanted. He didn't want "a mess of conversation. I didn't intend to get distracted." So he would avoid chatter with others including, or especially, his excitable employer, George M. Steinbrenner III.

ALBERT LEONARD ROSEN, called Flip in his playing days, had lived a life that was thrilling but touched with pain. His grandfather, a Polish immigrant, ran a department store in Spartanburg, South Carolina, a mill town set among the foothills of the Blue Ridge Mountains. Soon after Al was born in 1924, his grandfather died, the Great Depression came, the store went bad, and the family moved. The Rosens settled in Miami, Florida, in a neighborhood without other Jews. Rosen's father left the household when his son was eight. Rosen cannot recall the first time he heard "Jewboy," but the word was part of his childhood. "What is it?" he still wonders. "Is it because your nose is a little bigger, or your hair is a little curlier, or you don't go to Sunday school on Sunday morning, or you're not in regular school on Yom Kippur? What is it?"

As he grew older and rougher in Miami, he began spending time in a boxers' gym. He watched professionals, studying them, and, after a while, sparring with them. His Jewish education was measured in jabs and hooks. He went out for football at a Miami high school. After one early practice, he and six or seven other boys piled into the coach's car. "Rosen," the coach said, "what are you doing out for football?"

"I love to play the game," Rosen said.

"Rosen," the coach said, "you're different from most Jews. Most Jewboys are afraid of contact."

Two years later Rosen enrolled at Florida Military School, a prep in St. Petersburg, on an athletic scholarship. His mother was tremendously proud. He lettered in baseball, basketball, football, and boxing and made the dean's list. "Some of my best friends at prep," he says, "were gentiles." After the army he had some college, but he wanted to be a ball player. He played in Thomasville, Georgia; Wilkes-Barre, Pennsylvania; and Pittsfield, Massachusetts; and Oklahoma City and Kansas City and San Diego on a long, grinding journey to the major leagues. He remembers that sometimes during that struggle he wished his name were something other than Rosen. Smith, Jones, Abernathy. Anything but Rosen. Being Jewish was just one more handicap on top of all the other things that made it so damn tough to reach the majors.

Then in 1950 he broke through with the Cleveland Indians: 37 homers and 116 runs batted in. He did even better in 1953: leading the American League with 43 home runs, 145 runs batted in, and missing the batting title by a single point, .336 to Mickey Vernon's .337. After that he sometimes wished that he had a name even *more* Jewish than his own, perhaps Rosenthal or Rosenstein. He wanted nobody, least of all the bigots, to ever forget just who and what he was.

Before the confrontations of 1978, he had some history with Billy Martin. "I was playing for San Diego in the Pacific Coast League, and Martin was a skinny infielder with Oakland. An Oakland pitcher drilled me, and when I glared, he called me a Jew cocksucker, and I went for him. A lot of people got into that brawl. In the middle I noticed, I don't know how, Martin sneaking up to me trying to blindside me with a punch. He never did."

Often in 1978, Martin tried to challenge Rosen's authority. The chain of command ran upward from field manager (Martin), to general manager (the diffident Cedric Tallis), to president (Rosen) to principal owner (Steinbrenner). From the start, Martin said in saloons and elsewhere that Rosen didn't know what he was doing, had no business holding down the job of president, and, after a while, that he, Martin, was no longer speaking to Rosen. "If I want to send word upstairs, I talk to Tallis." For a time Rosen was tolerant. Then he said, "All right, Billy. Here's what we do. Just you and

me. Bare knuckles. At home plate. Either right before or right after
a game. We'll give the fans a little something extra for their money."

That story, even the mere headline, has appeal:

NEW YANKEE PRESIDENT FLATTENS

YANKEE MANAGER IN BRIEF BOUT

AT SOLD-OUT YANKEE STADIUM;

RETURN MATCH HELD UNLIKELY

That headline never ran for one reason. Martin did not accept
Rosen's challenge.

THE WARRIOR PRESIDENT of the Yankees awoke on October 2, 1978,
instantly aware of many things, including the fact that this was a
high Jewish holiday. It was Rosh Hashanah, the Jewish New Year, an
occasion generally marked by solemnity. Although there are many
varieties of Judaism in America, almost all regard Rosh Hashanah as
a spiritual day, properly spent in prayer and contemplation, and
certainly not spent working. "I was aware of that," Rosen said. "I
thought how will this look. The Jewish president of the New York
Yankees goes to a ball game on a high Jewish holiday. I was also
aware I had a job to do. I went to Fenway." There was only one unpleasant consequence. Rosen handled it with skill and humor.

Rosen felt tense when he entered the box behind the Yankee
dugout, and his mood did not lighten when he saw a pale,
expensively suited man sitting in his seat. "You'll have to move,"
Rosen said. "You're in my seat."

The man stayed where he was. "Don't bother me," he said.
"I'm a personal friend of George M. Steinbrenner. Who do you
think you are?"

"The president of the New York Yankees," Rosen said. "Move!"
He spoke so fiercely that the intruder, Roy Cohn, lawyer, hustler,
and once deputy to the infamous Senator Joe McCarthy, did as he
was told.

Rosen looked out at the field. Lovely day. Fresh breeze from left. He considered the ball players warming up on the green and brown and white texture before him. Lou Piniella. Hot tempered but a student of hitting. A competitor. Graig Nettles. He had some nasty moments, but he could pluck 'em at third and he could hit. Thurman Munson, the stocky, mustached, sometimes angry catcher, an Ohio kid who'd come round for help handling his money when Rosen ran an investment business in Cleveland. All excited about his private jet plane these days. A gamer. Munson could play like hell through pain. Bucky Dent. Maybe not up with the others, but he got the job done at shortstop and he never quit. A nice kid and a quiet pro. And Reggie Jackson; he'd torn a nail off a finger and he couldn't play outfield, but he could DH and this was Reggie's time of year. He owned the autumn. Last season in October 1977 he had hit five homers, *five,* in a six-game World Series. One homer for every four times at bat. Nobody had done that before in a World Series. Probably nobody ever would again.

These fellers, my fellers, Rosen thought, can play. But here are the Red Sox and their stumpy, gritty manager Don Zimmer. Some were saying this was the greatest Boston Red Sox team ever assembled. He had been through a lot in baseball and beyond, but suddenly Rosen felt more tense than he ever had at a ballpark. His stomach was a knot of twine. He reached for a package of antacid tablets and shoved a couple into his mouth. Was this tight stomach divine punishment for going to work on Rosh Hashanah? Who knew? A bulky man made his way into the Yankee box.

"Hello, George," Rosen said. "Now that you're here I guess we can begin to play the ball game."

▼

CHAPTER TWO

THE NEW YORK RED SOX
(AND OTHER CURIOSITIES)

IN JANUARY 2002 George Steinbrenner entered his thirtieth season as "principal owner" of the New York Yankees. Since the
franchise dates from 1903, when it began as the Greater New
York Club of the American League, Steinbrenner has been running the Yankees for just about one-third of the team's lifetime. He
has surpassed the previous ownership record, Jacob Ruppert's
twenty-four years, and, at this writing, has no plans to change his
management technique, let alone to step down from ruling what
his media people call "the most storied franchise in sports."

He has made his share of mistakes and behaved outrageously
at times. But a fair balance sheet on Steinbrenner and his era
shows first a man who rescued the Yankees from incompetent
management and even—though this may be extreme—ruin. In
the rescue process, Steinbrenner played the developing free-agent
market better than anyone else. He has kept the team in the Bronx,
not always happily, and he has preserved the historic ballpark
where they play. After that, but only after that, do we get to the
chaos and the swordplay.

Because of Steinbrenner's big-bang style, some, particularly
among the younger generations, may wonder if prior to his emer-

gence the Yankees existed at all. As a matter of fact, or many facts, they did. Indeed they did. Before Steinbrenner swept out of the Great Lakes into New York on a chill January day, the Yankees had already won twenty of their twenty-six world championships. No other team comes close to that mark. The St. Louis Cardinals, who share second place, have won the World Series nine times. So have the Athletics, who won five for Connie Mack in Philadelphia and four for Charley Finley in Oakland. The Dodgers, like the Yankees an extremely rich franchise, have won six, one in Brooklyn and the others in Los Angeles. (They have also lost the Series to Yankee teams eight times.) The Red Sox have won five Series but to the ongoing grief of New England, none since 1918, when they defeated the Chicago Cubs exactly one month before an armistice concluded the bloodshed of World War I. At twenty-six, the Yankee Series mark may be the least approachable of all team baseball records. When I was growing up a gambling man offered me two tips: Never bet against the Yankees or Notre Dame. That still seems to make sense today.

I FIRST ENCOUNTERED the Yankees professionally on March 25, 1952, when I covered one of their exhibition games against the Brooklyn Dodgers in St. Petersburg for the *New York Herald Tribune*. The Yankees had won the World Series the year before, defeating the New York Giants, and won the year before that defeating the Philadelphia Phillies, and won the year before *that* defeating the Dodgers. The spring day half a century ago remains bright and vivid in my mind: a simmering Florida sun, an old-fashioned wooden grandstand entirely fenced in by chicken wire to protect old spectators from foul drives, and at the center of this sunbright and aged universe, one Charles Dillon "Casey" Stengel, all growls and wrinkles, sitting in the home dugout, flanked by large, intimidating men, who turned out to be the right-handed pitchers Vic Raschi and Allie Reynolds. My assignment that spring was to cover the Brooklyn Dodgers, an open and friendly team, but the *Tribune's* Yankee beat reporter, Rud Rennie, had suffered a coronary. So it fell to me that day to write a Yankee story. (I am embarrassed to report that during Rennie's illness, the *Trib*, in a spasm of penury, had been getting by on reports marked "special to the *New York Herald Tribune*," actually written by Arthur "Red" Patterson, the Yankee publicity man. In Patterson's dispatches the Yankees played either well or very well, even on the rare afternoons when they lost.)

I introduced myself to Stengel, who said, "I don't know ya, kid, so I wouldn't talk to ya, except the feller that got sick is a good man and I got to help him out. What do ya want to know?"

"Who will be your fourth starter this season?" Stengel had Raschi and Reynolds, I knew, and an artful lefthander, a former movie usher named Eddie Lopat, but the previous fourth starter on a great staff, Whitey Ford, had been drafted into the army.

"I seen pitchers from before you was born," Stengel said, as though I had challenged his competence, "which is different from other players." Suddenly Raschi and Reynolds broke my focus. They began to spit tobacco juice around my freshly shined loafers. No words. Just spit. They were control pitchers and accurate spitters. They never hit the loafers, merely ringing the toe box of each shoe. Stengel didn't yet know who would be his fourth starter, which is what my story would say, and there was nothing particularly hostile in his words or even in the spitting of the tobacco-chewing pitchers. I was the new boy, from another team and another league. They were the Yankees. "We knew perfectly well who you were," Allie Reynolds told me years later. "We just wanted to make sure you knew who we were. Not the Brooklyn fucking Dodgers. The New York Yankees. The World Champion New York Yankees."

In time I came to know these Yankees, and I even met a few times with their remote millionaire owners, Dan Topping and Del Webb. Topping was a big, square-jawed sort, who had inherited a copper fortune. He was renowned at the Stork Club and El Morocco, two exclusive supper clubs, where he could be seen squiring pretty women who were interested in square-jawed sorts who had inherited a fortune of any kind. Tall, myopic Del Webb was a prosperous building contractor, based in Phoenix, who gave the press corps free subscriptions to *Arizona Highways,* a visually resplendent magazine designed to lure fresh settlers to the Southwest. Webb seemed proud that his company had built one of the concentration camps in which Japanese-Americans were imprisoned during World War II and had completed the job ahead of schedule.

After these men sold the club to CBS in 1964, I enjoyed conversations with their successor, the charming, eloquent, and ineffectual team president, Michael Burke, who liked to quote the poetry of William Butler Yeats and offered up an interesting story of his life, some of which was true. Burke is the man who went to Steinbrenner for financing when the Yankees became available in 1972. At this writing I've watched and interacted with the Yankees first hand for fully fifty years. I've seen the franchise change from that impersonal Topping/Webb machine, lightened by the public relations gifts of Stengel, to the roiling institution of Steinbrenner & Co. that we have today. I doubt if Topping or Webb would recognize the current Yankees. I have no doubt that both would be delighted by the current Yankee annual reports.

Fifty years is a very long time in baseball, a world in which men go from rookies to grizzled veterans inside a decade. But to be sure, well before my personal history with the Yankees began, the Greater New York Club of the American League had a life story of remarkable distinction and some turmoil. The most dynamic of all home-run hitters, Babe Ruth, once a pitcher, matured—as much as he ever did mature—as a Yankee. The might of Ruth's swing and the overpowering Ruth personality forced the Yankees to pay him $80,000 a year during the late 1920s. After the stock market crashed in 1929, someone asked Ruth if he realized that he was earning a higher salary than the $75,000 then paid to Herbert Hoover, the president of the United States. Ruth's response was free of false humility. "I had a better year than him." The great slugging first baseman, Lou Gehrig, starred as a Yankee for seventeen seasons. For sixteen of those years he never missed a game. Gehrig had dimples, an Ivy League background—sportswriters called him "Columbia Lou"—astonishing muscles, and an introverted, somewhat aloof personality. His early death from amyotrophic lateral sclerosis, a degenerative disease of the central nervous system, stirred the nation and struck some as a heartbreaking enactment of Housman's great poem, "To An Athlete Dying Young."

The career of Joe DiMaggio, the Yankee Clipper, became a splendor in the Bronx. DiMaggio joined the Gehrig team of 1936 and played, mostly brilliantly, through 1951, the year that Mickey Mantle joined the club. Although Mantle's final seasons were marred by pain, he lasted through 1968 and became, beyond question, the greatest switch hitter ever. His career rang with some of the longest home runs in history. From the coming of Ruth to the retirement of Mantle, a span of forty-nine years, the Yankees always had a resident superhero. No other team has had a run like that or even come close. Yet another superhero, the mighty and mightily vulnerable Reginald Martinez Jackson, came charging onto the Stadium scene just nine years after Mantle left, creating with Steinbrenner and Billy Martin an unusual, alarming, electric ménage à trois.

The Yankee sluggers were, to quote Lawrence Ritter's evocation of Ecclesiasticus, "the glory of their times." But there also existed a distinctly darker side. Harold Homer (Prince Hal) Chase played first base for the Yankees—then called the Highlanders—from 1905 into 1913. He managed the team briefly in 1910 and for all of 1911. My father, a college infielder, remembered Chase as the most graceful first baseman he had ever seen. Chase was a steady .290 hitter and swift; he stole forty bases in 1910. Unfortunately, he was, also in my father's term, "an unmitigated scoundrel." He was addicted to betting on baseball and was often accused, but never convicted, of throwing games. Chase left the major leagues in 1919, utterly unmourned, but his misdeeds were largely forgotten and overwhelmed when the Chicago White Sox threw the World Series that same year. A highly romantic picture of Lou Gehrig's life endures in the movie *Pride of the Yankees*, maybe the best film for young athletes ever. Hal Chase's unadorned story, "The Shame of the Yankees," has not yet made it to the screen.

Carl Mays, the only major-league pitcher ever to kill a batter, did it while he was a Yankee. Mays, a righthander, threw hard and three-quarter underhand, earning him the nickname "Sub," as in submariner. That style has fallen out of favor but Mays's pitches were intimidating. By reputation he was a head hunter, keeping batters alert with fast balls hurled toward the skull. On August 16, 1920, the Yankees were playing host to the Cleveland Indians at the Polo Grounds, the home field they rented from the Giants. The Indians were leading 3 to 0 when their shortstop, Ray Chapman, led off the fifth inning. Chapman crowded the plate. With the count at 1 and 1, Mays threw a fast ball that slammed into the left side of Chapman's head. (Batting helmets lay thirty-five years into the future.) Chapman had either lost the ball or frozen in fright. He dropped slowly, eyewitnesses—including my father—said. "It took him an eternity to hit the ground." After receiving first aid he regained his feet. He staggered as he tried to walk to the dugout. In the clubhouse the Cleveland trainer applied ice packs. Chapman said, "Tell [my wife] Kate I'll be okay." The trainer called for an ambulance. Emergency surgery failed. Chapman died at 5:00 A.M. of a fractured skull.

"I wanted that pitch to be a low fast ball in the strike zone," Mays told Bob McGarigle, who wrote the book *Baseball's Great Tragedy.* "But as my arm reached the farthest point of my back swing, I saw Ray shift his back foot into the position he took for a running bunt, a push bunt [up toward first base]. So at the last split second I changed to a high and tight pitch [that would be more difficult to bunt]. Usually a batter falls away from such a pitch, but Ray didn't. There was a sharp crack... Now, nobody, it seems, ever remembers anything about me except one thing—a pitch I threw caused a man to die." When Detroit followed the Indians into the Polo Grounds, a clubhouse boy came up to Mays bearing a folded note from a Tiger outfielder. "If it was within my power I would have inscribed on Chapman's tombstone, HERE LIES THE VICTIM OF ARROGANCE, GREED AND VICIOUSNESS." That message was signed TY COBB.

THE AMERICAN LEAGUE opened for business in 1901 as a rival, not a partner, of the National League, which had been organized in 1876. Today's fused, conglomerated major leagues—Baseball, Inc.—did not exist in the buccaneering boom-and-bust baseball business of long ago. But even a hundred years back, for a major league truly to be major, there had to be a franchise in New York. The American League, which evolved from the essentially Triple A Western League, was not able to establish a New York franchise until 1903. Andrew Freedman, a real estate speculator who owned the New York Giants—he bought the team in 1895 for $48,000— was well connected with the Tammany Hall political organization that ran New York; he and his political allies at first barred the American League from New York City. Freedman was a loud and assertive owner who comes down to us as a sharp businessman and a baseball ignoramus. Under him, the Giants tried to make Christy Mathewson, arguably the greatest pitcher who ever lived, into a first baseman. The Giants tied for sixth in 1901 and finished last in 1902. During the throes of the 1902 season Freedman hired John McGraw to manage for a then unheard-of salary: $11,000 a year. Under McGraw, the Giants moved up to second place in 1903

THE NEW YORK RED SOX (AND OTHER CURIOSITIES) ▼ 39

and won the pennant in 1904. After that they remained a reigning power for decades.

On January 10, 1903, representatives of the National League and the American League met in Cincinnati and signed an agreement of mutual recognition that brought most of their warfare to a close. Why would National League fat cats bother to deal with the aggressive American League newcomers? The American Leaguers had been raiding the National League for talent; then McGraw reversed the process, dipping into American League rosters for ball players to help his Giants. These raids made for lively newspaper copy and, to the growing horror of owners on both sides, they opened the gates to competitive bidding for players. Free agency was a fact of big-league life in 1902. The 1903 agreement closed down contract jumping and kept competitive bidding, some would say free enterprise, out of major-league baseball for the next seventy years, from the bluster of Teddy Roosevelt clear through Richard Nixon's adventures in Watergate. This same agreement also provided specifically for an American League franchise in New York.

One Frank Farrell, who owned a racing stable and was famous as a heavy bettor, joined with William S. Devery, a real estate speculator and former New York police chief, in posting $18,000 for the Baltimore franchise, which, as the leagues had agreed in Cincinnati, was transferred to New York City. Thus the original Yankees, a bastard child of the original Orioles, were had for $18,000, a fact that occasions surprise today when no fewer than eighteen major-league athletes individually earn $12 million or more a season. It is no overstatement and may even be true to say that $18,000 is tip money to Alex Rodriguez ($25.2 million), Derek Jeter ($18.9 million), or Mo Vaughn ($13.3 million). I hedge a bit here because tipping habits among professional baseball players vary.

During the long-ago winter of 1902–03, construction crews began to battle an unlikely ballpark site at 168th Street and Broadway, one of the highest spots on Manhattan Island. A contemporary description was furnished by the weekly *Sporting Life*:

> A plot of hilly ground, dotted by large and small boulders and trees, many of them dead, with a pond extending along one side that will have to be filled in. Masses of rock are grouped where the grandstand will be erected. There is not a level spot ten feet square on the whole property. From Broadway looking west, the ground starts in a low swamp filled with water and runs up into a ridge of rocks twelve to fifteen feet above the level of Broadway. The rocks will be blasted out and the swamp filled in, while 100 trees will have to be pulled out of the ground.

After some lively months of digging and dynamiting, the New York Highlanders, the Pleistocene Yankees, opened their maiden season at Hilltop Park before a crowd of 16,243 on April 30, 1903. The new playing field was raw and rocky. The new wooden stands were raw and creaky. Bayne's 69th Regiment Band played "Yankee Doodle." Spectators waved tiny American flags that had been distributed at the gate. The Washington Senators lost the ball game, 6 to 2.

There is a tendency these days to denigrate the poor old Highlanders. "Everything the New York Yankees are now began with Babe Ruth," Robert Creamer of *Sports Illustrated* wrote in a regrettable moment. As a sharply opinionated Ruth biographer, Creamer perhaps can be forgiven for composing a sentence that is exclamation-point writing rather than accurate history. The Yankees adopted their trademark pinstriped home uniform in 1912 before Ruth had even entered organized baseball. (The story that the pinstripes were chosen to camouflage Ruth's watermelon belly is a canard.) The Yankees found millionaire owners in 1915 when Ruth was a still a mean young fast-ball pitcher with the Boston Red Sox. (He won eighteen that year and hit four home runs, the fourth highest total in the league.) No one denies that Ruth was the Baron of Bashers, the King of the Clouters, the Lion of Long Balls, the Sultan of Swat, but when he finally did come into his own and into New York, he was joining a healthy, wealthy, growing franchise.

From the beginning, Byron Bancroft (Ban) Johnson, the founding president of the American League, wanted a strong team in New York City and worked behind the scenes—a gray eminence dealing deals—to help Farrell and Devery fashion a winner. He brought in Clark Griffith, called "the Old Fox," to manage and transferred a fiery shortstop, Norman (the Tabasco Kid) Elberfeld, from the Detroit Tigers. Two established stars, the pitcher "Happy" Jack Chesbro and the great slap-hitting outfielder "Wee" Willie Keeler, had earlier decided to kangaroo out of their National League contracts. Both became charter members of the New York Highlanders.

Ban Johnson's design—an American League pennant in New York City—fell one-and-a-half games short of success in 1904. The first outstanding sportswriter to provide a written record of the early Yankees, Grantland Rice, was working in Atlanta when the 1904 Highlanders took spring training there. "Fairly nondescript," was his summation. Rice wrote in 1951, "I remember particularly Clark Griffith, their manager and a veteran pitcher at that time; the little sharpshooter, Wee Willie Keeler; and 'Happy' Jack Chesbro, the smiling right-handed pitcher who went on to win 41 games that year. As I watched them under the warm Georgia sun, I, of course, never realized that I was watching the formation of the greatest baseball dynasty of them all." As the season proceeded and the team found its stride, other sportswriters were more impressed. Some began calling this long-ago ball club the New-York All-Stars.

On the final day of the 1904 season, the Highlanders awoke in second place, a game-and-a-half behind their opponents, whom they would meet in a doubleheader at Hilltop Park. Those opponents were the Boston Somersets or Pilgrims, the early Red Sox. Rice reported that "28,540 pushed their way into an arena built for half that number. They packed the stands and crowded around the outfield, standing on benches and boxes. They saw [in the opener] one of the most famous games in American League history."

In the ninth inning the teams were tied at 2 with two out and Lou Criger, the Boston catcher, on third. Jack Chesbro, making his third start in four days, fired two fast-ball strikes past Freddy Parent, Boston's 5-foot-5-inch shortstop. Trying to put everything he had on a spitter, Chesbro threw the pitch high over the head of his catcher, John "Red" Kleinow, and Criger scored what proved to be the decisive run. Boston had won the pennant. The Highlanders finished a noble second. It is certainly fair to suggest that this early "famous game" foreshadowed the great and more recent "famous" Boston–Yankee game, their duel in the sun of October 1978. Though forgotten today, it was the beginning of the great New York–Boston rivalry, played when Babe Ruth was all of nine years old. (McGraw's 1904 Giants ran off with the National League pennant, but McGraw refused to allow a World Series with the "minor leaguers from Boston." In a prepared statement to "the fans of New York," McGraw declared: "Now that the New York team [the Giants] has won this honor [the pennant] I will not see it tossed away like a rag.") Actually Boston had won the first modern World Series from the Pittsburgh Pirates in 1903; the position of McGraw and the new Giant owner, John Brush, fell short of a critique of pure reason. Brush, a clothing merchant from Ohio, had paid Andrew Freedman $200,000 for the Giants before the 1903 season started. He had a nasty past history with Ban Johnson. So did McGraw. The 1904 World Series was canceled not to preserve the sanctity of the National League pennant, but as a matter of personal pique. Subsequently the major-league agreement was amended to ensure an annual World Series, and this worked through two World Wars, a Great Depression, an earthquake, in short, everything but the labor–management dispute of 1994.

The early Highlanders could not keep pace with jarring John McGraw. His 1905 Giants won 105 games and won three more pennants in the next ten years. The Highlanders managed to finish second in 1906 and 1910, but most of the time they were a second-division club. Still, things were happening in the lower depths. The nickname "Highlanders" proved ungainly, particularly in news-paper sports departments, where an eleven-letter word made an ill fit into a one-column headline. Rice said that the name Yankees be-came popular "around 1908." The team formally assumed its new name, the New York Yankees, in 1913, a year in which the team fin-ished seventh and the owners put the nine-year-old Hilltop Park up for sale. The newborn Yankees became renters in the Polo Grounds, at 155th and River Avenue in Manhattan; it was a bigger and better arena, and McGraw did not feel threatened by sharing space with an inconsistent team that drew fewer than four thousand fans a game.

Frank Farrell and Bill Devery were chronic gamblers. "When-ever the Yankees made them some money, they'd go out and lose it to bookies at the racetrack," Grantland Rice told me years ago. Sometimes when they needed yet more cash, they borrowed, using the Yankees as collateral. Presently Farrell and Devery found them-selves broke. Even after the sale of Hilltop Park, the franchise was mired in debt. Still trying to develop a powerful ball club in New York, Ban Johnson stepped in and found two eager, and solvent, buyers. One was Jacob Ruppert, who had inherited a family brew-ery that produced vast quantities of revenue and beer at its installa-tion on the Upper East Side. The other, Tillinghast L'Hommedieu Huston, was a soldier of fortune who had made millions mysteri-ously as an army engineer in Cuba after the Spanish–American War. Each man put up $230,000. On January 11, 1915, they ac-quired the Yankees for $460,000 and became equal partners.

That did not work. It seldom does in baseball, a business of hunches, opinions, and guesswork. With a few exceptions—Hank Greenberg and Bill Veeck putting together a pennant-winning White Sox team—equal partnerships in baseball lead to disagreements, feuds, and stalemate. Ruppert, a natty bachelor, affected baronial airs. "When I bought the Yankees," he said, "I went into it in a sporting spirit, like buying a lake or a shooting preserve." Ruppert disliked being called Jake; he preferred Colonel, the rank he held in the New York State National Guard. Huston was "Cap," his old army rating; unlike Ruppert, he liked to run about and drink with the ball players and the writers covering the team. When American entry into World War I loomed during the spring training of 1917, Huston imposed marching drills on his players, substituting bats for Springfield rifles. "He even had some of the newspaper crowd marching around with Louisville Sluggers on their shoulders," Rice reported, "an experience that Damon Runyon and myself, among others, never forgot."

When war came, Huston rejoined the army and went off to France. Ruppert, looking for a sound baseball man, asked Ban Johnson for advice on a manager. Johnson recommended Miller Huggins, called the Mighty Mite, an intense and intelligent man who stood perhaps 5 foot 5 and weighed 140 pounds. After Ruppert signed Huggins, Huston yelped in France, "My partner has got us a dwarf." On his return, he and Ruppert argued, then stopped speaking.

At the end of the 1920 season—the Yankees finished a strong third—Ruppert hired flinty, thick-browed Edward Grant Barrow, sarcastically called "Cousin Ed" (he was nobody's friendly cousin), as general manager, opening an era of Yankee–Red Sox relations that bore a discomfiting similarity to illicit intimacy. Barrow had been managing the Red Sox. The Yankees had money. The Red Sox, owned by one Harry Frazee, had talent and what Frazee's show-business friends called "the shorts"—not underwear, boxers, or briefs, but a shortage of cash.

Frazee wanted to become a successful Broadway producer. He invested his baseball money in shows that flopped until there was no more baseball money left. Then he slouched to the marketplace and peddled athletes. In a four-year stretch, from 1919 to 1922, the Red Sox dealt the Yankees the three outstanding pitchers Carl Mays, Herb Pennock, and Waite Hoyt; an all-star shortstop, Everett Scott; an all-star third baseman, Jumpin' Joe Dugan; a sturdy catcher, Wally Schang; and, most famously, George Herman Ruth, the Grand Bambino. The 1923 Yankees won the World Series. The 1923 Red Sox finished last, thirty-seven games out of first place.

Frazee initiated the Ruth deal with a letter to Cap (now Colonel) Huston offering the big man's gifts for $125,000 and a loan in the form of a $350,000 mortgage on Fenway Park. Huston had the letter forwarded to Ruppert, who personally brought it to Miller Huggins. The manager is said to have leaped into the air and, upon landing, shouted: "He's cheap at twice the price. Grab him." After Ruppert quietly got Ruth to sign a three-year Yankee contract, the deal was announced on January 3, 1920. Frazee issued a public statement: "The Yankees are taking a gamble. While Ruth is undoubtedly the greatest hitter the game has ever seen, he is likewise one of the most selfish and inconsiderate men ever to put on a uniform. It would have been impossible to start next season with Ruth and have a smoothly working machine." That protest didn't wash in New England. Like the base Indian, Frazee had cast away a pearl richer than all his tribe, and people knew it right away. With Babe Ruth gone, was anything in Boston safe? Sarcastic FOR SALE signs appeared on historic Faneuil Hall and the Old North Church. "If Harry Frazee had been a bag of tea," author Ed Linn, a native New Englander, observed, "he'd have been trundled into a frigate and thrown into Boston Harbor."

The conflicts of interest at play might startle even a politician. With a mortgage on Fenway, the Yankees de facto owned a chunk of the Boston franchise. Can you have honest competition when one club is holding a rival's ballpark in hock? It doesn't seem so to me.

Probably the most painful episode, lye rubbed into wounds still gaping 'round old Back Bay, came during the 1923 World Series. Former Boston pitchers—the so-called Red Sox "transfers"—started five of the six games for the Yankees. They won four. Ruth hit three homers during this Series. Joe Dugan got four hits in game five. Wally Schang and Everett Scott each hit an impressive .318. As I noted earlier, the Yankees won the 1923 Series from McGraw's Giants, four games to two, beginning what sportswriters call the Yankee Dynasty. But as Ernie Shore, a Boston pitcher sold to the Yankees in 1919, put it, "The Yankee dynasty was really the Red Sox dynasty in Yankee uniforms."

In 1925 Frazee used the remaining proceeds from the Ruth deal to produce one of his few Broadway hits, *No, No, Nanette*. Not many cared in Boston. That year the Red Sox lost 105 games and finished last. As Ruth dominated baseball, Frazee protested to friends that the big feller had really forced his hand. The Boston police, he said, had to pick up a drunken Ruth in some gutter every night and take him home. A remarkable and knowledgeable Red Sox fan, the late Lib Dooley, told Ed Linn that Frazee knew such things "because he was such a notorious drunk and skirt chaser himself." It was patently symbolic that when Frazee died in 1929, his new best friend, Jimmy Walker, was at his bedside. *Mayor* Jimmy Walker, the mayor not of Boston but New York. It was also telling that in 1929 the Red Sox finished last for the fifth consecutive time. To this day Frazee is remembered in New England as a man of infamy, but it is nonsense to claim that he let Ruth go for a few pieces of silver. The sale price and the mortgage equal at least

$10 million today. There has never been a bigger deal in baseball history.

CHARLES H. STONEHAM, a securities speculator who dabbled in bookmaking and ticket scalping, bought the New York Giants and the Polo Grounds for "somewhat over a million dollars" in 1918, dealing in John McGraw as part owner. Before Babe Ruth joined the Highlanders/Yankees, the team had never drawn as many as 620,000 fans in a season, never averaging as many as 5,000 fans a game. With Ruth in 1920, the Yankees broke a million, attracting 1,289,422 paying customers to the Polo Grounds, outdrawing the Giants by the sizeable number of 359,813. Miffed, McGraw told Yankee management that the team was no longer welcome at the Polo Grounds, and Ruppert began to look for a new playing site. Huston, who wanted no part of a larger investment, or Ruppert himself, sold his half interest in the franchise. Ruppert paid him $1.5 million. The Yankees, baseball, and Babe Ruth were big business.

After considering several places in Queens and another at 135th Street in West Harlem, Ruppert purchased a tract of flat terrain in the South Bronx that had been owned by the estate of William Waldorf Astor. The location, today 161st Street and River Avenue, was only a fifteen-minute walk east of the Polo Grounds, across the McCombs Dam Bridge. It was accessible from most of New York City via the Interborough Rapid Transit subway line, which ran from an outpost in east Brooklyn under tunnels to Manhattan, then up both the East and West side and finally, emerging as an elevated line, clear up to Woodlawn Cemetery at the top of the Bronx. Yankee Stadium opened with a Red Sox game on April 18, 1923, a chilly day. Attendance figures were reported variously from 60,000 to 74,217. Either way, this was the largest assemblage to see a baseball game up to that time, although it was markedly lower than the crowd (90,000) that had watched

Jack Dempsey knock out George Carpentier in boxing's first million-dollar gate two years earlier.

(To set straight a persistent misconception, during the 1920s Dempsey, not Ruth, was the greatest box-office attraction in American sport. Dempsey earned as much as $900,000 for a single fight; Ruth's highest annual wage was $80,000. Overall, Ruth earned $1,076,474 in salary during a twenty-two-year playing career and another million dollars, but no more than that, from ghost-written articles, endorsements, and personal appearances. At a time when the federal income tax was just a whisper, Ruth's total gross ran to about $2.1 million. Dempsey earned at least $2.7 million in boxing purses, plus another $3.5 million for newsreel rights to his fights and movie appearances, a formidable total of $6.2 million. For a time Dempsey personally could have bought Babe Ruth. But not for a long time. When the stock market went over Niagara, Dempsey told me with a wan grin that he lost an even $3 million—more than Ruth earned in his lifetime—and found himself "broke like everybody else and eating sixty-cent blue plate specials for dinner.")

Fred Lieb of the *New York Evening Telegram* was the first man to call Yankee Stadium "The House That Ruth Built." Lieb saw the new ballpark as a mighty fortress. "Unlike the Polo Grounds, which is built in a hollow [under Coogan's Bluff]," he wrote, "the stadium can be seen for miles as its triple-deck grandstand majestically rises from the banks of the Harlem [River]." A *New York Times* reporter called the Stadium "a skyscraper among baseball parks." Ray Kelley, then with the *New York Post,* found a nice way to illustrate the stadiums's size. "The best indication of the immensity of the new plant," he wrote, "was furnished by the music of the Seventh Regiment Band, working hard in the corner of the left-field stands, with only snatches of the tunes reaching the crowd near home plate. It was like hearing the music of a parade on Fifth Avenue from an office window on a cross street." Triple-decked, copper-facaded, framed by steel and concrete, Yankee Stadium was like no ballpark seen before. It was baseball's Flavian Amphitheater, its coliseum. When new, the playing field ran 487 feet to dead center field and 500 feet at the deepest point in left center, but coming toward the right-field foul line, the stands cut sharply toward home plate so that straightaway right field was only 344 feet away from the batter. The length down the right-field line was a very modest 295. This vast and overwhelming new stadium came complete with a convenient short porch in right, a beckoning target for powerful left-hand-pull hitters such as Babe Ruth. On that distant day when the stadium first opened its gates, the Yankees defeated the Red Sox, 4 to 1. The winning margin was Ruth's three-run homer into the porch.

DURING THE RUPPERT–BARROW YEARS, a span of roughly three decades, the Yankees won the World Series ten times. They were the mightiest of ball clubs. They played in the grandest of ballparks. Ruppert and Barrow ruled skillfully, harshly, and with disdain. When Ruth's playing career wound down, he asked Ruppert to appoint him Yankee manager. "You can't take care of yourself, Ruth," Ruppert said. "How can you take care of a whole team?" Ruppert did offer Ruth a minor-league job managing the Newark Bears, saying, "Newark, Ruth, or nothing."

"Nothing," Ruth said. The Bambino went home to his apartment on Riverside Drive, where he burst into tears.

Joe McCarthy, the Buffalo Irishman who managed the Yankees to eight pennants under Ruppert and Barrow, was generally tightly controlled. But in the argot McCarthy was "a bust-out drinker." During one spring training McCarthy set forth on a bender and didn't show up at the playing field in St. Petersburg for a week. Desperate, Mark Roth, the Yankees' traveling secretary, telephoned Barrow in New York. Barrow's response was prompt and decisive. "Don't tell the goddamn writers."

The writers already knew. A few had even written that McCarthy was suffering from the flu. Many were spending two months in Florida with their families, all expenses paid by the Yankees. As surely as the Yankee barons tamed their ball players, they also co-opted the press.

Joe DiMaggio blossomed in 1937, his second season with the Yankees. He hit .346 and led the major leagues in home runs with forty-six, a remarkable total for a right-handed batter slugging into the deep prairie that was left field in the Bronx. He had earned $15,000 for 1937. The Yankees' first offer for 1938: $15,000. After talking things over with his older brother, Tom, DiMaggio decided that he wanted $40,000. Ruppert let a few favored reporters know that he was now increasing his offer to $25,000, but that DiMaggio would get "not a button more." At home in California, DiMaggio told Tom Laird, the sports editor of the *San Francisco News,* that he didn't actually *have* to get $40,000 but as a matter of pride and dignity he did need to extract an offer for more than the $25,000 written into the most recent contract the Yankees had mailed to him.

"Where is that contract now?" Laird asked.

"In the city dump," DiMaggio said.

Spring training began with DiMaggio unsigned. Ruppert engaged a private Pullman car and departed for Florida, attended by a valet and several other servants. DiMaggio missed all of spring training and on opening day the *New York Herald Tribune* published an editorial:

> The Yankees, led by the popular Mr. Joseph McCarthy, are as usual very strong. The immortal Lou Gehrig will be at first base. To be sure the Yankees will be missing the brilliant California youngster, Joseph DiMaggio, until he decides to be reasonable about his salary demands. He will eventually come to terms. They nearly always do. But even so he has hurt himself with his New York admirers, trying to get too much money out of poor [sic] dear Colonel Ruppert.

A smaller story in the *Tribune* reported that "beginning tomorrow when the Yankees open in Boston DiMaggio's stubborn behavior will start costing him $162.33 a day." That was the $25,000 offer worked out on a per-game basis. Two days later, out almost 325 Depression Era dollars, DiMaggio wired Ruppert: "Your terms accepted. Arriving 7:30 Saturday morning." He was coming by train. He had bought his own ticket.

Having earlier rejected Babe Ruth, Ruppert now orchestrated the humiliation of Joe DiMaggio. On April 25, Ruppert met privately with DiMaggio at the brewery, then invited the press into his office. "We're going to review this contract right before your eyes," Ruppert told the sportswriters. "DiMaggio has signed it. It calls for a salary of twenty-five thousand dollars." Then, sharply, "DiMaggio, is there any bonus for you here?"

DiMaggio shook his head. Ruppert looked at the contract. "DiMaggio," he said. "Put in your full address." DiMaggio had printed the address of his new home on Beach Street, but had neglected to add "San Francisco, California."

"Joe," a reporter said. "When you met with the colonel alone, was he peeved?"

"If he was, so was I," DiMaggio said. Ruppert shook his head, like the father of a talented, spirited, but poorly disciplined child. He then told the writers that DiMaggio would not begin collecting any salary at all until "we decide that he is in playing condition."

"Suppose he makes a trip with the team?" a reporter said.

"Until he's in condition," Ruppert said, "if DiMaggio wants to travel with the team, he has to pay his own way." By the time the Yankees did let DiMaggio return to center field, he had lost eleven days' salary, roughly $1,800. After that DiMaggio batted .324, hit thirty-two homers, thirteen triples, and threw out twenty base runners from center field. The Yankees won the pennant by nine-and-a-half games and swept the 1938 World Series from the Chicago Cubs.

Ruppert's death in 1939, at the age of seventy-one, had no immediate effect on the Yankees. He had built an organization as mighty as his stadium. Flinty Ed Barrow remained general manager. Cold, skilled George Weiss continued to run the farm system. The Yankees won pennants in 1941, '42, and '43, before selective service broke up the team.

After World War II, Ruppert's heirs, Mrs. Joseph Holleran, Mrs. J. Basil McGuire, and Miss Helen Weyant, put the Yankees on the market for $3 million. Leland Stanford "Larry" MacPhail, called the Roarin' Redhead, was a brilliant, hard-drinking baseball man who had built pennant winners in Cincinnati and Brooklyn. He brought night baseball to New York when he installed lights at Ebbets Field in 1938, and he recognized, before anyone else in the city, that broadcasting ball games was sound marketing. Before MacPhail arrived, the accepted wisdom held that New York fans would not buy tickets to a game that they could hear free over the radio. MacPhail made his own point by hiring Red Barber, who became a splendid sportscaster and, coincidentally, a master ticket salesman.

Larry MacPhail's son Lee, a former president of the American League, picks up the story. "My father offered three million dollars and the lawyers for the Ruppert estate were delighted. But, of course, my father didn't have three million dollars. He never was able to hold on to money. He did have a backer, but that fell through. The backer was too close to racetrack people, too close to gambling. So Dad had this great deal with Colonel Ruppert's estate, three million for the Yankees and the stadium. All he was lacking was the cash."

MacPhail took his problem to the bar at the 21 Club, where he encountered Dan R. Topping, the black-haired, square-jawed Anaconda Copper heir. Topping instantly was interested "for a third." He had a friend, a contractor in Arizona named Del E. Webb, who would surely take another third. Webb agreed and called his financial manager in New York. "I've decided to join the deal for the Yankees," he said. "Where can I get my hands on a million dollars quickly?"

"Why don't you drop in on the Chase National Bank," the money man said. "They're holding a million dollars worth of bonds that belong to you." With $2 million up front, raising the balance was no problem. On January 25, 1945, the troika of MacPhail, Topping, and Webb purchased the Yankees for a final price of $2.8 million. They acquired the franchise—the monarch of franchises—plus Yankee Stadium, which was later sold, plus the land under Yankee Stadium, which was sold in a separate deal, plus contracts signed by characters named Rizzuto, Henrich, and DiMaggio. It was as good a business deal as anybody in baseball could remember, and it was recognized as a great deal at the time. Put simply, the Yankees went on the block at discount in an estate sale. The same fate sometimes befalls Aubusson rugs.

Change, action, and constructive chaos were Larry MacPhail's hallmarks. He forced Cousin Ed Barrow to retire and took over running the ball club himself. Soon his box office was handing free nylon stockings to women who bought tickets. He had lights installed, and the first night game at the Stadium on May 28, 1946, drew 49,917. He hired a spectacular character named Jackie Price who shot baseballs to great heights with an air cannon, then jumped into a tan jeep and caught the monstrous fly balls in a glove while steering with the other hand. It made for a great show and raised eyebrows. John Drebinger of the *New York Times* told me, "Price was good all right. Still I couldn't get over the feeling that he belonged in the circus." The Yankees finished a distant third in 1946, but drew almost twice as many fans as any Yankee team in history, attracting a major-league record attendance of 2,265,512. They won the 1947 pennant by twelve games and took an exciting seven-game World Series from the Brooklyn Dodgers. Then in the clubhouse and during a victory party in the grand ballroom of the Hotel Biltmore, Larry MacPhail's brilliance exploded in a barrage of manic flashes that abruptly, some would say tragically, brought his baseball career to an end.

A minute after Dodger catcher Bruce Edwards bounced into the double play that ended the Series, MacPhail stood in front of the Yankee dressing room, ignoring his players and making a speech to the sportswriters. "You fellows have been just wonderful to me," he shouted, waving a bottle of beer. "Aw, hell. Just wonderful." He began to sob. "I'm out of the picture now. I got what I wanted. We won the World Series. I can't take any more. My health. My health."

Inside the clubhouse MacPhail guzzled champagne. "Here, you guys," he shouted at the reporters. "I want you to say this in your stories. I'm the guy that built up the losers, the Brooklyn club. Here's the man who really built the Yankees." He raised George Weiss's right arm. Still guzzling, he climbed onto a trunk to address the ball players. "I want to congratulate you fellows. Nobody beat you three in a row all season. Isn't that something! The two Joes [DiMaggio and relief pitcher Joe Page]. Just wonderful. I wanted to leave at the top. You fellows made it possible. I'm through, fellows. I'm quitting right now." He started crying again and wandered about until he found the Dodger president, Branch Rickey, in the center of a circle of reporters. "You've got a fine team," MacPhail said. "I want to congratulate you." Rickey leaned in very close. His whisper was ice. "I'll shake your hand because I have to with all these people watching. But I don't like you, sir. Don't care for you at all."

MacPhail was drunk when he arrived at the victory party. He dropped into a chair next to John McDonald, a diligent minor official who had also worked for him in Brooklyn. "That Rickey," he said, "is a Bible-quoting, hypocritical, tightwad son of a bitch."

"I got no complaints with him," McDonald said. "Rickey looks after people he likes."

"Stand up, you Judas," MacPhail said. He swung a right into McDonald's left eye. The two were separated. MacPhail lurched about and spotted George Weiss, the man he had praised a few hours earlier. "You gonna do what I tell you from now on," he said, "or are you gonna quit?"

"We've all been drinking, Larry," Weiss said. "Why can't we talk tomorrow?"

"I'll give you tomorrow. Stop in my office tomorrow for your final check. Weiss, you're through."

"Oh, dear," said Weiss's wife, Hazel. "Larry, please. We need the job." Hazel Weiss, a woman of wit and dignity, began to cry.

"Stay away from me," MacPhail said. He resumed lurching about the room and spotted big Dan Topping, big Anaconda Copper Dan Topping of New York and Southampton, who had paid cash for his third of the Yankees. "Hey, Topping," MacPhail said. "You know what you are? You're a guy born with a silver spoon in his mouth who never made a dollar in his life."

Topping stood up and seized MacPhail's left arm. "Listen, you," he said. "We've taken everything from you that we're going to take." Topping wrestled MacPhail into the ballroom kitchen. He was bigger than MacPhail, younger by twenty years, physically stronger and substantially more sober. He shook MacPhail roughly, punched him with a few body blows, and ordered him to behave. "If you act up again, Larry," Topping said, "I'm gonna knock your head off. Now go into the washroom and clean yourself up and for Christ's sake, comb your hair."

Half an hour later MacPhail returned to the ballroom, properly groomed. He walked up to the relief ace, Joe Page, who was sitting with his wife, drinking slowly. "What were you, Joe, before I picked you up?" MacPhail said. "A bum. You and this broad here were nothing. I bought a home for you. You're wearing nice clothes now. You're drinking my champagne. But without me, the two of you would be starving." Like Hazel Weiss before her, Mrs. Joe Page burst into tears. Topping approached the table with a murderous look. MacPhail weaved away from the couple. Then this remarkable, bizarre, wondrous character staggered out of the victory party and out of baseball.

In the sports section of the late and extraordinary New York newspaper *PM*, which accepted no advertising, Tom Meany commented the next day, "The World Series and MacPhail finished simultaneously. Larry was sobbing when he announced that he was through. He set a record for sobbing in a seven-game series."

Before the self-destruction, MacPhail had been talking with Wall Street firms Bear Stearns and John J. Bergen & Co. about selling Yankee stock to the public. He produced books showing that the 1946 Yankees had earned $1.35 on each (privately held) share. The shares had a par value of $10; the team was returning better than 13 percent. The figures for 1947, with proceeds from a seven-game World Series, would be even better. MacPhail wanted to sell the public three hundred thousand shares—just under fifty percent of the club—at $15 a share. The three partners would retain control and pocket $1.5 million each. MacPhail wanted the money to expand a horse farm he had purchased in Bel Air, Maryland. But after the crack-up at the Biltmore, the idea for a public offering died. Topping and Webb liked privacy and neither needed the money.

In the spring of 1952, I spent a day with MacPhail, who had just become president of Havre de Grace racetrack. I was a young newspaperman, just turned twenty-four, and MacPhail was gracious, vital, and uncomplaining after a long siege of radiation for throat cancer. During a shining afternoon we tired the sun with talk. He was hoarse, to be sure, but his voice crackled with vitality and his ranging mind was a wonder. When MacPhail died in 1975, it surprised me to learn that he was flat broke. "What Larry wanted most," Tom Meany told me, "was not just to be a winner. He wanted to be a squire, like Thomas Jefferson, only richer."

Topping and Webb bought out MacPhail for an even $2 million. Webb lived in Arizona; his building business was prospering. Topping, based in New York, replaced MacPhail as president and day-to-day CEO. Neither man approached MacPhail in solid baseball knowledge, or in charisma. Webb, in fact, was as shady as Pete Rose. But they delegated brilliantly and across the twenty years of the Topping–Webb regime, the Yankees won another fourteen pennants and another nine World Series. Such phrases as "the rampaging Yankees," "the Bronx juggernauts," and "the Lordly Bombers" became stock stuff in sports pages. At one cocktail hour during this period, an unemployed actor at the Players' Club remarked to Walter "Red" Smith of the *New York Herald Tribune*, "How can you root for the Yankees? It's like rooting for U.S. Steel."

Up close the organization was somewhat less than tranquil. Aside from constructing concentration camps for nisei in the western wilderness, Webb had built hotels with gambling casinos in Las Vegas, working for and with mobsters, which I suppose is one reason that, except for those free subscriptions to the glossy *Arizona Highways*, he had nothing to do with the press. I tried to interview him at a Wisconsin lake resort during the 1958 World Series—Yankees vs. Milwaukee Braves—when he was sitting with a fluffy brunette show girl who had just arrived by seaplane. He glared and said did I want to leave him alone or would he have to call hotel security? The late Joe David Brown of *Sports Illustrated* had somewhat better luck two years later. In a first-rate article called "The Webb of Mystery," he described Webb as a man who sat on the boards of 43 companies, belonged to 14 social and country clubs, and "has so much money he almost never has to touch the dreary stuff." There was also a distinctly darker side. Webb admitted to having built the Flamingo Hotel in Las Vegas for the mobster Benjamin

"Bugsy" Siegel, which led to some sort of partnership with Meyer Lansky, a titan of the underworld, and later dealings with a Detroit Mafioso named Joe Zerilli. Robert Goldwater of Phoenix, who ran a department store and was brother of the late Senator Barry Goldwater, once described Webb as "an ignorant son of a bitch who built a million-dollar business with a hammer and a nail and a case of whiskey thoughtfully distributed in Washington." These days when people suggest that some of George Steinbrenner's excesses "besmirch the Yankee tradition," I'm tempted to remind them that a former co-owner of the team figuratively went to bed with mob gamblers, two at a time. There was something distinctly ominous about the man. For whatever reasons, various commissioners of baseball chose not to notice.

Topping was cleaner, a former Marine Corps Captain, more approachable and marginally more polite. When we talked, he usually made me feel that he was already late for an appointment with someone more important than I and that I was holding him up. He sidestepped baseball questions and always concluded by asking me to send his regards to my boss, the very social Robert Barbour Cooke, sports editor at the *Tribune,* and in an earlier time, Yale's hockey captain.

Topping and Webb put dour, chipmunk-cheeked George Weiss in charge of baseball operations. Weiss quickly fired the manager, popular, low-key Stanley "Bucky" Harris, replaced him with Charles Dillon "Casey" Stengel, and brought in Arthur "Red" Patterson, late of the *Herald Tribune,* as public relations director, the first full-time major-league publicist ever. Patterson took over the 21 Club on October 12, 1948, and introduced, or reintroduced, Stengel to the New York press. Stengel had played outfield for the Dodgers and Giants. He later managed Brooklyn for three seasons without finishing higher than fifth.

"It's just twenty-five years to the day," Patterson said from a dais which he shared with Joe DiMaggio and other worthies, "since Casey hit his second homer [for the Giants against the Yankees] in the 1923 World Series." Dan Topping followed and introduced Stengel as "the man who's going to lead our great Yankee club to a pennant."

Stengel stepped to the microphone, looked at Dan Topping, and said, "Thank you, Bob." Topping had a brother named Bob who never worked but won renown as a playboy. Following an uncomfortable pause, a reporter asked how Stengel felt about "managing a great player like Joe DiMaggio." Stengel said, "I can't tell you much about that, being as since I have not been in the American League so I ain't seen the gentleman, except every once in a very great while." DiMaggio, whose ego was as mighty as his bat, grimaced. After that he and Stengel never got along.

"Most observers," John Drebinger reported in the *New York Times* the next day, "[started out as] kindly disposed toward Stengel. But after the press conference they were viewing his forthcoming performance with misgivings." Frank Graham, Jr., was more succinct. He wrote, "Uneasy lay the crown upon that old gray head."

"Patterson was trying hard," Stengel told me years later. "And so was I. But I know writers, and I kept hearing a hum from the writers in the room. And the writers were looking at me, damn near sixty years old, and they're saying in this hum: 'That old bum managed nine years before in the major leagues and he ain't never got out of the second division once.'" Stengel would manage the Yankees for twelve seasons and never fall out of the *first* division once. Under him the Yankees won ten pennants. In his first five Bronx years, the Yankees won the World Series five times. Twenty years later George Weiss told me he was not surprised. "I knew what I was getting," he said. "I was not hiring a comedian. In the minors Casey was wonderful working with veterans and great with difficult youngsters like Billy Martin [whom Stengel managed in

Oakland]. He had this uncanny knack for getting the right hitter up at the right moment, handling pitching, running a game. He learned a lot playing for John McGraw. Everybody agreed Casey did a great job managing in the 1949 season. But what did the goddamn writers think, that he had learned how to manage all at once in 1949?"

This Weiss–Stengel baseball partnership was superb and Topping and Webb were smart enough to leave it alone. But their own sophisticated business sense led to a series of deals in 1953 that changed the structure of baseball. Historically, major-league teams owned the ballparks in which they played. The Giants owned the Polo Grounds, the Dodgers owned Ebbets Field, the Cubs owned Wrigley Field, and the Yankees owned the Stadium. On December 17, 1953, after the Yankees' fifth consecutive World Championship, Topping and Webb sold the Stadium, the land under the Stadium, and some collateral property to a financier named Arnold Johnson. The price was $6.5 million. Topping and Webb essentially had doubled their investment, *and they kept the franchise.* After further brokering, the Knights of Columbus acquired the land under the Stadium and richly endowed Rice Institute of Houston, Texas, bought the Stadium itself. Topping and Webb, sometimes dismissed as an odd couple, had scored a phenomenal business coup. They recognized that the Yankees had no need to own acreage or steel or mortar. All the Yankees needed was a team and a place for that team to play. Webb and Topping pocketed more than $3 million apiece and leased back playing space on favorable terms. And, as I said, they kept the franchise. They would have to pay rent, but these fees flowed painlessly out of the profits earned by a team now drawing more than a million-and-a-half fans a season and earning another $750,000 a year from broadcast and television rights. Although this transaction may seem simple enough in the telling, it moved the earth under the world of baseball. Like the tungsten filament finally glowing for Edison, it at last became clear: A team didn't have to own that expensive facility called a ballpark. All it had to do was rent space. Soon Walter O'Malley sold Ebbets Field to a real estate developer, shocking humble, idealistic fans in Brooklyn. "I mean," one asked, "what's next? Will the Roman Catholic Church sell Lourdes?" But led by the Yankees, the businessmen who ran baseball quickly marched to the beat of the new drummer. Horace Stoneham got the city fathers of San Francisco to build a new field, Candlestick Park, for the Giants. Today twenty-seven of the thirty major-league clubs play in facilities they do not own, but rent.

This new way to do the business of baseball echoed a story popular in the last days of World War II when Del Webb's crews were building El Toro Marine Base in California. A lonely GI, wandering across the Parisian street Place Pigalle, spotted a voluptuous lady of the evening under the inevitable lamp post. War-weary, lonely, the GI eschewed preliminaries and asked the girl directly, "How much?"

She quoted a very hefty figure.

The GI said, "We got a little misunderstanding, lady. I don't want to buy it. I just want to rent it." It's a fair assumption that some years after the war this GI found a job in baseball.

CHAPTER THREE

▼

STEINBRENNER UNBOUND

MICHAEL BURKE, the seventh president of the New York Yankees and the man who immediately preceded George Steinbrenner into the Bronx corridor of power, was telling a story about a time and place that was far from the growls of Ruth, the stares of Joe DiMaggio, and the soft memories of dimpled Lou Gehrig. In 1944, it seemed, Mike Burke parachuted out the belly of a B-24, a lumbering four-engined, twin-tailed World War II bomber called a Liberator, and plummeted through chill and black night air. Falling, he remembered that, above all, he was not to pull the ripcord until he came to within five hundred feet of the drop point, a meadow that colonels in the Office of Strategic Services had decided was a good area for landing, hard by the Vosges Mountains in northeastern France. In 1944 that territory was occupied by Nazis. Burke hit the ground, rolled, and buried his chute. He carried a pistol, emergency rations, a pint of brandy, and the address of a house that would be friendly. His mission: Mobilize and energize the French Resistance in the area, which up to that time, Burke told me, had been "sheeplike."

As Burke, whose French was fluent, began to rally natives and take out some of the invaders, the *Abwehr* dispatched a regiment of Ukrainian collaborators to pacify the region, find the resistors, and kill them all. No prisoners survived this kind of clandestine action. The Nazi plan went sour when the Ukrainians defected to Burke's mountain band. He was telling me all this calmly during the summer of 1971 while the Yankees kicked away a game to the Chicago White Sox on a large television screen in Burke's Manhattan penthouse. Terrible game. Great conversation.

It was very bad behind the Nazi lines. "Mike," I said, "did you ever look a man in the face and shoot him dead?"

"I had to do that at least eight times. But the ethical problem eased up for me after the Gestapo grabbed one of our people. They put one hundred fish hooks into his back and pulled them out one by one. Then they blew off his face with a shotgun."

On the screen tough Thurman Munson was digging in to hit. Suddenly, in counterpoint to Mike Burke's story, Thurman didn't seem so tough at all.

"France," Burke said, "was worse than Italy. There they sent me behind the lines in a PT boat to see about getting the Italian fleet to surrender. A lot of the Italian captains did and I ended up with the Silver Star. After I talked a little about that one, Hollywood wanted my story. They made a movie called *Cloak and Dagger* and they hired Gary Cooper to play me.

"Damn," he said, suddenly switching from war to baseball after Lindy McDaniel came in to relieve the Yankee starter, Fritz Peterson. "This guy McDaniel tells me baseball is only the third most important thing in his life. First comes his family and his church, then baseball. I hope he can concentrate on number three tonight. No. Damn." A fork ball hung and Carlos May of the White Sox crashed a double into the right center-field gap.

Burke shook his head and said, "Rough business."

"War?" I said.

"That, too, but I was talking about baseball."

———

DURING THE TOPPING–WEBB REIGN, the Yankees dominated as no team has before or since, winning the pennant fifteen times in the eighteen seasons between 1947 and 1964. Every autumn in New York, the weather cooled, the leaves turned russet, and the Yankees marched off to play the World Series. But during the early 1960s change threatened this established way. The nature of the South Bronx shifted with great speed: What had been middle class and safe slid down toward slum. Mickey Mantle's speed, durability, and power declined. In 1961, the year of Roger Maris' sixty-one homers, Mantle hit fifty-four. After that he never again hit as many as forty. Along with Mantle, other stars of his era, Yogi Berra and Whitey Ford, were fading.

Casey Stengel had been fired in 1960. ("It was because I made the mistake of being seventy years old," Stengel said. "I won't make the same mistake next year.") The Yankees won two straight World Series under their new manager, Ralph Houk, and then opened the 1963 Series against the Los Angeles Dodgers with a swagger that had become as traditional as their pinstripes. The score of the Dodgers' first-game victory, 5 to 2, does not indicate how Sandy Koufax, the great Dodger lefthander, presided at Yankee Stadium. Bobby Richardson, a fine high-fast-ball hitter, was batting second. Koufax threw Richardson three high fast balls and struck him out. Then he looked into the Yankee dugout. I was sitting behind the dugout. I saw the Koufax look. It said, "I'm gonna pitch it to your power and I'll *still* strike you out." Right then Mickey Mantle said to Richardson, "We are not going to win this game." Koufax struck out fifteen, setting a Series record. The Dodgers swept the Series. In the four games the Yankees scored a total of four runs and struck out thirty-seven times. Hard as it was to believe, a Yankee team had been outclassed. Next fall, 1964, the Yankees hit better, but Bob Gibson pitched two complete games for the St. Louis Cardinals, who clinched a seven-game Series on October 15. Little more than two weeks after that, on November 2, 1964, Topping and Webb sold the Yankees to CBS. The final price, Mike Burke said, was $14 million. Bill Veeck was offering $10 million. A brokerage house—Burke did not remember which one—had talked about putting up $20 million and then taking the Yankees public, but what Burke called "tax complications" killed that deal.

Topping and Webb got out of baseball for several compelling reasons. The declining stadium neighborhood was significant. "We were all concerned that the colored people and the Puerto Ricans moving into the Bronx couldn't afford our ticket prices. We were concerned, too, that they would scare off our good box-seat customers from downtown and Westchester County," George Weiss told me. At forty, Yankee Stadium was showing its age. Cracks appeared in the concrete. By the standards of the time far too many seats offered bad views obstructed by pillars. An expensive remodeling was coming due. Finally, and most seriously, the Yankee pool of young talent, refreshed by seemingly eternal springs, had run dry. Some have attributed this to a sort of borderline racism: a reluctance to recruit black and Latin players as vigorously as other franchises. That probably is true to a degree. But an equal factor was simply age: The great scouts hired by Barrow and Weiss, the men who brought in Gehrig, who recommended DiMaggio (when others worried about his bad right knee), the bird dogs who found Mantle and Berra and Ford, were growing old. The 1964 Yankees, the team the Cardinals defeated in the World Series, were a fine facade of a ball club. Behind the front-liners, there was little vital pressure from young talent, patching critical weak spots, driving veterans to hustle for their jobs. In 1965, Mike Burke's first year as president, the Yankees finished sixth. In 1966 the Yankees finished last, their first last-place finish in fifty-four years. One September day in 1966, the Yankees played the White Sox at the Stadium before a paid attendance of 413.

"The blame is mine," Burke told me in his penthouse. "I'd run a circus, moved on to CBS, and become the right-hand man to the boss, William Paley. When I heard the team was available—the word was all over town—I urged Willie to buy it. It was my suggestion, but it was Paley's fourteen million dollars. Did I know a last-place finish was coming? No. Not at all. Never. If you conclude that when I took over as team president, I simply did not know enough about major-league baseball, I can't argue. I developed an awe for baseball as a boy playing the game at Kingswood Prep in Hartford, but Kingswood isn't the Yankees, as I've learned at some expense to myself and the very patient Mr. Paley." Smart and literate as Burke was, he never carefully checked out the Yankee minor-league system. When CBS bought the team and put him in charge, the farms were barren. Burke's Yankees (1965–73) never won a pennant and finished second only once. Mike was a wonderful companion, a true war hero, a gentleman of vision, culture, and lyricism. Unfortunately, at the major-league level, he was no baseball man. Perhaps his tragedy was that he thought he was.

Two of Burke's accomplishments endure. It was he who worked with Mayor John V. Lindsay in organizing the 1970s renovation of Yankee Stadium. Lately that deal, like other government–sport collaborations, has come under fire from urbanologists. One academic writer, Neil J. Sullivan, attacks Lindsay as a poor negotiator and a naif who failed to bargain with Burke as shrewdly as he might have. Lindsay did volunteer city funds, tax dollars as they say, to pay for the reconstruction, which was projected to come in at $24 million. Before the remodeled Stadium opened on April 15, 1976, the final cost, the real cost, had risen to $106 million. John Lindsay's personal integrity can hardly be at issue. That was demonstrated most poignantly when he spent his last days in severe circumstances, struggling to pay his medical bills. Some of the $106 million was devoured by inflation. A significantly larger amount went through many hands to the mobsters then running New York's construction unions. That is ugly, of course, but only part of the story.

In City Hall one spring day in 1971, John Lindsay told me that he had a dream. Lindsay was a tall, handsome, fair-haired man who glittered when he spoke. He saw the South Bronx springing back to life around a magnificent new Stadium, a shining jewel of a ballpark, a model for baseball people and urban planners everywhere. Along with this great stadium would come the necessary parking ramps and, beyond them, new inviting shops and restaurants, attracted by the baseball crowds. In a much wider area— where rat-infested abandoned buildings stretched for scores of city blocks—would come new housing. "Stadium Apartments," "Yankee Arms" were two names with which Lindsay played. He spoke for almost an hour with what I remember as great candor—we had known each other for ten years—and concluded with controlled passion: "You know as well as I that no white people live in the South Bronx, no white people go there for anything except baseball. Unless we do this thing with the Yankees, the Bronx will become the most foul and segregated ghetto anywhere in the country. That would be nothing less than a disgrace to the city I've been elected to govern."

Academicians now point out that sports arenas do not appear to revive neighborhoods. But no one knew that thirty years ago, and I have a hard time faulting John Lindsay for his idealism.

BURKE'S SECOND exceptional achievement was finding somebody to buy, or rather pay for, the Yankees. Construction contracts with New York City were signed in 1972, and they provided for a thirty-year lease on a remodeled Stadium, running from 1976. But 1972 was also the season in which a drab Yankee team finished fourth and attracted fewer than a million fans. Proceeding from the Yankee problems, *Forbes* magazine suggested that major-league baseball "could well vanish from the scene in twenty years." About that time William Paley told Burke that he, that is to say CBS, intended to sell the Yankees as quickly as practically possible. "The team just doesn't fit into any niche in our company," he told Burke. Put more directly, the Yankees, now losing about a million dollars a season, had become a stye in the eye that was the CBS logo. Paley also told Burke that CBS was willing to take a $4 million loss and accept an offer of $10 million. Rather than risk the possibility of a public auction, which could take on the embarrassing look of a fire sale, Paley offered the franchise exclusively to Burke and told him to go out and find the financing.

"I knew a lot of people," Burke told me, "but I couldn't find any serious backers, not a one, even among financial exotics. Did I have ten million dollars myself? Not even close." His search for capital finally led him to a forty-two-year-old Midwestern sports buff, a shipping man recently cited by *Fortune* magazine as one of twelve "Young Movers and Shakers of the Nation." That mover and shaker was and is George Michael Steinbrenner III.

As Burke told the story, Steinbrenner made two phone calls. Bunker Hunt, of the Texas silver-straddle Hunts, said fine, he was in for $2 million. Lester Crown, an insurance and real estate megamillionaire from Chicago, said sure, he was in for another $2 million.

"How did you get the rest?" I asked Burke.

"George got the rest. But as soon as we had that first four million dollars, the banks fell all over themselves dropping interest rates to give us the other six. After you find the front money, everything goes easy."

In early January 1973, the Yankees held another press conference at "21"to confirm that "a limited partnership has purchased the Yankees." The "managing general partner" was Steinbrenner. The best-known baseball man in the group was Gabe Paul. "Most of my own work is in Cleveland," Steinbrenner said. "We're shipbuilding people. Mike Burke has agreed to stay on as president. Mike Burke will continue to run the team."

Three weeks later Burke resigned, offering the press an elegant, if not entirely relevant, recital from Yeats' "An Irish Airman Foresees His Death":

> *I know that I shall meet my fate*
> *Somewhere among the clouds above;*
> *Those that I fight I do not hate,*
> *Those that I guard I do not love.*

Burke accepted a 9 percent interest in the Yankees as a reward for past efforts and, I suspect, as an inducement not to make a fuss. Burke: "It was early apparent that George and I could not be compatible, so we elected to part in adult fashion." Steinbrenner: "I brought in Gabe Paul to handle the baseball stuff. I mean, look at Burke's baseball record. I wanted Mike limited to public relations work. So he left us, but with a handsome reward in his wallet." Paul began in baseball as a shoeshine boy outside the ballpark in Rochester, New York, home to a renowned minor-league club called the Red Wings. "Then I moved up to water boy. I carried bats. I lugged equipment. I don't want you to think I started at the top." Paul moved on to Cincinnati, where in time he ran the Reds, then on to Cleveland. He had a soft voice, a seemingly gentle style, and a charming wife named Mary, in whom he took much pride. When he assumed the Yankee presidency in 1973, he became the first Jew to run a ball club in New York since the Andrew Freedman days at the dawn of the century. Some said cynically that Steinbrenner was hiring a Jew to win the affection of Jewish sports fans in New York. Actually Paul was the best baseball man Steinbrenner knew. That Gabe was Jewish (and that his wife, Mary, was an elegant high WASP) was not a primary consideration.

The following April a federal grand jury in Cleveland indicted Steinbrenner on fourteen counts related to illegal contributions, with the implication that he was trying to buy influence within the

Richard Nixon administration. As a shipbuilder, Steinbrenner clearly wanted to sell ships. Both the U.S. Navy and Coast Guard purchased ships. One senses a connection. After hard bargaining by his lawyer, the renowned Edward Bennett Williams, Steinbrenner pleaded guilty to violating Section 610 of the Federal Elections Code, a felony. He was fined a modest sum, lost his right to vote, but avoided prison. The *Wall Street Journal* reported: "Legal authorities say they are certain that the prosecutor's staff had been confident Steinbrenner would receive a jail term." That is journalese. The anonymous "legal authorities" the *Journal* cited were the federal prosecutors themselves.

Baseball Commissioner Bowie Kuhn suspended Steinbrenner for two years, but let him keep his Yankee stock. He lifted the suspension eight months early in March 1976. That was not time off for good behavior, as some wrote, but it may have been an *ex-post thank you*. Earlier, during the summer of 1976, Kuhn had needed Steinbrenner's vote to stay in office. He got it.

YANKEE BIOGRAPHIES are not in short supply. Under the keyword "Babe Ruth," the Barnes & Noble website posts eighty-nine titles. There are twenty-eight listings for Mickey Mantle, twenty-seven for Billy Martin, and seventeen for Reggie Jackson. Autobiographies (with collaborators) have flowed from the pens, so to speak, and the hearts, one hopes, of Jackson, Sparky Lyle, Graig Nettles, Billy Martin, Ron Guidry, Thurman Munson, and Goose Gossage, among others. But here is a curious thing. Punch the name of George Steinbrenner into a major book website and almost nothing happens. You draw a 1999 work called *Patton on Leadership: Strategic Lessons for Corporate Warfare*. Steinbrenner wrote the preface. Then comes a 1997 book by Brandon Toropov, *101 Reasons to Hate George Steinbrenner*, which is moving at an extremely modest clip: As of this writing, Barnes & Noble reports its sales rank as 537,349. After that the websites subside. They list no autobiography, no critical biography, no full-length book of any sort devoted wholly to the life and times of the most dramatic baseball executive of recent times. (A purported biography was written in 1981 by the late Dick Schaap, who tossed ethics to the winds and secretly let Steinbrenner review and edit his manuscript. That work has disappeared. Schaap spent hours on television that year belittling Ed Linn's volume, *Steinbrenner's Yankees,* which Schaap regarded as competition. Linn, always fair-minded about the books of others, was deeply hurt.)

The absence of a serious Steinbrenner life story cannot entirely be attributed to the traditional lack of interest by publishers in off-the-field people. Biographies of MacPhail, Branch Rickey, and Bill Veeck exist. Four baseball commissioners have published memoirs. Besides, Steinbrenner ranks with his best ball players in having the quality that glows golden in the offices of contemporary book publishers: celebrity. There is no Steinbrenner book mostly because George has not wanted a Steinbrenner book and through various means he usually gets his way.

He and I met in suburban Cleveland in 1965—neither of us recalls the exact date—at a small, upscale party to which I came as the guest of Frank Ryan, then quarterback for the Cleveland Browns and still the only professional football player to have earned a Ph.D. in theoretical mathematics. George was husky, bluff, intense, and charming. As I remember it, he was very much a midwestern feller. I had flown in from New York; my title was editor-at-large at the *Saturday Evening Post,* then selling about seven million copies a week. Steinbrenner probably wanted to make enough of an impression so that I, and the national magazine I represented, would not forget him. We talked sports, journalism, and politics, but Frank Ryan was the star of that party. He had just passed the Browns to a division championship in the National Football League and in a few weeks he was going off to teach a course in topology at Case–Western Reserve.

The twenty-first-century George Steinbrenner is much more

of a corporate type than the intense, hustling midwesterner I met in Cleveland, and about equally remote from the character who appeared at the Yankee Stadium Restaurant in 1973 as the new and unknown CEO of the Bronx ball club. Over the years I've had enough conversations with him to understand Steinbrenner on several levels and to know, perhaps as well as anyone outside his intimate circle, the pleasant aspects of the private man. There is more serious music lover and poetry enthusiast—in short, aesthete—within Steinbrenner than ever makes the daily papers.

With timing appropriate for a Yankee Doodle Dandy, Steinbrenner was born on July 4 in a prosperous Cleveland suburb called Bay Village. The year was 1930, Depression time but not for the Steinbrenner family. George's father, Henry, once a hurdler at MIT, owned a five-ship inland fleet that carried ore and grain across the Great Lakes. The family roots were German and Irish. According to George, his father was stern but tightly controlled. No tantrums thrown at the children, but no allowance, either. When George was nine, his father bought him a variety of chickens and said, "Look after them. You can make your spending money selling eggs." The boy worked hard, built an egg route, and prospered. He called his egg business the George Company. To this day he can and will describe the differences between a Buff Wine Dot, a Plymouth Rock, and a guinea hen.

At thirteen, before he went off to secondary school, Steinbrenner sold the George Company to his two younger sisters, Susan and Judy. "They renamed it the S & J Company," he said once. "I don't remember the price I got from them, but it must have been pretty good. My sisters still don't speak to me." The specific prep the family chose for young George is significant. It was Culver Military Academy in Indiana, where boys from prosperous homes were dispatched to acquire toughness and discipline. Walter O'Malley, the merciless buccaneer who ripped the Dodgers out of Brooklyn, was another Culver product.

Apparently some rebellion ensued. After Culver, Steinbrenner's paramilitary education ended when he enrolled at Williams College in the Massachusetts Berkshires and majored in, of all programs, English literature. At Williams he developed, he says, a fondness for the novels of Thomas Hardy, a love for the poetry of Keats and Shelley, and a passion for Shakespeare. I have heard him talk softly of Hardy's "peony-lipped maidens." He sang in the Williams Glee Club, along with Stephen Sondheim. ("I had a better voice," Steinbrenner volunteers.) He wrote a sports column for the *Williams Record*. ("I was not a knocker.") Like his father, he ran hurdles. As a senior he made the football team at halfback. Following graduation, the family expected that regardless of his ranging interests, George would join his father in the shipping business, Kinsman Marine Transit, and enter a quiet life of obscure affluence.

But after a service hitch, spent as a general's aide in Columbus, Steinbrenner broke away. He became a high school football and basketball coach in Ohio. In 1955 he moved up and became an assistant football coach at Northwestern, and later he coached backfield at Purdue. He gave up life as a Big Ten jock only, he says, after an elegant lady—one of the Kettering (as in Sloan Kettering) girls—dumped him, remarking that she would not settle for a lifetime spent as Mrs. Assistant Coach.

He joined his father at Kinsman in 1957, but he could not or would not abandon sports. He found enough backers to raise $125,000 and buy an industrial-league basketball team called the Cleveland Pipers that moved into the American Basketball League. When the league collapsed, the Pipers went bankrupt. Although he had no legal responsibility to do so, Steinbrenner subsequently repaid his backers $50,000 out of his personal funds. He dismisses suggestions of nobility. "That was a price I had to pay," he says, "if I was going to keep on doing business in Cleveland."

During the late 1950s Kinsman Transit ran into buffeting days. The big steel companies were building fleets of their own to transport ore from Duluth down toward the big mills in Ohio and Pennsylvania. Some independent shipping companies folded. After three years "when my father and I really beat the bushes looking for business," Kinsman signed a contract with Jones and Laughlin Steel of Pittsburgh guaranteeing considerable annual tonnage. George had saved the family business. He was thirty. Seven years later he led a group that took over the American Shipbuilding Company, a mighty enterprise with yards in Tampa, Cleveland, and a half-dozen other cities. After that he became a forceful spokesman and lobbyist for his big company and the shipbuilding industry at large. This was a rocket rise to wealth, but all the while part of his focus stayed on sports. In a sense, sport to George was like that beckoning green light Jay Gatsby saw and sought on a dock he could not reach. Or so it seems to me.

MARSH SAMUEL, long a prominent Cleveland publicist and a Steinbrenner associate, says, "George was a Cleveland boy and what he really wanted was to buy the Indians. But an even richer Cleveland boy, Vernon Stouffer, owned the team and Stouffer was taking a long time to decide whether to sell. The Indians were idling into the 1970s. They sure could have used fresh energy, but as I say, Stouffer procrastinated and patience never was George's long suit. Then this Yankee thing came up and then the trouble." Details of "the trouble" exist in court records. On April 14, 1974, in Cleveland the federal grand jury charged Steinbrenner with making illegal contributions to CREEP—the infamous Committee to Reelect the President (Nixon)—during the 1972 campaign. The indictment further accused him of doctoring records, ordering officials of American Shipbuilding to make false statements, and obstructing a federal prosecutor's investigation. Steinbrenner responded: "I am totally innocent and will prove it in court." As events demonstrated, that statement was not entirely accurate.

According to federal prosecutors, the facts were something other than a civics lesson. Steinbrenner personally contributed $75,000 to CREEP. He paid "bonuses" of $25,000 to each of eight executives working for him at American Ship and ordered them to transfer the bonus money to CREEP. Such forced contributions are illegal but not unheard of in big-time, big-fisted corporate America. Compared to sums generated to influence government by drug companies, banks, the tobacco industry, and oil cartels, the Steinbrenner donation may have been illegal, but it was modest. Worse, from Steinbrenner's standpoint, the aggregate contribution—$275,000—did him no good. He would have been better off using the money to buy a vacation hideaway, except, of course, George Steinbrenner seldom hides away and never vacations.

When the federal investigators began closing in, Steinbrenner allegedly doctored books at American Ship to cover his tracks and asked several executives, including Robert E. Bartlome, Matthew E. Clark, Jr., and Stanley Lepkowski, to join him in the cover-up. Or so these men told the FBI. They all refused to perjure themselves and when they went as a group to tell that to Steinbrenner, he put his head in his hands and said, "I'm ruined. The company is ruined. I might as well jump off a bridge." He did not mention the Yankees. This, in brief form, is the prosecution version of what happened. But an underlying question is acutely troubling. With all the megamillion high-rollers in all the board rooms in all the towers skirting campaign finance laws, why did the federal government investigate Steinbrenner in the first place? As funding in presidential races goes, the money put up by the former CEO of the George Company was chicken feed.

One sunny afternoon Steinbrenner provided me with his explanation. He was, he said, not a Republican at all. He was an independent Democrat. He regarded the late Thomas "Tip" O'Neill, Democratic Speaker of the House, as a good friend; he also was close to Senator Ted Kennedy. Across 1969 and 1970 he organized fund-raising dinners for Democratic congressional candidates in the Cleveland area and, George being George, raised about $2 million. Then, as the 1972 presidential election approached, Richard Nixon's Republican henchmen, Harry Robins "Bob" Haldeman, John Daniel Ehrlichman, and the rest, sprang. Steinbrenner told me, "The Nixon people were very annoyed at my Democratic fund-raising." Now they demanded he provide them with whatever dirt he had on O'Neill, Kennedy, George McGovern, Fritz Mondale, and other eminent Democrats of the time. "Rough stuff," Steinbrenner said, "not only stories about the politicians but about their wives. Drinking. Sex. Very damn distasteful, if you ask me."

George told me that he refused to deal in dirt. Nixon's men threatened an antitrust investigation of American Ship. The steamers might lose licenses to dock in important ports. Steinbrenner, his company, his executives, and just about everybody close to him would undergo income tax audits—audits à la Nixon. (These voracious IRS proceedings became known as "punitive audits.") Faced with the possible destruction of his company, his fortune, and, indeed, the fabric of his life, Steinbrenner decided to buy his way out with the contributions to CREEP. But still, Steinbrenner insisted to me, he would tell no tales on his Democratic friends. The Nixon response, he says, was the fourteen-count indictment, accelerated when he bought the Yankees, in the expectation that it would drive him out of baseball. If you accept Steinbrenner's story, Nixon and his henchmen become wanton characters, almost beyond belief. But that may be why so many of them went to prison.

▼

CHAPTER FOUR

MANUMISSION

BASEBALL SLAVERY ENDED in two installments. Part one proceeded from the arrogance of Charles Finley, an autocratic insurance millionaire out of Chicago, who bought the Kansas City Athletics, moved the franchise to the unlikely setting of Oakland, and built a fine ball club by the bay. (Gertrude Stein, who once lived in Oakland, complained famously: "There's no there there.") Shrewd though he was, Finley underestimated the intelligence of a Carolina country-boy pitcher called James Augustus Hunter and nicknamed (by Finley) "Catfish." Finley believed ball players should have nicknames and one day he said to Jim Hunter, "When you were a kid you ran away from home with your fishing pole and when you came back you had two catfish, understand?" That seemed harmless enough. The pitcher nodded; "Catfish Hunter" was born. But Hunter's docility ended in 1974, precisely at the point where Finley played games with his contract.

Part two proceeded from a business blunder committed by Walter Francis O'Malley, who didn't make many. O'Malley was dark and devious, but he also possessed great roguish charm. When I caught him uttering a set of false statements once, he smiled without embarrassment and said, "You have to remember that only half the lies the Irish tell are true." As CEO of the Los Angeles Dodgers, O'Malley, called the Big Oom, let a bright young righthander named Andy Messersmith, a physician's son from Toms River, New Jersey, pitch for the entire 1975 season without signing a contract. Messersmith won nineteen for the Dodgers, but at the end of the season of '75, he was under contract to no one.

When the Hunter and Messersmith affairs finally were settled, baseball's reserve-clause system was history. As with Aquarius, this was the dawning of an age, in this case, the new age of free agency. Quicker than anyone else, more shrewdly than anyone else, more decisively than anyone else, Steinbrenner moved into the free-agent era, pen and checkbook poised. Before you could say Catfish or Martinez or Goose, Jim Hunter, Reggie Jackson, and Rich Gossage were wearing Yankee pinstripes, and with a difference.

FOR STEINBRENNER, settling the criminal indictment was an exercise in agony. He says Nixon's gang was after him, and there is no reason to disbelieve that, but as Watergate's blood-red glare erupted, it was finally the special prosecutor, Leon Jaworski, who probed the Steinbrenner case. A more reasonable man than the later prosecutor Kenneth Starr, Jaworski, a Texas lawyer and a Democrat, was hardly Nixonian. Probably it is accurate to say that Steinbrenner, a good way from the epicenter of Watergate, got caught up in a nasty aftershock.

As everyone from Bill Gates to Monica Lewinsky has learned, the power of federal investigators is disquieting. They can threaten, indict rightly or wrongly, and enlist roguish Internal Revenue auditors as artillerymen. John Marshall summed that up as well as anyone: "The power to tax involves the power to destroy." Steinbrenner's statement that he might jump off a bridge does sound like a melodramatic cry of despair. But transient despair. Once Big George walked out on that bridge, he would have looked to see if its toll booths were sufficiently jammed with traffic. If they were, he would have bought the damn thing. Another Steinbrenner statement may be more telling: "I was the only person outside of Washington, D.C., to be indicted in the mess that followed Watergate."

There is no doubt that he faced a measure of potential ruin. The federal indictment threatened him with public disgrace, particularly humiliating for a man who wore patriotism on his blazer sleeve. A serious conviction would have battered his shipbuilding business. A stern judge might have imposed years in prison; jail time would almost certainly have led to his expulsion from the coveted closed universe of major-league baseball. When Fred Saigh, the feisty owner of the St. Louis Cardinals, went to prison for income-tax irregularities in 1953, the lords of baseball forced him to sell out, which he did to August Busch of the Budweiser Busches. Now, twenty seasons after that, an imprisoned Steinbrenner could similarly have been forced to sell his team, the team he liked to call his *Mona Lisa*.

Except, except...Edward Bennett Williams, a big, bluff Irishman, a sports buff and a hearty, enjoyable drinking companion, was one of the greatly gifted attorneys of his time. Williams died of cancer in 1992, and no one knows exactly what tactics he employed on Steinbrenner's behalf. Particularly with a client like George, Williams would not tell the client everything. But after Williams maneuvered, cajoled, bullied, fasted, wept, and prayed, Steinbrenner was permitted to plead guilty to a single felony count and to another count that been had been reduced to a misdemeanor. On August 30, a federal judge named Leroy Contie, Jr., settled the case by fining American Shipbuilding $20,000 and fining Steinbrenner $15,000. Even allowing for inflation, that is pin money.

Bowie Kuhn, then the commissioner, has stated, "A jail sentence would almost certainly have ended Steinbrenner's days in baseball." But following the fines and several meetings with the redoubtable Ed Williams, Kuhn decided on suspension, rather than expulsion. In November 1974, he issued an interesting order:

> Within 20 days Mr. Steinbrenner shall delegate to a person satisfactory to this office all of his powers, duties and authority to manage, control and make all decisions affecting the business and assets of the New York Yankees... Mr. Steinbrenner shall not visit or be physically present in the Yankee clubhouse or offices [or] confer, consult, instruct, advise or otherwise communicate with the person to whom such powers are delegated. These prohibitions shall not be interpreted as prohibiting Mr. Steinbrenner from associating with such persons on a purely social basis during which [author's italics] *there shall be no discussion of the affairs, financial or otherwise, of the New York Yankees or baseball.*

Within twenty days, Steinbrenner replaced himself as managing partner, installing Pat Cunningham, the Democratic leader of the Bronx and the chairman of the New York State Democratic party. Gabe Paul, the sound baseball man who came from the Midwest to New York with Steinbrenner, remained club president, in charge of day-to-day baseball. Steinbrenner disappeared from press conferences, dugouts, and the clubhouse, but as surely as Alexander Graham Bell invented the telephone, Steinbrenner remained in charge. Red Smith wrote: "Giving him a two-year 'suspension' that costs him nothing is like sending a naughty boy home from school for the Christmas holidays." Ed Linn, going deeper, wrote: "Allowing him to retain his [majority] Yankee stock but to have no say in running the club is a ruling so absurd, so unenforceable that it strains credulity to believe there was any intention of it being enforced."

Why was the penalty so light? Kuhn says Steinbrenner spoke to him openly and candidly and that helped his case. Ed Williams argued for no suspension at all. Kuhn commented, in somewhat befuddling prose, "Perplexed as I was by the court's leniency, I still

Ron Guidry, baseball's best pitcher in 1978, ▲
shows the grace and power of his delivery.
Corbis

From the heels. Reggie Jackson
demonstrating his power stroke.
Corbis ▼

► Lou Pinella, one of the club pros on the '78 Yankees, called "the best slow outfielder in baseball."

Baseball Hall of Fame Library, Cooperstown, NY

Thurman the Grump is concentrating as he gets ready to hit.

▼ *Ira Golden*

And in this corner . . . Martin (*left*) and Jackson almost come to blows ► during a 1977 game with the Red Sox at Fenway Park.

Corbis

▲ George M. Steinbrenner, one formidable boss. A sign on his desk read: "Lead, follow or get the hell out of the way."
Baseball Hall of Fame Library, Cooperstown, NY

Gabe Paul, the first Yankee president under George M. Steinbrenner, never lost his ability to smile under pressure. ▲
Baseball Hall of Fame Library, Cooperstown, NY

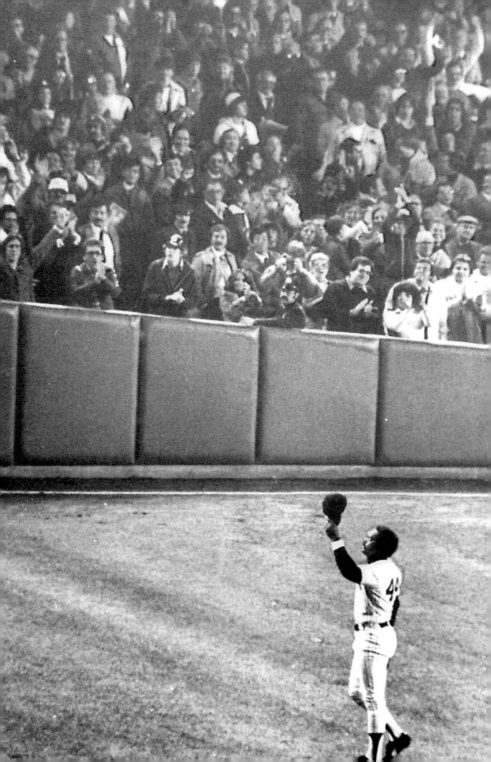

Power pitcher Rich "Goose" Gossage unloads one of his ▲
97-mile-an-hour fast balls. "He scares hitters," Jackson said.
Baseball Hall of Fame Library, Cooperstown, NY

◄ After hitting three homers on three swings in game six of the 1977
Series, Jackson acknowledges the jubilant crowd at Yankee Stadium.
Associated Press

Cy Young Award–winning relief pitcher Sparky Lyle. *Baseball Hall of Fame Library, Cooperstown, NY*

The Cleveland Connection: Key Indians in their 1954 pennant season, (*from left*) manager Al Lopez, third baseman Al Rosen, and pitcher Bob Lemon. Rosen moved east and became president of the 1978 Yankees, bringing in Lemon as manager. *Corbis*

decided that a substantial suspension was necessary." Other sources, who do not wish to be named, tell me that Williams faced the commissioner and slammed home powerful points. Sure, his client had made a mistake, but it wasn't a very big mistake. That's why the fines were so light. Now, if Kuhn ordered Steinbrenner to divest himself of Yankee stock, Williams would take *that* matter to court. If Williams knew the law business at all, he would see that the proceedings went beyond Steinbrenner's situation and subjected Kuhn and Baseball, Inc., to a complete judicial review of the extralegal, some said feudal, structure of baseball. To the rulers of the baseball business, the implications of that approach, pursued by one as adroit as Ed Williams, were catastrophic. Even fighting off the ropes, Steinbrenner and Williams were intimidators. Briefly put, they slugged their way to a sweetheart suspension beyond compare. One thinks, perhaps hyperbolically, of the great Jack Dempsey crawling back through the ring ropes and nailing mountainous Luis Firpo, "the wild bull of the Pampas," in what is arguably the greatest fighting comeback ever.

AS WHAT WOULD BECOME the remarkable 1978 Yankee team began assembling—it took three or four seasons to come together—Steinbrenner ran the show mostly by phone. He is a master of the demanding 2:00 A.M. call. Did he fire off memos? Only, I'd guess, in disappearing ink. But was his power still there? Did his will still dominate the Stadium? One might as well ask if the phantom really attended the opera. Gabe Paul remained the on-scene baseball man. The designated boss pro tem, the stand-in, Pat Cunningham, offered the finest impersonation of the Invisible Man performed anywhere since the death of Claude Rains. Pseudosuspension or no, Steinbrenner presided. Of course he did.

DURING THE SEASON OF 1974, the Yankees began to show vital signs. They had previously acquired Graig Nettles, a powerful and improving young third baseman, in a one-sided trade with the Cleveland Indians. (That date was November 27, while Gabe Paul was already negotiating to leave the Indians for the Yankees. More than one baseball man expressed suspicions. Paul always denied that his pending move to New York was a factor.) Grumpy, mustached Thurman Munson, up from the farm system, was coming into his own as a big-league catcher. The '74 team finished a close second to Earl Weaver's Baltimore Orioles in the American League East and paid attendance reached 1,273,075—the highest in ten years. The number was not entirely remarkable. In Los Angeles the Dodgers drew more than twice as many people—2,632,474. But the Yankee return was under way.

The team lacked a dominant pitcher. "No team," Gabe Paul remarked over a pleasant lunch back then, "ever has enough pitching."

"Except for the [1960s] Dodgers of Koufax and Drysdale," I said.

"As a matter of fact," Paul said, "I was running the Reds in those days and [Dodger general manager] Buzzie Bavasi was after me all the time to see if there was one more available good pitcher I could send him."

Catfish Hunter was arguably the best of all pitchers in 1974. He won twenty-five for Oakland, led the league with a 2.49 earned run average, and pitched six complete-game shutouts. When the Athletics won a five-game World Series from the Dodgers, Hunter saved the first game and won the third. He was not a dramatic missile hurler like Nolan Ryan, nor did he throw a cosmic curve like Sandy Koufax. Hunter worked in an understated way with a variety of breaking pitches and moving, though not overpowering, fast balls. He employed guile and he possessed control. Hunter knew how to throw the right pitch to the right spot at the right time. He was a master of that part of pitching called the head game.

His 1974 salary was a flat $100,000, half to be paid during the season and the other half to be deferred as Hunter specified. In August, Hunter's lawyer, J. Carlton Cherry, the sixty-eight-year-old senior partner of Cherry, Cherry, Flythe and Evans in Ahoskie, North Carolina, instructed Finley to use the second $50,000 to purchase an annuity. Hunter passionately wanted an annuity to guarantee a college education for his young children, Todd and Kim. After discussions with other baseball executives, Finley decided to ignore Cherry. Instead he handed a $50,000 check to Hunter, who returned it with a brief note: "My attorney advises that this check must go directly to the Jefferson Insurance Company." The ensuing dispute combined issues of contract, taxes, and insurance. Finley had learned belatedly that the IRS refused to allow an annuity payment as an immediate business deduction. In a contract simply calling for deferred payments—Finley signed one of those with Reggie Jackson—the owner retained the use of his money until payment time came round, some years into the future. But now Finley would lose the use of the $50,000 he had agreed to pay to Hunter's specifications, and he couldn't even get a write-off on the money. Finley's millions came from his own insurance business. Fury seized him. He had mishandled what was turning into an insurance matter. He was a caustic, foxy man who now found himself outfoxed by a farm-boy pitcher and a country lawyer. The Oakland A's were playing fine baseball, but Finley fumed with a persistent larval glow.

When the regular season ended, Hunter led the American League in victories (25) and earned run average (2.49), but Finley still was refusing to set up the annuity. On October 7, a day off during the Athletics' play-off series with Baltimore, Dick Moss, the lawyer for the players' union, wrote Bowie Kuhn stating that Finley was in breach of contract and asking the commissioner to declare Hunter a free agent. Tone deaf to the times that were a'changin', Kuhn refused. The union filed a grievance which came before a scholarly arbitrator named Peter Seitz, a passionate fan of the Bayreuth opera of Wagner and the comic-opera Dodgers of his own youth in Brooklyn.

On the afternoon of December 13, Seitz announced that James Augustus Hunter, perhaps the best pitcher in baseball, was now a free agent. His decision ran for fifty-five pages. Bowie Kuhn commented with neither grace nor understanding: "To forfeit the contract over a few days' delay in paying the $50,000 is like giving a life sentence to a pickpocket."

Drinking coffee with Seitz in his handsome apartment on Central Park West that winter I said, "I thought you might fine and reprimand Finley, but you'd let Hunter stay with the Athletics."

"A fine would have been appropriate," Seitz said, "if Finley had failed to provide Hunter with those nice white understockings ball players wear. But he refused to follow the contract in a somewhat more serious way, wouldn't you agree? In nonlegal terms, Mr. Finley went back on a fifty-thousand-dollar promise. He welshed. Do you happen to know how many fans the A's attracted last season?"

The number was 845,693.

"So Mr. Finley certainly possessed fifty thousand dollars. I believe a synonym for welsh is swindle. Have some more coffee, or would you like a J & B?"

Finley tried to overrule Seitz in court. He lost quickly. Kuhn tried to ban open bidding for Hunter. He had to back down. This was again Runnymede, June 12, 1215. Finley and Kuhn were fighting to squelch the Magna Carta.

JAMES AUGUSTUS HUNTER, the youngest of a sharecropper's eight children, was an unlikely sort of revolutionary. He grew up outside Hertford, a village in the North Carolina lowlands sixty miles south of Norfolk, Virginia. Fields of soybeans and peanuts reach for miles. The Alligator River flows to the south. To the north lies the Great Dismal Swamp, a 750-square-mile tangle of vines and bald cypress, black tupelo, and white cedar trees, alive with bear, deer, gray fox, opossum, and snakes. But the dry land around Hertford is flat—classic Carolina hardball country where center field seems to extend to the horizon.

Hunter matured quickly and starred in three sports (track, football, and baseball) at Perquimans High School. Pitching for an American Legion team in Ahoskie one summer he struck out 138 batters in eighty-seven innings. That sort of performance draws scouts even, or especially, to backwaters. Clyde Kluttz, once a journeyman big-league catcher, later a Carolina bird dog for Finley, befriended the young star, helped him with pitching grips, and composed such radiant scouting reports that Finley himself traveled to Hertford. For all his sandpaper edges, Charlie O. was a pretty good baseball man. Three other teams were interested in Hunter. But now in a tenant farmer's stark home where twenty dollars was a lot of money, the owner of the faraway Oakland Athletics produced a check for $75,000. He signed his pitcher.

Hunter did not become an instant star. Soon after the signing, he was hunting with his brothers in the swamp when a downward-pointed shotgun discharged accidentally. He lost the little toe on his right foot and that year, 1964, he could not pitch at all. Finley stayed with Hunter, who recovered and gradually, over five or six seasons, developed a feel for the art form that is fine pitching. The remarkable lefthander Warren Spahn described one aspect of this touch and made it sound more simple than it is. "Hitting is timing. Pitching is upsetting timing." Hunter could make his fast ball sink and move in or out. He had a variety of breaking pitches. He was forever changing speeds. Starting in 1971 he won twenty-one games for three consecutive years. Then in 1974, he won his twenty-five. By the end of 1974, the season of Finley's blunder, Oakland had taken three straight World Series and Hunter's Series record was estimable. Four victories. No defeats.

Now that this premium pitcher was a free agent, panic spread among baseball's old guard. "The Hunter thing is terrible," said Walter O'Malley, grand vizier of the Old Guard. "It threatens the whole structure of the game." Steinbrenner, the new kid, wasted no time on rhetoric. He directed Gabe Paul to sign Hunter for "whatever it takes." George did this quietly, of course. The Bowie Kuhn pseudo-suspension remained in effect. By now Hunter owned a 110-acre farm outside Hertford and in December, when the last legal questions on his free agency were settled, he began commuting from his front porch to Ahoskie for a daily meeting with Cherry, most of whose other clients were peanut farmers.

The manhunt was without precedent. Others followed as free agency became a rule of the game, notably the Pete Rose gold rush of 1978, when Rose elected to leave his hometown Cincinnati Reds. But then Rose, like a political candidate, flew from town to town with his lawyer, carrying videotapes of himself into a dozen front offices before deciding that his heart belonged to the Philadelphia Phillies. Hunter, wholly a different man from Rose, felt no need to promote himself.

Hunter and Cherry put out word that they would entertain no offer of less than one million dollars. Twenty-four clubs were playing major-league ball in 1974. Twenty-three bid for Hunter's services. Structure of baseball be damned, Walter O'Malley was among the bidders. Charles O. Finley was not.

BEYOND CASH, some teams tried special pleas. Hunter recalled a phone call placed to him by Don Sutton, the Dodger star, on orders from O'Malley. Hunter said Sutton seemed embarrassed by having to telephone and spoke for about ten seconds. "I know you don't want to hear my bull, but the Dodgers are a good organization. Best of luck." Then Sutton hung up. Thurman Munson, the Yankee catcher, was more prolix. "Cat," he said, "you know I'm a good catcher. Would you rather throw to me or to catchers who're a hell of a lot worse?"

Brad Corbett, a multimillionaire manufacturer of plastic piping, owned the Texas Rangers (which he would later sell to Eddie Chiles, who still later sold the Rangers to a syndicate organized by one George W. Bush). Corbett sent a delegation of seven men to Ahoskie. Each presumably carried a checkbook. Others who made the pilgrimage included Gene Autry (California Angels), Ruly Carpenter (Phillies), Al Campanis (Dodgers), present Baseball Commissioner Bud Selig (Milwaukee Brewers), Gabe Paul (Yankees), and Peter Bavasi, son of the Dodgers' highly successful general manager, who was trying to pump life into the San Diego Padres under their crusty owner, Ray Kroc, an ice-eyed man who had built the McDonald's hamburger (some would say cholesterol) empire. Bid followed bid. The Angels went to $2 million. The Phillies moved to $2.6 million, plus lifetime hunting privileges on the Carpenter family's vast acreage in South Carolina. The Red Sox went to $3 million. In the end Kroc agreed to a complex offer which Carlton Cherry estimated was worth no less than $4 million. Although this was by far the richest package offered to a ball player since the Mesozoic Age, Hunter turned it down. "Tell him I'll throw in a free McDonald's franchise," Kroc, who was deaf, screamed at Peter Bavasi. Cherry checked with his client and reported back. Hunter had no interest in selling Egg McMuffins.

From an accountant's point of view, the Yankee offer was second or third best. (With such things as annuities, insurance policies, and deferred income measured against inflation, it is impossible precisely to quantify the package offered Hunter.) Two, possibly three, factors tipped the scales. Clyde Kluttz, Hunter's old mentor, had moved on from Oakland to the Yankees and become director of the farm system. With the Yankees, Hunter knew he would have a friend high up on the command post. Then, country boy or not, Hunter recognized that New York was America's media and advertising capital. That could translate into just about as many commercial endorsement deals as he had the energy and inclination to undertake. Finally, as his focus on annuities demonstrated, Hunter was a staunch family man. "If I play in New York," he told me, "I can fly to Norfolk, pick up my car, and be home in a couple of hours. If I play in San Diego, what? I'm gone for half the year."

Not that the Yankee contract was penurious. It provided a $1 million cash bonus, payable immediately; a $1 million life insurance policy also paid up immediately; $50,000 each in annuities to underwrite college tuition for the Hunter children; $750,000 in salary, payable over five seasons at $150,000 a year; and another $500,000 in deferred income. In addition, the Yankees paid J. Carlton Cherry of Ahoskie $200,000 for his professional time. The worth of all this is generally set at $3.35 million. Good-bye grits. Hello, Oysters Rockefeller. Hunter responded to his change of fortune with imposing calm.

A few days after the Yankees announced the signing, Hunter flew to New York on January 2, 1975, for a so-called "media day" introducing his new persona, *Catfish Hunter, Sudden Yankee, Instant Millionaire*. Robert O. Fishel, the team publicist for many years, was an earnest and gentle sort. He left six months after Steinbrenner arrived. Marty Appel, who replaced him, was young, energetic, perhaps more resilient than the older Fishel, and very bright. (Within three seasons, Appel also left Steinbrenner's employ.) I was writing a monthly essay for *Esquire* magazine at the time, and I asked to spend the entire media day with Hunter, whom I knew slightly. "I'll set it up," Appel promised.

Hunter and I met near dawn for coffee at the Essex House on Central Park South. He was big, but not outsized, a solid six-footer.

He wore a tan double-knit suit over an open-collared shirt that depicted hunting scenes. "What is this about?" he said pleasantly.

"I write a monthly essay, eight or ten pages, for *Esquire*," I said, "except the editor calls it a column because that way he can pay me less."

"Sounds like baseball," Hunter said.

I considered his attire, neat but decidedly country. "You like hunting?" I said.

"When you hunt," he said, "you get your mind off everything. You just worry if your dog does good." Then tersely and without complaining he recounted the specifics of his accident eleven years before. He was tramping in wetlands with one of his brothers when the other man's shotgun discharged. The blast knocked Catfish sideways into hip-deep water. He felt as though a hammer had slammed his toe. "Dammit, dammit, dammit," Hunter said. "You done shot me. Get me the hell out of this hole." His brother fainted.

"So you've become the greatest nine-toed righthander in baseball history."

He grinned. "And there's something else. Losing that toe kept me out of the army and probably being sent to fight in Vietnam. I knew some country boys got killed over there."

Early that morning Rusty Calley, the former army lieutenant charged in the My Lai massacre, was defending himself on ABC's *AM America*, the first stop on Hunter's media circuit. In Vietnam, like everywhere else, Calley was saying, the top army brass protected itself and let blame fall on junior officers like himself. We were sitting in a green room. Jesse Jackson walked in, and Hunter stood to shake hands.

"I thought you'd be bigger," Jackson said. "When you were beating the Dodgers for Oakland in the World Series you looked twelve feet tall."

"I'm about as big as I have to be," Hunter said.

"I root for the Dodgers," Jackson said, "because they signed Jackie Robinson, but knowing about Charlie Finley, I sort of rooted for you guys, too. You know I'm against slavery."

Bill Beutel, the ABC interviewer, had been poorly briefed. He asked Hunter several times whether all major-league ball players would now make themselves free agents. "They can't," Hunter said without impatience. "We all have contracts. To become a free agent, there's got to be a breach and you've got to prove that there was."

"Well, what is this going to mean?" Beutel said.

"It means owners are going to start reading the contracts they write," Hunter said.

In the cab to Shea Stadium—Yankee Stadium still was being remodeled—I asked Hunter how he liked being interviewed. "During the season," he said, "I'll do anything the Yankees ask. Television, talks, anything. But off season, I'm really gonna be off. All that huntin' makes me do a lot of hard walkin' and a pitcher got to have strong legs. That's how it's gonna be."

A blur of photographers milled outside the ballpark. Fourteen Nikons chattered as Hunter walked into the catacombs of Shea. He met Pete Sheehy, the Yankees' clubhouse man, and passed photographs of old Yankees in their glory: Ruth, Gehrig, DiMaggio, Mantle, and Whitey Ford, the old lefthander who was then serving a term as pitching coach. Someone asked Ford if, in view of all the millions of dollars, he would treat Hunter differently from his other pitchers. "Not at all," Ford said. "Absolutely not. Except, of course, I'm going to call him sir."

Hunter put on a Yankee uniform, number 29, while obeying a confusion of directions. "Look this way, Catfish. Smile Catfish. Look serious, Catfish." He walked onto the field, patched with ice, and lobbed a baseball for twenty minutes. "Now look like you're really pitching," a photographer ordered. Hunter went into a full windup and threw. Then he jerked his head and looked forlornly toward the right-field fence. It was a perfect pantomime of a pitcher who has just given up a home run.

We rode back to Manhattan for a luncheon press conference and the questions came in bursts. Had he been hearing from his old teammates? "A few. Gene Tenace's wife cried because we couldn't all be together any more. But I've had to change my number. Some fan kept calling with advice at three A.M."

What about pressure? Everyone would be expecting everything from the first million-dollar pitcher. "I'm just gonna do what I always did. Take the games one at a time. Do my damn best. That's all I can do. What else can I do?" In an anteroom he did nine separate interviews for radio and television, most repeating the same questions. By the time he finished at 4:00 P.M., his eyelids were drooping and he suggested we relax over a beer.

He told me that when he was growing up, at the end of one year of tenant farming his father showed a profit of seventy-five cents. "We ate what Dad grew, corn and turnips. Dad had some hogs. I ate a lot of pork. Winters he did some logging. Pine and cypress. That brought in maybe two thousand dollars. There wasn't much money but we had plenty of food. It was a good way to grow up." After a while I asked Hunter how he felt about Charlie Finley now. He smiled a hard smile. "How do you expect *you'd* feel when you're treated like an animal and the keeper don't feed you when he's s'posed to."

The Yankees had gained one formidable feller, and I called Marty Appel to tell him how interesting I'd found Hunter. "He was great," I said, "but it's still overwhelming to think of one ball player being worth three million dollars."

"What the hell," Appel said. "We needed a right-handed pitcher anyway."

▼

CHAPTER FIVE

THE DARK PRINCE

IEWED COLDLY and perhaps a bit cruelly, Catfish Hunter was a disappointment in New York. At 1970s prices, three million was supposed to buy a pennant; the 1975 Yankees finished third. That year the Boston Red Sox led the American League East and Baltimore came in second. Hunter won twenty-three and pitched thirty complete games, but still the Yankees lagged twelve games behind the Red Sox, who went on to play a memorable World Series against the Cincinnati Reds. (Cincinnati, then called the Big Red Machine, defeated the Sox in seven rousing ball games.)

To the disappointment of the Yankees and more sharply of the pitcher himself, after 1975 Hunter never had a twenty-victory season. Shoulder miseries gradually robbed him of his edge and he elected to retire at thirty-three after an embarrassing performance during 1979, when he completed one of nineteen starts and won only two games all year. Hunter's pitching arm and his Yankee contract expired at just about the same time.

As a novice club owner back in 1975, Steinbrenner may have been seduced by the notion that one great pitcher all by himself could cure a team's ills. But the Yankee squad Hunter joined was dogged by problems. Graig Nettles, who had come over from

Cleveland in 1972, was developing into an all-star at third and Thurman Munson was flourishing behind the plate, but for every positive, as Isaac Newton postulated, there was a corresponding negative. The starting shortstop, Jim Mason, batted .152. Rich Coggins, who played some center field, hit .224, a blasphemous performance in a spot once manned by Joe DiMaggio and Mickey Mantle. Solid pitching or not, pennant winners must be made of sterner stuff beyond the mound. But while Hunter's New York career did not work out as divinely as Steinbrenner had hoped, his acquisition was an important statement. Steinbrenner was willing to fix the broken CBS Yankees by spending great sums, his own and those of his limited partners, some of whom complained at the assessment levied on them to meet the Hunter contract. It is sometimes argued in baseball that "you can't buy a pennant." But the Yankees, of course, did buy Babe Ruth from the Red Sox and Joe DiMaggio from the San Francisco Seals, changing the course of pennant races for thirty years.

A CHARGE DIRECTED at the third-place 1975 Yankees was lethargy, a deadly sin in the world according to George M. Early that August. As the Yankees were falling out of the race, the *New York Times* ran a headline: LETHARGIC ATTITUDE BLAMED BY SOME FOR YANKEE DECLINE. A synonym for the word "some" here is the name Steinbrenner. After dumping Ralph Houk, who succeeded Casey Stengel and managed the Yankees for eleven seasons, Steinbrenner tried unsuccessfully to hire Dick Williams, a bristly martinet of a manager. Eventually he settled for Bill Virdon, a former outfielder who had been managing the Pirates for two seasons. Perhaps Virdon's chief failing in New York City was that he was a Pittsburgh sort of guy.

The Yankees scheduled an old-timers' game for a Saturday in August in their rented quarters at Shea Stadium, middle-aged Yankees facing portly opponents for three innings. Virdon had agreed to suit up with the opponents; playing against the Yankees in the 1960 Series, he had hit a modest .241. But at 7:10 that Saturday morning, when Virdon entered the Yankee clubhouse, he came to pack his gear. He thanked Pete Sheehy, the clubhouse chief, for past favors and he was gone at 7:30, before any ball players arrived. He had been fired at 1:00 A.M. The new Yankee manager, hired at 1:30 in the morning for $72,000 a season, was Alfred Manuel "Billy" Martin, who himself had gotten dismissed just ten days earlier as manager of the Texas Rangers. "This is a very exciting move," said Gabe Paul, speaking for a guarded and probably anxious Steinbrenner. Others were not so sure. Martin's managing approach, later called *Billy Ball* when Martin managed in Oakland, began with aggressive play and an induced paranoia. "He works on the players singly and in groups," one baseball man said to me, "and tells them the people they can't trust. The press, of course. He'd let the ball players know the press wasn't out to help them; the press was out to sell newspapers and didn't much care who got hurt. Then there were the other athletes. A lot of them, Martin said, were out only for themselves. Those were guys you had to watch out for. Aside from that, there were the coaches, good guys maybe, but some were just looking to get the manager canned so they could move in and get the big job." Martin said such things day after day in clever and obscene ways. He'd warn whites about black ball players. "Nigger" was a staple of his vocabulary. Were there some Jewish ball players on the squad? He'd tell the non-Jewish players to be careful of the Jews; not all Jews, of course, just the scheming ones. So it went, day after insufferable day until Martin had his athletes thinking just the way he wanted them to think. The only man in baseball they could assuredly trust was... Billy Martin.

How could such an approach be accepted and tolerated by mostly grown-up men? Because in the curious world of the big leagues Billy Ball worked. Minnesota hired Martin to manage in

1969 and the Twins promptly won the American League West. Detroit hired Martin to manage in 1971 and a year later the Tigers won the American League East. Texas hired him in 1973, where, suddenly partial to cowboy boots, Martin moved the Rangers up from last place to second in the American League West. All of a sudden, he became a lone cowhand and if his legs weren't bowed and his cheeks weren't tanned, shucks, the Bay Area of California where he came from was really sorta Rio Grande North, if you thought of things the way Martin wanted.

Unquestionably Billy Ball worked, but as Martin's itinerary demonstrates, it never worked for long. After he won the division in Minnesota, the Twins fired him. The year after he won the division in Detroit, the Tigers sacked him. After he hauled Texas up to second place, the Rangers dismissed him in the middle of the following season. Few mortals, Mickey Mantle and Whitey Ford excepted, could stand Billy Ball or Billy Martin for an extended period. Nor was this a development simply of Martin the manager. After some rousing early seasons in the Bronx, his playing career disintegrated into a travel agent's dream. The Yankees traded Martin to Kansas City on June 15, 1957. Kansas City traded him to Detroit on November 20, 1957. Detroit traded him to Cleveland on November 30, 1958. Cleveland traded him to Cincinnati on December 15, 1959. Cincinnati sold his contract to Milwaukee on December 3, 1960. Milwaukee traded him to Minnesota on June 1, 1961. Across eleven seasons in the major leagues, he batted .257 and played for seven different teams. Everywhere he went he made enemies. Still, there is no denying Gabe Paul's statement. Bringing Martin to New York to manage the Yankees was indeed "exciting," along with several other things that can be better expressed in stronger language or, for the moment, be left unsaid.

AS THE HUNTER CONTRACT indicated Steinbrenner's willingness to spend, hiring Martin demonstrated his willingness to risk. In his third year as managing partner, the Yankees were going nowhere in the pennant race. During Walter O'Malley's reign as president of the Brooklyn Dodgers, he sometimes pronounced, "In Brooklyn you're either in first place or you're bankrupt." That is not precisely so for all New York City teams, of course, but it is a good hyperbolic guideline. Even with Willie Mays, a mediocre Giant team drew only 600,000 fans to the Polo Grounds during the 1950s and without their famous move—first projected to Minneapolis, then amended to San Francisco—"we might have gone under," Chub Feeney, their general manager, told me. Now in rented quarters at Shea, the Yankees were drawing less than 1.3 million fans a season, roughly 400,000 fewer than the Mets were drawing and only half of what the transplanted Dodgers were attracting in Los Angeles. Steinbrenner recognized that his attendance figures were anemic for a team operating in a metropolitan area of fifteen million people, and he signed Martin in part because he was impatient and somewhat desperate. Martin surely would shake the Yankees out of their lethargy. He might also improve coverage in the New York media, which at that time seemed to show more interest in the Mets than in the Yankees. By signing Martin, "the Yankees reached into their rich but distant past," Joe Durso observed in the *New York Times.* "The 47-year-old Californian [was] the controversial 'brat' of Casey Stengel's infields in the 1950s ... He moved into the office under the first-base grandstand and took up the dream that has haunted the Yankees since their last pennant in 1964." Durso's Yankee dream was winning the pennant. A larger dream was winning the World Series, which the Yankees had not done since 1962. That stretch, almost two decades without a World Championship, was the longest arid period Yankee teams had known since 1923 when Babe Ruth's muscles prevailed over the intellect of John McGraw.

If Steinbrenner was desperate, he was also a sound enough businessman to feel concern. He had his lawyers insert a variety of good-conduct clauses into Martin's contract, covering, among other things, drinking and outbursts to the media. One clause specified that if Martin criticized Steinbrenner to the media he could be "immediately dismissed without further compensation." The written restrictions annoyed Martin mightily, but at his first press conference as Yankee manager he said with great passion on a sunny summer day, "This is the only job I ever really wanted."

MARTIN WAS BORN on May 16, 1928, in Berkeley, a long way from the dialogues and sophistication of the university campus. He grew up on Seventh Street in the western part of town, a neighborhood of small frame houses, old factories, and empty lots, populated mostly by Italian immigrants and their offspring. Martin's ethnic background is clouded. His father probably was one Alfred Manuel Martin, a fisherman of Italian and Portugese descent, who played guitar and sang and is said to have resembled the definitive Latin lover, Rudolph Valentino. Martin's mother, Joan Salvini Martin Downey, told the sportswriter Maury Allen, "I threw him [Martin's father] out. I found out he was sleeping with girls from the university. I busted up his car with a hammer. Then I threw all his clothes out on the street. I'll piss on his grave. He can count on it."

The family name on Billy Martin's birth certificate is Pisani, taken from Joan's first husband, Donato Pisani. Joan had divorced Pisani, describing the relationship as an arranged marriage that did not work, and then divorced Martin before Billy's birth. "But I used Pisani on the birth certificate because I didn't want that bastard [Martin, the likely biological father] being connected with my baby." At the same time, she named the infant after the man she said she so detested. "Ambivalence," a thoughtful psychiatrist, the late Charles Fisher, used to say, "is the common fabric of life."

On November 5, 1929, Joan made a third marriage to Jack Downey, a truck driver out of Toronto, who came to California after taking a change-of-pace job: cook on a cruise ship. Billy Martin said many times, "Jack Downey was the person I considered to be my real father." If this genealogy is confusing to those unraveling it, imagine how much more confusing and traumatic it was to a child trying to understand his own background. Martin was an attractive, dark-eyed little boy and his maternal grandmother, Raphaella Salvini, called him "Bellis," an Italian term for beautiful that evolved into the English first name he adopted. That, then, is how a child named Alfred Pisani on a Berkeley birth certificate became the rugged Yankee baseball man Billy Martin. He liked being addressed as Billy and wanted no one ever to call him Alfred, which, to enter the late Dr. Fisher's province, certainly appears to be a commentary on the father who abandoned him. He could have been Al Martin, Jr. He chose not to be. In early stories, a few reporters referred to "Al Martin." The subject sought out each writer. "It's Billy," he said. "That's my name. Get it right. *Billy* Martin." If he was cowed by the New York press, he hid it, even from himself.

Predictably, he grew up as a street kid, wiry, tough, and less beautiful as his nose began developing into a beak. "There was always enough food and we made our own wine in the backyard," he told me, "but there wasn't any money for the stuff middle-class kids have, roller skates and bikes. Instead of skating or bicycling, we kids used to fight. I could always fight good. I hit hard. I never quit. I could beat up the other kids and then they didn't want to fight me any more and that gave me time to concentrate on baseball." Martin was no better than a fair student at Berkeley High School. "I woulda dropped out and probably got into a pile of trouble, except for baseball. I made the varsity and when I was a senior in 1946, I hit .450. I played third. I loved playing ball. I loved figuring out how you played ball. I read a book, I never read a lot, called *Lou Gehrig, A Quiet Hero* [by the sports columnist Frank Graham]. That gave me my dream. To be a New York Yankee."

At 5 feet 10 and 160 pounds Martin lacked the substantial stature big-league scouts prefer, but a successful Pacific Coast League team, the Oakland Oaks, signed him. After two years in the lower minors he moved up to the Oaks, one step below the major leagues. There he encountered the baseball roustabout Casey Stengel, who was managing Oakland in 1947. No one better described Stengel's reputation at the time than Stengel himself in his remark I cited earlier: "That old bum managed nine years before in the major leagues and he ain't never got out of the second division once." But not everyone breaks out of the gate like a quarter horse. Herman Melville published a book called *Redburn* and another called *Mardi* before he got around to writing *Moby-Dick*.

Stengel's great baseball knowledge thrilled Martin and this grizzled character warmed to Martin's defiant, belligerent spirit and aggressive style. Once Stengel tramped to second base and showed Martin the precise footwork he wanted used on the pivot that is the hinge of the infield double play. Martin argued. He did not like being told what to do. Finally he snapped at Stengel, then fifty-six, "Hey, if you can't do it yourself, don't knock it." Thus challenged, some managers might fume and bench the upstart. Stengel, secure in his own knowledge, was amused. In time Martin began to pivot as Stengel directed.

When the Yankees hired Stengel to manage in 1949, Charlie Dressen, another experienced big-league discard, replaced him at Oakland. Though not Stengel's equal, Dressen was a skilled field general, particularly adept at stealing signs. In Martin's three seasons at Oakland, he never hit .300, topping out at .286, nor did he lead the league in any significant department. (By contrast, Martin's idol, Joe DiMaggio, batted .398 for the San Francisco Seals and was voted Most Valuable Player in 1935, before the Yankees obtained his contract for $25,000 and five career minor-league journeymen.) But what Martin did do at Oakland was enroll in a post-graduate course in the science and tactics of baseball. Stengel learned from John McGraw. Dressen learned from that ultimate pool hustler, Leo Durocher. Young Billy Martin absorbed enormous baseball knowledge at Oakland, and if he never became a great big-league player—he did not—he did develop into a skilled performer, notably dangerous in clutch situations.

At Stengel's insistence the Yankees acquired Martin after the 1949 season. When someone asked Stengel to describe the rookie, the manager said, "He's a hard-nosed, big-nosed kind of player." But that winter Martin underwent plastic surgery and when he reported for spring training, his nose, while not a Scandinavian pug, was smaller than anyone, including Stengel, expected.

The 1950 Yankees won the second of Stengel's five consecutive World Championships and Martin couldn't crack the starting lineup. He played in just thirty-four games and batted .250. But as Martin was fierce, he was also capable of great charm, and he managed to befriend Joe DiMaggio who was nearing the end of his playing days, suffering from arthritis and generally aloof from rookies. No one on the Yankees had seen anything like it before, their senior star, polished and calculating, suddenly having dinners on the road with a scruffy kid. "He just liked me," Martin said, "and not only because we were both Italians from California. I think he kind of respected my passion for the game."

In 1952, Jerry Coleman, the Yankees' regular second baseman, was recalled by the Marine Corps to fly fighter jets over Korea. An unpretentious patriot, Coleman reported without complaint, losing prime earning years and, of course, putting his life at risk. Billy Martin moved in at second base in the Bronx and played competently; he hit .267 and made only nine errors over 109 games. He also made two plays that won the World Series.

The Brooklyn Dodgers were leading, two games to one, but the Yankees' Allie Reynolds, part Creek Indian and called the Superchief, was blazing in game four and carried a 1-to-0 lead into the fifth inning. Then Andy Pafko singled to left, Gil Hodges walked, and Carl Furillo's sacrifice put runners on second and third. Joe Black, the best Brooklyn pitcher that season, came to bat and Charlie Dressen signaled for a suicide squeeze. Pafko was to break from third with the pitch; and as long as Black bunted the ball on the ground in fair territory, the score would be tied. In the Dodger dugout Dressen grabbed his throat and shouted at Reynolds, "Hey, Wahoo. You're choking." The shout was a decoy. By clutching his throat Dressen was signaling for the suicide squeeze. It was a tricky sign, a splendid sign, its purpose camouflaged by annoying inelegant words about choking. It was, in fact, the same splendid squeeze sign that Dressen used in 1949 when he was managing Billy Martin in Oakland. Now at Yankee Stadium, when Dressen grabbed his throat, Billy Martin spotted the move from second base. "Squeeze," he screamed. Reynolds threw his fast ball three feet wide of the plate. The pitch was impossible to bunt because it was impossible to reach. Black lunged but couldn't get his bat close to the ball. Pafko stopped in his tracks and began moving back toward third, but Yogi Berra burst out from behind the plate and ran him down. As John Drebinger put it in the *New York Times,* "When the squeeze attempt blew up in the face of the astonished Dodgers, that, to all intents and purposes, was the ball game [which the Yankees went on to win, 2 to 0]." How could a supposedly shrewd baseball man stay with a sign that an opposing infielder, who had once played for him, might recognize? Quite simply, amid all the pressure of a great rivalry, Charlie Dressen forgot some of his history with the skinny, street-smart second baseman. Billy Martin remembered.

That was the ball game but not the Series. The teams moved on and tied at three victories each. The Yankees led the seventh game in Brooklyn, 4 to 2, when the Dodgers loaded the bases with one out in the seventh inning. Their next batter was Duke Snider, who had already hit four home runs in this Series. Stengel summoned a journeyman lefthander named Bob Kuzava to face Snider. Next to me in the Ebbets Field press box, Red Smith, said, "Kuzava sounds like some kind of melon." Stengel knew, but had not been saying, that Kuzava—no melon, he—had enjoyed good success against Snider when the two faced each other four years earlier in the International League. Kuzava threw a rising inside fast ball. Snider's left-handed stroke was a thing of beauty. But now the pitch jammed him, and he popped out to third baseman Gil McDougald.

Jackie Robinson followed Snider. Now Smith, myself, and other resident authorities without portfolio expected Stengel to bring in the right-handed Johnny Sain to face the right-hand–hitting Robinson. Sain had been the starting pitcher against the Dodgers on the bright April day in 1947 when Robinson became the first African American to play major-league ball in the twentieth century. That afternoon Sain held Robinson hitless, throwing what Robinson said were "the best curve balls I ever saw."

After the Snider pop fly, Kuzava said, "I turned and looked for Sain. But Casey kept me in the game. I had to pitch to Robinson. I threw hard, going for the corners." The count went to 3 and 2. The Brooklyn crowd sat rapt and prayerful. The Dodgers had never won a World Series. As Robinson fouled off three or four full-count pitches, fans squirmed and hyperventilated. With two out and a full count, the runners broke with the pitch every time. Then Kuzava threw a hard breaking ball, knee high and to the outside corner of the plate. Trying to line a game-tying single to the opposite field, Robinson hit a pop fly close to the first-base line. "I saw the ball all the way," Kuzava told me. "I coulda caught it myself. But this is the major leagues. The World Series. Pitchers don't chase down pop flies. I hollered, 'Joe, Joe'[to first baseman Joe Collins]." Collins did not move. Blinded by the late afternoon sun, he had completely lost the baseball. A brisk autumn wind blew the pop fly back toward home plate, but Yogi Berra, hearing Kuzava's shout of "Joe," assumed that this was Collins's play and didn't remove his catcher's mask. Enter Billy Martin, running full speed, racing, straining, lunging until finally, with the three base runners and Jackie Robinson moving in full stride, he caught the abandoned pop fly at his shins, perhaps a foot above the ground. And that is how Billy Martin saved the New York Yankees' fifteenth World Championship and defeated what was the second-best baseball team that ever played for Brooklyn.

The following season the New York Giants sagged to fifth, and Brooklyn ran off and won the pennant by thirteen games. These were the classic boys of summer in their prime; they led the National League in runs scored, homers, batting average, stolen bases, fielding percentage, and strikeouts by one pitching staff. This team, the Dodger team, collectively batted .285. But in October they ran into a strong, wiry Yankee infielder (who had hit only .257 that season). Billy Martin's triple with the bases loaded was critical in the first game. His home run helped the Yankees win game two. His two-run homer helped the Yankees win game five. He came to bat in game six during the ninth inning with the score tied and a man on second and rammed a single up the middle and the winning run came home. He finished that World Series with a six-game batting average of .500, better than Mickey Mantle (.208) and even surpassing the formidable Berra (.429). And that is how Billy Martin won the Yankees' sixteenth World Championship from the best baseball team that ever played for Brooklyn. ("A lot of the other Dodgers cried in the clubhouse after Martin's hit," Pee Wee Reese said some time later. "Not me. I didn't cry till I got home.")

If someone had been able to come up with a nickname from the future, young Billy Martin would have been called "Mr. October," the feller who wins the games that count the most. But no one did. For all Martin's heroics, and in a sports sense playing great baseball during a World Series truly is heroic, a sour counterpoint sounded in the background. Up from the mean streets of west Berkeley, twice the star of a World Series, Martin, newly famous and in demand, developed a passion for the fast life: upscale night-clubs, good whiskey, flashy women. To quote the splendid wrestling sportswriter Ben Epstein, who traveled with the Yankees for a decade, "Billy was never any more a playboy than ninety per cent of the ball players I've known, and I've known plenty. It's just that he talked a lot and the bluenoses in the front office decided that he was. Myself, I'm getting to be fifty years old and here is my best move on the road. I stand in a hotel lobby and throw the room key into the air. The girl who catches it, any girl, she can have me."

Martin's first specific misstep came after the Yankees' 1953 pennant party when he and some of his teammates, including Mickey Mantle and Whitey Ford, decided to extend the evening with a second, free-lance victory celebration. They chose the Latin Quarter, a big, brassy New York nightclub, with sizable chorus girls and prices to match. After some time, and some rousing bumps and grinds, a prodigious bill arrived at the ball players' table. Credit cards were not then in general use and Martin said, "Hey, I got a load of cash. I'll get it." Another ball player suggested that the group split the bill. Martin turned out to be the only one with ad-equate cash. They were seated up front, close to the abdomens of the chorus girls, and when the discussion became loud, a head-waiter appeared and said, "You boys can sign this thing. Just sign all your names and we'll mail you the bill." Everyone signed.

"Firm name, please."

"We're Yankees," Martin said. "You know that."

"We still need your employer's name."

At this point, Martin said, he himself fell silent and another Yankee—it could have been Mantle—grabbed the check and signed the name of Yankee president Dan Topping, saying, still ac-cording to Martin, "Send this to Topping. He's got a million bucks." Topping was a veteran nightclubber on his own, but when the ball players' Latin Quarter bill reached his desk in the Yankee offices on Fifth Avenue, he responded with penurious and puritan anger. After talking with George Weiss, Topping decided that Martin must be to blame and had items planted into gossip columns. *Yankee Brass Fuming at Martin's Brass.* Summoned into Topping's office, Martin said, "It wasn't me. I didn't sign your name, Mr. Topping. I never have. Bring in a Bible. I'll swear on the Bible I'm telling you the truth."

"Get the hell out of here," Topping said.

A second incident occurred two years later when Martin, Mantle, and a few others missed a Yankee charter flight out of Logan Airport in Boston. The group was drinking in an airport bar; they were still drinking when the plane took off. "I'll take some blame there," Martin said. "We missed the plane. But it wasn't like we missed a game. They fined me and Mickey two hundred and fifty bucks each, but their attitude was like it was me that was making Mickey drink. Hey, *nobody* ever had to urge Mickey to take a drink."

The third and fatal episode, a *cause célèbre* of the 1950s, was the Battle of the Copacabana on Martin's twenty-ninth birthday, May 16, 1957. By way of brightening the spring, Martin organized a party for himself, which swelled to a group of eleven: five Yankees with wives and Martin, whose first marriage had come apart, flying solo. The players began with dinner in a steakhouse, proceeded to drinks at the Waldorf-Astoria, and then moved on to the Copacabana, another large, popular nightclub, and its 2:00 A.M. show featuring the young, newly popular entertainer Sammy Davis, Jr. This was a fast lane of New York night life in the fifties, when there were not many things better than being young and being a Yankee.

Mantle and Ford were in the group, along with the essentially tranquil Yogi Berra, the rugged outfielder Hank Bauer, and a young pitcher out of Hoboken named Johnny Kucks. Seated behind the

Yankees was another sporting group, seventeen bowlers, who were celebrating some sort of championship in a league of their own. The bowlers chattered loudly through Davis' act until the entertainer walked to the front of the stage and said, "I wish you people would either keep quiet or leave." One of the bowlers said that no nigger was going to tell him what to do. Bauer glared at him and said, "Why don't you guys just shut up or get out." A stocky bowler, one Edwin Jones of Manhattan, said to Bauer, "Why don't you make me?"

Both men rose and proceeded to an alcove away from bright lights. A minute or so later Edwin Jones was lying on the floor, unconscious and suffering from a brain concussion. To this day, Berra, Ford, and Bauer all repeat a similar version, along these lines: as Bauer moved toward Jones, Ford and Berra grabbed the outfielder's arms and began trying to wrestle him back. While this was going on, one or possibly two Copacabana bouncers decked Jones with professional dispatch. Speaking of his teammates, Berra said and says, "Nobody did nothing to nobody." Unfortunately for the ball players a gossip columnist named Leonard Lyons was working his night beat, looking for noise. The next day Lyons' paper, the *New York Post,* ran a front-page headline YANKEES BRAWL AT COPA. Within a month, Billy Martin was playing for Kansas City.

George Weiss, the Yankees' stern general manager, didn't care much for Ford, whom he dismissed as a "smart-alec New York kid." Weiss suffered Mantle's sloppy training habits in silence. But these two Yankee nightriders were great and irreplaceable stars, moving surely toward the Hall of Fame. The third, the bony kid from Berkeley, was batting under .250. Weiss liked things neat and quiet. Personally he shunned the press. With the enthusiastic endorsement of Topping and a grudging concession from Stengel, Weiss dealt Martin to the (then) Kansas City Athletics in a seven-player June trade that brought the Yankees a fine relief pitcher in

Ryne Duren and left Martin with profound feelings of rejection and abandonment. Where on earth had been his champion, his second father figure, Casey Stengel, when he most needed a champion and a father? That year the Yankees, with young Bobby Richardson playing second, won the pennant, but lost the World Series. The Athletics, with fiery Billy Martin in the infield, finished seventh. The glory of Martin's playing days lay buried in the Bronx. He was not yet thirty years old.

A magazine editor subsequently asked me to write a story under the title, "Why They Broke Up Billy Martin's Gang." Proceeding into the Kansas City clubhouse, I found a forlorn figure, blatantly out of place in an Athletics' uniform, trying to mask his feelings and not really understanding why the Yankees had banished him. My characterization of him at this relatively early time of stress seems relevant in the present context: "Alfred Manuel Martin is sensitive and brash, defiant and humble, angry and soft voiced. He has not lived like a Trappist monk but to picture him as an inveterate hell-raiser, completely surrounded by chorus girls, comfortable only on ball fields and in saloons, would be a considerable exercise in inaccuracy."

At the time the late *Sport* magazine, for which I was to write, had not been outpaced by *Sports Illustrated*. Among others, ball players, managers, and club owners read *Sport* and Martin was avidly aware in our conversations that he was addressing an important nationwide audience. "The trade was rough," he said. "I mean one day I was a Yankee and all of a sudden I was in a different uniform. You know baseball. You see other guys being traded. All of a sudden you're one of the other guys. I don't think I ever once stopped to think how it would feel if it happened to me. To tell you the truth, I don't know how I feel."

"Numb?" I said.

"Yeah. Maybe."

"Bitter?"

"I ain't bitter. It's one of these things in baseball that happens, one of these unexplainable things." I asked Martin to make a stab at explaining it to me. He was sitting in the visitors' locker room at Yankee Stadium on an unpainted three-legged stool, the kind associated with milkmaids and old ball players. He leaned back and began a stream of consciousness. He seemed to trust me. He did not subscribe to Joan Didion's cynical dictum that writers are always selling somebody out. "I read stories that say I was a bad influence on Mick [Mantle]. We roomed together and hung around together and he led the league in everything. I only wish he influenced me like I influenced him. In my first six years with the Yankees, the team wins six pennants. How can you be a bad influence on six pennant winners? A bad influence, year after winning year after winning year. I mean, come on, where's the poison? Where in hell is the goddamn poison? I like to drink but I was always in shape come game time. I play every day. I play to win and maybe I get some people upset, but the idea is to play to win, or am I wrong? I like girls. All right. I been divorced. I'm a single man. Can't a single man like girls? Mostly on the road, you're playing night games and running to catch a plane. A lot of the time when people thought Mick and I were chasing girls, we were trying to cool out at a movie. Good movie, bad movie, any movie. That's a good way for a ball player to relax. They say I showed Mick the hot spots. Listen, when it comes to living hard Mick don't need me or nobody to show him how. I took him to the Stage Delicatessen [in midtown Manhattan]. That's a hot spot. They got hot pastrami sandwiches. I took him to church a couple times. Church. He wears a St. Christopher medal I gave him. That's pretty hot. It don't strike me as fair that a guy should be rapped as a bad influence by people who don't know what they're talking about. I'm not knocking George Weiss. He makes trades year in year out and look at all the Yankee pennants. I'm not knocking Weiss because you can't knock success. But I know I'm not a bad influence and it's a serious thing to say I am and there's nothing I can do about it. Nothing! I got the rap, even thought it isn't fair, dammit."

His mood swung. "Next time this team comes to town, let's see if you and I can have dinner."

"I'll check the schedule, Billy."

He grinned a little. "Don't worry. I won't get you into trouble."

He telephoned a day later and asked if I could get *Sport* to publish a brief personal statement. Here is Martin's first farewell to New York City from the summer of 1957:

> Could you just print my thanks to the people around New York City. I mean a lot of people, just guys on the street, shook hands and said they'd miss me and the first time I came to bat for Kansas City in Yankee Stadium, they gave me a terrific hand. It made me feel good just to stand there and hear them cheering. It made me feel a little bit like Joe DiMaggio must have felt. I can't explain it right. I just want to tell all of them thanks.

After Martin's playing career ran down, whatever uniform he wore, he talked ceaselessly about his Yankee days. He signed on as a scout with the Minnesota Twins, he moved up in the organization, and in 1969 took over as manager of a fine team with such solid stars as Harmon Killebrew, the great slugger Rod Carew, and the splendid batsman Tony Oliva, one of the finest of the early Latin players. But Baltimore swept the Twins in the league playoff and Cal Griffith, who owned the team, publicly questioned why Martin had chosen one Bob Miller, not Jim Kaat, to start the final game (which Baltimore won, 11 to 2). "Why?" Martin responded to some sportswriters. "He wants to know why. Here's why. Because I'm the manager." After his comment hit the *Minneapolis Tribune* and the *St. Paul Pioneer Press,* he was not the manager any longer.

Martin signed to manage Detroit in 1971 and took a strong team to a divisional title in 1972. But for a second time he found disaster in October. Oakland won a close and exciting American League Championship Series, three games to two. The Tigers stayed with their manager, but a season later, as the team sagged, Martin prattled endlessly about how Joe Cronin, the president of the American League, was letting Cleveland's Gaylord Perry get away with throwing an illegal pitch. "Perry puts Vaseline on the ball," Martin said. "No way Cronin should let him do that. I don't know what it is. Cronin has the authority. What he doesn't have is guts." San Francisco Irish Joe Cronin remained composed until an August series that matched Cleveland against Detroit. Then a story spread that Martin was directing two of his starters to throw spitballs whenever they pitched against Perry. When that report reached the pages of the *Detroit Free Press,* Cronin ordered Martin suspended for three days. Subsequently Jim Campbell, the Tigers' general manager, fired Martin. "I'd be crazy to hire him again," Campbell said. "I was crazy to hire him in the first place. But what the hell. This is a crazy game."

Martin surfaced managing the Texas Rangers late in 1973 and a year later in 1974 he drove a weak team all the way up to second place. But presently Brad Corbett, a Bronx native who had made millions in the plastic pipeline business, bought a majority interest in the Rangers and in the classic manner of plastic pipeline millionaires, Corbett decided that he knew baseball. Soon he and Martin were bickering about personnel and strategy. At length Martin told Randy Galloway of the *Dallas Morning News,* "I can't win with the players Brad is forcing on me." In the formal announcement, Corbett said Martin was being fired "for disloyalty." Considering Martin the manager, one remembers the Sean O'Casey character who "couldn't let the silence sing a song of peace."

After George Steinbrenner read about Martin's latest, calamitous onslaught on authority, he told Gabe Paul, "The man is a fiery manager. I want him here."

"You'd be making a mistake, George," Paul said.

"I want him."

Certain psychologists describe Martin's behavior—always creating a terminal fight with his employer—as "repetition compulsion." It is, they say, difficult to treat. But we are considering baseball ahead of psychology. On August 2, 1975, Billy Martin's first game as manager, the New York Yankees defeated Cleveland, 5 to 3.

DURING THE DETROIT DAYS, *Sport* sent Irv Goodman, afterwards a prominent literary editor, to compose "The Sport Special," a 10,000-word "definitive" story about Billy Martin. In the course of one Tiger trip to New York City, Martin stopped at an extremely fashionable nightclub, El Morocco, to deliver an autographed baseball to "a friend" who was dating Linda Christian. (The friend's name seems to have been lost.) Christian had been married for a time to the implausibly handsome movie star Tyrone Power. A great beauty herself, she posed bare-breasted for a Mexican sculptor when toplessness was still exotic. She surfed with millionaires and princes, and Billy Martin, after delivering the baseball, got to shake her hand.

"Do you know Linda Christian?" he asked Goodman the next day in a taxi riding out to Shea Stadium.

"Nope."

"She's been dating some mighty rich fellows," Martin said. "Must be great to be rich, huh?" He slumped and rested his feet against the front-seat partition. "I wonder if I have any royal blood. Could be, you know. That would be the life."

Keeping the conversation going, Goodman mentioned the general excellence of Italian-American baseball stars and Martin said, "We're good because we take things personal. We got pride. We try to do our best." As the cab rolled toward Queens, Martin looked back at pudgy tugboats and a familiar skyline and said, "I got too much pride to be only a ball player. I must be royalty. Gotta be. Way back from my Italiano ancestors. Some day I'm gonna look it up. I know what I'll find; I'll find what I am. Prince Billy. And tell me, don't that sound fine?" Irv Goodman fell silent then, but now, all at once, it sounds does fine and preposterous and poignant.

▼

CHAPTER SIX

R. MARTINEZ J.

T HE FORTY-SEVEN-YEAR-OLD California street tough who began managing the Yankees during the summer of 1975 initially appeared in the subdued guise of St. Billy the Good. Martin took over a third-place team and began simultaneously analyzing the ball club, courting the media, considering future trades, and damping his temper. Martin's self-control was more significant than the discomfiting truth that the Yankees played no more successfully under him than they had for Pittsburgh Bill Virdon. (The team finished with Martin where it started with Martin, in third place behind the Boston Red Sox and the Baltimore Orioles.) Even with Steinbrenner and Martin figuratively oar to oar and side by side, the Yankee scene was quiet for a time. But in New York baseball somebody somewhere always raises hell. Earlier that season it was Cleon Jones of the Mets, an outfielder who once batted .340 but whose career had been sagging, at least around home plate. During spring training, Florida police bearing flashlights found Jones sleeping in the back of a van wearing, the cops said, only socks. The woman slumbering beside him, one Sharon Ann Sabol, wore nothing. The situation was not helped by the consideration that

Jones was married to somebody else or by two other considerations: Jones was African-American and his van companion was white. The police booked both for indecent exposure. In addition they charged Sabol with possession of marijuana. Ten days later the charges against Jones were dropped on the grounds of "no information," Florida legal jargon for insufficient evidence.

Yogi Berra had been managing the Mets since 1972, the year of Gil Hodges' sudden, shocking death, and Berra had taken the team into the 1973 World Series. Underneath his humor and affability, Berra is a determined and disciplined man; he found Jones' parking-lot indiscretion beyond forgiving. The Mets fined Jones $2,000 and forced him to read a statement to the press at Shea Stadium. "I wish to apologize publicly to my wife and children," Jones said, "to the Mets' ownership and management, my team, to all Mets fans and to baseball in general for my behavior." A number of African Americans expressed dismay. Although the criminal charges had been dropped, Jones still was being fined. (He had, of course, to put this gently, broken training.) His apology, actually composed in the front office, was so obsequious some said it sounded servile.

Berra used Jones sparingly that season and Jones simmered. One day in August Berra sent Jones to pinch-hit against Atlanta and then told him to go out and play left field. Jones refused, remarking that Berra hadn't let him play all year and he sure didn't feel like playing now. Almost the entire Mets squad heard Jones defy his manager. Subsequently Berra approached M. Donald Grant, a remote man with a Wall Street background who was the Mets board chairman and C.E.O., and asked him to sell, trade, or at least suspend Cleon Jones. Grant refused. He was concerned, Grant said, that Jones might file some sort of grievance with the players' union. Significant portions of the New York black community could well read bigotry into the Mets' handling of Jones. Berra, a man without discernable prejudice, said color had nothing to do with the situation or with the need to penalize a ball player for refusing his manager's order. It was all about team morale and obeying rules. Neither Berra nor Grant would modify his position and finally Berra said, "It's him or me." Three days after the Yankees hired Martin, Grant fired Berra. Joseph Durso, the senior baseball writer at the *New York Times,* composed an impassioned column under the headline YOGI BERRA AND HIS ASSASSINS. The Mets, Durso wrote, fired "a sound baseball man who caught almost every Yankee game for 13 summers, played in 14 World Series and 15 All-Star Games, managed both the Yankees and Mets to pennants and helped pay bills with an image probably matched only by Casey Stengel in our time." Within hours the telephone rang in Berra's home on Highland Avenue in Montclair, New Jersey. "You got a job with me," Billy Martin said. "I want you to coach for me next season." Berra says he first thought Martin was teasing him and then asked if Martin had run this offer past Steinbrenner. "I don't have to," Martin said. "You got a job with me." Actually, neither Gabe Paul nor Steinbrenner wanted Martin to hire anyone above the rank of batboy without consultation and approval, but in this episode, the public relations situation gave them no choice but to accede. Just three years earlier Berra, a St. Louis native who became a bona fide New York Yankee hero, had been elected to the Hall of Fame. Vetoing Martin's hiring now would anger New York fans, the fans that the Yankees still were laboring to win back after the dark ages of CBS. (During the early and middle 1970s, the Mets consistently outdrew the Yankees by about a half million paying customers a year.) Further, Berra was a great favorite not only with Joe Durso, but with just about every local sportswriter. Red Smith, the reigning columnist, even invented a game he called "L. Peter B.," which he played over and over during the long annual auto trips to and from spring training. The idea was to supply a ball player's first and last initials and full middle name and ask the other participants to identify the athlete.

Smith's favorite entry was L. (for Lawrence) Peter B. (for Berra). Yogi, of course, is a nickname. Other elementary offerings included H. Louis G. (Gehrig); J. Roosevelt R. (Robinson); W. Howard M. (Mays), and so on, far down the Pines-to-Palms highway, until you hit such stumpers as A. Bluford W. (the Dodgers' back-up catcher, Albert Bluford "Rube" Walker).

Even though Martin ignored channels and exceeded his authority, his hiring of L. Peter B. held firm and Berra would again put on Yankee pinstripes, this time as a coach, for the season of 1976, which coincided with the reopening of Yankee Stadium. For the next few years Berra, along with his old teammate Elston Howard, provided the Yankees with some quiet comfort and a sense of the team's remarkable tradition. In April of '76, as promised, the old view-blocking pillars were gone, but the revamped Stadium looked and looks eccentric, at least to this non-architect. From outside the lower portion appears much as it did in 1923, but the upper portion smacks of a different vintage. The effect suggests a Swedish modern coffee cup set on a saucer of Dresden china. Still, the Yankees were back in the Bronx and Berra was back in the appropriate uniform and on reopening day, April 15, 1976, Billy Martin's Yankees defeated the Minnesota Twins, 11 to 4. "We're first," Martin said, "and we're gonna stay there."

Dealing with great skill, the Yankees acquired the splendid lead-off hitter and centerfielder Mickey Rivers plus the fast-improving right-handed pitcher Ed Figueroa from the California Angels. In exchange they gave up Bobby Bonds, a gifted outfielder who never quite lived up to his potential (except perhaps in another context, by fathering Barry Bonds). They traded a right-handed medical student, George "Doc" Medich, for Dock Ellis, a righthander with no degree but imposing stuff, and second baseman Willie Randolph, a former Brooklyn schoolboy star who would play strong Yankee infield for thirteen years. Finally, they acquired Ken Holtzman, a solid left-handed pitcher with a notably fine World Series record, four victories against only one defeat. Martin brought the Yankees home first in the Eastern Division by ten-and-a-half games. When the team took a close five-game playoff from Kansas City, the Yankees had won their first pennant since 1964, when they had been managed by, of all people, Yogi Berra.

After his initial courting of sportswriters, Martin began drawing lines to cut off the players from the press and establish his trademark climate of paranoia. One day he announced that no reporters would be allowed in the clubhouse during the twenty minutes immediately preceding games. "The players voted on that one," he said. A veteran baseball writer asked a veteran Yankee if there had indeed been a vote.

"Did Billy say there was?" asked the player.

"Yes."

"Then I guess there was."

One lounge area, away from the lockers, was marked "Players Only." Now Martin decreed that a sort of anteroom with a couch and some comfortable chairs also would become off limits to reporters. That was too much for Dick Young, the crusty baseball writer with the *Daily News*. As Martin lingered in the anteroom, Young started across the new invisible barrier.

"Hold it," Martin said.

"Fuck you," Young said.

Martin swung his right but in mid-swing his future flashed before him and he opened his fist. The result: a hard shove to Young's left shoulder. The appeasement was too little and too late. A few days later Young wrote that Martin was certain to be fired in a matter of days or at most weeks. Not entirely aware of the fiery politics at play, I visited Yankee Stadium the day after Young's story appeared, mostly just to watch a game. Martin saw me in the clubhouse. I don't think we'd crossed paths in fifteen years. Now he approached and said with urgency and intimacy, "Back when you were covering the Dodgers, did Jackie Robinson consider Dick Young a bigot?"

Robinson detested Young for a litany of reasons and, although I didn't agree, Robinson did regard Young as a prejudiced man. Now with that restless, racing mind, Martin had put quite a few things together in a hurry. For a time Young and I both covered the Brooklyn Dodgers. Robinson and I had been close. Four years after Robinson's death he was becoming both saint and legend. Without thinking carefully, I said, "Yes, Billy. Jackie believed that Dick Young was bigoted."

"That does it," Martin said.

"That does what?"

"I'm calling a meeting, I'm gonna tell my whole team that Jackie Robinson considered Young a bigot."

"You can't do that, Billy. You're just gonna make a lot of trouble for me with Young."

"Fuck you," he said, not unpleasantly. "You said it."

"But Billy, for Christ's sake, that was off the record." I started to laugh. Here I was telling the manager of the New York Yankees that something *I* had said was off the record. I didn't laugh for long. I telephoned upstairs and a few minutes later George Steinbrenner came into the clubhouse, nodded grimly toward me, and talked to Martin behind a closed door. The special players' meeting to announce that Jackie Robinson regarded Dick Young as a bigot never was convened, nor for that matter was Martin fired in a matter of days or weeks.

In sum, with relatively few bursts of shrapnel, Martin enjoyed an excellent season, but his World Series unfolded as a disaster. A good Yankee squad came up against one of the strongest teams ever assembled, Cincinnati's Big Red Machine, starring Johnny Bench, Joe Morgan, and Pete Rose. The '76 Reds had led the major leagues in victories, doubles, triples, homers, batting average, and fielding percentage. They led the National League in stolen bases and pitching saves and some wondered if this was the best baseball team of all time. The night before the World Series began in Cincinnati, I had dinner with George "Sparky" Anderson, the Reds' manager, an outgoing, prematurely gray character, and detected anxiety in his manner. "I'm in a corner," Anderson said. "I've got a great team. I'm expected to win. If we win, I'm only doing what's expected. But if we get beat, and any team can get beat in a short series, they're gonna say the manager messed up." A few years earlier in his minor-league days Anderson had worked winters selling used cars in California and he said he'd hate to go back to doing that. I said I suppose there was some cheating in the used car business and Anderson's eyes flashed. "Damn right. And you know who the worst cheats are? The customers."

Martin started a journeyman named Doyle Alexander in game one. "I like him because he has a herky-jerky motion that could bother the Reds." It did not. Joe Morgan homered in the first inning and Cincinnati won easily, 5 to 1. As the game began Martin dispatched three Yankee scouts with walkie-talkie radios into the press-box area, supposedly to position Yankee outfielders from on high. Word reached Commissioner Bowie Kuhn that Martin's scouts actually were staring at TV monitors, trying to steal signs flashed by Johnny Bench. Kuhn ordered the scouts out of the press box. Meeting the media later, Martin denied that his scouts had broken rules.

"Aren't you sticking your neck out disputing the commissioner?" a reporter said.

"I'm telling the truth," Martin said. "Can they hang me for that?"

Would he request permission to use scouts in the stands for the next game? "No," Martin said. "I'm not going to ask him no more. The commissioner's word is no good. I wouldn't ask him for permission if my heart was on fire."

"About pitching," someone said. "When is Ken Holtzman going to pitch?" Martin ground his teeth and glared. "When I fucking tell him to get up." He looked as though he was about to spring at the reporter and he said again, "When I fucking tell him."

The second game, played on a Sunday night marked by a sharp wind and a temperature of 40 degrees, turned out to be the closest of the Series. Catfish Hunter, coming off a mediocre (17-and-15) season, had lost some of his old velocity and the Reds scored three times in the second inning. But the old competitive fires still burned. Hunter settled down and the Yankees tied the score in the seventh inning. As the bottom of the ninth began Martin moved about in the dugout shouting encouragement to Hunter. But with two out the Yankee shortstop protem, Fred "Chicken" Stanley, threw away a bounder hit by Ken Griffey, Sr., and Griffey raced to second base. Left-hand-hitting Joe Morgan, a .320 hitter, was next to face the right-handed Hunter. Martin walked to the mound and directed Hunter deliberately to walk Morgan, after which right-handed Tony Perez singled home the winning run. "Bloopers," Martin said later. "They hit bloopers that fall in. We hit line drives and they catch them."

"Which hits would you call bloopers, Billy?"

"Weren't you at the game?"

"Yeah, but they didn't look like bloop hits to me."

"Come to batting practice on Monday," Martin said, "and I'll show you what a blooper is." The temper was flaring again. Martin seemed to regard each question as a personal attack. Some reporters were cowed; while not a particularly skilled boxer, Martin was certainly a dangerous brawler and he had a long history of throwing the first punch. But one newspaperman persisted, "Would you call this Cincinnati team awesome?"

"Awesome?" Martin said, dismissing a great rival team with scorn. "Awesome? The only awesome team I ever saw were the Yankees of the 1950s."

The Reds won game three at Yankee Stadium, 6 to 2, and Johnny Bench's two home runs powered them to an easy victory in the final game, 7 to 2. Across this Series, Bench batted .533 and George Foster hit .429. In all seven of the Reds' starting nine, every regular except Pete Rose and Ken Griffey, batted over .300. Their play was—there is no way around this—awesome. Martin spent much of game four shouting complaints at home-plate umpire Bill Deegan. In the top of the ninth, Martin picked up a foul ball near the Yankee dugout and hurled it at Deegan. Stocky Bruce Froemming, umpiring at first, thumbed Martin out of the game. The manager charged Froemming, who stood his ground, chest to chest, until three other umpires reached the scene. They knotted around Martin, pinned his arms, and ordered him off the field. For a time after the game Martin became invisible. Thurman Munson, who had hit nine singles in the Series and batted .529, represented the team during a mass interview. That went about as badly for the Yankees as the ball games. Munson walked in just as Sparky was answering a reporter who asked him to compare Munson and Bench. "Munson," Anderson said, "is an outstanding ball player and he would hit .300 in the National League. But don't compare anybody to Johnny Bench. Don't ever embarrass nobody by comparing them to Johnny Bench." Munson moved to the microphone. "To win four in a row and rub it in my face, that's class," he said. "I never compared myself to Bench, but if I played in the National League I just might be the best offensive player over there."

Steinbrenner walked about the Yankee clubhouse doing a part of the manager's job: comforting the players who had lost. When Martin finally came out of the trainer's room half an hour later he was drinking a Scotch. "I'm sorry, gentlemen," he told a few reporters. "I was just too upset. Bill Deegan started the crap. When he tossed a used ball out of the game, he threw it right at my face. He called a brutal game. But I should have gone after the umpires who grabbed ahold of me. They're not supposed to do that."

His eyes were red. In the trainers' room he had been crying. "I'm not ashamed," he said. "I'm an emotional guy. It hurts my pride, my ego to lose like this. Hey, if winning and losing weren't so fucking important, why do they bother to keep score?"

A few weeks later, still agitated and confused, Martin left his wife, Gretchen—they had a home in Texas—and moved into a single room in a Sheraton Hotel in Hasbrouck Heights, New Jersey, near the George Washington Bridge. He said he wanted to stay close to Yankee headquarters, but like so many married men starting over in a hotel room alone, he suffered episodes of depression. He drank hard, not in the genial manner of Casey Stengel, the Grand Imbiber, but in the chaotic, angry manner of a man on the edge of a nervous breakdown. Despite the pennant, he was ripe, even overripe, for firing. In that brief World Series he had attacked the commissioner of baseball, charged an umpire, lashed the media and, not least important, managed poorly. All season he had the Yankees playing exciting running baseball; they stole 163 bases, or slightly more than one a game. But in the Series, intimidated by Bench's powerful arm, the Yankees stole only once, and that came in game four when their cause had become hopeless. Martin was awed by a team he declined to describe as awesome, a manager who was alternately frightened and enraged.

Red Smith had taken to calling George M. Steinbrenner III simply George III. Like many, Smith found Steinbrenner overbearing. But within George, the rough tough leader, the would-be tank commander, there also dwells a sensitive aesthete who loves the still, sad music of Keats' odes and the heartbreaking beauty of *Jude the Obscure*. That Steinbrenner, the old Williams College English major, reached out to Martin, not as a friend or as an equal, but as a tormented, gifted character who needed, and perhaps even deserved, help. Historically harsh Christian missionaries behaved in a similar manner. Far from dismissing Martin, Steinbrenner said to him, "What will it take for you to win the World Series next year?"

"This was a fucking fluke thing," Martin said.

"What will it take?"

"I need more pitching and more power," Martin said.

"You also need help at shortstop," Gabe Paul said.

"[Joe] Rudi is the guy I really want," Martin said. Rudi, a solid left fielder good for fifteen or twenty homers a year, had decided to leave the Oakland Athletics and try free-agency.

"I was thinking of Reggie Jackson," Steinbrenner said.

"I don't need him. I got plenty left-handed bats right now. Nettles, [Chris] Chambliss, Rivers. I want Rudi."

"We're signing Jackson," Steinbrenner said.

"I'd prefer Joe Rudi, dammit," Martin said, "but okay. I'll give you this. Jackson hit good against the clubs I managed."

Jackson had moved from Oakland to Baltimore, as centerpiece of a six-player trade at the beginning of the 1976 season. The deal upset him, Jackson said, because it was rejective and unfair. He had been playing in Oakland for eight seasons, during which "I hit two hundred fifty-four dingers [home runs] for that man [Charley Finley]. Besides, I like the Bay Area and I liked the guys on the team, Sal Bando and Rollie Fingers." With Jackson dominating the lineup, the A's had taken their division title five straight times and won three World Series in a row. "I took that ball club uptown," Reggie said. Without Jackson they would fall back, an ordinary team, second in 1976 and dead last in '77. Oakland attendance dropped from 1,075,518 in '75 with Reggie to 495,599 two years later when one Jim Tyrone stood in Reggie's gigantic right-field footprints. How, then, could one possibly deal away Reggie Jackson, a ball player who embodied crowd appeal, excitement, and triumph, the power and the glory, in the rousing patterns of G. H. Ruth? Jackson did talk about himself a lot, which bothered Finley, who liked to talk about *himself* a lot, but as Dizzy Dean, another baseball man uncomfortable with silence, put it, "If you can do something and you say you can do it, that ain't braggin'." Beyond the gabble, Finley could not shake his skinflint ways and Reggie was becoming increasingly expensive. When Jackson turned down $140,000 to play in Oakland during 1976, Finley raged, cut Jackson's pay to $112,000, and shipped him, or anyway his contract, some three thousand miles east to Baltimore. Finley could do that in what were the last hours of baseball feudalism. As the attendance figures show, it would have been far better business to pay Jackson and keep him in Oakland, but as we saw with Catfish Hunter, Charlie Finley at his worst—and he was at his worst in the end games with Hunter and Jackson—was an absolute master of false economies.

Jackson said he did not want to go to Baltimore. He wasn't even sure he wanted to keep on playing ball. He had other interests, he said, philosophy and sociology. His IQ had been measured at 160. Baseball was not his whole world. "If my team loses a big one, and I strike out with the winning runs on base, are you aware that one billion Chinese don't care?" he told one reporter, leaving the man flummoxed. But facing fiscal reality, under pressure from his agent, and getting pleas to come east from Baltimore's prime stars, Jim Palmer and Brooks Robinson, Reggie agreed to join the Orioles under a new contract that would pay him $190,000 for 1975 and after that let him become a free agent. Jackson hit twenty-seven homers for Baltimore in '76 (Graig Nettles hit thirty-two for New York) and the Orioles finished a distant second to Martin's Yankees. But Reggie is not simply the sum of his homers, his doubles, or, for that matter, his strikeouts. Reggie is all by himself a star, a constellation, a galaxy, and—returning to our planet—an earth force lightly filtered through a personality. At one point, while wearing a Baltimore uniform, he famously told a group of reporters, "If I played in New York, they'd name a candy bar after me."

As Martin wanted the Yankees to sign Joe Rudi, Gabe Paul stumped for Bobby Grich, who could play second base or shortstop very well. But Grich said he felt uncertain about coming to

New York and, besides, Steinbrenner was inexorably drawn to Jackson. To Martin's discomfort, Paul pointed out that Rudi was slow afoot and didn't have much of a throwing arm. The Yankees passed on Messrs. Grich and Rudi, worthy ball players but not great ones, who went on to play fairly well for a variety of teams, all of which failed to win a pennant.

In November of 1976, Jackson traveled to New York to be fitted for some menswear by a high-fashion clothier whose suits he was being paid to wear and endorse. Steinbrenner asked Jackson to meet him for talk and a beer at an apartment he maintained in the Hotel Carlyle on the Upper East Side, an elegant, tasteful spot that won notoriety during the 1960s as a a favorite trysting place for President John Kennedy and his assorted actresses, society girls, and strumpets. When George met Reggie at the Carlyle romance of a wholly different stripe was born, although later Reggie did say that George came after him "like someone trying to hustle a girl at a bar."

Reggie is a handsome character, with a wonderful smile and a steady gaze that makes you feel you are very important to him. (Ronald Reagan had that same striking quality.) Jackson is, as he has confessed, exceptionally bright, quite warm, witty, and informed. When we were talking for this book, he asked me if I had been taught writing in a formal way. "I studied at Bread Loaf, near Middlebury College," I said, "under Robert Frost."

Reggie gazed at me and said:

> The woods are lovely, dark and deep
> But I have promises to keep,
> And miles to go before I sleep,
> And miles to go before I sleep.

"You are the first right fielder ever to quote poetry to me," I said, and Reggie's smile was as fresh as an April morning. He says in 1976 when he first met Steinbrenner, he was something of a hick. "My idea of lunch was a tuna sandwich and corn chips."

Steinbrenner took Jackson to lunch at the 21 Club, explaining that this was where New York's movers and shakers gathered. Steinbrenner, who is a fine hand at recognizing star quality, was totally taken with Jackson and began negotiating ardently. A story has sprung up that has Steinbrenner saying, "I want you with the Yankees more than anything else in the world, Reggie. What do you want more than anything else in the world?"

Supposedly Reggie said, "The top-of-the-line Rolls-Royce. A Rolls Corniche" [which then sold for about $60,000].

"Play for the Yankees and you get one as my personal gift." The rest, goes this story, was easy. But appealing as that tale might be to a movie maker, that is not exactly the way matters went. Reggie was mightily impressed by what he later told Mike Lupica was Steinbrenner's uniform "blue blazer, gray slacks, blue shirt, Yankee tie, killer gray hair and the way he looked me in the eye." But Reggie was too smart to make a deal on the spot. He asked George to speak to his agent, Gary Walker, and then the two, Steinbrenner and Jackson, went for a walk in midtown Manhattan on a warm Indian-summer afternoon. Time and again complete strangers approached them. "Hey, George. Hi, Reggie. You gotta play for us, Reg. We need you." Drivers leaned out of taxi windows. "Come on, Reggie. This is your kind of town." Jackson said New York's bursting ebullience swept him away. Steinbrenner picked this up and as the two walked along Madison Avenue in the sixties, Steinbrenner said, "This is what it's like. The greatest city in the world. Can't you feel how much New York wants you?"

As negotiations proceeded, Jackson and Walker set up a private headquarters at the Hyatt Water Tower Hotel in Chicago, on Wednesday, November 24, the day before Thanksgiving, to consider bids and make a decision. As Reggie remembers it, the Montreal Expos offered "about $5 million" for five years. San Diego came in at $3.4 million. But New York had Jackson's heart. Steinbrenner flew to Chicago and signed Jackson for five years at the rather odd total of $2,960,000. Reggie had in fact mentioned the Rolls Corniche during one conversation, but Steinbrenner was damned if he'd personally buy an auto for a ball player. So the final $60,000 in the contract was the money with which Jackson could go out and buy the Rolls on his own. (Some accounts make Steinbrenner's offer somewhat higher. Whatever, soon Reggie would have his car.)

Details were drafted by hand on a Hyatt hotel napkin. At the bottom Reggie wrote: "I will not let you down, Reginald M. Jackson." And when February passed, and spring training began for the Yankees under Billy Martin, Jackson drove into the camp in Fort Lauderdale at the wheel of a new brilliant silver Rolls-Royce Corniche. It was spotless. Reggie had washed the car himself the night before. That same morning Cahen Car Rental on South Federal Highway in Fort Lauderdale offered 1977 Gremlins "with factory air and unlimited mileage" for fifty-nine dollars a week. At that rate, you could have driven one of Cahen's Gremlins for 1,017 weeks before reaching the tab for Jackson's chariot, although there is no record of any Gremlin ever built actually having lasted that long.

"I'm glad to be here," Jackson announced, "but I'm not joining the Yankees to become a star. I'm bringing my star with me." Did Billy Martin have some warm welcoming words? "I never say no to getting a Reggie Jackson," Martin said, "because he can help us win. Hell, I'd play Hitler or Mussolini, if it would help us win."

REGINALD MARTINEZ JACKSON was born in a mostly Jewish Philadelphia suburb called Wyncote on May 18, 1946. "My father," he remarked once as we shared a late-night pizza in Cooperstown, "is as white as you." Martinez Clarence Jackson, the son of a black man and a white Spanish woman, ran a tailor shop until, when Reggie was seventeen, he was convicted of distilling corn liquor in his basement below the store on Greenwood Avenue. He was sent to prison for six months. Reggie, seeing his father led away, burst into tears. Jackson adored and still adores his dad. In times of trouble he turns to his father and to prayer (and in truth sometimes to sympathetic strangers). Having a parent imprisoned was not the first harsh trauma visited on a gifted and sensitive young man. He was only six when his mother, Clara, walked out, taking four of the family's five children with her but leaving Reggie to grow up with Martinez.

"There is a reason I'm mentioning my father's color," Reggie said over the Cooperstown pizza, as a throng of fans stood outside, pressed their noses to the window, and gaped at him as some have gaped at the Hope diamond. "I think there's an important book in me. Not a baseball book. I mean there's baseball in it, of course. But boyhood. Growing up, which I'm still doing. The great baseball years and moving on to today. I work for Compaq, increasing market share. Bill Gates is a friend of mine. I live in Pebble Beach. I own my own private jet. I'm talking about a book with serious sociological and psychological and implications."

Reggie says that from pretty much as far back as he remembers he was an outstanding athlete, but even on the fields of sport there was no escape from trauma. At thirteen he was starring for the Greater Glenside Youth Club, near Wyncote, and he was the best ball player in the neighborhood, or as he puts it, "hell, in all the neighborhoods." The Wyncote-Glenside area was white, peopled by prosperous residents who commuted to Philadelphia. These white commuters were his father's dry-cleaning customers. Each year Glenside played a team from Fort Lauderdale in what was called locally the "Dixie Series." The Glenside coach refused to let Jackson play in the Dixie Series of 1959, lest his presence offend young ball players from the still intensely segregated South. Reggie took off his spikes, tied the shoelaces together, slung the gear over his shoulder, and walked home in street shoes, weeping. Sometimes these days Jackson muses, "I couldn't play that day because I was colored. A few years later I was a negro. Today I'm a black. That's three things in one lifetime. It gets confusing."

Reggie played football, baseball, and basketball and ran track at Cheltenham Township High School, where he pitched three no-hitters and batted .550 in his senior year. He ran a hundred-yard dash in 9.7 seconds, just four-tenths of a second behind the world record. He could hit and throw and run as well as any high school athlete in memory and, as he puts it, "I was the most famous kid in the area." His father told Reggie baseball was great, especially since the big leagues were opening up to blacks, but nothing was more important than a college degree. The surest path there, Martinez said, was through football. On his graduation Reggie was drafted by Finley and the Athletics but chose instead to accept a football scholarship to Arizona State. There he ran into a coach named Frank Kush, who possessed some of the sadistic qualities found in Vince Lombardi. Kush turned off Jackson. But the baseball coach, Bobby Winkles, fair though demanding as a drill sergeant, turned Reggie on, and Reggie responded with mammoth power hitting.

Under the Organized Baseball rules of 1965, Jackson was eligible to be drafted again for the season of 1966, when he would reach his twenty-first birthday. As the second draft approached, Winkles summoned Jackson and said he was certain to be selected in an early round. The New York Mets, who had lost 112 games in 1965, the end of Casey Stengel's quarter century of big-league managing, would have first pick but, Winkles said, they were not going to select Jackson. "I understand they're concerned because you have a white girlfriend," he said. Her name was Jenny Campos, she was studying elementary education, she was Mexican-American, and her skin indeed was white. The Mets drafted one Steve Chilcott, who never made the major leagues, and Charlie Finley signed Jackson for a bonus of $85,000 and a maroon Pontiac. As a twenty-two-year-old with Oakland in 1968 Jackson hit twenty-nine homers; a year later—the season Billy Martin was winning the division in Minneapolis—Jackson hit forty-seven and led the major leagues in runs scored. The onrushing A's were moving toward a dynasty.

In his rookie major-league year, Jackson married Jenny Campos, but in yet another of the rejections that seemed to be his fate she divorced him in 1972. Reggie says that essentially he was so focused on his career, he didn't make much of a husband. After the break he pleaded repeatedly for a reconciliation. Jenny, embarked on a teaching career, said that she respected Reggie, admired Reggie, but simply did not want to be married to him, now or ever again. As she tells the story, Reggie's calls persisted. One summer she decided to vacation at a far meridian, where his communications and commanding presence could not intrude upon her. She chose Nepal and a lodge in the foothills of the Himalaya Mountains. There, after a bracing day of hiking, she paused before dinner and picked up copy of *Time* magazine from a rack in the lobby. Reggie was having a very big year. Hard by the shadow of Mount Everest, Reggie's visage smiled at Jenny from the magazine cover. "Halfway around the world," she told a friend. "Two miles into the sky. And I *still* can't get away from the guy." They never reconciled, nor has Reggie married again.

IN TROUBLED TIMES with the Yankees, Jackson was inclined to look back on his Oakland seasons as a sea of tranquility. The team won its division championship every year from 1971 through 1975 and, as we've noted, won the World Series three years in a row. In Jackson's memory the Oakland A's were a band of merry musketeers, all for one and one for all, bonded in unjudging camaraderie, if not quite whistling French mountain airs on the road to Burgundy. But the record indicates that this was not precisely the way things were. Glenn Dickey, a columnist with the *San Francisco Chronicle,* covered the A's intensely and pronounced in a 1973 *Sport* magazine article that Jackson was not yet a superstar and maybe never would be for reasons that had nothing to do with raw ability. As Sal Bando, the A's captain, told Dickey, "There are two players on this club who are physically better than *anybody*—Vida Blue and Reggie Jackson." Catcher Dave Duncan said that Jackson was "so unbelievably strong he should be able to hit thirty homers a year, just by accident." Reggie himself declined to play the role of blushing violet. During the 1972 season, he began referring to himself as "Mr. B. & B." That was not a reference to a country lodging with home-cooked egg-and-sausage breakfasts. Reggie meant b-for-bread and b-for-butter, implying that he was the man who drove in the important runs. One problem with the nickname was Jackson's performance. After hitting the forty-seven homers in his sophomore year, 1969, he averaged fewer than thirty a season up to the time of Dickey's story, 1973. Jackson's annual runs-batted-in total worked out to fewer than 75. (Benchmarks here were set by Lou Gehrig, who batted in 184 in a single season, and Hank Greenberg, who once knocked in 183. Gehrig and Greenberg each concluded distinguished careers averaging 92 runs batted in per season.) What, Glenn Dickey wondered, was preventing Jackson from becoming another Greenberg, or Gehrig or Hank Aaron or Willie Mays? A technical problem was Jackson's undisciplined swinging. "He strikes out," Duncan said, "on pitches over his head and in the dirt." But a deeper difficulty, Dickey suggested, was the way Jackson let his emotions trample good sense. In a salary feud with Finley, he told reporters that he needed neither his employer nor baseball. He could make a fine living selling land in Arizona. At one point he cursed at Finley, who then began to talk of shipping Jackson back to the minor leagues. Indeed he might have, except that Jackson, finishing strong in '73, was voted Most Valuable Player in the American League and Most Valuable Player again in the seven-game World Series the A's won from the New York Mets.

He was not humble in the sweep of success. "I can do it all," he said with great passion to a reporter. "There are others who hit more consistently or harder, who run faster, field better or throw better. But there's no one who does as many things as well as I do. I used to dream how good it would be to be Willie Mays or Mickey Mantle. My dreams have died. Even the rotten [World Series] rings aren't what they're supposed to be. I'll buy my own diamonds. I can afford it now. I can do it all and I create excitement in a ballpark just when I walk on the field."

Mike Epstein, the A's mighty 220-pound first baseman, found Jackson, in a word, "impossible." One of Finley's frugal rules was that players could get free tickets only for their immediate families. One day when Oakland was playing in Texas, Epstein left four tickets for friends of his father, whose name was Berman. Perusing the pass list before a game, Reggie said, "Who put down all these tickets for Berman? We have no Berman on this squad."

"I did," Epstein said, "and it's none of your business."

"I'm appointing it my business," Jackson said.

"Don't buy any more than you can handle."

"I'm assistant player representative for this team," Jackson said. "I'm crossing Berman off the pass list."

By now both men were standing. Epstein threw a punch and landed four more before the manager, Dick Williams, charged into the clubhouse and broke up the battle. Later Jackson got into a fist-fight with Oakland outfielder Billy North. Breaking up that one, catcher Ray Fosse pinched a nerve in his neck and missed half a season.

"These confrontations come because of the owner we have," Jackson said after contemplation. "Other persons wouldn't believe him and they couldn't play under the conditions we have on this club. Cold weather. Bad ballpark. Lack of attendance. Unbelievable cheapness and a tense air between management and players. To survive this has become a very loose ball club." I don't think "loose" is the right word for those Oakland squads. The championship A's always were on edge. They seemed wired. Winning, but wired. "On some teams," Catfish Hunter said, "you might look into a corner of the clubhouse and think, that son of a bitch is loafing, that son of a bitch isn't carrying his load. On every club probably some players think that about others. But on the Athletics, you didn't just think it, man. You fucking *said* it." Candor is a strong point with Jackson. Discretion is not. His detractors claimed that he was disruptive, but with all those championships it equates as a kind of positive disruption. A similar quality has existed in Jackie Robinson and George Steinbrenner. The disrupted Reggie A's were a World Championship team.

In Reggie's defense, Sal Bando said, "At times on this club you need someone to speak up. When no one else is willing, it's Reggie who has the guts to say what has to be said. I admire him for that." Nor did the free-swinging Jackson stay angry at teammates for long. After the fight with Epstein, Jackson sat next to him on a plane ride and began, "You hate my guts, don't you? You ignore me."

Epstein said, "I just don't want to have anything to do with you."

"It bothers me that you don't like me."

"It's not that I don't like you. I tolerate you."

"Well, that's not enough," Jackson said. "I really want to be a leader on this club."

"There are no leaders here," Epstein said. "We all play to win."

When *Sport* magazine assigned a reporter named Murray Olderman to write another profile of Jackson in 1974, Olderman concluded an interesting piece with a description of Reggie's condominium in the Berkeley Hills and its splendid view of Oakland, San Francisco, the bridge and the bay. More than the vista, Olderman seemed interested in a young blonde named Mary "who spends her spare hours with Reggie." When Olderman visited, Mary sat in the lotus position wearing a green bikini. Olderman noticed copies of *Playboy* and *Penthouse* magazines alongside a Bible atop the television set. Jackson took the writer's commingling of a bikinied girl, skin magazines, and the Holy Bible in a magazine article as a slap at his religious belief. He recalls Olderman asking how he could consider himself a Christian when he was living with a woman out of wedlock. After the story appeared in September 1974—REGGIE JACKSON: BLOOD & GUTS OF THE FIGHTING A'S— Jackson decided never to speak to a journalist from *Sport* again. But he did, and as a Yankee. The results were volcanic.

IN MARCH 1977, *Sport* dispatched Robert Ward, a little-known gifted writer, to compose a piece about Jackson among the Yankees. I imagine that three stories on one athlete across four years was a *Sport* magazine record. Bob Ward would go on to compose *Red Baker*, a solid novel of blue-collar life, and become "story editor" of the popular television series *Hill Street Blues*. The Hollywood job called for him to shape up screenplays of the police stories that fueled the series, polishing works of fiction until they sounded authentic. That touches the core issue of Ward's memorable article, "Reggie Jackson in No-Man's Land." How much was fiction and how much was fact?

Ward worked his assignment hard, appearing before, during, and after Yankee workouts at Fort Lauderdale Stadium, loitering in the lobby of the Galt Ocean Mile Hotel, tirelessly trying to create a relationship with Jackson. Reggie remembers Ward as "nondescript and harmless looking," but Reggie also remembered that *Sport* magazine had bruised him. For two or three days he told Ward, nothing personal, you understand, fella, but I don't intend to cooperate with *Sport* ever again. Ward said that he wasn't out to get Jackson, that the story would be positive, and Reggie remembers thinking that all journalists say the same things. "I mean, can you imagine someone coming up and telling you he simply had to interview you because he was going to write something *negative*?" Ward told Jackson that if he came back from Fort Lauderdale without a story, it would make him look bad, hurt his career. He may even have said—there is no agreement on this—"Please help me with the piece. My family needs the money." Within Jackson's mighty chest beats a brave heart that is no stranger to kindness. Jackson found himself feeling sorry for Ward. He either invited Ward to join him at a Fort Lauderdale bar called the Banana Boat, or Ward tracked him to the place—there is no agreement on that point, either. Whatever, Ward started a conversation, which was really an interview, and Jackson responded.

In the background, Mickey Mantle, Whitey Ford, and Billy Martin were drinking enthusiastically, and playing and kibitzing at backgammon. The Yankee nightriders had started carousing early. Jackson, who doesn't drink much, ordered beers for himself and Ward. He was wearing a gaudy T-shirt; capital letters across the chest read SUPERSTAR. That was a gift from the producers of a network television show on which Jackson competed with a half dozen other athletes in a kind of miniature made-for-TV Olympics. Great fun to some observers. Garbage sport to others. Jackson flagged a waitress and told her to send a round of drinks on him to Mantle, Martin, and Ford. She returned quickly and said that Whitey Ford appreciated the offer of a drink, but would much rather have Reggie's SUPERSTAR T-shirt. Jackson grinned, stripped off the shirt, and hurried bare-chested across the room. When presented with the shirt, Ford said thanks and gave Jackson something of his own, a pink cashmere sweater. Ford is gregarious by nature, outgoing like Martin, without the paranoia, and humorous like Mantle, without the nasty, hung-over edge. Still in that spring-training atmosphere of boozy baseball, Jackson was doomed to be the outsider. Mantle, Martin, and Ford were playing big-league ball together, and drinking together, a quarter century earlier, when Jackson was five years old.

Jackson returned to the bar and said that he was thrilled to have a sweater "from Whitey Ford, a Hall of Famer." No one had asked if he knew how to play backgammon. Ward steered the conversation to baseball friendship and after a while Reggie said that Graig Nettles had seemed aloof when he and Reggie met during the Superstars TV Competition. If team captain Thurman Munson sounded gruff, Reggie said, he looked forward to playing with him because Munson was such a great competitor when Reggie was playing *against* him. According to Reggie, he then picked up a glass and compared the Yankees to a cocktail, a Planter's Punch, made with syrups and several varieties of rum. "Or it may have been a banana daiquiri. The important thing is that I absolutely remember putting the mix of a ball club into the context of the mix of a cocktail." Holding the glass, he says, he talked about Munson, Rivers, Catfish, and the others and what they could contribute. Then, according to Reggie, he said, "I've got the kind of personality that can jump into a drink like this and stir things up."

Ward's account, published in the June 1977 issue of *Sport,* was significantly more dramatic.

"[Jackson] seems to be talking directly from his bones. 'You know,' he says, 'this team...it all flows from me. I've got to keep it all going.'" Then, memorably, "'I'm the straw that stirs the drink. Maybe I should say me and Munson...but really he doesn't enter into it. He's being so damned insecure about the whole thing.'"

The planter's punch or banana daiquiri seems to have been lost in the journalistic process. Ward had Reggie go on to say that he could read Munson and that he would not talk to the Yankee captain just yet. There followed more remarkable stuff, supposedly from Jackson's mouth:

"I'll wait and eventually he'll [Munson] be whipped...I'm a leader, but leader isn't the right word...It's a matter of PRESENCE...Let me put it this way: No team I am on will ever be humiliated the way the Yankees were by the Reds in the World

Series!...Munson thinks he can be the straw that stirs the drink, but he can only stir it bad."

Ward said he asked Jackson, "Are you sure you want me to print that?" He said Jackson replied, "Yes. Print it. I want to see that in print. I want to read that." Reggie says he doesn't remember saying any such thing. He does remember "this character Ward, all the time we were talking, he didn't take a single note."

Early copies of the June 1977 *Sport* magazine showed up in the Yankee clubhouse on May 23 at the start of a series with the Red Sox. Someone in the front office sent word that the Jackson story "could start a real fuss and Munson sure is not going to like the piece." Groups of Yankees gathered about copies of the magazine, read as quickly as they could. A few began to curse. Someone said Jackson was a dirty son of a bitch. Munson took a copy into the trainer's room, from which reporters were barred. He came out looking shocked. "I just go out every day and play hard," he said. "I helped the Yankees win the pennant last season. I was voted MVP. What's so bad about that?"

Francis Xavier Paul Healy, a backup catcher out of Holyoke, Massachusetts, whose career was winding down, was as good a friend as Jackson had on the team. "Maybe they quoted Reggie out of context," Fran Healy said.

Munson smiled without mirth. "For three pages?" he said. "For three fucking pages?" Jackson himself dressed quickly and hurried onto the field. Some Yankees, moving past his locker, kicked his equipment bag and stomped his shoes. The Red Sox beat the Yankees, 4 to 3. After the game Jackson said he had not read Ward's story. Reporters pressed. "But you did talk to this fellow Ward?"

"Did I talk to this fellow Ward?"

"You gave Ward an interview."

"I gave Ward an interview?"

"You met him at a bar. People saw you."

"I met him at a bar? People saw me?"

"Come on, Reggie."

"Si, señor." After that Jackson would answer questions only in Spanish.

No other piece of journalism ever so isolated a great star from so many teammates. Numerous Yankees stopped speaking to Jackson. One day I heard Jackson say to Willie Randolph, "What time's batting practice supposed to start?" Randolph, a controlled, street-smart athlete, stared straight ahead as though deaf. When Jackson repeated the question, Randolph stared some more. Jackson's old Oakland teammates, Catfish Hunter and Ken Holtzman, stood back. They were civil to Jackson but unwilling to patrol no-man's-land in what might turn out to be a Munson-Jackson war. In his dignified way, Ron Guidry, just coming into his own after six seasons during which the Yankee organization didn't seem to know what to do with him, was accepting of Reggie. But Guidry was a quiet man who made his biggest impact from the mound with hard sliders. Sparky Lyle, the loud, mustached relief ace, was openly hostile. Manager Billy Martin came down on Jackson with bursts of sarcasm. Captain Thurman Munson said the magazine article revealed that Jackson, not he, was insecure.

Jackson defended himself to some new Manhattan friends by saying that the Yankees were coarse and crude and nasty. "I go up to the batting cage one day," he said. "Kenny Holtzman is jogging in the outfield. Four or five of them around the cage, including Billy Martin and Thurman Munson, are pointing at Holtzman and making Jew jokes. That was one of the most disgusting things I've encountered anywhere." But obscene as some Yankees were—unedited baseball humor tends to be cruelly sexual or harshly ethnic—the larger issue here was Jackson's pain. At length he went to Gabe Paul and said that the Yankees obviously were right for a lot

R. MARTINEZ J. ▼ 139

of people but they were just not right for him. "Trade me, please," Reggie said. "I want out. George said if I wanted out, you'd take care of it."

Paul leaned back with a mild smile. "Reggie," he said, "don't look at the hole in the doughnut. Look at the doughnut as a whole." Reggie stayed. He moved into a costly Fifth Avenue apartment, near the Metropolitan Museum of Art, and spent hours on the terrace looking out on Central Park, trying to understand his situation. He walked the Upper East Side, dropping into antique shops, bookstores, and galleries, chatting with pretty receptionists and asking questions about the work of such artists as Joan Miró. He left some of the women breathless, but still he always seemed to end up back on that very expensive terrace, very much alone. Was bigotry the primary force that was isolating him? Was it his color? He remembered the season he spent with Birmingham in the Southern Association where one night on the road he was barred from joining his white teammates in a honky-tonk redneck diner. The manager, John McNamara, ordered a meal for him and carried it out, making a nice little joke about room service before the two ate together on the team bus. McNamara's support made bearable an ordeal by racism. The Yankees had played blacks since 1955, but by tradition black Yankees were quiet, respectful, sometimes even servile, especially before their white bosses, and carefully bland to the media. He wasn't the first black Yankee, but he was the first *outspoken* black Yankee. He felt that Ward, nondescript, harmless-looking Robert Ward, had played him for a chump. Then other white New York writers were jumping on every mistake in the field, every strikeout, "Certainly not a great hitter and maybe not even a good one," commented Roger Angell in the *New Yorker*. A stronger writer, Red Smith, described Jackson as "an *opportunistic* hitter," which is a better description, but one that also meets the standards of Alexander Pope's damning "with faint praise." (Jackson would finish with 563 home runs, more than Mickey Mantle, Ted Williams, and Stan Musial, three white stars who almost always are referred to as great hitters.)

In his first months as a Yankee, Reggie's throwing arm hurt with a persistent toothache pain. Munson went around saying that Jackson's pain was "bullshit, just like the rest of the guy." It was impossible to sort out everything, but Reggie decided that if life were a science-fiction story, his Yankee role would be clearly marked. He was the alien.

Sometimes, as he eased the silver Rolls-Royce into the cement handball-court lot reserved for the cars of players and prepared to walk through the gates of Yankee Stadium, feelings of rejection and dread consumed him. More than once despair caused him to weep. But he stayed a Yankee; he stayed through what he later called the worst year of his life. Which is how it happened that he refused to shake his teammates' hands after hitting a dramatic home run; that he almost punched out Billy Martin on national TV; and that finally, in the World Series of 1977, he put on the most amazing show of power hitting in all the storied annals of major-league baseball. Reggie was, you see, the straw that stirred the drink.

▼

CHAPTER SEVEN

THE DOUGHNUT AS A WHOLE

THICK-NECKED, GLOWERING Thurman Lee Munson had a reputation for grumpiness and irritability. Moss Klein, who covered the Yankees for the *Newark Star-Ledger,* recalls a night when the Yankees flew "commercially"—as opposed to flying charter—from Kansas City to Chicago after a tough one-run loss. That meant the defeated ball players had to mingle with civilians. Sitting in the second row of the coach section, Munson began playing country-and-western music on a tape deck and twirling the volume control. At length a businessman wearing a suit, who was seated in the first row, turned and said, "Would you mind lowering that a bit?" Munson responded, "Mind your own business, fuckface." The impression Munson frequently created was just that: *Neanderthalis Americanus.* But when I met him off season in 1971 I got another, possibly truer and certainly less forbidding, picture: a young man with his pockets full of dreams.

He had driven fifty miles from home in Canton, Ohio, to meet Al Rosen, then running an investment business in Cleveland. Munson was coming off an outstanding rookie year, in which he batted .302 for the Yankees. He was a truck driver's son and now that a richer life was opening, he was calling on Rosen for advice. Stocks? Bonds? Real estate? Which investment made the most sense? He looked burly, he *was* burly, but mostly in a wood-paneled big-city financial office Munson looked uncertain. Rosen said warmly that he was a terrific young ball player. Munson said thanks. He and I talked a bit. I mentioned the Yankee tradition of wonderful catchers—Bill Dickey, Yogi Berra, Elston Howard—and Munson said that it was nice to be thought of in their company. He was wearing a jacket and tie, but kept tugging at his shirt collar, as though uncomfortable in business clothes. He seemed to be a courteous small-town kid, anxious to succeed and painfully afraid that he would not. "He's a good young guy," Rosen told me later. "A little hardheaded, but a good young guy." I didn't then spot the anger bubbling within Munson and I don't know if Rosen did, either. (Of course, when channeled into competitive drive, anger becomes an asset for a big-league ball player. Ty Cobb and Ted Williams, to mention just two celebrated Hall of Famers, brimmed with rage.)

Late in Munson's Yankee tenure, after the anger had erupted for all to see, he decided to write an autobiography with Marty Appel, the Yankee public relations director from 1974 through 1977 (who would also collaborate with the fallen commissioner, Bowie Kuhn). Six other Yankees lent their names to books back then and a few sold well. One element that distinguishes the Munson memoir is the jacket copy, which, by a long tradition of American publishing, decks the protagonist with sprigs of laurel. Billy Martin's ghosted memoir proclaims: HE'S A WINNER ... HE'S A FIGHTER ... HE'S A LEGEND. But here, after describing Munson as "gritty and determined," the publisher continued: "Some fans also mistakenly regarded Munson as a snarling, arrogant, self-serving prima donna." Perhaps, but I never heard any fan put it quite so tartly. (With a publisher like that, one wonders, who needs enemies?) Within the pages Munson protested that he was a strong but equally tender sort who wrote poetry while in high school. "I don't mean 'Casey at the Bat,' either. I'd write about children or God or things that required some sensitivity. I was rather proud of my efforts." A chaotic image—Edna St. Vincent Munson—quickly materializes and even more quickly dissolves.

"Actually," Appel wrote me, "I HATE the book, mostly because he withheld too much and it should have been far better. It was a struggle just to reach book length because Munson insisted that we stick to season after season of statistics and total wins and loss. After a while the numbers repeated after numbers get boring." Munson deleted a critical story describing the June day in 1968 when Lee MacPhail, the chief baseball man under Mike Burke, arrived in Canton bearing a Yankee contract. When Thurman let MacPhail into the house, Munson's father, Darrell, lounged on a couch in his underwear. He did not rise to greet MacPhail. When the contract appeared, Darrell Munson shouted, "He ain't too good on pop fouls, you know!" Shortly afterwards Munson's father left Ohio and the two, father and son, never again spoke.

Munson said he never sought the Yankee captaincy and when Billy Martin bestowed the title on him in 1976 he shrugged and said merely, "Okay with me. Thanks." Later he learned that numbers of outstanding ball players, Joe DiMaggio, Yogi Berra, Mickey Mantle, had *not* been appointed Yankee captain. The preceding captain was Lou Gehrig and after Gehrig died in 1941 manager Joe McCarthy said that the title would be permanently retired as a gesture of respect. It was Steinbrenner who defined Yankee permanence and told Martin to reactivate the the captaincy. Munson was a good handler of pitchers. He had already made a point of telling Martin that he, not the manager, should call pitches because he had studied opposing batters, understood the Yankee staff, and knew just what should be thrown where and when. "I don't think you're as qualified to call pitches as I am. Give me a few days to show you and you'll see I'm right." After the few days Martin agreed. Munson became increasingly proud of his leadership qualities and with that his new title as team captain; Reggie Jackson's comments, as *Sport* magazine reported them, flashed like bright arrows aimed at his pride. With Fran Healy serving as matchmaker, Munson did sometimes eat dinner with Jackson when the team was traveling, but the two never became friends. "It's a shame," Munson said, "that Reggie doesn't just let his bat do the talking for him." He later told Appel that he himself had come to regard baseball as a fantasy world, less significant than his "real" world, which he defined as family life with his wife Diana and their three children, relationships with old friends, and his business career—mostly real-estate investing—that was growing fruitful in the Canton-Akron area. Jackson, Munson said, not letting the issue between them die, had no real world; he had only the fantasy world of baseball. According to Munson that caused Jackson to envy him; jealousy lay behind the *Sport* magazine remarks. Whether one agreed with him or not, Munson was capable of fairly sophisticated thinking. But in this instance anyway, it is difficult to accept his conclusion, even aside from Munson's shameless, if understandable, fudging on the real relationships within his own family.

I think that Jackson was bruised by his rejection at the hands of Martin, Mantle, and Ford. Consequently he lashed out, insisting that in one way or another he was the most important Yankee. This included asserting, probably parenthetically, that he was more important to the team than captain Munson. Bob Ward is a strong writer and I suspect that in keeping with a longtime, usually denied practice in journalism, he "juiced" Jackson's quotes for maximum impact. Ward denies this and has denied it for more than twenty-five years. But at this point no one can be certain. In *Founding Brothers* the academic Joseph J. Ellis describes "the postmodern contention that no such thing as objective truth exists, that historical reality is an inherently negotiable bundle of free-floating perceptions." Absent a tape recorder on the bar of the Banana Boat—and there was none—"a negotiable bundle of free-floating perceptions" describes the situation we encounter, looking backward here.

Even before the Ward article appeared, Munson wanted to argue with another set of perceptions. Munson thought he was a helluva catcher, and he *was* a helluva catcher, although not quite as good as two of his contemporaries, Carlton "Pudge" Fisk of the Boston Red Sox and the Reds' Johnny Bench, just about the best catcher anybody ever saw. Munson wore number 15 on his broad back, but it bothered him that baseball people and sportswriters regarded him as big-league catcher number three.

He developed a confident, needling manner with his teammates, most of whom enjoyed him, but he was inconsistent with sportswriters. Sometimes he answered their questions. Sometimes he refused to talk. Sometimes he cursed them out. He either didn't understand, or couldn't accept, the reality that part of a major-league captain's job is maintaining civil relations with the media, not only for himself but for the good of his team. (The late Heywood Hale Broun, who covered the long-ago Yankees, told me that the real "Columbia Lou" Gehrig looked at reporters with disdain, as opposed to the saintly "Hollywood Lou" Gehrig who appeared in *Pride of the Yankees.* "But within that arrogance," Broun said, "Gehrig was civil enough and he certainly did not curse out anyone.")

On April 5, two days before the 1977 season began, Gabe Paul completed what he later called "my best Yankee trade." After weeks of bantering with Bill Veeck, Paul shipped a bulky young righthander named LaMarr Hoyt and a power-hitting right fielder named Oscar Gamble to the White Sox along with a minor-league pitcher and a check for $200,000. Veeck was underfinanced for the free-agent era. He hated the idea of helping Steinbrenner, but he needed money. That season in Chicago, Gamble batted .297 and hit thirty-one home runs. Some time later Hoyt won twenty-four games. But in '77, Paul's final year in New York, the Yankees wanted a pennant and a World Series victory right away, pronto, this season, by October 20 next. "I'll admit," George Steinbrenner has said, "that patience may not be my longest suit." What Paul obtained from Chicago was a championship shortstop, Russell Earl "Bucky" Dent, a gifted competitor and a quieter sort than most other leading Yankees. Still he certainly fit one mold; Like Martin, Jackson, and Munson, Dent was a product of a troubled family. Trim and dark-haired, Dent was so handsome he became an idol to a nubile crowd of Yankee fans who greeted him with or-giastic squeals. Few knew of his long history of isolation.

Dent's birth certificate reads "Russell Earl O'Dey" (his mother's maiden name). His birth followed a breakup between his mother, named Dennis, and his father, one Russell Stanford, that was so angry neither parent would raise the child. Dent did not discover until he was ten years old that the couple raising him in Florida, Sarah and James Earl Dent, were not his parents at all but his uncle and his aunt. He did visit his mother in Savannah, Georgia, from time to time, and the confusing fiction here was that he was told she really was an aunt. Riding a bus from Savan-nah back to Florida in 1962, the real mother turned and said— Dent remembers that her tone was cold—"Those people you live with aren't your parents. I'm your mother."

"At first," Dent, a pleasant, even-tempered man, told a sports-writer named Richard O'Connor, "I didn't know what to think. I was shocked, but I had no special feeling for her and consequently I couldn't accept her as my mother. I continued calling my aunt and uncle 'Mom' and 'Dad.' They brought me up. They deserved the titles. But sometimes when a lot of relatives were around I was afraid to call out 'Mom' because I wasn't sure who'd turn around. It was really strange." Dent is a private person. He said he was will-ing to tell personal things to a journalist because " I came to real-ize there were millions of kids in the same situation I'd been, missing a parent, maybe missing two. I thought maybe my success could be an inspiration to children who felt lost and discouraged."

At Hialeah High School near Miami Dent starred in baseball and football. "I had so much going for me there that other kids didn't. Yet they had something I didn't have: a father. Every kid has the right to know where he comes from." None of his relatives would help Dent search for his dad. None even supplied a picture. He focused on baseball and won a scholarship to Miami Dade North Junior College, where he became an All-American infielder. "But finding my father became almost an obsession. Someone said he was a Cherokee Indian and that his nickname was 'Shorty'— not much to go on." Finally in the winter of '76–'77 Dent told his mother with considerable anger, "Once and for all I want to know who and where my father is." He had worn her down. She told him his father's name and directed him back to Savannah, where Dent found a listing for Russell Stanford in the telephone book. Dent traced him to his job in an upholstery shop where the receptionist paged Russell Stanford. Presently a short gray-haired man appeared. Dent was trembling. "You probably don't know me, but I'm Bucky Dent."

"You're Russell Earl," said Shorty Stanford.

"You know," Bucky said, "I've been looking for you for fifteen years."

"And I've been living in Savannah for fifteen years," Stanford said.

That night they went to dinner. Happiness lights Dent's face as he concludes, "And we talked endlessly."

OPENING DAY 1977 broke amid fiery bursts of shrapnel. Center-fielder Mickey Rivers said he wanted to be traded. A reporter found out that the '76 Yankees had cut their batboys out of World Series shares, giving them only $100 each. (Batboys for the '76 Cincinnati Reds received $6,591 apiece.) Inevitably some called the

Yankees the Bronx Cheapskates. Fred "Chicken" Stanley told reporters he was "damn unhappy" that Dent was supplanting him at
shortstop. (Stanley had batted .238 in '76 and hit .167 during the
Series.) Larry Keith wondered in the pages of *Sports Illustrated*
whether Jackson and Munson "would beat each other bloody with
their Most Valuable Player trophies."

Martin's technique for dealing with fires was a generous appli-
cation of gasoline. Now he could not restrain himself from
needling Jackson. "Reggie has to understand the way I do things.
I'm going to win or lose but whatever happens I'm gonna do it my
way. I might bat Reggie fourth when he's hot, but with our running game it's best to have a fourth-place hitter who does not
strike out a lot." It was common knowledge that Jackson had led,
if that is the word, the American League in strikeouts four times.
Still his prodigious power always dictated that he bat fourth, the
clean-up spot. No fewer than seven big-league managers had previously hit him clean-up. There had been no issue about that before Martin. It was also common knowledge that Jackson had been
personally romanced by Steinbrenner. When reporters asked him
to comment on Martin's comment, Jackson issued a restrained
and ambiguous response. "It's important for me to get along with
my boss. I'm going to have to take a certain amount. Well, I'll take
it, but I won't eat it." Ostensibly Jackson's boss was Martin, but the
boss of bosses was Steinbrenner.

"I'm a driver," Steinbrenner told a reporter, as if doubt existed.
"I'm a firm believer in the old adage that if you're going to lead,
lead. You know, or don't you know, the saying? *Lead, follow or get
the hell out of the way.* I'm involved with everything from the ush-
ers to the dining room to the players' equipment bags. I raise hell
if the rest rooms are dirty. On the field I've been letting Martin do
things his way. But I know his record. I got Martin because he was
what we needed at the time. His record has been instant success
and I knew he could put it together in a hurry. But then there's al-

ways been a drop. It's my job to see that Martin's drop is not allowed to happen here." Following this resounding no-confidence
vote, Martin led the Yankees to 3-to-0 victory on opening day over
a last-place team, the Milwaukee Brewers. He started Catfish
Hunter and got a shutout. Neither McGraw nor Stengel could
have managed better than that. Then, playing mostly the Brewers
and an expansion club, the Toronto Blue Jays, Martin's Yankees
lost eight out of their next nine. "I could see in spring training we
had too many distractions," Lou Piniella said. "I could even see
some players being complacent. I knew we weren't going to get off
to a good start." By April 19, the Yankees had collapsed into last
place, five and a half games behind the suddenly (and temporarily)
competent Brewers. Larry Keith summed up the groundswell of
doubt: "A dream of New York's rivals seems to be coming true...
If the Yankees got off to a bad start, their explosive personalities
would set off a disastrous chain reaction, with the players squab-
bling among themselves and Martin locking horns with Steinbrenner and eventually getting the axe." Keith presented an essentially
sound forecast, but he was just about fifteen months premature.
No chain reaction developed, and on May 7, 1977, the Yankees defeated Oakland, 11 to 2, and moved into first place by half a game.
Munson explained the rapid turnaround as well as anyone:
"People talk about our egos and our salaries, but they forget we're
also ball players who've had success and care for what we do. Pride
doesn't allow us to let down. When you start getting killed on the
field [the team] and booed by the fans [Jackson], if you're a ball
player who's had success, your pride takes over." Emotions aside,
these were outstanding physical athletes and another factor in the
turnaround was talent. But a few victories and even, as we would
learn, a lot of victories did not end, or even muffle, the ragging.

On the day that the *Sport* magazine article became public,
Jackson hit a seventh-inning home run at the Stadium, a long
drive to right that drew the Yankees even at 2 to 2 with their great

rivals, the Boston Red Sox. It was only May, but first place hung in the balance. Suddenly Jackson's teammates forgot that they were angry and crowded to the home-plate side of the dugout to shake his hand. Jackson jogged toward the group, abruptly made a 45-degree turn, and entered the dugout from the first-base side, where nobody was waiting for him. Then he sat down. Jackson was refusing to accept congratulations. It may not be *pure* cause and effect, but the Yankees lost the game, 4 to 3, and they didn't get back into first place until June. Jackson's conduct was an oddly shocking, blatantly public illustration of the fratricidal aspect of this Yankee team. I'm reminded of Branch Rickey's comment on an earlier tempestuous character. "Leo Durocher," Rickey said, "has an infinite capacity to go into a bad situation and make it worse."

Six days later in Chicago first baseman Chris Chambliss, a soft-spoken "old-style black" Yankee, secured a victory over the White Sox by driving out a home run with Munson on base. Jackson, the on-deck hitter, moved toward home plate and extended a hand. Munson chugged right by it. Afterwards, Jackson tried to deflect reporters by saying, "Chris shook my hand. I guess Thurman just didn't see my hand out there."

"Sure I saw it," Munson said. He assumed an angry glare that foreclosed the questioning.

A writer remarked to Jackson that it was hard for him to grasp Jackson's real feelings toward Munson. What was Reggie's deep-down attitude, anyway? "My deep-down attitude toward Munson," Jackson said, "is that I'm trying to be a good Christian." (To play off Mike Nichols' phrase, Reggie regards his friend, God, as "a kind of a nice guy.")

As the season proceeded, Martin batted Jackson fifth, sixth, third, every slot but fourth. This was needling, more than managing, and it was also an exercise in destructive behavior. The needling helped nothing and nobody, not Martin, not Jackson certainly, and not the team. Besides that, it riled Steinbrenner, who wanted Reggie batting clean-up. Steinbrenner had already broken up with Ralph Houk and Bill Virdon. In someone's hyperbolic, inelegant, but catchy phrase, George changed managers as often as a hooker changes partners. Martin was weaving the strands of his own noose.

The Yankees played the Red Sox in Boston on Saturday, June 18, with first place on the line. The NBC network was televising the game; executives estimated that "thirty, maybe fifty million" people would be watching. It was a hot, sunny afternoon and 34,603 paying customers jammed Fenway Park, the largest daytime crowd gathered there in twenty years.

Jackson had hit safely in thirteen straight games and was feeling ebullient. Bucky Dent missed a bunt the night before on an early-inning squeeze play and a few minutes before the first pitch Jackson sat next to him in the dugout to show support. Martin came over and said to Dent, "Forget the busted squeeze." Dent nodded. Martin looked at Jackson. "I thought I made a good call. What do you think?"

"If you really want my opinion," Jackson said, "I think he feels that when you make him bunt that early in the game you take the bat out of his hand." (Translation: in essence, you destroy his confidence. You make him feel as though he doesn't know how to hit.) Martin stalked away. He may have wanted a Jackson opinion, but he did not want the one he had just heard. In the game the Red Sox pounded the big righthander, Mike Torrez; Carl Yastrzemski, Bernie Carbo, and George Scott hit homers and the Red Sox were leading, 7 to 4, in the sixth inning. With Fred Lynn on first base, Jim Rice checked his swing on an outside fast ball, but made contact and lifted a soft fly into short right field. Jackson looked toward the infield, as though expecting second baseman Willie Randolph to race down the looper. Then he broke slowly, picked up the ball on a few bounces, and soft-tossed it toward the pitcher's mound. Rice pulled into second base. The ball was not catchable.

There was no call for Jackson to make a frantic, diving lunge. But had he broken smartly, he could have held Rice to a single. It was a poor play, the play of a ball player whose mind was out of focus.

Martin walked to the mound. He was lifting Torrez for Sparky Lyle. He also dispatched Paul Blair, a gifted outfielder but a mediocre hitter, to right field. He told Torrez, who had not asked, "I'm pulling that son of a bitch for not hustling." Munson nodded in agreement. Martin was benching Jackson during an inning and in plain view of a sellout crowd and an enormous television audience. When Blair reached right field, Jackson said, "You coming in for me?"

"Yeah."

"What the hell is going on?"

Blair, sometimes called "Motormouth," turned laconic. "You got to ask Billy that."

Jackson set his jaw and began running toward the dugout with powerful, purposeful strides. The television cameramen in center field and alongside the Yankee dugout followed him, step by jolting step. Martin leaned forward on the bench, waiting, a coil of anger. Jackson closed with him, spread his hands as though bewildered and said, "What did I do? What did I do?"

Martin rose and said through a snarling look, "What do you mean, what did you do? You know what the fuck you did." (Lipreaders, including nuns and precocious children, picked up these syllables from their television sets.) Jackson moved past Martin as if he had heard nothing. Then he said, "Why did you take me out? You have to be crazy to embarrass me in front of fifty million people."

Martin said, "You want to show me up by loafing? Then I'm going to show *your* ass up. Anybody who doesn't hustle doesn't play for me."

Reggie said he hadn't been loafing. "Confused, maybe. But that doesn't matter to you. Nothing I could do pleases you. You never wanted me on this team. You don't want me now. Why don't you just admit it?" On the mound Sparky Lyle threw warmup pitches. The ten or twelve Yankees in the dugout sat silent. They were watching, just like the Fenway crowd, just like the television millions. In the truck, one of the NBC men said, "We're getting one helluva show. This should be prime time." (It would make pretty much every evening news show in the country.)

Martin moved toward Jackson, who stood his ground. The veins bulged in Martin's neck. He screamed, "I ought to kick your fucking ass."

"Who the fuck do you think you're talking to, old man?"

"What? Who's an old man? Who are you calling an old man?"

"You're forty-nine years old and you weigh one hundred sixty. I'm thirty and I weigh two hundred ten. Let me tell you something, Martin. You aren't going to do shit. What you are is plain crazy."

Coach Elston Howard had quickly marshaled a peace corps. He and Berra grabbed Martin from behind. The wiry thick-armed outfielder Jimmy Wynn grabbed Jackson. Nobody got to throw a punch. (Although some claim to have seen Martin launch a roundhouse right, the tape replays I've watched show tempers, but no punches.) Reggie shook free and tramped into the clubhouse. By the time he got there, he says, he decided that after the game he would punch Martin silly.

Mike Torrez, 6 foot 5 and 220, sat on a stool in front his locker. He'd heard the encounter described on Boston radio. "Why don't you go back to the hotel?" he said to Jackson. "Just keep away from Billy for a while."

"Maybe," Reggie said, and walked into the trainer's room, where he found Bucky Dent dressed in street clothes. Earlier Martin had lifted Dent for a pinch hitter. "I can't take any more of this," Dent said. He had made a plane reservation to Chicago, where his son was still attending school, and had called his wife,

Karen, asking her to meet him at O'Hare. "Martin never lets me swing with men on base," Dent said. "I've had enough. I'm jumping the club." (Reggie's pregame comment on the consequences of taking that bat out of Dent's hands were coming true in a whirlwind rush and in spades.) Big Fran Healy, the bullpen catcher who was named after three saints, Francis, Xavier, and Paul, appeared and in the next few minutes earned his season's pay. Jackson spoke to him about the humiliations he was suffering. "He wants me to make a hard throw on a nothing play like that? I've had three cortisone shots this season. I have to save my arm for when it counts." Jackson went on with his litany. Healy said sincere, placating things. Listening, Bucky Dent felt less isolated, less the lone victim of a strange and willful manager. He called Karen, a spirited young woman nicknamed "Stormy," in Chicago for a second time. He loved her, he said, and he had decided to stick with the club.

Steinbrenner missed the game. He was in Cleveland attending a funeral. But he saw the encounter on television and immediately telephoned the Fenway Park press box and demanded to talk to Phil Rizzuto. There was no phone connection between the press box and the radio booth and Bill Crowley of the Red Sox, who answered the call, assumed the loud character on the other end was "some nut." He hung up. He hung up on George M. Steinbrenner III. The phone rang again. A frightened Fenway operator began, "I have to know who it was that just hung up." A strong voice drowned her out. "This is George Steinbrenner." In the end Steinbrenner reached not Rizzuto, but a Yankee publicity man. "Have Gabe Paul call me right away," he ordered.

Paul recalled that Steinbrenner was distraught and wanted to fire Martin "immediately, if not sooner." The man was a disgrace, Steinbrenner said. He had completely lost control of himself on national television. His language was disgusting, "a terrible example for American youth." Paul said he couldn't disagree, but there were other factors to consider. If Martin were fired, it could seem that Jackson was running the team. Munson might organize, or anyway try to organize, some sort of nasty rebellion. "We don't need a *firing* right now, George. What we need is a *cease-fire*. Let me meet with Martin and Jackson in the morning." Then, speaking slowly and clearly, Paul said, "If you fire Martin now, I won't be able to deal with the consequences. If you fire Martin, I'll resign." This would have left the Yankees without a manager or a president. Like Hannibal, Caesar, and Patton, Steinbrenner knew that not often, but every once in a great while, one beats a strategic retreat.

In Paul's suite at the Sheraton, Martin again challenged Jackson to fight. "I'm going to kick the shit out of you right here. Get up, boy."

"Hey, Gabe," Jackson said. "You're a smart guy. Why don't you tell me what you think he meant when he called me 'boy'?" Martin started toward the door. Paul rose and ordered him to sit. After a while Jackson said to Paul, "I know you're not trading me because you would have done that already. I know I'm going to be staying. I assume Billy is staying, too. I've talked to some friends and my father. The only recourse I have is to bust my ass for this guy regardless of what he tries to do to me." As Jackson was leaving the suite, he remembers Paul sounding his secular anthem: "Don't look at the hole in the doughnut. Look at the doughnut as a whole."

The Red Sox swept the series from Yankees, who fell, two-and-a-half games out, into third place. The team flew to Detroit, where Steinbrenner was waiting at the Ponchartrain Hotel, breathing heavily between growls. He called Martin to his suite. "I thought Jackson was dogging it," Martin said. "If I let Jackson get away with it, they all will. I'll lose my team." (Twenty-five ball players, the storied New York Yankees, Munson, Piniella, Nettles, Randolph, Dent, and the rest, all loafing on the job in midseason? That may have been possible in the fantasies of Billy Martin. It was not possible in reality.) Martin continued, "You're just mad, George, because we got swept by the Red Sox. You're the only owner that wants to fire the manager every time the team drops out of first place." Still considering Paul's counsel that a cease-fire was the best course, Steinbrenner suspended judgment. He encountered Jackson walking through the lobby and in a few intense minutes, Jackson told him that firing Martin would cause more problems that it would solve. "It will make it look as though I'm running the club."At length Steinbrenner called over Martin and issued a command. Martin and Jackson were to ride out to Tigers Stadium in the same taxi. "And," Steinbrenner said, fiercely, "make sure all the sportswriters see the two of you getting into the one cab." Later Gabe Paul told me, "Actually George wanted Martin to take a taxi to the Sahara Desert by himself. He never entirely forgave me for not agreeing with him."

Paul left the team in Detroit and flew to his home in Tampa. He was the president of the Yankees. He was giving himself a little vacation; surely he had earned it. Quiet, temperate Gabe—it was said no one had ever seen him lose his temper, except perhaps his wife, Mary—was worn out by all the ranting, but quiet temperate Gabe was at his core a shrewd, audacious man. He was acutely aware that he was leaving the team at a time of crisis. The players were difficult, the manager was on the way to becoming a full-time drunk, but Paul felt that he could handle these matters. What bothered him were reports that Steinbrenner was saying vituperative things behind his back. "I'd been hearing," he told me, "and you know I have a lot of sources, I'd messed up with Martin and that George had had to bail me out. And I heard he was telling people that I was over the hill, that I was getting senile, that my mind had been affected by a stroke. I'll put up with a lot, but there are limits even for me." The Yankees lost two more games in Detroit, falling four-and-a-half behind the Red Sox. They came home and managed to lose the Mayor's Trophy game to the New York Mets, 6 to 4. That was a charity exhibition, devoid of championship significance, but in the years before interleague play it was heavy with local symbolism. As it happened the '77 Mets were one of the weakest teams in baseball. They would finish last, thirty-seven games out of first place, with a rookie manager widely regarded as an ambulatory disaster. As Red Smith remarked, "The only apprentice who seems less suited for managing than the Mets' novice, Joe Torre, is the Atlanta amateur, Ted Turner." Turner had managed the Braves, which he owned, for a single game in 1977. The Braves lost it and, just like the Mets, finished thirty-seven games out of first place.

After Detroit and the lost exhibition game the Yankees were to play three more against the Red Sox, this time at the Stadium. Another Boston sweep would just about end their season. From Detroit, Steinbrenner flew to Tampa, following Paul. He owned a team of renegade ball players, with a captain wrapped up in himself and a manager increasingly erratic. Deep down, within the macho, three layers underneath the bravado, Steinbrenner knew he needed help. He asked Paul when he would come back. Paul said only when he was assured that the backbiting would stop. Steinbrenner apologized, or at least apologized sufficiently to placate the Yankees' president, and Paul agreed to go back to work on June 24, when the Yankees opened against the Red Sox at night in the Stadium.

Jackson had been swinging at some bad pitches and he had misplayed a line drive in Detroit. At Martin's suggestion, he visited an ophthalmologist on June 23. His eyes turned out to be fine. It surprised him the next night to see his name missing from the lineup. The Red Sox were starting the left-handed Bill Lee and at first Martin told reporters that Jackson had been having trouble with lefthanders. Someone pointed out that in nine turns at bat against Lee so far this season, Jackson had belted five hits, including two homers. "But his eyes," Martin said. "He had them dilated by the doctor. The trainer says they still look dilated. I'm sitting Reggie because I don't want him getting hurt. I'm doing this for his own good." Hearing that, Jackson jogged to the outfield without a glove. He didn't want to be pressed by the sportswriters.

During the second inning Gabe Paul arrived at the Stadium. The Red Sox were leading, 3 to 1, and Jackson was sitting on the bench. After listening to explanations, Paul summoned the Yankees' team doctor, Maurice Cowen, and told him to check Jackson's eyes. Not long afterward, Paul telephoned the dugout. He told Martin: "I've just talked to Cowen, Billy. Reggie is *available*." Not needing to listen further, or so he hoped, Paul hung up. Martin sent Jackson up to pinch-hit in the ninth inning with the Yankees down by two runs. The Stadium crowd numbered 54,940. Jackson drew a fortissimo of boos. The substantial redneck element in the Yankee fan base, often identified a bit simplistically as beer drunks from New Jersey, didn't care for an outspoken and, dammit, *snooty* black guy. Jackson grounded out. Then Carl Yastrzemski misplayed Willie Randolph's fly into a triple and Roy White hit a hanging screwball into the left-field seats, tying the score. Jackson came to bat in the eleventh inning with runners on first and second and rocketed the first pitch into right field for a run-scoring single. Reggie (and Gabe Paul) had won a very big game in eleven, 6 to 5. The Yankees went on and swept the Red Sox.

But August brought dog-day afternoons when the Yankees stumbled against weak teams on the West Coast and again fell five games out of first place. The team flew to Syracuse for an exhibition against their Triple-A farm team, the Chiefs, and the minor leaguers beat them, 14 to 5. In one corner of a rough-hewn bush-league clubhouse, Gabe Paul talked to Martin. The customary geniality had fled. "Why don't you cut out the horseshit now, right now, and start batting Reggie clean-up?"

"His strikeouts will mess up my running game."

"Your running game? That was last year until you came up against Johnny Bench. This year your running game is *already* messed up. You aren't playing running baseball." Paul shook his head. He seldom spoke coarsely, and the sudden sprinkling of crude language now made his sentences more strong. "I told you, Martin, cut the horseshit. I'm too damn old to be fucked around." (The '77 Yankees would steal a modest ninety-three bases. Six other American League teams stole more than one hundred.)

"As a matter of fact," Martin said, backpedaling as rapidly as he could, "I been thinking of putting Jackson in clean-up myself. He's swinging good." (At this juncture Jackson, batting .243, was not swinging particularly well.)

"I don't mean for one day," Paul said. "I'm talking about the rest of the year."

"That could work."

"You're five games out and you keep platooning Lou Piniella. He's hitting .330. You need Piniella in your lineup every day."

"I was thinking the same thing myself." Martin knew that he was close to being fired. For the moment Steinbrenner had become irrelevant. Gabe Paul stood powerfully in command. No bluster. No notable eloquence. Just a man who knew baseball and knew how to run a big-league team, which he'd been doing here and there for thirty years. Right now, Martin must have realized, another firing would make four—four big-league firings in just eight years. Not only that, but losing the Yankee job would be the mother of all firings. Afterward? Back to scouting, probably, sitting on creaky wooden benches in a hundred bush-league fields. Driving the two-lane blacktops through the night. Tank-town meat loaf. Dingy bars, where your drink came with a wooden swizzle stick and the blondes had crackly hair and sandscraper skin. You saw that when you got them in the light. "One thing," Martin said. He was close to tears. "You gotta help me here. I need Art Fowler to be my pitching coach." John Arthur Fowler of Spartanburg, South Carolina, had pitched professionally until he was forty-eight years old, after which he joined Martin in Minnesota and followed him to Detroit and Texas. He had become companion and confidant and crutch. "You should have asked before," Paul said. "I don't have a problem hiring your buddy."

A few days later Ron Fimrite of *Sports Illustrated* found Martin and Fowler sitting in the manager's office at Yankee Stadium dead sober and apparently relaxed. Pictures of Casey Stengel crowded the walls. A classic campy movie, *Hercules,* starring Steve Reeves, was playing on a large televison set. Splitting his vision between the strong man and the writer, Martin said, "I been trying to get Art here for two years. I'm happy to have him at last."

"Has your relationship with Steinbrenner improved?" Fimrite asked.

"I don't want to discuss that," Martin said. "I have nothing to gain from discussing that." On the screen, an actress playing an ancient Hellenic beauty and wearing a stole said, "Very well, Hercules, but there is one thing you can't take away from me—the love we shared together." Fowler shook his head. Martin whooped and grinned. His piercing, unbearable intensity, if not his anger, seemed to be gone. With Fowler aboard, with Piniella playing every day, with Jackson batting clean-up, and with Martin watching movies in the afternoon, the 1977 Yankees swept thirty-nine of their next forty-nine games, a triumphant .796 pace. One reporter maintains that the conflict between Martin and Jackson never abated, but simply went underground: "Billy would take some drinks and say, 'If you want to know what I think, Reggie is shit.' Then he would say, 'That's off the fucking record.' Reggie, when you asked him and sometimes when you didn't, took you off record, too. 'Personally,' he'd say, 'I regard Billy as a motherfucking bastard. I'm just telling you that so you know. You can't print it.' Of course my paper wouldn't have printed the actual words, but they did know how to print dashes." As John McGraw pointed out that managing is not a popularity contest, so a winning big-league ball club is not necessarily a lineup of nine or ten former eagle scouts, all with citations for superb deportment. Everyone does not have to like everybody else for a team to succeed, but clearly it helps to keep high-bounding egos under some measure of control. At length, with their fussing and feuding damped, rather than extinguished, the Yankees won one hundred games and their second consecutive Eastern Division championship, and moved into a play-off against a tough, young Kansas City club, managed by the gifted Dorrel Norman Elvert "Whitey" Herzog.

For some reason, good Kansas City scouting, emotional exhaustion, whatever, Reggie Jackson suddenly stopped hitting. Across the 130-odd years of organized professional baseball, slumps have appeared during periods of pressure and humbled even the greatest hitters. In the primordial World Series of 1884, Dave Orr, a slugging, 250-pound first-base star of the New York Metropolitans, got one hit, a single, in nine trips, a dismal batting performance of .111. In the World Series of 1907, Ty Cobb batted .200 (and didn't steal a base). Babe Ruth went 2-for-17 in the 1922 World Series (and didn't hit a homer). The 1946 World Series brought a classic match between the best batters of the time, the Cardinals' Stan Musial and the Red Sox's Ted Williams. Across seven games, Musial hit .222. Williams, matching Cobb, hit an even .200. ("But *between* us," Musial told me deadpan years later, "we batted over .400.") In the 1952 Series, Gil Hodges, the Brooklyn Dodgers' strongest right-handed slugger, went 0-for-21. Put differently, Hodges went 0 for October. Explaining why such things happen could fill a volume, or two or three. Briefly, hitting against major-league pitchers is the most failure-prone activity that exists in sport. Many have pointed out that a successful batter, a .300 batter, succeeds only 30 percent of the time. The other 70 percent of his efforts end in fly balls, ground outs, whiffs. This observation is accurate as far as it goes, but understates the point by just a bit. On an average turn at the plate, a batter gets two or three swings. Arbitrarily, give him three swings per at bat. Viewing things now in the proper light, we realize that a .300 hitter connects safely in only about one out of ten swings. *Nine out of every ten swings that a fine major-league hitter takes become sweaty, grunting failures.* Imagine a golfer hooking drive after drive out of bounds, or a tennis player netting 90 percent of his ground strokes. Neither happens, even at the modest country-club level of athletic performance. When I first stood in against big-league pitching, after a boyhood of ball playing on the sandlots, I wondered how in the world you could hit this stuff. Presently I came to realize, you don't.

The astonishing failure rate of big-league batters unfolds against a mixed bag of pitchers. But in the big series, the bag is not so mixed and outstanding pitching is frequently the rule. Outstanding pitching actually carries many teams into the play-offs and the World Series. In addition, the post-season scouting reports are meticulously detailed. If you have trouble with an inside fast ball, thumb high, then in a big series that is what you will see, *ad nauseam.* Bothered by a hard slider low and away? Get ready for a gelid menu of hard sliders, low and away, mixed from time to time with a brush back, lest you lean in. There is a venerable saying that good pitching stops good hitting, which is not always so, but does hold true most of the time. So, given the difficulty of hitting, the sophistication of modern scouting, and the historic primacy of pitching, Jackson's play-off slump was disappointing rather than surprising.

When a star hitter goes south, loses his touch, traditionally a manager stays with him even, so to speak, into the Mato Grosso. "Truthful Jim" Mutrie stayed with big Dave Orr in 1884 because Orr had led the team in homers. No one thought of benching Cobb or Ruth or Musial or Williams or even Hodges during their mournful Octobers. Slumping or not, any one of them could win a ball game with one swing. The rule here, a good and venerable rule, says: If you're going to lose, don't lose with the backup players, the "scrubinis." Make the sons of bitches beat your best.

The Royals were a speedy, plastic-turf club, and when they split the first two play-off games on the real grass of Yankee Stadium, they became heavy favorites. During the regular season they had won four of five from the Yankees on the ultra-fast Astroturf of Royals Stadium among the waterfalls and fountains of the Harry S Truman Sports Complex. The Royals won the third game but then the Yankees staggered back from the edge when a superb relief stint by Sparky Lyle carried them to victory in game four. Herzog started his crack lefthander, Paul Splittorff, for the fifth and deciding game. The rangy Splittorff had led the league in winning percentage and—one can pretty much see this coming—Martin responded by benching Reggie Jackson. Up to that point in the Series, Reggie was one for fourteen, a batting, or perhaps non-batting, average of .071. "He has trouble with certain lefthanders," Martin said. "Splittorff is one of them." Other Yankee left-handed batters—Graig Nettles and Chris Chambliss—also had trouble with Splittorff, who was in his prime, but only Jackson was benched. Martin did not tell Jackson face to face. He ordered coach Elston Howard to bear the news and told Fran Healy to keep Jackson calm. Reggie avoided reporters until he had a full grip on his composure. Then he said: "If you're out of a big game like this one, you've got to be down. Your pride has got to be hurt. But if a man tells me I'm not playing, I don't play. I sit down and pull for the club. I'm not the boss. I'm the right fielder." A severe look came here and Reggie said, "Sometimes."

Going with his best for a must game—one of the gospels fervently articulated by Saint Casey—Martin started Ron Guidry and, when Guidry looked arm weary, quickly followed with big Mike Torrez. But after three innings the Royals led, 3 to 1, and they held that lead into the eighth. Then Willie Randolph singled off the righthander Doug Bird, who had just relieved Splittorff. Bird struck out Munson, but Lou Piniella singled Randolph to third. Abruptly Martin barked, "Reggie. Go pinch-hit." Jackson singled to center, bringing home Randolph. In the ninth inning the Yankees scored three more runs and won a very exciting ball game, 5 to 3. (For the

record, Jackson finished the play-off set 2-for-16, an average of
.125. Among the lefthanders Martin declined to bench, Nettles
went 3-for-20 [.150] and Chambliss went 1-for-17 [.059].)

During the Yankee clubhouse celebration Martin shook a
bottle of champagne and doused Steinbrenner, who was wearing
his signature custom-tailored blue blazer. "That's for trying to fire
me," Martin shouted.

When Steinbrenner spoke his voice was hard. "What do you
mean try? If I want to fire you I will."

Gabe Paul stepped in, raised a cup of champagne to Martin,
and offered the Italian toast, "Salute!"

Martin responded in Hebrew, "L' chaim!" [to life]. It was a
lovely moment but Martin kept talking until he spoiled it. "Stick
with us dagos," he said to Paul, "and we'll makes dagos out of all
you Jews." Paul shook his head. Steinbrenner vanished. "Hey,"
Martin said to a crowd of reporters. "We just won two pennants in
a row. If I was them, I'd sign me right now to a five-year contract."

THE YANKEES HAD NOT won a World Series since 1962, when
Mantle and Maris were playing in the outfield. The Reds, as we've
noted, obliterated them in 1976. Now the Yankees started this Series unevenly, defeating the Los Angeles Dodgers 4 to 3 at the Stadium but losing the next day, 6 to 1, when the Dodgers knocked
out Catfish Hunter. Perhaps worse, before game one somebody, or
everybody on the Yankees, neglected to leave Joe DiMaggio's tickets at the pass gate. DiMaggio was supposed to throw out the first
ball. The Great Man would accept no explanations; he wheeled,
stepped back into a limousine, and headed downtown. Whitey
Ford threw out the first ball. When Steinbrenner telephoned
DiMaggio to apologize, he had no sooner identified himself when
DiMaggio hung up. Long before Jackson, Munson, and the rest,
Yankee Stadium had been home to egos as big as the Ritz.

The Dodger squad is best remembered for a fixed and constant infield: Steve Garvey at first, Davey Lopes at second, Ron Cey at third, and Bill Russell at shortstop, a group that stayed together for ten years. Although the Dodgers were not a great team—a soft, beach-boy quality persisted—they were a good one and would become consistent contenders for the National League pennant as the Big Red Machine ran down.

The Series moved to California, where Torrez and Guidry won the next two with complete-game efforts. Starting to roll, Jackson supported Guidry with a double and a home run. Don Sutton pitched game five for the Dodgers, shutting out the Yankees for six innings. He was ahead, 10 to 2, when Thurman Munson homered in the eighth. It was then, with the Yankees trailing by seven, that the curtain went up on the Incredible, Unprecedented, Mind-boggling, Stupendous, Utterly Fantastic But Absolutely True Reggie Jackson Show.

Sutton saw, or thought he saw, a swagger in Jackson's manner. This annoyed the Dodger ace, probably the strongest character ever to emerge from Clio, Alabama, and he decided that he would embarrass Jackson right here and now at Dodger Stadium in full view of 55,955 fans and the customary national television audience of millions. Before the catcher, Steve Yeager, could put down a sign, Sutton looked at Jackson and made a small, thrusting motion with his right hand and wrist, the universal signal for fast ball. Pitchers use that sign when warming up, to tell the catcher what kind of pitch is coming. But here in a brash and naked dare Sutton was telling Jackson—*the hitter*—that now he was going to throw his fast ball. *I'll tip what I'm going to throw, you swaggering s.o.b., and you still won't be able to hit it.* That is not precisely what happened. Sutton threw his fast ball and Jackson hit a huge, high drive that cracked into the top of the right-field foul pole. "Through all the twenty-five years I caught," Johnny Oates, then with the Dodgers, told me, "that was the single hardest-hit ball I ever saw."

Still, Sutton and the Dodgers won, 10 to 4, and with the Yankees ahead three games to two, everybody flew back to New York. There, on the off day, Gabe Paul announced that Martin would be back managing the Yankees in 1978. Martin was getting a $50,000 bonus plus a Golden Jubilee Lincoln Mark V (worth $13,000) and the Yankees would henceforth pay the four-hundred-dollar monthly rent for his apartment in New Jersey. Paul was making a supportive point, in hopes of relaxing his wired manager. Martin did *not* have to win the World Series to keep his job. (Of course at some level, Martin still would boil because, to put matters in *Billy-Ball* language, Reggie was driving a fuckin' Rolls and he had to settle for a fuckin' stinkin' Lincoln.)

To outward appearances, the Dodgers were far from dead. They stood two games away from winning the World Series, where the Yankees were one game shy, and the outlook remained dicey for both clubs. In game six the Dodgers were starting a big Texas righthander named Burt Hooton, who was early in a string of five winning seasons. The Yankees countered with the even bigger Mike Torrez, who four days earlier in Los Angeles had become the first Mexican-American to win a World Series game. A *week* earlier in New York, Joe DiMaggio had sworn never again to speak to George Steinbrenner or to enter Yankee Stadium. But when his Sicilian temper subsided, DiMaggio agreed to throw out the first ball for game six. He accepted Steinbrenner's effusive greeting at the pass gate, then proceeded into the Yankee clubhouse and sat down to chat, not with his old caddy, Billy Martin, but with the new feller in town, the right fielder, Reggie Jackson, whom he had known slightly during the season he put in as an Oakland coach. DiMaggio was sixty-two years old, graying, trim, poised and magisterial. To be in his presence was to experience, well, to experience Joe DiMaggio. Here in the flesh—and beautifully tailored conservative clothing—was the Yankee Clipper, Joltin' Joe, the Greatest Living Ball Player (as he liked to be introduced) and—not the least element in his aura—the man who had bedded and wed America's Blonde. (When Marilyn Monroe died, it was DiMaggio who organized her quiet funeral, barring such prospective attendees as the leader of the Rat Pack, Frank Sinatra, and the mighty Massachusetts Kennedys. When asked why, DiMaggio spoke briefly and said volumes: "Because they killed her.") Now this Olympian character was seated on a three-legged milkmaid's stool telling Reggie Jackson, in a number of ways, that he thought Reggie was a great ball player. Praise was as oxygen to Reggie and this praise flowed from the highest imaginable source. After Jackson jogged out to the field, spikes barely touching earth, he embarked on the most remarkable batting-practice session in the annals. No precise record exists, but he took approximately forty swings and hit about twenty baseballs into the seats. Drive after drive exploded from his thirty-six-ounce bat. As the exhibition continued, the Stadium crowd began to chant, *Reg-gie, Reg-gie, Reg-gie.* Other ball players gazed, trying to conceal their awe. Finally Willie Randolph said what some Yankee inevitably was going to say: "Hey, would you maybe save a little of that for the game?" Reggie nodded intensely and said, concluding his memorable overture, "I'm feeling good. I mean I'm feeling great."

Burt Hooton saw Jackson's display. He paid court in the second inning by walking Jackson on four pitches. The Dodgers had taken a two-run lead in the first. Chris Chambliss followed the walk to Jackson with a home run and tied the score. Reggie Smith's homer gave the Dodgers a one-run lead in the third. Munson led off the Yankee fourth with a single and Jackson stepped in. His last swing (in a game) had produced that booming home run off Sutton on the far side of the continent. Now he swung again and crashed a ferocious line drive into the lower deck in right. Two swings. Two homers. The Yankees regained the lead.

Before Jackson came to bat in the fifth, a strong Dominican righthander named Elias Sosa relieved Hooton. While Sosa took his warmup pitches, Jackson went to the dugout phone and spoke to the Yankees' scout, Gene Michael.

"What's this guy throw?"

"Hard slider, Reggie, and a good fast ball." Jackson decided that Sosa would try to get ahead of him with a fast ball up and in. But Sosa did not get ahead of him. Reggie lined the first pitch, a fast ball, even harder than his previous drive into the right-field lower deck. In the press box someone suggested that this smash approached the speed of light. "I was still in batting practice," Reggie said. "That's how I felt." But it was not practice, it was a game, a World Series game. He now had hit three World Series home runs on three consecutive swings. The failure element that governs big-league hitting did not apply to Reginald Martinez Jackson this October. The law of averages had been repealed.

Jackson got a final turn at bat in the eighth inning. He had driven in four runs. The Yankees were leading, 7 to 3. Charlie Hough, a knuckleball pitcher, was on the mound and Jackson remembers wanting to shout at Tommy Lasorda, the Dodgers' very loud manager, "Hey, Tommy. Don't you know I love swinging against the knuckler?" He did not shout or even speak. Hough threw his knuckler. Jackson bashed the ball 475 feet to dead-center field into an area of black concrete risers. Drives into the black come seldom. "That was a helluva pitch," said Lasorda, who was shaken clean out of his syntax. "When I seen him hit that pitch that far I seen the greatest performance I ever seen in a World Series." Four World Series home runs on four swings had not happened before, not once. No one had even come close. Some ask now if Jackson's towering feat will be equaled in the years ahead. A line from *King Lear*'s final scene provides an answer. As the ancient king cried out: "Never, never, never, never, never."

The Yankees won the ball game, 8 to 4.

▼

CHAPTER EIGHT

THE GATHERING STORM

"To MAKE MATTERS even more difficult," Richard "Goose" Gossage, the great relief pitcher, was saying, as he remembered the Yankee season of '78, "before that year was over they started letting women into the locker room. All of a sudden you had young women walking up to naked ball players. But to be fair, you also had naked ball players walking up to young women." The collision between militant, or anyway activist, feminism and the hidebound Barons of Baseball was yet another symptom of the changing times. The leader of the feminist charge—she had worked as my research assistant three years earlier—was Melissa Ludtke of *Sports Illustrated*, a soft-spoken reporter out of Amherst, Massachusetts, by way of Wellesley and Berkeley, who looked not like a firebrand but rather like a well-scrubbed preppie. (As a matter of fact, she was both.)

During 1978 the country was governed by President James Earl Carter, who had captured the White House from Gerald Ford in 1976, although Carter won only 48 percent of the popular vote and only twenty-three of the fifty states. After forging the Camp David Accords in what was clearly a great running start, the Carter administration had been backsliding, unable to brake inflation and getting caught in a series of feuds with Congress, although the Congress, like the president, was nominally Democratic. A man with a warm smile and a brittle manner, Jimmy Carter later complained from the Oval Office of "a national malaise," unintentionally offering a straight line that not every American could resist.

Isaac Bashevis Singer, a New York West Sider, won the 1978 Nobel Prize for literature, marking the first time an author who wrote in Yiddish was so honored. A few years earlier Singer's wife had worked as a department-store sales clerk to help feed the family. Now, with his budget and future secure, Singer said in Stockholm: "In a figurative way, Yiddish is the wise and humble language of us all, the idiom of frightened and hopeful humanity." Halfway across the world in the small South American country of Guyana, the madness lurking within cult religion came clear when nine hundred followers of a fundamentalist Christian named James Warren Jones voluntarily drank a concoction of powdered fruit juice, water, and cyanide. Everybody died. In distant Afghanistan, Marxists seized power. During the coup they murdered President Mohammad Daud Khan. In England the first "test-tube" baby was born, alarming many fundamentalist Christians more acutely than did the madness of James Warren Jones. Dominating 1978 was both a sense of change and a sense of trouble for Mr. Singer's frightened, hopeful humanity, a group that included George Steinbrenner's champion New York Yankees, who were just as frightened and just as hopeful as everybody else, beneath various cloaks of macho swagger.

Their first World Series victory in fifteen years brought with it no tranquility. Steinbrenner continued to harbor reservations about Martin and now Gabe Paul's new independence seemed to be making him uncomfortable. He did not forget that Paul had de facto quit the team in June, forcing him to plead like a supplicant for Paul's return. Steinbrenner did not regard himself as a supplicant. He was a boss and there was room for only one of those in the Bronx.

Martin stepped up the pace of his drinking and managed to sleep through the *Sport* magazine luncheon at the Plaza Hotel where Reggie Jackson was honored, amid a swarm of media, as the most valuable player of the Series. *Time* magazine reported that Jackson would not play for the Yankees again if Martin was retained as manager. The source of the story, someone at *Time* conceded over a drink, was not Jackson but Steinbrenner, or anyway one of Steinbrenner's friends. Before *that* flurry passed, Jackson told reporters: "Hell, Martin deserves the Nobel Peace Prize for managing this team." He was being diplomatic. The sixth game of the World Series had been the greatest evening of Jackson's life but a few days later he was wondering how strained things would be next year. As he saw it, whenever Martin felt pressure the manager followed a three-point program. Go to bar. Start drinking. Attack Reggie. Accepting the car given by *Sport,* Jackson suppressed his concerns, ignored Martin's absence, and spoke in a lofty and unusual way. "I'd like to be thought of as a hell of a person," he said, "a great person more than a ball player. And maybe my accomplishments could be interpreted humanistically. What they mean for people, for mankind, for poor people, for black people, for white people. About togetherness." Some found this grandiose. Listening, I remembered the Spanish-accented words of Roberto Clemente, another great athlete who had felt the whips of bigotry, when he won the same award after batting .414 in the World Series of six years before. "I am thirty-three years old," Clemente began his passionate address, "and this is the first time I have ever been asked to speak in New York City..."

A three-column headline in the *New York Times* acclaimed Jackson as BLACK SUPERSTAR ON THE FRONTIER. The writer of the accompanying story, Roger Wilkins, discussed Jackson "in relation to four other black athletic giants—Jack Johnson, Joe Louis, Jackie Robinson and Muhammad Ali." Johnson, a great heavyweight who held the championship from 1908 through 1915, had been vilified for, among other things, enjoying white women. Authorities sent to him Leavenworth for "transporting a [white] woman across a state line for immoral purposes," even though he later married the lady. Still later, he married two other white women. When he died in an automobile accident in 1946, John Lardner wrote memorably, "Jack Johnson crossed a white line for the last time." Unlike Johnson, Louis, heavyweight champion from 1937 to 1949, possessed a humble manner, and though he did have an affair with the gorgeous bottle-blonde actress Lana Turner, he kept quiet about it. (Turner did not.) Outside the ring, Louis appeared never to give offense. When he donated several rich boxing purses to army and navy charities during World War II, a reporter asked how he felt about fighting for nothing. "I'm not fighting for nothing," Louis said. "I'm fighting for my country." He was still champion when Robinson tore apart baseball's cotton curtain, integrated the game, and and set the stage for the movement to integrate the country.

"Ali," Wilkins wrote, "clearly profited from Robinson's groundbreaking... When Ali chose an apparently threatening religion [the Muslim faith] and then refused to go to war, he too was made to suffer. But most of his outrageous behavior was explained away as brilliant salesmanship. Often he seems like a playful child, no threat to the white male psyche.

"Now with Reggie Jackson a certain circle [with Jack Johnson] has been completed... Though he makes the East Side scene with fair-skinned beauties, Jackson is something more than an empty-headed bon vivant. He is an intelligent, complex, driving and sometimes immature human being who forces the world to take him on his terms. Though a ball player with lesser skills might be constricted, Jackson is not diminished by what society expects a black man to be. And that does transcend the ball field." After the 1977 World Series, Reggie was a king in New York, at least protem, but rather than reign he retreated to his condominium overlooking San Francisco Bay where he could cool out, see some friends, and play with his cats.

Back in Ohio captain Thurman Munson announced on a Canton radio talk show that he didn't intend to be a Yankee anymore. He would play only for the Indians because Cleveland was closer to home. If the Yankees did *not* trade him, Munson said, his anger percolating, he was going to pack it in and quit baseball. These words made headlines in New York sports pages and Gabe Paul commented, a little wearily, "Munson has made that kind of statement before. He knows our position. We're not just going to give him away and I don't see any deal for him that I'd like to make right now with the Indians [a second-division team, light on talent]. Will Thurman really quit? That's his decision, but looking at the economics of the situation, can anyone believe he really will?" Paul's term with the Yankees seemed to have drained him of outrage. But here, after winning two pennants and one World Series, the team captain, Steinbrenner's handpicked leader of the pack, was threatening to abandon the pack he was supposed to lead. It is just about impossible to imagine other, less self-obsessed team captains—Lou Gehrig of the Yankees, Pee Wee Reese of the Brooklyn Dodgers—behaving so disruptively. In the end, to be sure, Munson did not quit; the threat was a tactic to force the Yankees to give him a new contract and bring his income closer to that of Jackson. The tactic was not only inappropriate. It failed.

AL ROSEN WAS ALL ABOUT runs batted in. During his first five full seasons playing third base for the Cleveland Indians, he batted in more than a hundred runs a year. Rosen was not only a stout-armed power hitter—he twice led the American League in home runs—but also a batter possessed of great hitting intelligence. He varied his stance with the game situation and the count, a tactic also practiced by Yogi Berra but not by that many other power hitters because it is extremely difficult to pull off in the big leagues. Early Wynn, the late Hall of Fame righthander who pitched in Cleveland for ten years, told me, "People think Mickey Mantle is the toughest hitter in the league, but I can usually get him if I don't make a mistake. The real toughest clutch hitter is Berra. As you change speeds and move the ball around, Berra moves right with you. Rosen does the same thing, but fortunately he's playing third behind me so I don't have to pitch to him. Believe me, the two best clutch hitters in the game are Berra and Rosen. Most of us pitchers wish to hell they'd switch to golf."

My friendship with Rosen dates from the long-ago spring of 1954. I covered the New York Giants as they barnstormed across the country, from Phoenix to the East Coast, playing an exhibition game against the Indians every afternoon for eighteen days. We slept in private Pullman cars—hygiene and laundry became serious issues—and to stay in some sort of sensible physical condition, Louis Effrat, a sportswriter with the *New York Times,* and I developed a ritual game of catch, far down the right-field line, while the major leaguers took their daily batting practice. (Jogging had not yet crashed the national consciousness.) On a sunny day in Beaumont, Texas, Effrat and I were flinging sandlot fast balls at one another's faces when a very large Texas Ranger approached and said, "You'll have to get off the playing field."

"Press," Effrat said. Then, with much authority, "I represent the *New York Times.*"

"You'll have to get off the field," the Ranger repeated.

"What the hell for?" I said. "The gates aren't open yet. There's nobody in the stands."

The Ranger spoke very slowly and carefully, as though using unfamiliar words. "You are making a travesty of the National Game." He advanced toward us. He wore jack boots and was armed with a .45-caliber pistol. He spoke again, still slowly. "You are making a travesty of the National Game." As we retreated, Effrat tossed over his shoulder, "The *New York Times* is going to hear about this." The Ranger seemed unimpressed and we trudged off the field and into the right-field stands, as ordered. By chance I happened to look toward home plate. Near the batting cage Rosen was all but doubled up with laughter. He had given the Ranger five dollars (and a script) to evict us. Effrat, who suffered illusions about his sporting skills, felt offended. I thought and think the prank was pretty damn funny.

Rosen played baseball with exuberance and joy. Injuries cut short his big-league career when he was only thirty-two, a misfortune he accepted without complaint. He signed on with a brokerage firm in Cleveland, then started his own investment company. When that hit rough seas he took a position as vice-president of Caesar's Palace, then the dominant hotel in Las Vegas. This job involved press and public relations and, more important, building a sports program that would bring to Caesar's customers who were not sufficiently lured by slot machines, show girls, or the hunky, hokey pseudo-Roman statuary that towered over visitors in a lobby slightly smaller than the Coliseum. During 1977 Rosen was part of a group that booked the rugged heavyweight Ken Norton into the Sporting Pavilion of Caesar's to meet Jimmy Young, who early in the year had defeated George Foreman. Before their fight Muhammad Ali grabbed the ring microphone and said that his next defense of the championship would be against "whichever of these guys wins tonight."

Norton and Young topped an imposing program on the night of November 4. Starring on the undercard, future champion Larry Holmes knocked out Ibar Arrington; Jerry Quarry, a sort of professional heavyweight contender, knocked out one Lorenz Zanon, and the speedy, stylish future middleweight champion, Sugar Ray Leonard, won his fifth consecutive professional bout by knocking out Augustin Estrada of Mexico. As advertised, this was an all-star card. Ken Norton won the featured fight, gaining a close decision by crowding Young and body punching very hard. "What saved the show at Caesar's Palace," Pat Putnam wrote in *Sports Illustrated*, "was fifteen rounds of unremitting action [between Norton and Young]." Writing in the *New York Times*, Leonard Koppett called the decision "razor close."

Among the sports buffs flying to Las Vegas for the fights was George Steinbrenner, late of the Cleveland suburbs, who just happened to wind up at ringside beside the old Cleveland hero Al Rosen. "What happened next was not pre-planned," Steinbrenner told Russell Schneider of the *Cleveland Plain Dealer*. "It was all on the spur of the moment." Whatever. Afterward, over drinks, Steinbrenner asked if Rosen had ever thought about getting back into baseball. Out of that question came an offer of a reported $100,000 for Rosen to leave Las Vegas and become executive vice president of the Yankees. Rosen knew that Steinbrenner could be a difficult employer, but his passion for baseball prevailed and he accepted. Now Steinbrenner had Rosen, an experienced baseball man although at the time a novice baseball executive, to submarine, as the saying is, good gray Gabe Paul.

(As for the boxing subplot, Ali refused to fight Norton, choosing what he thought would be an easier bout, against Leon Spinks in New Orleans on February 15, 1978. But Spinks won a clear decision and with it the championship. Then when Spinks also declined to fight Norton, the World Boxing Council stripped him of the title and awarded it to Norton on March 29. Next Larry Holmes outpointed Norton in Las Vegas on June 9. After that Holmes dominated heavyweight boxing into the middle 1980s, when Mike "Tyrannosaurus" Tyson rumbled into view.)

GABE PAUL WAS FACED AT LAST with only a hole in the doughnut. There was no doughnut as a whole. Martin privately dismissed

Steinbrenner a rich fan, who happened to own the team, and he resented Steinbrenner's intrusion into baseball matters. But Steinbrenner believed he knew the game and felt he had every right to intervene. As the indispensable middle man, essential to both Steinbrenner and Martin, Paul could function with a certain sense of command. But now, with another solid baseball professional moving into the Yankee executive suite, Paul's authority inevitably would diminish. That December he resigned and accepted the presidency of the Cleveland Indians. We had known each other for a quarter century and Gabe invited me to a farewell lunch at one of those fine Italian restaurants on Arthur Avenue in the Bronx. Back in Cincinnati, he said over veal Marsala, he had run the Reds for Powell Crosley, "a man with all the money in the world, but he wouldn't put a dime of his own into the team. I made the operation much more profitable. The Reds' dividend went from twenty-five cents a share to eight dollars. But I couldn't sign the kids I wanted because there was no money for the bonuses that would take. Hell, I knew all about Koufax. He was a student at the University of Cincinnati, for goodness' sakes. But I couldn't bag him for the Reds when all I had to offer was loose change. Same sort of situation when I ran the Indians. Here in the Bronx is the first time I've had money to work with.

"To be fair, Steinbrenner was strongest for bringing Reggie here. I knew Jackson and Martin would be bad chemistry. My role there finally was talking Martin out of saying no Reggie and demanding Joe Rudi. I'd say the best free-agent deals we made were Catfish Hunter and now, of course, Reggie. The worst was Don Gullett; we gave him two million dollars and then he tore his rotator cuff. Pitchers are always dicey. Trades? I made how many, fifteen, twenty. Two really good ones were getting Lou Piniella for Lindy McDaniel and taking Bucky Dent away from Bill Veeck. A great one—my best—was getting Willie Randolph for Doc Medich." Sitting with this self-effacing man it became notably

clear as it sometimes does that money by itself is not the key to
major-league triumph. In the 1970s as today, the key is money
well used by someone who knows the game and knows what he is
doing.

Finally, Paul told me, he had urged Steinbrenner to let Mike
Torrez ($1.5 million) go and to invest as much as it took (about
$2.7 million) to acquire Goose Gossage. "Torrez had a couple of
good World Series games, but he's thirty-two and that's an age
when power pitchers can begin to lose their edge. Gossage is five
years younger—a big five years."

I asked what he intended to do with the Indians, a team that
had just finished twenty-eight-and-a-half games behind the Yankees. "Build," he said. "You know some of these young newspaper
kids come up and ask if George Steinbrenner hasn't damn near
driven me nuts. They're way off base. What *would* drive me nuts is
retiring. Cleveland used to be a great baseball town and it will be
again. Right now it's a sleeping giant. I'm going to start making
some good deals for Cleveland and build another winner."

He never did.

WHILE AL ROSEN WAS settling in as the new on-site keeper of the
zoo, Steinbrenner became more visible and more available to the
press. He thought the Yankees needed additional right-handed
power hitters and he went for strapping Dave "Kong" Kingman,
who had once hit thirty-seven homers for the Mets. But Kingman's relations with the New York media were chilly and then the
Cubs, of all teams, topped Steinbrenner's offer, purportedly $1.5
million for three years. Kingman went to Chicago (where in 1979
he led the National League in homers). "I'm not through beefing
up this club," Steinbrenner told reporters. "We won the last World
Series and we intend to win the next one, too. We've brought in
Gossage, just a great relief pitcher, and now we're involved in

something *really* big." He meant Vida Blue, a premium left-handed starter. Charlie Finley, again feeling impoverished in Oakland, was taking bids for Blue's contract. The Athletics had drawn only 459,599 fans in 1977, fewer than half of what they had been attracting before Finley blundered and lost Reggie Jackson.

Commissioner Bowie Kuhn, consistently outmatched by the strategists at the Players Union, uncomfortable coming to grips, so to speak, with feminist sportswriters, had established a strong and sensible policy on players being sold and traded within the major leagues. To prevent the poorer owners from selling off their talent to the richer ball clubs, a practice dating, you may remember, from Connie Mack's Philadelphia fire sale of 1914, Kuhn arbitrarily set a limit. The most that one team could pay another for a player's contract would be $400,000—a microscopic sum judged against current baseball numbers and even in the 1970s not much big-league money. (Free-agent ball players could make their own deals, as they can today. The courts had taken free-agent contracts out of the commissioner's jurisdiction.) Whatever strategy Steinbrenner tried to snooker Vida Blue from Oakland to the Bronx—details remain fuzzy—didn't work. Then George, like everyone else in baseball, figuratively yelped in surprise when a Cincinnati spokesman announced that the Reds were acquiring Blue's contract for Dave Revering, a minor-league first baseman, and, just by the way, $1.75 million. Kuhn immediately ordered a hearing and Robert Howsam, a hard-nosed baseball man who ran the Reds, argued this was basically a trade, Blue for Revering (a trade, incidentally, that would have brought Cincinnati another pennant), and that the money was incidental. I am told Bob Howsam said that without giggling. Kuhn would have none of it. He summarily vetoed the deal. Later Finley ferried Blue's contract across the bay and shipped the pitcher to the Giants for seven players and $390,000. That transaction did hold up and Blue went on to win eighteen for San Francisco. "I know for a fact," Kuhn told Marty Appel, who shaped his interesting biography, *Hardball,* "that my $400,000 rule finally deterred George Steinbrenner and the Yankees from pursuing Blue." Perhaps if Gabe Paul had still been working at the Stadium, he could have cobbled a Blue package that would have pleased Steinbrenner and been acceptable to Kuhn. Paul was a great rule bender, but in point of fact he was gone.

As with almost everything on the early Steinbrenner Yankees, Paul's departure and the ascension of Al Rosen proceeded with some confusion. Paul announced his intention to leave New York for Cleveland in early December but his Yankee contract ran until January. In addition he possessed Yankee stock, perhaps 5 percent, which baseball rules allowed him to sell at leisure because a quick forced sale might sharply cut the price. For a time Paul appeared to be serving two masters. He was getting some affectionate farewells, but Dave Anderson of the *New York Times* wrote, with uncharacteristic harshness, that Kuhn should at once bar any and all transactions between the Yankees and the Indians, lest there be a conflict of interest. Speaking behind their hands some asked if Paul had shipped Graig Nettles from Cleveland to New York after the 1972 season knowing that he himself would be moving on to New York. Paul, a fine raconteur, was equally skilled at saying, in one way or another, "no comment" when he was on the spot.

The annual "winter meetings" of major-league officials boosted the economy of Honolulu during December 1977. Here rules would be reviewed, trades would be discussed, managers and coaches might be hired and fired, and, since this was Hawaii, there would be some drinking and cooling out in the midocean sunshine. The Yankee delegation included Paul—or was he representing Cleveland?; Al Rosen, now executive vice-president; Cedric Tallis, now general manager, and, lest we forget, Billy Martin. The exact chain of command appeared indistinct. Reporters assumed that since Tallis was general manager, a job that had not existed under Gabe Paul, he would be running the baseball transactions. That is what people called general manager do. Rosen then would concentrate on the so-called business side. This seemed logical to the sportswriters since Rosen had spent fifteen years in the investment business. But before that Rosen was a baseball man and it was ingenuous to think that he would limit himself, or allow himself to be limited, to reviewing television contracts and setting the price of hot dogs.

The Yankee meetings within the major-league meetings did not go smoothly. Martin wanted to be the man who made the deals or at least the man who could veto any deals he didn't like. Neither Rosen nor Tallis would cede him that power. Traditionally the front office picks the team and the manager works with the players he is given, keeping his reservations to himself, like a good soldier. Martin's response was to spend time at poolside drinking Scotch. When a reporter asked what was going on with the Yankees, Martin said, "I got no idea. I'm boycotting the meetings." I doubt if he would have made that remark, which offended Steinbrenner, Rosen, and Tallis, when stone sober. But paranoia, whiskey, and hostility aside, which is one enormous aside, Martin was a smart baseball man. Dealing without him in the winter of 1977–78, the triumvirate of Steinbrenner, Rosen, and Tallis made only one good move out of four. After the Kingman transaction fell apart and Vida Blue proved unattainable, the Yankees acquired first baseman Jim Spencer from the White Sox. He was a journeyman; in fifteen big-league years Spencer never batted .300 or hit as many as twenty-five home runs. He would hit a soggy .227 in '78. They signed the right-handed relief pitcher Rawly Eastwick, who had twice led the National League in saves, to a five-year contract worth $1.1 million. Eastwick had lost the hopping edge on his fast ball; in June he and his contract moved on to Philadelphia, which, if nothing else, was close to Eastwick's hometown of Camden. By 1982, with still a year to run on his Yankee contract, Eastwick was out of baseball. In addition the Yankees acquired Andy Messer-smith, the handsome righthander so influential in bringing about free agency a few years before. He'd possessed a fine fast ball then. By this time it was history, like the reserve clause.

In essence the Yankee high command had spent a lot of money to acquire a left-handed hitter the team didn't need and two pitch-ers who were on the edge of retirement. How to explain this inep-titude? Years later when he built pennant winners at Houston and San Francisco, Rosen proved to be an outstanding executive, but at this point his position and authority remained ill-defined. Tallis had once won an award as "Baseball Executive of the Year." Stein-brenner himself was 50 percent owner, 50 percent fan, and 100 per-cent businessman. That totals 200 percent, which is both shaky math and perhaps another indication that George is larger than life.

Even the one fine deal for a major talent, Gabe Paul's acquisi-tion of the mighty Rich Gossage, was not to Martin's taste. In Sparky Lyle the Yankees already possessed a skilled reliever, who had just won a Cy Young Award and whose personality—unpre-tentious, crude, and combative—was what the manager liked. In a single year at Pittsburgh, Gossage had blossomed in relief as he never had as a starter for Bill Veeck, posting a 1.62 earned run av-erage in seventy-two games. But rather than rejoice in a bounty of new talent, Martin could see only trouble for the team and for himself in integrating two alpha male relievers on a single staff. As he later put it to his biographer, Peter Golenbock, "How was Sparky going to react to Gossage's getting all that money when he was already fighting with George over money." Another question turned out to be just as pointed. How was *Martin* going to react to Gossage's getting all that money? In a word, abysmally.

MELISSA LUDTKE CAME into baseball out of a massive publishing company, Time, Inc., which owned three of what were once the most prosperous magazines in America, *Time, Life,* and *Sports Il-*

lustrated. For almost half a century Henry Luce, the company's granitic founder, decreed policies that effectively barred women from writing, just as effectively as the Barons of Baseball had once barred blacks from the major leagues. In Harry Luce's patriarchy, men wrote and men edited and men laid out pages and men composed headlines. With very few exceptions women at Time, Inc. performed only the laborious and sometimes demeaning work of checking facts in stories men had written. Supposedly separating the writing of sentences from factual responsibility would reduce the number of errors that found their way into print. A writer trying to "juice" a story would encounter a researcher who actually could require him, at least in theory, to stick to the facts. The male writers were encouraged to concentrate on style and they were permitted to leave blank as many facts as they chose. The women, originally "research assistants" rather than reporters, were then required to fill in the holes. The late Otto Friedrich mocked this practice in an essay entitled "There Are 00 Trees in Russia." If Friedrich actually had written his beguiling title sentence in an article when he worked for *Newsweek* or later *Time,* his research assistant would have been required to come up with the accurate number of trees existing in the then Soviet Union although, as Friedrich remarked to me in his quiet way, "I don't believe that any such accurate number can be found, do you?"

Among the many changes ruffling the sporting scene during the 1970s was the appearance of Patricia Ryan as articles editor at *Sports Illustrated.* Luce had died in 1967. Despite her sex Pat Ryan was permitted to commission and edit articles and she quickly won a reputation as a competent "writers' editor," encouraging, informed, and very good. The previous high-water mark for women's editorial efforts at *Sports Illustrated* came with the 1955 publication (in a special section printed on bonded paper) of a short story by the powerful and seductive Claire Booth Luce, who was married to the boss. The story, which ended with the drowning of an unpleasant male scuba diver, was not the second Mrs. Luce at her best. Some even read it as an act of naked revenge, Claire publicly fantasizing the death of a younger lover who had jilted her. I don't believe she again cracked *Sports Illustrated.*

A generation later in 1976, Pat Ryan asked if I would do a series on the overall state of baseball. We narrowed the focus a bit and soon I found myself moving from Puerto Rico to Oregon and from the Berkshire Hills to Los Angeles on what was one frequent flyer of an assignment. Toward September I swung into the Midwest to catch up with the White Sox and Bill Veeck, still buoyant and fearless after a dozen amputations performed on his right leg. He was wounded as a Marine in the South Pacific during World War II and after that untreatable jungle rot kept eating into the bone. Veeck never complained and it was a pleasure later to salute him as William the Unconquerable.

After Chicago I intended to move on to Cincinnati, where an improving Dodger team, running second to the Big Red Machine, would be arriving for an interesting series. When I mentioned that I could not be in the Cincinnati and Dodger dugouts at the same time and might need to hire a helper, one of *Sports Illustrated*'s male editors suggested that their best staff baseball researcher, Melissa Ludtke, travel with me. Undertaking on-scene baseball reporting still was new for women—not only at Time, Inc., but everywhere. I said thanks and the editor, trying the sort of humor one seldom hears today, said, "Take her for the whole trip. You can do anything you want with her, just so long as you return her in two weeks." Not knowing how to respond, I chose silence.

The White Sox (with Goose Gossage as their top *starting* pitcher and Bucky Dent playing shortstop) never got untracked in '76, but when Melissa and I reached Comiskey Park, Veeck was still spouting hope. He'd had the scoreboard programmed to explode in fireworks as soon as the White Sox won a game. Whenever a

Sox homered, Veeck's organist played a *forte* version of Handel's "Hallelujah Chorus." "If I can't give my fans a winner yet," he said, "at least I can make a show of our good moments. The fan has probably had plenty of bad moments all day on his job."

At the pass gate Melissa picked up credentials good for the press box and the field. Mine covered press box, field, and clubhouse. Upstairs I sat beside Veeck, who was chain-smoking mentholated cigarettes. Melissa parked herself in the second row of the press box and quietly kept score. Some old-line baseball writers variously stared and ogled. One writer came up and said intensely into my ear, "Your girlfriend doesn't belong here. You know that. What do you think this is, ladies' night at the Turkish bath?"

The White Sox were taking on Whitey Herzog's Kansas City Royals, the strongest team in the American League West. Veeck was not funded for free agency and his team lagged in the cellar. Making the best of a bad situation, he activated Minnie Minoso, once a gifted outfielder, who had reached the age of fifty-three. Saturnino Orestes Minoso, called by some O! Restless Minoso, was a great favorite of Veeck's, which was why he was being given a chance to become the oldest person ever to hit safely in the major leagues. "My reasoning," Veeck told me, "was that it was a good promotion all by itself. Besides, it's been interesting to see this fifty-three-year-old man hustling down to first on a pop fly. For some of our younger men who are less enthusiastic, it's made for object lessons."

Suddenly Charlie Finley was upon us. Although Finley ruled as emperor of the Oakland Athletics, he resided in Chicago, where he had made his fortune by selling an epidemic of health insurance policies. His white hair glistened in the sort of mane film directors demand of central casting when they are looking for an actor to play an honest judge. "Veeck," Finley said, "since you've activated Minoso and made a joke out of the game, it's time for all us old men to activate ourselves. I'll activate me and you activate you."

Veeck nodded but did not smile. "You know the rules," Finley said. "No artificial aids. That means you gotta hit without your wooden leg."

"And you," Veeck said, "will have to bat without your hairpiece." Finley turned florid, retreated, and did not return. The White Sox played some sloppy defense and going into eighth inning, Kansas City was leading, 4 to 2. Then two runners reached base and the beefy first baseman Jim Spencer came to bat for Chicago. (Spencer would become a Yankee following the 1977 season.) Steve Mingori, a Kansas City lefthander, threw a slider and Spencer pulled a drive to right, not very high or even very hard, but just high enough and hard enough to clear the rail in front of empty box seats. Three runs scored. Veeck's Sox would win. The scoreboard awoke. Explosions rang. Fireworks lit the South Side night. Mingori looked at his shoes and drew his spikes across the mound. Suddenly every speaker at Comiskey Park erupted into Handel's great chorus. "Hallelujah," I said to Veeck above the din. He winked and said, "It's supposed to be fun."

After the game, I brought Melissa into an old-fashioned press room—I think a photo of Ring Lardner, Sr., hung on one oak-paneled wall—to share the pleasures of hearing Veeck hold forth over drinks and also so that Melissa, not I, would have to take and subsequently type the notes. I stopped at the bar, asked for a drink, and ordered a Scotch and water for Melissa. A few sportswriters glared at her and then at me and though I knew some of them, no one offered a nod or even a friendly look. It was as though I had brought a harlot into the temple. But Melissa was hardly a harlot and the press room was hardly a temple; we stood quietly waiting for Veeck. After a bit the bartender motioned me aside and whispered, "Sir, your secretary will have to drink outside in the hall." I snapped, "She's not my secretary, she's a reporter, and if she has to drink in the hall I'll drink there, too." The old bartender, small, white-haired, docile, and black, suddenly looked miserable. "I don't make the rules, sir. I'm only telling you what I've been told to tell you."

"Sure. Sure." Guilt rose. I tipped the man two dollars. "Come on, Melissa. We'll drink Mr. Veeck's whiskey in the hallway." But the hallway was airless. Paint was peeling. We soon moved on. In the morning I telephoned Veeck, whose wife, Mary Frances, had been the publicity director of a hugely popular ice show, where more than once she had been a woman in a locker room. To my surprise, he pleaded that by tradition the White Sox "let the baseball writers make all the rules concerning the Bards' Room. They could even throw me out if they wanted to." For just about the only time in our thirty-year friendship, Veeck was waffling. "Come on, Bill," I said. "Don't make me go to war over this." I don't know exactly what Veeck did next but that night Melissa was welcomed into the Bards' Room and sat with Veeck, who smiled at her and said that the most beautiful thing in the world was a major-league ballpark full of people and didn't she agree? (Oh, yes, Minoso got a base hit on September 12, a single against the California Angels. That was "kind of beautiful also," Veeck said.)

Almost twenty years later, in conversation with Anne Ritchie of the Washington Press Club Foundation, Ludtke picked up the story of her reporting adventures and how they led to a formidable lawsuit which weighed freedom of the press against what Bowie Kuhn called "the athletes' rights to sexual privacy." Backed by the legal guile and the treasury of Time, Inc., Ludtke brought an action against the Yankees, Kuhn, the American League, the Mayor of the City of New York, and the Commissioner of Parks and Recreation that was background music, background litigation, to the charged Yankee season of 1978. Before the furor passed, Melissa had become a a celebrity who was being widely interviewed herself.

"I had met Tommy Lasorda [then about to become manager of the Los Angeles Dodgers] when I'd been doing interviews for Roger

Kahn [in Cincinnati, 1976]," Ludtke told Anne Ritchie. "The day before the 1977 World Series started, a practice day for both teams, I went up to Yankee Stadium just to get my feet wet and catch up, you know, on what was happening and I was walking through the tunnels under the grandstand and just as I went by the Dodgers locker room, Lasorda walked out accompanied by Tommy John. I asked, I simply asked as a matter of curiosity, what Lasorda would think about giving me access to the locker room if I felt during the Series I really needed to see some players. He begged off and introduced me to Tommy John, who serendipitously was player rep [head of the Dodgers' chapter of the players' union]. Tommy John, who I came to know quite well as a compassionate and gentle soul, said, 'I can't make that decision by myself, but what I'll certainly do is get back to you after I call a brief meeting.'"

True to his word, John found Ludtke near home plate during batting practice and motioned for her to walk him to the backstop. There he said, "I can't tell you it was a unanimous vote. It wasn't. It wasn't by a long shot. But a majority of the Dodger players voted that if you needed access you ought to have it." Ludtke enthusiastically reported the news to the Dodger publicity director, Steve Brener, whose own enthusiasm was limited. "You can't go in the locker room just because the players say so," Brener said.

During the first game of the World Series, a loudspeaker summoned Ludtke from a temporary media section into the main press box. There Brener introduced her to Robert Wirz, director of what Bowie Kuhn called his "information department." Wirz told Ludtke that she could not have access to the locker room of either team. "If you need to talk to a player, we'll try to bring him out so you can talk to him in the tunnel. What you are asking is just not practical. Besides the wives of the ball players haven't been consulted."

"When was the last time ball players' wives ran baseball policy?" Ludtke said.

"Besides *that*," Wirz said, "if women can go into the dressing room, the ball players' children are going to be ridiculed by their classmates. It's our job to see that doesn't happen."

Time's lawyers later argued that the issue was equal access, rather than nudity, but Ludtke's feeling of the moment "was almost resignation. That's the end of the road. That's it." The road reopened on December 29 when Time, Inc., and Melissa Ludtke filed their suit in Manhattan Federal District Court charging that she was being deprived of an opportunity to cover baseball on an equal basis with her male colleagues and competitors "solely on account of her sex." Kuhn opposed the suit "as a matter of principle. I knew athletes would inescapably be placed in embarrassing situations by the presence of female reporters." The case was assigned to an African-American woman judge, Constance Baker Motley, who would have been old enough to remember that the Yankees had been the last New York City team to integrate, waiting eight long seasons after Jackie Robinson's debut in Brooklyn to sign the estimable Elston Howard.

Logically, Time and Ludtke should have directed their suit against the Dodgers. Dodger players, not Yankees, voted Ludtke into their clubhouse. The Dodgers' publicist, not the Yankees' publicist, barred the way and scampered off to Bowie Kuhn. But the issue was law rather than logic, with an additional *soupçon* of public relations. Time's lawyers believed that they could focus their strongest case against the Yankees because the Stadium and its clubhouses were municipal property leased from the City of New York. In excluding blacks, women, Jews, and even Irish Catholics from certain club memberships in Greater New York, a so-called privacy defense—private club, private property, private rules— had sometimes worked. Focusing on public property surely would weaken that defense. Besides, the Yankees played in the media capital of the cosmos. Breathes there a lawyer who abhors center stage? Legalistics and media aside, the Ludtke action stirred Yankee people from Steinbrenner to Rosen to Martin to Munson to Jackson toward one communal and possibly paranoid thought: If anything explosive happens in or around baseball these days, it sure as hell is going to happen to us.

WHEN SPRING TRAINING BEGAN, rugged Lou Piniella said he never wanted to endure another season like 1977. "This club can't take another year like that. It was the toughest year I ever had mentally. It felt like I was playing five or ten years in that one season. If the season had dragged on for two more weeks, I don't think I could have made it."

Usually spring training brings with it a heady sense of renewal. Old grudges are forgotten, or at least dulled. Everyone has safely fled the snows. Won-and-lost records are wiped clean. The best big-league team and the worst big-league team stand flat even, tied at a fault-free 0-and-0. Watching the tableau of spring workouts, hearts leap up, even the sometimes stony hearts of publishers. I once escorted Larry Kirshbaum, then president of Warner Books, onto a field in Tampa where the Cincinnati Reds were taking batting practice. The sky was bright. The sun was warm. Big Red sluggers belted pitch after pitch clean out of the zip code, 33607. Boldly going where he had not gone before, Kirshbaum looked spellbound. Then he turned and said breathlessly, and loudly, "These guys are good." One of the Cincinnati sluggers, Eric Davis, glared at me, as if to say, "Who's *that* dude?" But "these guys" were indeed good and are indeed good and considerably better than that. They are major leaguers, the best baseball players on earth. When spring training begins, I always feel some awe, not only at how far the fellows hit, but at how hard they throw, how fast they run, how lithe and graceful they are. Like a great orchestra, a big-league team is a collection of outstanding virtuosos. In spring the mood about these gifted folk is cheery, adventurous, and often

carefree. Managers predict big things. Rookies rush onto the field
unable to hide their wonder or their hopes. Veterans insist they are
good for five more years. Oh, what is so rare as a day in June? A
day in February, of course, and particularly the February day
when spring training begins.

Still, as Piniella's comment indicates, life in the Yankee spring
of '78 could not escape the traumas of the Yankee summer of '77.
So the gathering at Fort Lauderdale was not as lighthearted as those
at other spring camps. Ebullience existed, to be sure, but amid
cross-currents of foreboding, anger, narcissism, disorder, and,
these being the October Men, elements appropriate to a theater of
the absurd. Reggie Jackson arrived astride his great silver Corniche
on the last day of February, forty-eight hours after the other regu-
lars. He had been given an extension so he could work with people
from the Curtiss Candy Company on final plans for the forthcoming Reggie Bar. As you may recall, Jackson, the human quote
machine, mouthed a beauty during his brief stay in Baltimore: "If
I played in New York, they'd name a candy bar after me." He was
playing in New York and they had. For decades Curtiss produced
the Baby Ruth, that rough cylinder of chocolate, nuts, caramel,
and goo which sugared up the mouths of generations. The new
Reggie Bar, also nuts and goo, would be small, flat, tannish, and
dish-shaped. In the barnyard ways of baseball, players soon were
saying that the Reggie Bar "looks just like cow plop."

Less quietly Martin announced that after winning two straight
pennants, he was pursuing Casey Stengel's record: managing five
consecutive Yankee pennant winners. "The old man was my
teacher and in a lot of ways my idol," Martin said, as he sat with
reporters in his office at the little Fort Lauderdale ballpark. "If
Casey were alive, he'd get a tremendous kick out of seeing me beat
his record, although of course he wouldn't admit it." It was March
6. The '78 Yankees had not yet played an exhibition game. Martin
was fudging a bit. Stengel not only won five straight pennants for

the Yankees, he also won five consecutive World Series (from 1949 through 1953). As you may recall, Martin played on four of those teams.

"After I got traded (following the Copacabana brawl), I took it out on Casey for letting the Yankees trade me. I vowed never to talk to him again. I knew that would hurt him. I kept my silence for almost six years. It was killing me because I loved the old man. Finally in 1963 I was at the winter meetings in Houston as a scout for the Twins. I wanted to talk to Casey. I didn't want him to die thinking I hated him. I walked over to him in the hotel lobby and said hello and right away he said to me, 'Now as I was telling you about this young pitcher you got...' He never mentioned the years of silence. Just picked up right where we left off." Martin said that Stengel, in his final years, supported five old-time ball players who had become indigent. "He used to talk about converting his mansion in [Glendale] California into a home for old ball players who didn't have any other place to live. I bet that's in his will. I know he wanted to do it. But Casey's will has never been found. He kept a lot of things hidden away and as far as I know his will is still missing. [Stengel had no children and when he died in 1975, he was a widower.] Casey didn't trust too many lawyers, never did. Who knows, Casey could have left me his fortune. I'm still waiting to hear. Then I could buy the Yankees." Martin was ending with some humor, but the joke came with an edge—the suggestion that Billy as Yankee owner would be preferable to Steinbrenner. This was the spring training of the long knives.

"There isn't usually much tension connected to the exhibitions," Rich Gossage says. "Mostly you're just hoping that you don't pull a muscle or come down with jock itch." But with the October Men, tension—and hypertension—was the order of almost every day. On the afternoon before the Yankees were to play their exhibition game against the Texas Rangers in Lauderdale, Martin said he would be starting Ken Holtzman. Not Ron Guidry or Ed Figueroa but Holtzman, who had won just two games the year before. This was, in the baseball term, a showcase start, putting Holtzman on display, in the hope that he would perform well and set up a trade. As Holtzman sat in front of his locker, talking to reporters, Sparky Lyle came over, hand extended. "Hey, congratulations, Ken. You got your wish."

Long-faced, earnest Ken Holtzman looked startled. "You mean...?"

"You're starting tomorrow," Lyle said.

"I know," Holtzman said. "I thought you were going to say..."

"Nope," Lyle said. "Neither of us got traded today. But there's still hope." (Rain canceled the start. Holtzman remained on the Yankee staff until mid-June.)

Lyle had won the Cy Young Award in 1977, beating out such worthies as Jim Palmer of the Orioles and Nolan Ryan of the California Angels (who averaged more than ten strikeouts a game). But beneath what Gossage called "an overdeveloped sense of mischief" and a grating, macho swagger, Lyle was miserable. His salary, negotiated before free agency took hold, still was a quiet— in big-league baseball terms—$135,000 a year. Gossage's complicated contract was throwing off $460,000 annually. As Lyle saw matters, Steinbrenner was stiffing him by $320,000. Nor was Lyle's attitude helped by the fact that Rawley Eastwick, 5-and-9 as a reliever in 1977 and nobody's Cy Young nominee, had signed a Yankee contract worth $220,000 a year. "I gotta talk to Steinbrenner," Lyle told everybody who would listen. "We have nothing to talk about," Steinbrenner told everyone who asked. Whatever else the the Yankees accomplished during 1978, by the end of March they would lead the majors in discontented, agitated pitchers.

IN THIS EARLY VIEW OF Steinbrenner, who eventually characterized Paul as "the greatest baseball man I ever met," signing Eastwick to relieve along with Lyle seems to have be an enactment of

Paul's immutable *You can never have enough pitching*. If you can never have enough pitchers of all varieties, you certainly can never have enough strong-armed relievers. Or can you? Can you even have too many? As Paul knew in his bones, a great pitching staff is a complex and delicate creation, not simply a matter of numbers and muscular arms. The great closers, the pitchers who work the final innings with such dazzling skill, Hoyt Wilhelm, Bruce Sutter, Rollie Fingers, and indeed Sparky Lyle and Rich Gossage, are solo acts in a team game. They constantly walk into clutch situations— what Christy Mathewson called the pinches—with small if any margin for error. Then without appearing to be fazed by men on first and third in a one-run game with nobody out in the ninth, they get the pop fly and the double play. Hosanna! Break out the clubhouse beer. Describing this kind of performance, sportswriters and broadcasters tend to go aquatic. The hitters and the managers "are sweating bullets." But not the great closer. Why not? Because "he has ice water running in his veins." Actually great relievers get adrenaline rushes and rapid heartbeats, just like lesser men, but they control the effects of pressure and channel their excitement into a measured performance, just the way old Gary Cooper used to in the movies. It's always high noon for the great reliever, who walks alone down the dusty street, where gunmen, or anyway batters, await to do him harm. They're all Frank Miller toting lethal bats.

The high-noon scenario doesn't work when the protagonist is a committee. Teams very rarely win with two closers or three. You need one main man, a Hemingway hero, to do the job. During the winter of 1977–78, the Yankee front office was unsettled, the manager was drinking too much, and the boss, for all his intelligence, was still learning the ways of big-league baseball. When Paul said that a team could not have too much pitching, he didn't mean that a front office should randomly add characters to the staff. That nuance was lost on the early Steinbrenner. A great closer needs to believe in himself, but he also needs to know that his teammates and his ball club and his boss believe in him as well. You don't want to crowd a great closer. Praise him and give him room to take deep breaths. Lyle was never again as good as he was before big Rich Gossage joined the Yankees, crowding him, sharing his oxygen.

As it happened, on a March day when the Yankees were to play an exhibition game against Texas, Martin would trudge to the outfield where Gossage was shagging flies during batting practice, a routine and peaceful occupation. There he would tear into the pitcher with a ferocity that taxes belief. Gossage is a sensitive man. It would be months before he and the team recovered.

▼

CHAPTER NINE

A BICKERING SPRING

F ORD FRICK, a reformed newspaper man and ghostwriter for Babe
Ruth who became the third Commissioner of Baseball, created
the Cy Young Award in 1956 to celebrate annually the major
leagues' most valuable pitcher. Frick felt that pitchers too often
were overlooked in the selection of an overall most valuable player.
He drafted sportswriters to choose a winner of the new honor,
named after Denton True (Cy) Young, the storied early righthander who had recently died at the age of eighty-eight in the village of Newcomerstown, Ohio, which, to make its location clear,
lies ten miles east of Hardscrabble. (Young had a second nickname.
It was "Farmer.") As matters developed, Don Newcombe was so
dominant in 1956 and Sandy Koufax so dominant in 1963 that each
man won the Cy Young and the National League MVP *both*.

Soon after Frick's retirement in 1965, the Young Award multi-
plied, with one offered for each major league. Frick felt that two
awards diminished the value of each, but he was out of office,
replaced by an amiable former Air Force General, William D.
"Spike" Eckert, who quickly won a devastating nickname: "The
Unknown Soldier." If Commissioner Eckert is remembered at all
today it is for failing to cancel scheduled games following the as-

sassinations of Robert Kennedy and Martin Luther King. Eckert was fired in 1968, opening the job for Bowie Kuhn.

Even with dual Cy Youngs, relief pitchers continued to be neglected. Until 1970 only one reliever, Lindy McDaniel, received as much as a single vote, and that was what McDaniel garnered, one vote. But all that changed in 1974 when stocky, grouchy Mike Marshall, a righthander with a graduate degree in kinesiology, the mechanics of human motion, appeared in no fewer than 106 games for the Los Angeles Dodgers. He won fifteen and saved twenty-one. The Dodgers played 162 games that season. Working in two out of every three, Mike Marshall relief-pitched the team to a pennant. As someone remarked, "Marshall was not your everyday pitcher, even though he was your everyday pitcher."

Coming out of the bullpen, Albert Walter "Sparky" Lyle won thirteen for the 1977 Yankees and saved another twenty-six. He appeared in seventy-two games and finished every one, a performance comparable to Mike Marshall's prime year in effectiveness if not kinesiology. Put differently, Lyle was not knocked out of the box all year. Like Billy Martin, Lyle became a great Stadium favorite, particularly with the hard-nosed, blue-collared core of Yankee fans. These fans sensed in Lyle a beer-drinker after their own steins.

Presently Lyle won a close four-way race for the American League Cy Young Award, drawing 56½ votes out of a possible 252 and edging, as we've noted, such premier starters as Jim Palmer and Nolan Ryan. Directly upon hearing the news at his home in Demarest, New Jersey, some eight miles west of the New York State income tax line, Lyle told his biographer, Peter Golenbock, "My wife Mary and I got out the Dewar's and we started yelling and hollering and carrying on." When a reporter telephoned and asked what he intended to do with the plaque, Lyle said, "I'm gonna build a glass case on my front lawn with a big spotlight and display it. I'm only going to leave it out there for about ten years."

Lyle was a lefthander with a hard slider and strong opinions.

He came out of a Pennsylvania coal-mining town called Reynoldsville and he remembers that the miners "worked their asses off for not a hell of a lot of money." Reynoldsville High School did not field a baseball team, so in his teens Lyle traveled nine miles to DuBois and pitched for an American Legion squad. One afternoon while working the first fourteen innings of a seventeen-inning game, he struck out thirty-one. Major-league pitchers tend to do that sort of thing during their formative years. Lyle signed with the Baltimore Orioles in 1964 and after five minor-league stops moved on to the Red Sox, who on March 22, 1972, dealt him to the Yankees for the journeyman first baseman Danny Cater. That was the finest deal that Mike Burke completed for the Yankees and one that comes down to us as another painful spasm in the ongoing Red Sox saga of terrible trades. In his first Yankee season Lyle saved thirty-five; by the end of 1977 he had pitched in 621 major-league games without making a single start. Yankee publicists claimed, with some justification, Lyle was the greatest "pure reliever" of all time. On good days or bad Lyle was garrulous and accessible. He described Tom Yawkey, who owned the Red Sox, as "a nice person," but had a different take on Steinbrenner. The day after one of his infrequent bad outings, Lyle told Golenbock, Steinbrenner charged up to him and said, "What the hell were you doing last night? You looked like a monkey trying to fuck a football out there." If Lyle is to be believed, Steinbrenner had tramped rather a long way from the English lit classrooms of Williams College. (Golenbock insists Lyle was entirely believable. When their book, *The Bronx Zoo*, was published, he bought a dog and, in tribute to his mustached partner, named the animal Sparky. As I remember it, the dog barked quite a bit.)

When the Yankees brought in Gossage, Eastwick, and Messersmith for seven-figure multi-year contracts, Lyle's Cy Young euphoria faded fast. He had signed for three seasons, accepting a bit more than $400,000. He was earning $135,000 a year, "which wasn't bad money, but it wasn't a million bucks, either." His attempts to renegotiate led nowhere; he was under contract and had little leverage. When spring training opened in Fort Lauderdale in February, Lyle remained in Demarest. Missing spring camp was a common maneuver among star ball players of an earlier time when they were trying to pry more dollars out of management. Dixie Walker, an enormously popular Brooklyn Dodger outfielder, called by New York sportswriters looking down their typewriters at Brooklyn diction the "Peoples' Cherce," won a batting championship in 1944 and then refused to report for spring training the following season. Was he holding out? "Nope," Walker said from Alabama. "I'm just busy painting my house down here in Birmingham." When he drew a small raise, Walker immediately drove south. Someone else finished the shutters.

Lyle loitered in Demarest, telling those who asked that spring training was too long, anyway; he only needed two weeks to get ready. Who said it had to go on for six weeks? John McGraw? Hell, John McGraw was dead. Al Rosen telephoned from Florida and told Lyle to come down immediately. Steinbrenner issued a combative press release. "If Sparky Lyle isn't mature enough to understand that he has a contractual and moral obligation to the New York Yankees, we are certainly not going to waste one minute of our time attempting to find out where he is." This was reminiscent of the megamillonaire Jacob Ruppert's 1938 campaign against DiMaggio, but less effective. Everyone involved knew where Lyle was: at home in New Jersey. Having made his point, the pitcher flew to spring training later in the week and the Yankees marshaled a high school matching band, 100 people strong, to greet him at the Fort Lauderdale airport. The musicians played Lyle's old theme music, "Pomp and Circumstance." Nine baton twirlers pranced, showing pretty legs. Twenty-eight pom-pom girls waved fluff. Then a few boys in the band held up a sign, prepared by someone in the Yankee offices. It read: "Welcome to Fort Lauderdale,

Sparky—Finally." Lyle turned to his wife, Mary. "Imagine if we'd showed up *two* weeks late."

DiMaggio, increasingly a sure hand at public relations, at length carried his case to the powerful columnists who joined him at Table One, the port of honor in that ultimate Manhattan sports bar called Toots Shor's. Subsequently Bob Considine wrote for the Hearst Syndicate and a wire service that fed hundreds of newspapers: "If you were puzzled because Commissioner Landis said he would inquire further into the report that Joe DiMaggio is kicking back a piece of his salary to Joe Gould, the fight manager, even though DiMaggio and Gould both hotly denied it, the answer is that baseball has a perfect horror of any player's ever getting a mouthpiece ... The reason the average owner wants no part of a player's agent is that it would cost him money. When a green kid from Walla Walla comes face to face with an owner who has been around the baseball business for a generation, the kid winds up taking whatever the owner wants to pay him. Whereas if he had someone in there talking for him, as agents know how to talk, he could do a lot better. The big league bosses are afraid that the ball players will smarten up enough to hire fast-talking, tough-bargaining agents ... If that ever comes to pass, the ball clubs would have to pay all the blokes what they're actually worth." (That has come to pass.)

In 1978, neither Lyle nor his agent, fast-talking, tough-bargaining Doug Newton, had traction. Regardless of what anybody else made, Lyle was signed to play for $135,000. Al Rosen reminded him of that when they talked. "You're going to play for what you signed for—the money looked good to you then—and you're going to play for us. We're not going to trade the Cy Young Award winner." Lyle kept his temper, but thought, "Yeah, because if I go to Boston or Baltimore and beat you guys out of the pennant, you're gonna look like idiots." At length he said, "You don't have to trade me to a contender for some big star. This isn't about pride; it's about money. Trade me anywhere you want for a wet jockstrap. I don't care. I just wanna go where I can renegotiate my contract." On March 6, three days before the start of exhibition games, Steinbrenner gave Lyle a ten-minute audience. The pitcher made a number of points, some fresh, some not. With all the new arms, with Gossage and Eastwick added to the bullpen, he would not be pitching enough to be effective. "For my slider to work, I gotta throw steady."

"Come on," Steinbrenner said. "You know you'll be in there plenty."

After a while Lyle said, "George, I want you to trade me. I'll go anywhere you send me. I told Rosen and I'm telling you, anywhere just so long as I can renegotiate my contract with the new team." Lyle had fired his hard slider; Steinbrenner stayed with the pitch. "If you remain with the Yankees, playing ball in New York," he countered, "you have a chance to make the Hall of Fame. Have you thought about that? The power of the New York media to make a Hall of Famer? If you go somewhere else, your chance will disappear." (It was not until 1985 that the splendid knuckle-ball pitcher Hoyt Wilhelm became the first reliever inducted into the Hall. He first seized attention as a New York Giant.) Steinbrenner concluded by telling Lyle that he wasn't sending him anywhere. "Get in shape. We'll talk more later on." Lyle held his tongue, but fumed within. What the hell did *that* mean? Get in shape so we can have another pointless meeting? Running out of options, Lyle, like DiMaggio before him, turned to the press.

The spring training media tends to be relatively relaxed, like spring training itself, but among the October men, relaxation was rare as a deep-blue diamond. Munson, who wanted to be traded to Cleveland so he could play close to his hometown (and get away from Reggie Jackson), had decided to stop speaking to sportswriters. Here was the captain of the World Champion Yankees, the team captain, saying in effect go to hell, *Daily News*; take a hike, *New York Post*; sit on your thumbs, good, gray *New York Times*. (To this day I wonder why the managing editors didn't get together and respond in kind. *Go to hell, New York Yankees. Sit on your own outsized thumbs. We're calling our reporters back from Florida. Until you make your people shape up, no more Yankee stories in our papers. And, oh, by the way, good luck with your home attendance.*)

Lyle, vastly more outgoing than Munson, spoke candidly to several reporters. He told Moss Klein of the *Newark Star-Ledger*, "I reiterated [to Steinbrenner] my desire to be traded. We didn't discuss money, but that's what it boils down to. I want to go somewhere where I can get more money. I see what other pitchers on this staff are getting. That's why I want to get the hell out." Klein then published the salary figures that he had: Hunter, about $500,000 a year; Gossage about $460,000; Don Gullett and Andy Messersmith about $333,333; Rawley Eastwick about $220,000; Ron Guidry $200,000; Ken Holtzman $165,000; and Ed Figueroa $150,000. Almost at the very the bottom of the list—only the long reliever, Dick "Dirt" Tidrow, finished lower—came Lyle and his Cy Young Award at $135,000. Quite simply, eight Yankee pitchers were earning more than Lyle. He knew it. They knew it. Klein wrote, "In Yankeeland Lyle's contract is insulting."

On that same busy Florida day Steinbrenner later met with Thurman Munson. "You know," he said afterward, "I came down hard on Thurman at a banquet in Cleveland over the winter for saying he wanted to be traded to the Indians. I walked out of the banquet, in fact. Now everything is cleared up. Thurman is happy and proud to be a Yankee." Recently nicknamed Grumpy, Munson walked past a blur of reporters and photographers. "I got nothing to say to you fucking guys," the captain muttered. The marching band and the baton twirlers had returned to class, but—even

though Billy Martin was away, playing golf in a charity tournament—Camp Happiness had swung into full and strident session.

On March 10, the Dodgers traveled south from their huge base
at Vero Beach and, amid chilly winds, played the Yankees for the
first time since the World Series. In the opening inning Reggie
Jackson lined a first-pitch single off Doug Rau, giving him five
successive hits against the Dodgers on five consecutive swings. I
once watched Stan Musial line five consecutive hits against the
Dodgers at Ebbets Field but that must have taken place in a paral-
lel universe. All Musial's hits came with two strikes. In Florida, Ken
Holtzman worked two innings, "throwing the beans out of the
ball," according to backup catcher Cliff Johnson, but Los Angeles
hit Ed Figueroa hard and defeated the Yankees, 7 to 3. "It's always
nice to win," said Al Campanis of the Dodgers, "but this one came
143 days late."

In the exhibition that followed the Yankees beat the Baltimore
Orioles, 6 to 5, and the writers held forth on how sharp Andy
Messersmith looked, throwing three tidy innings. Fairly fast. Good
control. Only one bad pitch in thirty-nine. A headline in the *New
York Times* proclaimed: MESSERSMITH A STANDOUT. Catfish Hunter,
no better than a .500 pitcher in 1977, was next on the cavalcade of
(questionable) stars. He had recently been diagnosed as a diabetic,
which he conceded was a shock. "I don't want to be a sick guy,"
Hunter said. Speaking with more assurance than accuracy, the
Yankee physician, Maurice Cowen, said, "As long as he takes his
two insulin shots a day, there is absolutely no reason for concern.
His playing career won't be affected at all and beyond that his life
span will absolutely not be shortened." (Generally the medical
community recognized then as it does today that diabetes is potentially deadly. Combined with high blood pressure, it was the disease that first blinded, then killed Jackie Robinson at the age of
fifty-three.) After taking an insulin injection, Hunter started against
the Phillies and began with a home-run ball. Then he pitched two

pretty good innings. "You're looking terrific, Cat," Reggie Jackson said, "especially since I thought by now you'd be dead." The next day a headline in New York announced: HUNTER SHOWS THAT OLD GROOVE. He had thrown thirty-three pitches, the equivalent of one long inning. Chained to horseshoe-shaped copy desks, wearing green eye shades under a cold fluorescent glare, pale headline writers in the north dreamed of Florida. They paid little attention to applicable lines from *The Mikado*:

> *The flowers that bloom in the spring,*
> *Tra la,*
> *Have nothing to do with the case.*

Except for his announcement that he intended to surpass Casey Stengel, Billy Martin had been reasonably quiet, but the manager from Vesuvius would not stay dormant indefinitely, or even for very long. On March 13, before the third exhibition game, he erupted. The Texas Rangers traveled to Lauderdale carrying with them a great deal of impacted baggage. The Rangers, you may remember, were managed by Martin immediately preceding his return to the Bronx. After ninety-five games in 1975 the Rangers fired him with a public volley at his "disloyalty." (For the record, no tranquility came to Texas after Martin packed his cowboy boots and left. The Rangers went nowhere in 1976 and on the way to finishing second in 1977 the team played for no fewer than four managers. One, Eddie Stanky, a firebrand during the 1940s and 1950s, arrived in Texas sixty-three games into the season. He managed a single game, which the Rangers won. Then, reconsidering the tensions inherent in his new position, Stanky resigned, tying major-league records for managerial brevity and winning percentage.)

Dock Ellis, the big, talkative righthander whom the Yankees had unloaded in '77 and now was signed with the Rangers, set an appropriate tone before the Florida exhibition. "You know," he told a reporter, "I was one of the few guys really happy to be playing with the Yankees. I gave them a real good year [17 and 8] in 1976. All I wanted after that was a long-term contract. But they wouldn't give me one and they wouldn't tell me why. So I had to get out of there. *Had* to." His exit tactic startled even brash and mouthy Sparky Lyle. "I told a few reporters the truth," Ellis said. "I told them some Yankees were hoping that the next time Steinbrenner had to fly somewhere his plane crashed. That did it. In less than a week after my quote hit the newspapers, I had my wish. I was gone."

That night the Yankees defeated the Rangers, 9 to 3, but the story was not the game, the score, Ellis, Steinbrenner, nor anything else that the writers and broadcasters were able to pick up. Martin intended to use Gossage for a few innings and he walked out to left field during batting practice and called the pitcher away from the pursuit of flies. "I wanna talk to you," Martin began in an angry rumble. The manager put his hands on his hips and turned his back on home plate, not a prudent posture in the outfield during batting practice.

"Yeah, skip?" Gossage was keeping an eye on the batter at home plate, lest a high fly ball descend on his manager's skull.

"Goose, when you get in the game today and Billy Sample comes up," Martin said, "I want you to drill the little nigger in the head." William Amos Sample is a soft-spoken, notably affable man, a trim 5 foot 9, who hit .272 across a nine-year major-league career spent mostly as a Ranger outfielder. When Martin managed in Texas, Sample was a youthful prospect.

Startled, shocked, Gossage pretended that he hadn't heard. "What?" he said.

"I told you. Drill that little nigger, Billy Sample, in the fucking head."

Gossage took a deep breath. This was spring training, for gosh sakes, and besides here was a racial word that Gossage didn't care for at all. He took a few deep breaths, then said, "I'm not going to do that, Billy. I throw ninety-eight miles an hour. If I hit someone in the head I might kill him."

Martin flushed. The veins in his neck bulged. He looked up at Gossage, four inches taller than he, and began to rant. "You pussy. You cockeating pussy. I tell you to drill a guy and you say you won't do it. You gutless, motherfucking..."

After a while, Gossage said, "I don't know what this is about, Billy, but I won't fight your battles for you." To this day no one is certain what "this" was about. Sample, now a broadcaster for Major League Baseball Radio, recalls no clash with Martin in Texas. "I'm kind of quiet. Maybe I wasn't fiery enough for him." Gossage thinks Martin may have been imposing a loyalty test; asking him to to show that he would do whatever the manager demanded, however outrageous. That thought fits Martin's abiding overview: you were with him or you were against him. He figuratively saw the world and its people in black and white. There was no gray. (Although vastly more sophisticated than Martin, Steinbrenner sometimes sees things in that same dichromatic light.) Whatever, as Gossage recounted the story during one recent spring training afternoon, the experience still disturbed him. We were sitting side by side in an otherwise empty dugout looking out on a totally empty field. "I wonder," I said, considering Gossage's height, heft, and muscle, "if anyone had ever spoken to you in that manner before?"

"Not before," Gossage said, quietly, "and not since."

Gossage went out and pitched four hitless innings against the Rangers. The *Times* writer Murray Chass, a hard-working reporter whose prose style is a little wordy, then described him as "one of the more awesome pitching mortals in baseball at the moment." Reggie Jackson was more succinct: "Gossage puts fear into hitters." But the Martin-Sample episode had touched Gossage with fears of his own. As he put it, "Did Martin want his new, high-ticket closer—me—to fail? It became clear after I refused to drill Sample that he did." Presently Gossage came down with a staphylococcus infection in his right foot that required a week of hospitalization. Considered emotionally, physically, either or both, high-ticket Goose Gossage's first Yankee spring training was nasty.

More baggage surfaced soon afterwards when the Yankees played the Atlanta Braves in West Palm Beach. Bobby Cox had worked as a coach under Martin the year before. Now he was managing the Braves, who were coming off a last-place finish. "Everybody asks how I could leave a championship club for a last-place team, but that's really a silly question," Cox told reporters. "Here I'm the manager. On the Yankees I was just a coach." Moss Klein added in the *Newark Star-Ledger,* "There are other reasons that Cox didn't want to discuss, such as his silent feud with Billy Martin." Cox is a courteous man except when an umpire's decision inflames him, and he and Martin simply did not get along. Still, Cox told Klein, "When the rumors started about Martin getting fired, I told him he had my support. I'd managed in the Yankees minor-league system for a spell, but I wasn't after Martin's job. Steinbrenner made it awfully hard on him and I didn't think that was right. I guess I just wanted to get out of last season in New York without making too many enemies. I stayed aloof and did my job and tried to avoid the problems." Cox puffed air through his cheeks. "The Yankees should win easier this year. I see their division as strictly a two-team race, the Yankees and the Red Sox. Boston has a real good team, but the Yankees could be unbeatable, unless they go out and beat themselves." That was as insightful a comment as any uttered in the distant, chattering spring of '78. (As it happened, Cox's first tenure in Atlanta, 1978 to 1981, produced no winners, but his second term in Georgia, begun in 1990, has been so triumphant that at this writing he has won more post-season games than any manager in history.)

For all its attendant problems, the Yankee lure—Big Bucks, City Lights, Major Mystique—remained powerful. Before one exhibition game, Rod Carew of the Minnesota Twins, who batted .388 in '77 with 239 hits—that is to say more hits than Ruth, DiMaggio, Williams, Musial, Mays, or Aaron ever racked up in a single season—told reporters that he was "thinking New York." Carew said he intended to play without a contract during the coming season, which would then make him a free agent. Subsequently he wanted to sign with a new team, "perhaps the Yankees in 1979. Right after I moved to this country from Panama, when I was a kid playing in McCoombs Dam Park [an urban sandlot a block from Yankee Stadium], I remember the year Maris and Mantle were hitting all those home runs and I was thinking, hearing the cheers of the crowd inside the Stadium, I'd like to play for the Yankees myself one day." But by the time the auction took place, during the winter of 1979, the tumult of '78 still lingered. Forget Mantle and Maris. Carew told inquiring reporters that the Yankees resembled a zoo. Offended, Steinbrenner dropped out of the bidding and Carew finished his career hitting splendidly for the smiling cowboy, Gene Autry, out of Tioga, Texas, who owned the California Angels, a team that won two division titles but no pennants during Carew's illustrious tenure.

A day after the first Carew story broke, the Yankees mounted a chartered bus and traveled across Florida to play Bill Veeck's White Sox at Sarasota. This exhibition did not work out well at all. It had rained overnight and moving to cover first base on Ralph Garr's slow roller to the right side, Andy Messersmith, the Yankee starter, fell heavily onto his right shoulder. He rolled in pain and needed help getting to the clubhouse. I'd been watching in a box beside Veeck, who abruptly excused himself. "That's a good feller. I've got to see how he is." Twenty minutes later Veeck returned.

"Bad?" I said.

"Tears," Veeck said. The shoulder was separated. Messersmith never really recovered. His '78 Yankee record would be 0-and-3. Within two years he was out of baseball.

Injuries, the collateral damage of spring training, happen. Injuries happen every spring. "The amazing thing about '78," Moss Klein says, looking far back over his shoulder, "was not people getting banged up. It was that we saw so much turmoil on a world championship team that essentially was set. Except for the pitching staff, there wasn't much mystery. Jerry Narron could have looked like a Hall of Famer in Florida, but on opening day Silent Thurman would be parked behind the plate. Mickey Klutts had a fine spring, but Graig Nettles would be the opening-day third baseman. Reggie Jackson could have struck out in forty-eight straight exhibition at-bats. Opening day Jackson would start."

On St. Patrick's Day the Cincinnati Reds, wearing green uniforms to honor a fifth-century shepherd turned evangelist, and also to sell tickets to people named Murphy, beat the Yankees, 9 to 2, in Tampa. They bombed Gossage. Bill Bonham, a rangy Californian who was projected as the Reds' number-two starter (after Tom Seaver), pitched five shutout innings. Gossage pitched two and allowed seven runs. Although Catfish Hunter threw four impressive innings against this powerful Cincinnati team, with Johnny Bench, Joe Morgan, and Pete Rose, Steinbrenner refused to be impressed. Gathering with New York sportswriters at the Bay Harbor Hotel (which he owned and owns), he said this was St. Patrick's Day, all right, and he was sick and tired of Yankee blarney. "After seeing the inadequacies of a team that is supposed to be world champions, I think my complexion matches the other guys' green uniforms."

"Those uniforms cost $105 each," a reporter said.

Steinbrenner pressed forward. It wasn't his money. "We're at a point where Billy better start bucking down on them or we won't repeat."

"Billy says you stuck him with Messersmith and Eastwick," another reporter remarked. "He says they aren't winners any more. He calls them 'George's Boys.'"

"Billy better start bucking up and bucking down. There's no such thing in my organization as manager for life."

"George," the reporter said. "This is the *exhibition* season. You play twenty-four exhibition games and this was just exhibition number eight."

"No matter," Steinbrenner said. He was meeting the reporters on a cement deck, overlooking a large heated swimming pool. To the west sea birds milled about a sandbar. Sandpipers skittered ahead of slow surges of bay water. Gulls squawked as they circled against the sunset, looking, as gulls always look, for food. "We played badly today and we have been playing badly. We'll have trouble just winning the East Division. Our guys better start thinking of defending our championship. If we get complacent now... well, look, the Reds got complacent last year. The Dodgers jumped off to a big start and the Reds never caught up. Better team maybe, but they never caught up. I don't want that to happen to us with the Red Sox. It had *better* not happen to us with the Red Sox."

Presently someone carried Steinbrenner's words to Billy Martin in the Bay Harbor bar. The manager drained his glass of Scotch and said he was hearing one more example of how little baseball Steinbrenner knew. "I doubt if the Red Sox are strong enough even to finish second," Martin said. "They have good players but some are overrated, like Jim Rice. Their pitching staff is fairly worthless. Sparky Lyle didn't do great against them. That's the only team that consistently hit Lyle. But this year they'll see Gossage. Every series. Gossage is gonna blow fast balls right by their Boston nuts." How Martin loved the taste of danger. He seemed infatuated with a game, more risky than Monopoly, called *Bash the Boss*. In addition, on this occasion Martin was dead wrong. The "fairly worthless" Red Sox staff included such worthies as Dennis Eckersley, who

would win twenty; Luis Tiant, who would pitch five shutouts; Bill
Lee; and, most immediately significant, Mike Torrez, who had won
fourteen for Martin's '77 Yankees during the regular season and
then won two more during the World Series, including the sixth
and deciding Reggie Jackson game. (Although R. Maximus Jackson did everything else that night, he didn't pitch.)

The next time the Yankees played the Red Sox, I found Michael
Augustine Torrez, a very large, very amiable Mexican-American
out of Topeka, sunning himself on a bullpen bench. "You going to
have a loyalty problem," I said, "switching from the Yankees last
year to the Red Sox now? Do you feel that you're living on both
sides of the pennant race?"

He smiled a tolerant smile. "Not a problem," he said. "My loyalty in this game goes first of all to my wallet."

"What moved you to New England?"

Torrez continued to smile. "I don't mean to bore you, but the
answer is the same. My wallet."

We chatted some more—I was working on a column I owed
the *New York Times*—and big Jim Rice, the Red Sox's powerful
black left fielder, walked past. For reasons some, including Rice, attributed to racism, he'd been having a hard time with the Boston
press, even while hitting .300 and leading the league in home runs.
Torrez tapped me affectionately on the back and called, "Hey, Jim.
Come here and shake hands with a nice writer."

Rice approached and I offered a hand, which he took. As he
did Rice said, "There are no nice writers." Torrez laughed harder
than seemed absolutely necessary.

Presently Mike decided to have a bit more fun with his
ex–Yankee buddy, Ed Figueroa. "Figgy," he began, "you got to get
yourself traded like I did. They give you good money here, not like
those cheap Yankees." Torrez laughed again and Figueroa smiled,
then winced. By moving to Boston, Torrez had jumped his salary
to close to $400,000 a season. Still working the Bronx, Figueroa

was earning $155,000. "Over the last two seasons," Figueroa said. "I've won more games than any other Yankee [thirty-five]."

"Tell George I said he has to pay you more," Torrez said.

"My contract is up at the end of this season," Figueroa said. "If I can win twenty, next time around they'll have to give me good money."

"Don't count on it," said Mike Torrez, the smiling provocateur.

On March 27, Steinbrenner quietly promoted Rosen from executive vice-president to president. He made the announcement by way of a press release, mimeographed in one of the mobile homes that served as Yankee headquarters in Fort Lauderdale. Steinbrenner said later that he had admired Rosen first as a great Cleveland Indian competitor "back in the late 1950s." Rosen, he added, "is a great friend and he's going to be a great baseball executive."

Rosen walked onto center stage with poise. "When George and Gabe Paul took over the Yankees five years ago, it was one of the worst franchises in baseball," he said. "Now the Yankees are World Champions. Obviously. My job is to maintain what George and Gabe have started." Rosen's gray hair was close cropped. His voice and his features were strong. His was a powerful presence.

"But you've been out of the game for so many years," a reporter said. "How can you jump back in without missing a step?"

"I've never been that far away," Rosen said. "I was a director of the Indians for ten years. I've always stayed close to baseball." Inevitably, and properly in this instance, reporters asked Rosen for his ideas on ball-player salaries. He said neither he nor Steinbrenner had any objection to paying fair market value for talent, "but fair market has changed somewhat since I was playing ball." He remembered the great 1954 Cleveland team that won 111 games and reeled off names. Rosen himself, who led the American League twice in homers and twice in runs batted in, played third. A former batting champion, Bob Avila, played second. Cleveland had strong, gifted Larry Doby in center field, powerful Vic Wertz at first base, and carried four truly remarkable starting pitchers: Bob Lemon, Early Wynn, Mike Garcia, and Bob Feller. All but Garcia have been elected to the Hall of Fame. "That was thirty years ago," Rosen said easily. Then he threw his stun grenade. "Today Reggie Jackson makes more than the entire pennant-winning 1954 Indian team."

Presently Steinbrenner was insisting that from now on Rosen was in command. "*In command*," Steinbrenner said. "That's what being president of the New York Yankees means." As a perk, Steinbrenner gave Rosen a smattering of Yankee stock, making him a limited partner. Rosen was president, to be sure, but being in command was another story. Few things exist, now or then, that are as limited as the command of a limited partner, any limited partner, under Managing Partner George M. Steinbrenner III.

Billy Martin said pro forma things in praise of Rosen, but the tumultuous inner Martin roiled. Martin, as we've seen, had trouble with authority figures of all stripes. Now he would have to work under a new chief who was a member of his own ball-playing generation. (*Strike one. I could run this organization and manage the ball club, both.*) Further, this was an authority figure he'd tried and failed to sucker punch during a Pacific Coast League game nineteen years before. (*Strike two. I woulda landed if the feller wasn't so quick.*) Still further, Martin knew that if matters got physical Rosen, a skilled boxer, could beat him up. (*Strike three. I gotta watch it with this guy. But what was going on here? What the hell was going on? Three strikes or no, Al Rosen wasn't out. He was in. He was the fucking president of the New York Fucking Yankees.*) Consciously or not, Martin would try relentlessly to force Rosen out of his job.

A little Billy Martin resides in all of us, but most of us are able, most of the time, notably when sober, to keep the inner paranoiac suppressed. Ulcers or acne may develop in consequence, but most of us realize our best interest lies in getting along with the designated leader, whether he is a tyrant as severe as George S. Patton or a profoundly decent sort like Albert Leonard "Flip" Rosen.

What a bickering season. From February into April there passed an amazing assortment of distractions from the basic business of throwing, catching, hitting, and, as Gossage had pithily put it, "not coming down with jock itch." Distraction was the order of the time. Jackson arriving late because he had to "finalize" the Reggie Bar. *Let's see, people; how many peanuts do we put into this thing per bite?* Sparky Lyle demanding to be traded. Martin screaming at Gossage to throw a lethal pitch, then screaming obscenities when Gossage refused. Rod Carew lobbying to join the not-so-merry band. Ken Holtzman demanding to be traded. Munson deciding not to talk to the media. Mike Torrez agitating Ed Figueroa to complain about his salary, and Figueroa complaining. Martin trashing the archrivals from New England, violating a doctrine well put by Leo Durocher: "Don't get the other guys sore. They'll just play harder. In baseball you let sleeping dogs lie." Without hyperbole you can fairly call this period a spring training like no other.

At the end, Murray Chass wrote in the *New York Times,* "The consensus among the Yankees is no, they will not encounter the problems they had last year." Of course not. Last year was history; the Yankees would not fight the Battle of Bull Run, either. Chass and his supposed Yankee "consensus" missed a point, *the point,* that grew clearer almost every day: Even more lacerating problems lay ahead. The Yankees would open the championship season on April 8 in Arlington, Texas, where the ballpark lay close to the Dallas–Fort Worth Turnpike. Martin told Steve Cady of the *Times* that he looked forward to going to Texas so he could play a round of golf with Mickey Mantle, who lived near the Preston Trail Club in Dallas. He said his difficulties with Reggie Jackson were in the past. He added, with a straight face, that his relationship with Steinbrenner was "sensational." Cady printed Martin's statements. One definition of the word sensational is "arousing curiosity, especially by exaggerated or lurid details." In that sense, what Martin said was true.

CHAPTER TEN

▼

THIRTY BILLION CALORIES ON THE FIELD

B EFORE ORIOLE PARK at Camden Yards opened in 1992, inaugurating an era of splendid new ball fields, baseball architecture had slipped into a dark age. In 1964 Shea Stadium was christened with "Dodger Holy Water" from Brooklyn's Gowanus Canal, but once the water evaporated Shea looked cold and unfinished and more profane than sacred. Both Ebbets Field and the Polo Grounds were preferable. Two relatively recent indoor arenas, the Astrodome in Houston (1965) and the Kingdome in Seattle (1977), turned out to be so flawed they had to be abandoned. To any reasonably aesthetic eye the Hubert H. Humphrey Metrodome in Minneapolis deserves the same fate. Late in the 1960s officials in Philadelphia, Cincinnati, and Pittsburgh ordered multisport plastic-grass arenas that resembled cement coffee cups without handles. Upon entering any of them, you lost all sense of place. That also happens at motels and malls and in coach seats aboard jet aircraft, but can hardly be called a good thing. About the worst dark-age park, or so I thought, was Arlington Stadium near Dallas, a one-time minor-league field that was only modestly altered when the Rangers came into the American League in 1972. (Ted Williams managed that team, but no one batted as high as

.260 and the '72 Rangers finished last.) Arlington Stadium was grandstands without a roof, a hot sirocco blowing hard from center field, a scorched-earth infield, and outfield walls smeared with tawdry blotches of advertising signs. From behind a mask on the large Arlington scoreboard, an electronic version of the Lone Ranger materialized from time to time to lead the cheering. Tonto, a Native American of taste, declined to appear.

It was here, on the afternoon of April 8—the day on which former commissioner Ford Frick died—that the 1978 Yankees began what would become a clamorous struggle to retain their world championship, playing a Texas team strong enough to contend for a division title. Ron Guidry started against Jon Matlack, recently shipped southwest by the New York Mets, who were trying to rebuild under a novice manager, Joseph Paul Torre, hired just one season before.

A day earlier the Mets had begun in New York by defeating the Montreal Expos, 3 to 1, but the Mets story was not the score but the grandstands. For their opening day at Shea, the team drew only 11,736 paying customers. John Stearns, the catcher, said, "It's depressing, looking up at 45,000 empty seats." M. (for Michael) Donald Grant, the Wall Street broker who ran the Mets, blamed the nonattendance—this was the smallest crowd for any New York opener in memory—on "newspapermen hammering home the idea that the Mets are a last-place team." Outraged, Red Smith crouched over his Olivetti portable in chilly Shea and began throwing jabs. "Grant," Smith wrote, "is a dilettante among sports promoters, but in his limited experience he has learned one axiom of the fraternity. When business is bad, the press is responsible. Neither Gimbel nor Macy would expect to be rewarded for selling shoddy, but the proprietor of a bad ball club does not hesitate to demand sycophancy on the sports pages and 'loyalty' from the cash customers. It might have occurred to a deeper thinker that the perception [the Mets are awful] was created not by the press but by the team's last-place finish." Given a better ball club in the borough of Queens, squabbles between Grant and the sportswriters might have drawn interest away from the bickering Yankees. But bad teams, even raucous bad teams, seldom hold attention for very long, and the Mets were a bad club under a front office that had mindlessly discarded a splendid roster. Former Mets thriving elsewhere in 1978 included Tom Seaver, Dave Kingman, Nolan Ryan, Ken Singleton, Rusty Staub, Bud Harrelson, and Jerry Grote. You could create the beginnings of an All-Star team with players the Mets had abandoned. (Two, Ryan and Seaver, have been elected to the Hall of Fame.)

BACK IN TEXAS, Guidry gave up a run, then settled down and concluded a strong stint with four hitless innings. Matlack pitched hard sinking stuff that bothered the Yankees, including Billy Martin, who complained to the home-plate umpire that the Rangers had spread sand in front of home plate. "That's to slow the ground balls," Martin said. "That's to help Matlack's sinker. It's illegal." The umpire ignored Martin, who shook his head in anger. When Rich Gossage tramped in to close his first game as a Yankee, the score was tied at 1. Gossage retired the Rangers in the eighth, as advertised. Then in the last of the ninth he threw a high, hanging slider. Richie Zisk, a great moose of a slugger signed away from Veeck's White Sox, lined the hanger through prairie wind into the blue seats behind left field. Zisk leapt and waved stout arms in jubilation. Gossage and the Yankees lost, 2 to 1. Murray Chass wrote in the *New York Times,* "Richie Zisk ($2,955,000) won the battle of high-priced free agents with Rich Gossage ($2,748,000)."

Sport was becoming bigger and bigger business, which is what attracted such strident naifs as M. Donald (don't call me Mike) Grant. (Steinbrenner himself obviously enjoys making money, but, bulldozing aside all of that gold, he was and remains a sports buff at his core. The salary and bonus figures being paid to athletes—or close approximations—were available to reporters with good contacts, such as Chass, and the numbers frequently bobbed up in the press as stated or implicit evidence of rampant commercialism. But sports-page economics is not an accredited course. Less obvious than huge player salaries and their potentially deleterious effects was the influence exercised by television executives, those jocks and pseudojocks with Armani suits and corporate jets who live and die by ratings and the promotions that bump those ratings higher. From 1975 through 1977, CBS had staged so-called "winner-take-all" tennis matches featuring Jimmy Connors facing and defeating Rod Laver and John Newcombe, among others. The winner-take-all format was supposed to make the sets more desperately competitive. But would international tennis stars really risk serving, slamming, and lobbing for free? The Federal Communications Commission investigated and on April 9, 1978, one Gene F. Jankowski, president of the CBS Broadcast Group, cleansed some larceny from his soul with a confession. The matches actually had been winner take *most*. The promotion matter issued for the tennis by old, reliable CBS, the admired network of Edward R. Murrow and Walter Cronkite, had been 24-carat iron pyrite, *fool's gold*. In beating Newcombe, Connors earned $100,000. For playing three rotten sets, Newcombe was paid $60,000. "It was wrong and misleading to refer to prize money without disclosing that both players [in each of the matches] would receive substantial money just for showing up," Jankowski said. Then, announcing something others suspected, Jankowski added, "CBS is not infallible." A lesson, or one of many lessons, learned from this mendacity is that in 1978, like today, the salaries that athletes earn are as nothing compared to the profits harvested by the television companies from CBS to FOX to YES that market those athletes directly or through satellite or cable systems. "I'll concede that a lot of television sports and sports coverage is corrupt," Howard Cosell told me at the time, truth bursting through across a third martini. "But most of the TV corruption comes to light. That's the big difference between us and the newspapers. The newspapers are just as corrupt, but they know how to hide it better."

IN TEXAS ON THE second day of the Yankee season Reggie Jackson had a four-hit game and Ed Figueroa beat the Rangers, 7 to 1. But next night Doc Ellis, the Steinbrenner hater, handcuffed the Yankees, who then moved on to Milwaukee and lost two more to a strong Brewer club that included Sal Bando and Paul Molitor. The second Milwaukee loss was particularly troubling. In that game, which the Brewers won 5 to 3, a twenty-one-year-old righthander named Moose Haas struck out Jackson four times and Gossage again failed to close, throwing another home-run ball, this time to Larry Hisle. "It was a son of a bitch of a pitch," Gossage said. "A good fast ball at the knees on the outside. I don't know how in hell he hit it, but he did." With the Yankees at 1-and-4 and his personal record at 0-and-2, Gossage remarked on the flight east, "It's gonna be a great home opener, right, Kenny?"

Holtzman said, "You get big crowds in New York. The fans will be waiting for us."

"That's what I'm afraid of," Gossage said.

Steinbrenner often speaks up for Yankee tradition. On some level he is a traditionalist and, beyond that, he understands that tradition, like home-run hitting, attracts customers. For the Stadium opener on April 13, 1978, he brought in Mickey Mantle and Roger Maris to accept the World Championship Trophy on behalf of the team. Mantle, a heavy spender on such luxuries as, to use his term, "the broads," drew a retainer from the Yankees. To keep the checks coming Mantle always showed up on demand. Maris, a more conservative sort, left baseball for a Florida beer distributorship in 1968 when he was thirty-four. The Yankees had dealt him to St. Louis in 1966, five seasons after the extraordinary year in which he broke Babe Ruth's record of sixty home runs. The story of Maris' sixty-one homers in '61 became the basis of a television movie called *61 remarkable for intense promotion and thundering inaccuracy. Since Maris' convoluted problems go beyond the purview of this book I'll simply say, as one who saw him very closely on a long assignment from *Sports Illustrated*, that Maris trying to cope with the rewards and demands of fame was a case study in neurotic behavior. When Maris left New York and the Yankees he said, also neurotically, that he never intended to come back, that he would never revisit the scene of his great triumph. Now, almost two decades later, Steinbrenner's steamroller salesmanship had drawn Maris to the Bronx one more time, the return of the sort-of native. By the end of the first inning, however, Maris and his return were pretty much forgotten.

At long last Reggie Jackson had his candy bar from Curtiss. It was disc shaped—a "B cup," Sparky Lyle said in his tart way—and it came packed in an orange wrapper that depicted a mighty Reggie swing. Orange was a color favored by the Mets, not the Yankees, but this is corporate America and these things happen. Standard Brands Confectionery, the parent company of Curtiss, employed eighteen good-looking women described as "models and airline stewardesses" to stand at the Stadium gates and dispense free Reggie! Bars to all the incoming fans. Howard Stonesifer of Standard Brands said 70,000 Reggie! Bars were on hand. The Yankee Stadium of '78 could hold at most 57,500 customers so there was a margin of 12,500 bars. As it happened the Stadium crowd that day only reached 44,667; what happened to the surplus 25,333 bars seems to be lost to history. But each fan who showed up was handed a free Reggie! Bar by a pretty woman at the turnstiles. From there on the promotion went downhill.

With two men on in the first inning Jackson came up to hit against Wilbur Wood, a journeyman left-handed knuckle-ball pitcher with the Chicago White Sox. It was Jackson's first Stadium at-bat since October 18, 1977, when he hit those three home runs on three swings. Now he took two knucklers that dipped out of the strike zone. Then, on his first Stadium swing of 1978, Jackson cracked a home run to right center, over the glove of a leaping outfielder named Chet Lemon. That made four consecutive Yankee Stadium home runs on four consecutive swings. As well it might, the South Bronx erupted. Jackson's characteristic home-run lope was brisk. He had beaten the pitcher. That was enough. He had no need to jog in low gear and prolong the pitcher's pain. Down to first at a good clip. Dip the left shoulder. Turn toward second. And so on. Now Jackson had rounded third and was heading toward home when the first Reggie! Bar came spinning out of the stands. The modified discus shape was great for scaling. The idea swept the ballpark. Thousands of fans scaled thousands of Reggie! bars out of the stands. Within seconds the field was carpeted with candy discs in orange wrappers and play had to be halted.

"This is absolutely horseshit," the usually genial Bob Lemon said in the White Sox dugout, where he was putting in an unhappy term as manager. "But it tells you something about that piece of candy. The fans would rather throw it than eat it."

"Please stay in your seats," Bob Sheppard urged over the public address system in his senatorial tone. Youngsters were jumping onto the field and gathering more free Reggie! bars. "Please," Sheppard repeated. The crowd ignored him. "It was embarrassing," Al Rosen recalls, "but I didn't feel we could call on ballpark security. What were we going to do, arrest the youth of America?" Presently the Stadium ground crew went to work as candy scoopers and the volunteer youngsters were allowed to help, but it was six minutes before the game could be resumed. Bob Lemon walked up to the umpires, who were gathered at home plate in a dark-blue clump. "This is a terrible promotion," he said. "The stuff is slippery. One of my players could get hurt. If this happens again, I'm pulling my team. Besides, people are starving all over the world and we just had 30 billion calories laying all over the field." Red Smith picked up binoculars and focused on Jackson in the dugout. "He looked," Smith reported, "fairly immortal and altogether benign." Then, not exactly benign himself, Smith quoted a sharp comment that he attributed to Gordon Beard, a newspaperman working in Baltimore. "There isn't enough mustard in the world to cover the hot dog that is Reggie Jackson." Jackson was not amused. He was offended. He had hit four Yankee Stadium homers on four successive swings and the star sports columnist of the *New York Times* dubbed him not Hercules but hot dog. Reggie wondered to me if Smith would have cited Beard's cutting line had he been white. It is a painful but not entirely unreasonable question. Smith never applied the term *hot dog* to Babe Ruth, the loudest, gaudiest, most fully stuffed wiener of them all.

Slim, quiet Ron Guidry, nobody's hot dog, kept his composure and pitched a complete game as the Yankees defeated the White Sox, 4 to 2. "He wasn't as overpowering as I've seen him," said Bobby Bonds, the White Sox outfielder with a promising thirteen-year-old son. "But he utilized what he had very well. He threw fast balls to good spots and he mixed some off-speed sliders with some hard ones." Guidry said he was happy with his victory but not with his velocity. "I'm not really worried. The speed will come."

One mystery endures from Reggie! Bar Day. Who was it who scaled the first candy disc out of the stands? Was it an ebullient fan, as the newspapers suggested? Or was it a publicity man stirring things up in the service of the Reggie! Bar? Was this, then, spontaneity or hype? No one is certain of the answer, but the question itself is basic to much of modern American sport.

These intense, gabby, seriocomic Yankees were obviously good copy—great grist for the endlessly grinding mills that were the newspapers and wire services before an Internet existed. So, curiously or perhaps not so curiously, in a kind of counterpoint, was the earnest, awkward, essentially humorless administration of President Jimmy Carter. Whatever distance separated issues at the White House and the Stadium, the Yankees and Carter spent 1978 competing for newspaper space, often sharing columns of ink on the same front page as their various crises played out. On one level Martin's relationship with Jackson caused what one sportswriter called "serious concern"; on another level people worried about the neutron bomb, an atomic weapon that would not explode into a mushroom cloud from Armageddon, but instead issue torrents of radioactive matter. Neutron bombs dropped on New York City would harm very little real estate. The office buildings, the automobiles and street lamps, the brownstones and the bars, the concert halls and ballparks and garages would survive. But the people, eight million people, would perish. Radioactivity would kill them all. Against the advice of White House hawks, Jimmy Carter decided during April not to authorize the construction of American neutron bombs. He sent word to Moscow that he expected the Soviet Union to show similar restraint. At about the same time this very busy president worked toward devising a "more even-handed" Middle East policy; preached civil rights at South Africa; acted to return the canal to Panama; and, getting closer to the dugout, pressured Congress into appropriating $55.6 million to start revitalizing the South Bronx. The government, he said, would establish job-training centers, finance the teaching of English to Spanish-speaking residents, tear down blighted tenements, construct habitable housing, and underwrite commercial development on a large scale. "This program will take seven years," Carter said, "but you have my word. We will rebuild the Bronx." What happened to that program, and indeed what happened to the $55.6 million, remain mysteries. A quarter century later the principal crop of the South Bronx flatlands is still blight.

THE YANKEES HAD NO game scheduled on April 14, when their record was 2-and-4, and at Steinbrenner's insistence the public

relations staff scheduled a luncheon titled "Welcome Home, Yankees" at the Americana Hotel (now the Sheraton) on Seventh Avenue in midtown. Opening remarks. Introductions. Applause.
Smile for the fans. At most a two-and-a-half-hour stint for the ball
players. Profits from the proceeds would go to "instructional televison programs" produced by the Roman Catholic Archdiocese of
New York. The diocesan woman in charge, informally known as
One Tough Nun, was Sister Irene (Fugazy), the corporeal, or
earthly, sister of Steinbrenner's close friend William Fugazy. Ed
Figueroa, Catfish Hunter, and Jim Spencer got permission from
Billy Martin to skip Sister Irene's lunch. Sparky Lyle, Thurman
Munson, Graig Nettles, and Mickey Rivers simply didn't bother to
appear, and Roy White left early because he had an appointment
with his tax lawyer. Working to maintain order, Rosen fined each
absentee, and White, $500. With the Yankees being as talkative as
they were, word got out immediately. In keeping with his policy of
not talking to reporters, Captain Munson then kept quiet, but not
every Yankee did. Nettles said, "If they want somebody to play
third, I'm ready. If they want an entertainer for lunch, let 'em hire
George Jessel." Rivers said, "It was our first free day since before
spring training. We're trying to get settled. We don't need no frig-
gin' lunches and these fines ain't gonna help the team's morale.
Rosen is being lousy." Such indiscipline on a championship big-
league club was, to put this quietly, unusual. First key Yankee players, led by the captain, cut a public relations assignment. Then
the centerfielder criticized the club president to reporters. John
McGraw would have blanched. Branch Rickey would have blinked.
Larry MacPhail would have ordered a triple Scotch, then fired
everybody (rehiring them, of course, a day later). That night,
when the Yankees resumed their series with the White Sox, Nettles
and Munson sat on the bench. Mickey Klutts, who filled in at
third, went 2 for 2. Big Cliff Johnson, who caught, went 2 for 3.

Rivers did play and with Klutts at third in the eighth inning drove a fast ball over Chet Lemon's head in center field. The ball carried to the blue wall, then 430 feet distant from home plate. Rivers, slim and speedy, circled the bases and slid home head first, beating the relay throw by about a yard. The 20,965 fans roared an ovation; the runs provided the margin of victory and the *Daily News* ran a pleasantly brash headline: RIVERS HRS CHISOX 3-2; RAPS BRASS.

Promptly (and inevitably) a reporter asked Rosen to react. "Mickey's all right," Rosen said. "We're friends. He gets a little worked up sometimes. I know his vocabulary. I'm glad the worst he called me was 'lousy.'" The reporter wondered if Munson and Nettles had been benched "as a punitive action" for missing the lunch. "No truth in that," Rosen said. "Anyway, look at things positively. The manager decides who plays and it turned out to be a stroke of genius starting Klutts and Johnson. They got four of our six hits." As many noted, Rosen answered questions squarely, which is not to say that he volunteered every last scrap of awkward information. Angered by the fine, Munson told Martin that a cyst behind one knee was bothering him and he couldn't and wouldn't play. Nettles explained to teammates that he missed the lunch because he was tending his children while his pregnant wife visited an obstetrician. Also his entire wardrobe had disappeared in luggage lost between Milwaukee and New York. "Did they want me to show up in jeans and a T shirt?" He had neglected to make these explanations to Rosen, and then in the clubhouse Nettles insisted to Martin that he was suffering from the flu and would have to stay on the bench. Coughless flu? Feverless flu? Whatever. Nettles said he couldn't play. The *Daily News* put a merry headline on Phil Pepe's commentary:

EVERYTHING WELL

IN YANK FAMILY,

DISCORD RETURNS

This seemingly minor April episode, grown men behaving in erratic ways, would become a touchstone for much of the season. Steinbrenner wanted the lunch. Rosen fined the players who ignored the lunch. Martin, so fierce with Reggie Jackson, docilely bowed to Munson and Nettles, suggesting, in his bizarre, conspiratorial style, "Watch out for those creeps in the front office. I'm the only guy that's on your side." Who, then, was in charge of this ball club? Everybody was in charge and, since that never works, nobody was in charge. What were these Yankees anyway, a big-league team, a commune, an encounter group, a street gang? On a more tautly trimmed ship, Munson and Nettles would have been *required* to play against the White Sox, or face further and more severe punishment, suspensions without pay. Here key players acted up and after a tap on the wrist they got away with acting up further, not playing, without so much as a reprimand. The lords of baseball discipline lay bleeding in foul territory, but these Yankees had so much talent that they won a ball game anyway on backup strength and foot speed. Nothing succeeds like a game-winning, inside-the-park home run.

During this week of acting out word reached New York that Joe Gordon, the finest second baseman in Yankee history, had fallen to a fatal heart attack at the age of sixty-three. The date was April 14, same as the welcome-home (or go-to-hell) lunch. In the wakes offered for "Flash" Gordon, dissonance sounded between Yankee mores old and new. Gordon played in the Yankee infield from 1938 through 1946, when he was traded to Cleveland for the Superchief, Allie Reynolds. Trained as a tumbler and acrobat, Gordon made leaping, lunging plays that taxed belief. He had struggles with the front office but he handled them with dignity and a decent wit. After the Yankees won the 1941 World Series from the Brooklyn Dodgers—Gordon batted .500 in the five games—he approached the general manager, black-browed Ed Barrow, at the victory party. "I need to make a phone call, Mr. Barrow," Gordon said. "Can you lend me a dime against next year's salary?" Gordon generally was recalled as a profoundly genial person, but Rosen cited a moment in Boston when Gordon was something other than that. Rosen had beaten the Red Sox with a homer, and as he and Gordon sat in a hotel bar afterwards an overheated fan said he didn't like to see his team beaten by a Jew bastard. Before Rosen could react, Gordon (who was not Jewish) threw a body punch from his barstool that flattened the fan. Over and over in the remembrances of Joe Gordon the same word kept coming up, overworked but nonetheless appropriate. The word was *class*.

The sneezeless flu suddenly better, Nettles returned to third on the next night and singled home a run as the Yankees lifted their record to .500 with a 3-to-0 victory over the White Sox. Chass wrote in the *New York Times* that Nettles made "a remarkable recovery" from flu but then, flailing at the language once more, he continued, "Nettles seemed to want to talk about his action Saturday, as if words could expunge a deed he had not found altogether pure." Chass meant that Nettles tried to explain. Stopping well short of a gracious apology, Nettles told reporters, "They were wrong to fine me and I was wrong to sit out the game. Two wrongs don't make a right and we were both wrong. Last year I had my best year. I kept my hair short. I wore a tie on all the trips. I like to play as much as anybody, but I want them to respect me and obviously they don't." Listening carefully through Chass and to Nettles you could hear the spirit of classy Joe Gordon saying, "Don't whine."

The next day the Orioles knocked out Catfish Hunter and Gossage knocked down the Baltimore catcher, Rick Dempsey. Short, feisty Earl Weaver, the Lord of Baltimore, complained to Joe Brinkman, the home-plate umpire, who heard him out. After Weaver returned to the dugout, Brinkman summoned Martin to home plate and told him that he wanted the high, tight pitching stopped right now. Martin nodded, but he never liked being lectured to, particularly in public. He clenched his fists, and instead of walking toward Gossage or his own dugout, he strode toward Weaver. "You're making trouble, you little son of a bitch," he shouted.

Weaver himself was hardly tongue-tied. "I'm paid to make trouble for you," he said.

Brinkman and another umpire grabbed Martin and turned him 180 degrees. No formal statistic exists on major-league managers punching other managers during a ball game, but without Joe Brinkman, Billy Martin could have been the first. The *Daily News* continued its merry honking:

O'S BLAST CAT 6−1;

BILLY, EARL FEUD

Reggie Jackson's homer won the next game from Baltimore, 4 to 3, but playing uneven baseball, the Yankees remained in fourth place. Away from the baselines, Al Rosen abruptly had to defend Steinbrenner's organization against charges of chicanery that landed the Yankees on front pages again, alongside details from Jimmy Carter's prized Panama Canal Treaty. This was not the type of front-page spot baseball teams court. Harrison Goldin, the New York City comptroller, accused Yankee management of padding Stadium maintenance costs and "thereby cheating the city and its taxpayers out of rents rightfully due." According to the Stadium lease, negotiated by Mike Burke and John Lindsay during the dreary CBS days, the amount of rent the Yankees would owe the city fluctuated annually with the costs the franchise incurred keeping the Stadium in tolerable shape. The more the Yankees invested in runways, seats, restrooms—the physical plant—the less they had to pay in rent. Goldin leaked word that he was "investigating impropriety" and that the amount in question was not Peter Minuet's basket of trinkets, either. City bookkeepers, who kept themselves anonymous, suggested that the Yankees had overstated their maintenance costs so grossly that they now owed New York City $1.5 million. Secure in his Tampa shipbuilding office, separated from the Stadium and the courts of New York by nine state lines, Steinbrenner ordered Rosen into the breach.

The old third baseman offered a spirited, occasionally irrelevant, defense. "The Yankees are deeply concerned," he said, speaking from notes in his Stadium office, "about implications that this team is getting a free ride at the taxpayers' expense. During the lean years, the management under George Steinbrenner poured at least $3.5 million into the ongoing rebuilding of the Stadium. In subsequent outstanding years, 1976 and 1977, the Yankee partnership has never taken any dividends out of earnings. We all know that the '76 pennant winners and last year's world champions brought untold millions of dollars to New York hotels, shops, and restaurants. Mr. Goldin himself concedes that city and state taxes on our ticket sales, concessions, and parking last year totaled more than two million dollars. We are good citizens."

"Can you produce vouchers for the Stadium maintenance work you claim you've done?" a business reporter asked.

"Of course we can," Rosen said, "and we have. First only one agency [the Economic Development Administration] wanted to see them. Then just last month the Comptroller's Office reversed itself and asked for duplicate copies. We sent them over."

"Would you tell us how much profit the Yankees are making?"

As a partner, even as a limited partner, Rosen knew the answer. He also knew the first commandment of major-league management. *Thou Shalt Not Let Outsiders See Thy Books.* "Public corporations have to issue statements of profit and loss," he said. "The Yankees are a privately held partnership. They don't face that requirement."

"You could still tell us," the reporter said. He sounded plaintive.
"But I'm not going to," Rosen said pleasantly.

Afterwards a spokesman for Harrison Goldin announced, "Put simply we are running an audit on the Yankees. It's no more threatening than an audit from IRS. We will make our report public in June."

THE PLAYERS CONTINUED to simmer about the luncheon fines. Rosen agreed to rescind White's $500 because White had at least appeared, before fleeing to the bosom of his lawyer. But Rosen stuck to his position with Lyle, Munson, Nettles, and Rivers. Ken Holtzman, the seldom-used lefthander, the Yankee who most wanted to be traded, turned out to be the team's player (union) representative. After consulting the wording of the contracts, he decided to file a grievance. Clause 3 b stated "[Player] agrees to participate in any and all reasonable promotional activities of the club." A welcome-home lunch is surely reasonable, but there lurks a touch of Clarence Darrow in all of us, including seldom used left-handed pitchers. "We've got 'em," Holtzman said. "This wasn't a *promotional* luncheon. It was a *charity* luncheon. They can't force us to do one damn thing for charity." Passionate to lash management, the athletes embraced Holtzman's idea. The raw thinking of ball players does not always approach peaks of sophistication; the problems that might accompany taking a public position against charity does not seem to have entered anybody's mind. Indeed, the general clubhouse sense was to hell with charity (and possibly also faith and hope) just as long as management got hurt. Marvin Miller, the tough old trade unionist who ran the Players' Association, quickly modified the grievance to argue that the players could not be obliged to attend a *sectarian* function. That was how the complaint formally was filed with an arbitrator.

Somehow players worked in ball games. On the brisk Toronto

afternoon of April 19, with the temperature reading 48 degrees at game time and wind gusts reaching thirty-five miles an hour, Holtzman started, lasted into the fifth, and allowed three runs. Cliff Johnson lined a two-run homer for the Yankees in the sixth and the teams entered the ninth inning tied at 3. Gossage, delivering his best relief effort so far, had retired eleven straight Blue Jays. John Mayberry opened the ninth against him by lining a single to left center. Garth Iorg, who ran for Mayberry, became the potential winning run. Catcher Rick Cerone (who would become a Yankee in 1979) bunted and Gossage, going for the lead man, threw a one-hopper wide of second base that pulled Bucky Dent so far from the bag that he couldn't tag Iorg. First and second. Tie game. Last of the ninth. Nobody out. Strikeout time. But Dave McKay, a Toronto infielder, pushed another bunt. Gossage grabbed the ball and threw it a yard over the head of Willie Randolph, who was covering first. As the ball carried into foul and chilly wastes beside right field, Iorg scored, and Toronto took the game, 4 to 3. Gossage told the sportswriters, "I never in my life ever lost by making two errors in a row. Never." After the reporters moved on, Gossage wedged his large frame into his locker, closed his eyes, and began to cry. Presently he rolled out of the locker onto the floor and curled into the fetal position. His sobs carried through the clubhouse; he was still crying when he felt a tap on his shoulder. It was Hunter. Standing with him were Jackson, Munson, Piniella, and Nettles. "Get up, Goose," Hunter said. Strong hands lifted the losing pitcher to his feet. "Now get dressed," Hunter said. "You're down now, but you're going to come out of it."

"We all *know* that," Jackson said.

"We're going out to dinner," Munson said, "You're coming with us."

"Just pull yourself together," Nettles said, "and come on." Of this unusual and touching episode, Gossage says, "the guys picked me up literally and in spirit. Thanks to them I began turning things around." Still, the champions, in fourth place, fell below .500.

BETTY FORD, the former First Lady, issued a statement from a California Naval Hospital that "I am not only addicted to the medication I have been taking for my arthritis, but also to alcohol." She was undergoing treatment at the hospital's alcohol-abuse center and a bespectacled navy doctor named Joseph Pursch said, "Mrs. Ford is gutsy. I expect her to do very well." The National Basketball Association playoffs overran the early baseball season and the *New York Times* spun two interesting stories out of the Knicks' series against the Philadelphia 76ers. At thirty-two, Phil Jackson was retiring from the Knicks and Dave Anderson wrote a farewell column. "I was always apprehensive playing in front of a New York crowd," Jackson told Anderson. "The fans at the Garden had great expertise and they were very critical." Earl Monroe was "the most entertaining" player Jackson ever saw. Willis Reed was "the heart and soul" of the great Knicks club. Dave DeBusschere was Jackson's "teacher and my idol." Jackson remembered carrying pails of mountain water to the Montana cabin in which he lived as a child. Now, he told Anderson, he was going back to the woods around Flathead Lake, where he would construct a home for his family. "I've always wanted to build a house with my own hands." He did not wither in the wilderness. Jackson emerged and, of course, became the master coach of the NBA, first in Chicago where he worked with Michael Jordan and then in Los Angeles where he built a team around Shaquille O'Neal.

Samantha Stevenson, a spirited redheaded reporter, provided *Times* readers with a close-up look at Julius Erving, Dr. J., who was, she wrote, playing more "team-oriented basketball" than he had in the past. "There is a new Julius Erving," Stevenson wrote, "and, not coincidentally, a better 76er team." Women were permitted in the 76ers' dressing room and Stevenson did not stop this relationship at the lockers. Eventually she gave birth to a daughter, fathered out of wedlock by Julius Erving. The child grew into a graceful young woman playing on the professional tennis circuit as Alexandra Stevenson. This Philadelphia passion play bore out one of the dreads that made so many male sportswriters hostile to women journalists. In jock press-box terms, "They'll sleep with the guys, and come up with better stories in the sack than we can get in the clubhouse." Of course more than one famous female tennis star has slept with more than one male journalist, yielding up more than the secrets of her backhand smash. Issues of access, like issues of hormones, remain complicated.

AFTER TORONTO the hard news the Yankees generated fell mostly under the sports-page staple *Mound Woe*. Don Gullett, with a six-year $2 million contract, was fighting a losing battle with a rotator cuff. Hunter said he felt fine but his earned run average towered at 15.63. Rawly Eastwick simply didn't fit. Messersmith still was hurting. Holtzman said he had to work often to be effective, but since he was not effective Martin declined to work him often. On the theory that few turn to the sports section to read medical reports, some of the sportswriters tried to lighten matters by asking Martin if there was any history behind his attempted dash to hook and jab Earl Weaver.

"He scares me," Martin said. "I don't get excited when I'm dealing with stupid managers, but the smart ones, like Weaver, get me scared." Although Martin and Weaver were not friends, each respected how the other ran a game. "Weaver's a good manager," Martin said. Then he added, as if unhappy with a cease-fire, "As a player Weaver was strictly a minor leaguer and a bad minor leaguer at that." Someone called Weaver, who said maybe he wasn't Ty Cobb but one season in the minors he had batted in a hundred runs. Martin responded by telling the Yankee writers to look up his own record with Phoenix in the Arizona-Texas League during

1947. That year he hit .392, batted in 174 runs, stole 31 bases, and drove out 230 hits. Martin did not add that playing third base in that rollicking season he made fifty-five errors. Fifty-five. Wild throws. Missed grounders. Dropped pop flies. A top big-league third baseman, the Dodgers' Billy Cox, would make no more than six or eight errors a year. "Martin in Phoenix," Moss Klein wrote, "must have given his manager fits."

Back in New York, the Yankees won the Mayor's Trophy exhibition game from Joe Torre's New York Mets, 4 to 3 in thirteen innings. Catfish Hunter pitched well, or seemed to, but Lyle pointed out that the Mets were such a sorry team, you couldn't really tell. A physical examination revealed that Hunter was suffering from adhesions in his right shoulder, bits of tissue stuck together that should not be stuck together. These caused pain, robbed him of effectiveness, and led in time, as we shall see, to an unusual medical procedure.

As April melted into May the Yankees won five straight and moved up to second place. But then, to the ill-concealed horror of Steinbrenner and Martin, this very expensive team, this Rolls-Royce Corniche of ball clubs, slipped back into idle and loitered in third place week after week. Martin called meetings, profane pep rallies, and his stock theme went like this: "I'm tired of listening to you guys mouth off about money. Every one of you sons of bitches is making a helluva lot. Back when I was playing, hey, then money really was a problem. Good ball players had to take winter jobs, selling cars, selling suits, even working in factories. After the 1951 World Series, Mickey Mantle went down into the lead mines. His family was broke and his dad was sick. His dad was dying. A great ball player like Mickey had to work in the mines all winter because he needed the money and he did it and he didn't cry about it. Then I hear you guys. *Two hundred grand ain't enough. I oughta make four hundred grand.* Well, listen up. Forget the fucking money. Concentrate on baseball. The way you're playing, it looks like your bank accounts are so stuffed you don't even care if you win. Well, you better care. You better start caring right now. If you got something to say to me, get it off your chest now. If you don't like me, tough. You don't have to like me. You want to fight me, I'm ready. I'll fight one of you. I'll fight all of you." Martin's voice rose and cracked. When he finished the clubhouse fell silent. At about this time Martin had taken to wearing black leather jackets, like a motorcycle thug. His menace was palpable. But Martin had not been hired to be a menace. He was employed to win baseball games.

Raging at athletes was the tradition of a certain managerial breed. Such big winners as McGraw and Leo Durocher were great avatars of wrath. But powerful as the Yankee manager's personality was, frightening as was his willingness to brawl, the tide of the times was running against Alfred Manuel Martin. Feudal baseball was dead. So was feudal managing. Leo Durocher had barked its epitaph five years earlier in 1973 when he resigned from his last job, managing the Houston Astros: "Whatever happened to *shut up, sit down and listen?*"

McGraw and Durocher could enforce discipline with arbitrary fines, Martin could not. By 1978, on the insistence of the Players' Association, any fine of more than $400 was subject to arbitration. Fines of lesser amounts, in practice, were merely cosmetic. Ball players no longer worked like modern serfs who had only two options: *Do what you're told or get a job pumping diesel.* Faster than anyone else, the players recognized their own emancipation. They had agents now and lawyers and their union was every bit the equal of management. The union leader Marvin Miller, not Commissioner Bowie Kuhn, was widely regarded as the most potent figure in baseball. Baseball had undergone a revolutionary change. Martin was making fiery 1950s speeches into the heedless air of 1978.

Steinbrenner, the old Big Ten football coach, tried some rah-rah oratory himself. Classically club presidents stayed out of the clubhouse. It was spiky down there and rank and argumentative. Such powerful executives as Jake Ruppert and Walter O'Malley reigned imperiously from an executive suite. The great field marshals stay aloof from the trenches. But particularly when frustrated, Steinbrenner makes up his own rules. Following Gossage's Toronto collapse, Steinbrenner stamped into the Yankee dressing room and called for order. He stood over Gossage and said that certain people, he was naming no names, were getting paid a lot of money and playing terrible baseball. He repeated this point. He continued to stand over Gossage, and he continued to name no names of highly paid individuals who were not performing. As it happened Thurman Munson was seated behind Steinbrenner but directly in Gossage's line of sight. As Steinbrenner spoke, Munson began to mug and lip-synch, doing an excellent imitation of the wrath of George. Steinbrenner raged on; Munson continued to mimic and mug. Gossage told me that as difficult as 1978 was for him, listening to Steinbrenner, watching Munson, and not breaking out into great whoops of laughter was his hardest single achievement of the season. But it was important to stay silent and he did. "Under the circumstances," he says, "laughing in the boss's face could have led to fatalities."

▼

CHAPTER ELEVEN

THE NEW YORK CHOIRBOYS

THE YANKEE STADIUM lease furor died in howling hurricanes of noise that gave way to startling silence. After Mayor Edward Koch asked Congress to underwrite $2 billion worth of loans, William Proxmire of Wisconsin, the chairman of the Senate Banking Committee, studied the Yankee Stadium lease as part of an overall review of New York City finances. "This isn't a lease," Proxmire announced in his Washington office to Adam Clymer of the *New York Times*. "It's a knuckle-headed giveaway." Then, presented with a (happily) captive reporter, the senator began orating. "Come on, New York City. When you get less for leasing the Stadium than a batboy earns, you can't expect the taxpayers of Wisconsin, Kansas and Kentucky to give you a multi-billion dollar loan guarantee. This dim-witted contract will only make the Yankees richer so they can take the best players away from the rest of us." To Proxmire, whose views were seldom global, "the rest of us" meant the Milwaukee Brewers. Yankee phobia is a Milwaukee tradition, like bratwurst.

Koch went on a Manhattan radio program and said that it was true, the lease "practically gave away Yankee Stadium." But legally, he conceded, the lease was valid. "I hope," Koch said, "the Yankee

president, Mister um, uh, Steinbrenner, will consider altering it."
Mister um Steinbrenner responded with flare. "I'll be happy to
meet with the mayor on any and all problems that he feels are aris-
ing from the lease. But with one condition. I want to meet him in
the company of the Mets, the Jets and any other team that plays
in a city building." (The Jets have since moved to New Jersey, leaving New York City with no National Football League team in
residence.)

What seemed particularly to upset Bill Proxmire and Ed Koch
was the provision that allowed the Yankees to deduct maintenance
costs from their rent. That was, let us suppose, a tree. But Proxmire
and Koch were blind to the forest. Just twenty years earlier the
Giants and the Brooklyn Dodgers defected to California, robbing
New York City of two platinum baseball franchises and, some
feel to this day, a portion of its soul. Those Flatbush fixtures, Pee
Wee Reese and Duke Snider, suddenly had to play their home
games in a concrete Los Angeles arena designed for track meets.
Willie Mays, the pride of Manhattan, was uprooted from Harlem
and transplanted in San Francisco. The players were unhappy
but powerless. The fans of the two teams, franchises rooted in
nineteenth-century Brooklyn and New York, believed they had
been betrayed.

Those pseudo-Dodgers, the original New York Mets, were not
created as an apology to New York ball fans, but rather because, for
business reasons, the National League wanted to reenter the rich
New York market. As part of the painful birthing process that de-
livered the Mets, the city was required to construct Shea Stadium.
By the time Shea opened in 1964 it had cost $24 million. (The
nouveau Mets finished last for four consecutive seasons, leading
some to grumble along Queens Boulevard, "We shudda kept the
Dodgers and given California them crummy Mets.")

When the Yankees sagged under CBS, some, including Mike
Burke, talked about moving the team from the Bronx to the filled-

in New Jersey swamp called the Meadowlands, or places yet more distant. New York City would then have lost all three of its classic baseball franchises. John Lindsay was not going to let that happen on his watch and the deal he put together kept the Yankees in New York. He intended to provide exactly what the city had spent building Shea, $24 million, to modernize the Stadium. In the end, this turned out not to be as good a deal for the forces of government as, say, the Louisiana Purchase, but it was the best agreement Lindsay could cobble together at the time. For Proxmire and Koch to jump it years afterward strikes me as being about as moral as a mugging. Proxmire was a certified Wisconsin cheesehead with no feel for New York City and Koch neither liked nor understood baseball. Further (if a further is needed), Proxmire and Koch were Democrats. John Lindsay was a Republican.

Presently New York City's Democratic comptroller, Harrison Goldin, discovered that the Yankees had *not* been cheating on the lease. When he realized he was coming up empty, Goldin dropped the matter, without telling the media. Consequently, after the spate of stories about investigations, and suggestions of cheating by Steinbrenner, no headline, not one, proclaimed: CITY EXONERATES YANKEES. Between March 19 and April 20, the *New York Times* published six articles that were critical of the Stadium lease and then, when Goldin's audit came up empty, the *Times* simply walked away. A charge always gets more attention than the response, but in this instance the resolution of a skewed set of stories got no space at all. Silence was Goldin, which I do not mean to be taken as laudation. (To distribute blame equitably, I could have addressed the matter, probably should have addressed the matter, in one of my own random *Times* columns, difficult as it was in that institution to beat against the current. But I did not.)

Some politicians lose as badly as Billy Martin. The Lindsay lease made the city responsible for the cost of electricity used to light Stadium signs between the end of the baseball season and

February 1. The following December one of Koch's deputies spotted a lighted sign near the facade and ordered it extinguished. The Yankees complied, saving the city $10 a day. The offending sign had read: N.Y. YANKEES THANK 1978 FANS.

NO ONE WAS SUBPOENAED at the Stadium, where in-and-out Yankee baseball continued. Swift Ronald Ames Guidry, on the way to the best season accomplished by a left-handed pitcher since brilliant, glacial Sandy Koufax retired twelve years earlier, would win thirteen straight starts. Guidry's hard slider snapped into the bat handles of right-handed hitters, destroying their power and sometimes their bats. His fast ball hopped and buzzed. During Koufax's pitching seasons he was heavily muscled. One Dodger trainer, an osteopath named Harold Wendler, said Koufax had the strongest "lats"—*latissimus dorsi*, the long muscles running along the spine—that he had encountered in a forty-year career of ministering to athletes. Guidry weighed 155 pounds. No one talked about his lats, but neither could anyone remember another pitcher that lean who threw so hard, except for the young and skinny Satchel Paige. "Pitching isn't brute strength," Guidry says. "It's body rhythm and arm extension and a whole lot of small things that are boring to people who aren't pitchers."

It is also thinking a shade faster and more subtly than the batter. Someone has described great pitching as chess at ninety miles an hour; one of Guidry's favorite pastimes is playing chess, once with a board, today with a laptop computer. In conversation I wondered if he had done any special exercises to bolster his pitching. "I play drums," he said. "I found playing the drums kept my wrists loose. R and B, rhythm and blues. That seemed to help." He was also a great high school sprinter who turned down a track scholarship at Notre Dame "because baseball made more sense financially." In short, Guidry was a superb athlete, a focused man,

THE NEW YORK CHOIRBOYS ▼ 241

and perhaps the only major leaguer of his time intimately familiar with Longfellow's *Evangeline*, the saga that opens so splendidly in dactylic hexameter: *This is the forest primeval. The murmuring pines and the hemlocks*... Guidry's ancestry is French, by way of the Acadian district of Nova Scotia, and the journey from Acadia to Louisiana is central to Longfellow's poem. Guidry points out that "Cajun" actually is a Louisiana adaptation of the word "Acadian." He became a very good major leaguer at the age of twenty-seven and a great one at twenty-eight. During six earlier years in the Yankee organization he was mostly in the minor leagues, mostly pitching relief, so there surely was at least some reason for Guidry to complain that he had been mishandled. But that was not Guidry's way. He said in the early years he relied too much on his fast ball and made the mistake of trying to strike out every batter. But with better pitching coaches?... Guidry did not like to entertain that idea. Even in his time of triumph he was one quiet Cajun, an oasis of restraint near the center of the most hyperkinetic of teams.

On May 11, as the Yankees finally broke into a 7-for-8 roll, Fran Healy decided to retire. He had batted just once all season and struck out. Healy was only thirty-one but, he said, after an injury to his right shoulder four years earlier, "I've always had pain." Although he played in fewer than eighty games across three seasons as a Yankee, Healy was an important clubhouse figure, close to Reggie Jackson, and a peacemaker, a dove amid a crowd of raptors. He was joining Phil Rizzuto and Bill White on the broadcasting crew, so he would remain physically close to the team, but there was a jolt as he hung up his uniform, number 40, for the final time. "I've enjoyed my career," he said. "I know I'm young to quit but the timing feels right. I've met some great people along the way, including that interesting character who plays right field for the Yankees." Jackson said, "Without Fran last season would have been complete hell. I owe him a lot."

Still in third place, the Yankees flew to Kansas City in mid-May, and proceeded to lose the first game of a highly stressful series in an unusual way. They went into the ninth inning leading the Royals, the strongest team in the American League's Western Division, 3 to 2. With two out and bases empty, Ed Figueroa walked catcher Darrell Porter on four pitches. The winning run came to the plate in the person of outfielder Amos Otis and Figueroa missed with two more. Martin summoned Gossage, who threw a high fast ball that Otis lifted to right center, apparently ending the game. Paul Blair in center—Mickey Rivers had bruised a leg—was the Yankees' best defensive outfielder. He ran hard and gloved the ball just as Reggie Jackson, barreling over from right, dove to make the catch himself. Jackson's dive caught Blair in the legs. Both men hit the ground. The ball popped out of Blair's glove and rolled rapidly over Astroturf toward the center-field fence. Porter trotted home and Otis sped around the bases, scoring the winning run on what was ruled an inside-the-park homer.

"I've lost some tough games," Martin said, "but I don't think I ever lost a tougher one. The ball was in his glove. The game was over."

"Who do you blame?" asked Phil Pepe of the *Daily News.*

"There isn't any blame," Martin said, in a moment of genuine good fellowship. "Blair is the best centerfielder in the game. He's better than Willie Mays used to be, that's how great a glove I think he is. But how can you blame the other guy [Jackson] for hustling? He was trying his flat-out best to get to the ball. You like aggressiveness in the outfield. You can't discourage that and you can't fault Jackson for it."

"When the ball was hit," Jackson said, "my first thought was let him catch it. He's Paul Blair. He catches everything. Then I looked again and he seemed so far from the ball I thought he had no chance, so I made my dive." Jackson shook his head. "I feel like a fool," he said.

The next night Reggie rallied with a homer and three runs batted in and the Yankees defeated the Royals 5 to 2, with Gossage coming back and picking up the save. But on the following afternoon, tempers smoked and fellowship faded under the bright midwestern sun. Dick Tidrow, who started, didn't have much and Sparky Lyle replaced him in the fifth inning. If anything Lyle had less than Tidrow. In the sixth Otis, a solid but not spectacular outfielder out of Mobile whom sportswriters were starting to call "Yankee Nemesis Amos Otis," walked and went to second on shortstop Fred Patek's single. When Frank White bunted, Lyle fielded the ball and threw to Nettles at third. The play was close enough to bring Martin running out of the dugout, shouting at umpire Al Clark. Nettles joined Martin in braying. Clark said the man was safe and walked away. Yankee Nemesis Otis now took a long lead off third and broke for home on a bouncer to Nettles. He slid across the plate, arriving at the same time as Nettles' throw. "Sa-a-afe," bawled umpire Bill Kunkel, sounding the "a" long and harsh to Yankee ears. Munson leaped up, shoved his chest protector at the umpire, and said, "No way. He's fucking out!" Martin ran from the dugout, yelling at Kunkel and pushing Munson away from the umpire. Like Al Clark at third, Kunkel stayed with his decision.

Going into the last half of the ninth inning in this messy and intriguing game, the teams were tied at 9. Since Gossage had worked the night before, Martin did not want to use him again. He seemed never to want to use Rawly Eastwick. Instead, he chose Ken Clay as his closer. Clay was a rangy twenty-four-year-old righthander, a hard-throwing product of the Yankee farm system just feeling his way about the major leagues. The previous winter he had supplemented his modest baseball income—he was already the father of two—by working as a ring salesman in Lynchburg, his hometown in the foothills of the Blue Ridge Mountains. After a quiet eighth, Clay may well have wished he were back in the Old Dominion measuring the circumferences of fingers.

244 ▼ OCTOBER MEN

Clint Hurdle, the Royals' prize twenty-year-old right fielder, kept a picture of his mother over his locker. He was hitting .216 and he was afraid "Mom would get on me about my batting average." Leading off the ninth young Mr. Hurdle pounded young Mr. Clay for a line-drive double, his third hit of the afternoon. Yankee Nemesis Otis followed with a hard line drive to right center. Jackson started back, then looked around. He was not going to dive into anybody this time. The look cost Jackson a step or two and Otis's liner carried over his head. Hurdle ran home with the winning run and hurried into the clubhouse. There he telephoned Big Rapids on the Muskegon River in Michigan with all his best for a Happy Mother's Day. "How are you, Mom?" he said. "I got three hits."

Billy Martin tramped off the field, and stalked about the locker room in ferocious silence. Seeing Mickey Rivers and Cliff Johnson smiling during conversation, Martin screamed, "That's right. Laugh it up, you guys. We just got beat. Keep laughing." He moved into the trainer's room and threw three rolls of medical tape against a wall. When a reporter approached, Martin said, "I have no comment to make. No comments, period." Reggie Jackson said, "The ball carried fifteen feet over my head. I couldn't reach it." He looked over to first baseman Chris Chambliss in the next locker. "I couldn't get that one, could I, Chris?"

"I don't know," Chambliss said. "I wasn't out there." Jackson's expression went blank.

Munson broke his media silence long enough to say, "Otis was out in the sixth and he knows that he was out. Go ask him. I didn't tag him too hard because I didn't want to hurt him."

In the other locker room, Otis grinned and spoke mildly. "That call could have gone either way. But when he hit my leg, I thought my foot was on the plate. Either way. A nice ball game." Nearby Clint Hurdle was telling everyone who approached: "I got three hits today and I got three hits on Mother's Day a year ago. If they ever decide to call off Mother's Day, I'm in trouble." The *Newark-Star Ledger,* giving motherhood a rest, ran a forceful headline: YANKS JARRED IN 9TH, 10-9.

EACH MAJOR-LEAGUE team's season consists mostly of three-game series, slightly more than fifty three-game series in all, stretching through the mild months from April to October. A few odd contests added in complete the full schedule of 162 games. Barring rainouts, nobody splits a scheduled three-game series. One team or the other wins, usually two games to one, and that ongoing decisiveness is a wonder of every big-league season. Many extol baseball as independent of clocks. The games are played—to go metaphysical—outside of time. In W. P. Kinsella's fanciful novel *The Iowa Baseball Confederacy,* the game that drives the plot continues for thousands of innings. But tennis players and golfers also play without clocks. The matchless competitive quality of the major leagues indeed begins with games outside of time, but then continues into all those three-game series. Big-league ball games almost never end in ties and neither do the scheduled three-game series. A tie in sport has famously been described as "kissing your sister." These days it might better be described as kissing your sibling, but the point and the sentiment are unchanging. A tie in sport exemplifies an anticlimax. The nature and structure of major-league baseball piles one climax on top of another, which is what keeps the fans in chronic suspense.

Over the years the phrase "crucial series" has been pounded into a cliché, but sportswriters still have lively debates about when the word *crucial* properly may be applied. Many baseball men point out that a loss in April counts no more than a loss in September, which is, of course, mathematically so. But in April a team has months to make amends. Not so later on. As in Kurt Weill's poignant comment on love in *Knickerbocker Holiday,* the days grow

246 ▼ OCTOBER MEN

short when you reach September. I'd say that the Yankees' May set in Kansas City was absolutely crucial to their season. It did not decide the pennant but it spoke volumes about the team. Jackson won a game with his bat but lost at least one game in the field. When he turned for support to a teammate, none was forthcoming. Martin indulged himself in a nonproductive tantrum and after the second loss, on a flight to Chicago, he drank himself silly. That led to pointless confrontations with several players, including Munson.

The Yankees moved on to Toronto and even after they defeated a weak Blue Jay team, 11 to 3, on May 19, their clubhouse talk was barbed. Jackson took a fast ball into his right arm just above the elbow in the third inning and Paul Blair replaced him in the lineup. Chambliss and Dent powered the Yankee victory. Afterward Jackson sat in front of his locker, frowned, and shook his head. "Man, I was just crying every time Blair came up. I just sat on the bench and cried. Did you see all those runners Blair left dying there on base."

"Hey, I struck out on purpose," Blair shouted toward Jackson. "Couldn't you tell?"

Destructive behavior was threatening to cripple a World Championship team. I sensed that when I went to call on my old friend Al Rosen at his new presidential office in Yankee Stadium a few days later. The *New York Times* was demanding another "guest column." Our appointment was for 9 A.M. When I arrived Rosen said, "You're twenty minutes late."

"Overslept."

Rosen gazed.

"Can you get me some coffee, Al? The percolator at home broke down."

"Possibly. In the middle of a pennant race being president here keeps me on a full schedule. I imagine you can believe that. Whom do I have to thank for a day that's now twenty minutes out of whack? You? A percolator company? The *New York Times*?"

ACROSS HALF A CENTURY, my relations with America's Imperial Newspaper have been uneven. Although the staff of the *Times* has consistently included splendid people, "the institution," to quote one *Times* executive who does not want to be named, "is not as nice as most of the people who work for it." During my own newspaper years on the *New York Herald Tribune,* the *Trib* was more spirited than the *Times,* less arrogant, better written, and more comfortable with such novelties as a woman war correspondent and a Jewish city editor. *Tribune* people made fun of pomposity by calling the *Times* "the insurance company on 43rd Street." The various *Times* reporters I encountered, tall, short, plump, slim, had one attribute in common. They all complained that "the desk"—the copy-editing staff—was ruining their stuff. I don't imagine the *Times* people enjoyed being made fun of (or being rewritten), but passing years brought them a measure of revenge. When the *Herald Tribune* went out of business in 1966, the *Times* got to write its rival's obituary. Aside from that, the *Times* shot darts at *Tribune* types and others perceived as incorrigibly anti-*Times* in the form of book reviews composed with vitriol. I drew my share of those, but when *The Boys of Summer* outleaped *Times* Snide and went to the top of the best-seller lists, a different trumpet sounded from 43rd Street. James Tuite, the sports editor, invited me to lunch with an assistant managing editor and said the paper needed me as a sports columnist. "I've read your stuff," Tuite said. "I think you're a genius." Jim Tuite's flattery got him neither an argument nor a columnist. I thanked him and explained that I had not been a full-time newspaperman for decades. My focus had moved to books, I now lived by the rhythms of books, and I didn't think a regular newspaper column would work out happily for anyone.

"Books?" said the assistant managing editor, a pale fellow named Peter Millones. "Abe Rosenthal [the managing editor] says books are what you write before breakfast." I detoured into baseball talk and departed feeling concern. I had just spurned America's Imperial Newspaper; had I now guaranteed myself a fresh collection of sulfurous reviews? "There are two outfits you never want mad at you," counseled a sage old New York City police captain. "The first is us, the cops. We don't forget. The second is the *Times*. They don't forget either."

For a period the *Times* proved hard to discourage and when the paper's executives discovered sports in earnest during 1975 and started a separate section called "SportsMonday," Rosenthal asked me to step away from writing books long enough to deliver the lead column for the debut of the new section. I did, interviewing Walter O'Malley, the buccaneer who wrenched the Dodgers out of Brooklyn, on whether he would do it again, knowing that he had been hung in effigy on Flatbush Avenue. O'Malley, by that time worth hundreds of millions, agreed to lunch with me on one condition. I had to pick up the check. (Yes, he would do it again. He enjoyed being very rich. No he had never returned to Brooklyn for a visit nor did he intend to. In a burst of warmth—after I grabbed the tab—O'Malley chauffeured me from a restaurant on Wilshire Boulevard through nasty traffic to Los Angeles International Airport. His car was nice but not overwhelming, a middle-of-the-line Mercedes sedan.)

Abe Rosenthal greeted my piece with what he meant as humor, turning to his deputy Arthur Gelb and saying, "I'm surprised. This isn't bad." After that the *Times* periodically drafted me to do more of what they called "free-lance columns," some of which suffered because my focus remained on writing books. Tuite clashed with Rosenthal/Gelb and moved on. A logical successor, John van Doorn, didn't like working for them, either. At length the *Times* appointed a photo editor named Joe Vecchione to run the sports section, which he did, although, as Red Smith complained, "the feller's feel for the mother tongue is imperceptible." Vecchione was presiding late in May when I overslept on my way to see Al Rosen.

The Yankees had been beating up weak teams, such as Gabe Paul's Cleveland Indians, moving into second place behind the Red Sox. But angry noises continued, which I thought provided the basis for a reasonable discussion. Coffee arrived and Rosen looked out a window at the field. It had been raining. The Stadium looked soggy and depressing the way a wet, empty ballpark will, notably before coffee at 9:22 A.M. "Ball players always bicker and shout and call people names," Rosen said. "What do you think our ball club is, the New York Choirboys?"

"But this is a zoo," I said. "Right here in the Bronx you are the keeper of a zoo."

"In our day," Rosen said, "the disagreements were more private. We traveled by train. Who could sleep on a train? We'd go to the washroom and somebody would pull out a bottle and we'd talk baseball. What else was there to talk about but baseball? When we raised our voices it didn't make the papers. Our arguments stayed in the Pullman-car john."

"Looking backward," I would write, "you forget the bickering. You don't remember rainy ballparks either. Instead you see, in Jimmy Cannon's phrase, a perpetual afternoon of summer." But in reality Babe Ruth and Lou Gehrig sniped at one another. Gehrig thought Ruth was loud. Ruth thought Gehrig was cheap. (Both were right.) Joe DiMaggio welcomed Casey Stengel to his new job as Yankee manager by seeking out Arthur Daley of the *Times* and asking, in tones that made his own view clear, "What do you think of the new manager?"

"I never saw such a bewildered guy in my life," Daley said.

"That's what I think," DiMaggio said, "and damned if the other players don't feel the same way."

In his office at a bleak Stadium, Al Rosen grew intense. "Look at most winning teams," he said. "Disparate backgrounds. Strong talents. Gigantic egos. There'll be outbursts more often than not."

"But don't the outbursts on this team surpass the norm?"

"How's your coffee?" Rosen said.

Rosen was not simply a story subject, but a friend, which presented both a benefit and a conflict of interest. As a rule, friends talk more freely and honestly than strangers; that is the benefit. But on some level you are going to protect a friend, and that can get in the way of reporting, although not often in my experience, since I don't tend to become friendly with the sort of characters who warrant an exposé or a slam. As a matter of fact Rosen's friendship was more important to me than the columns the *Times* was stomping out of my typing fingers. When John Lardner died in 1960, A. J. Liebling of the *New Yorker* said, "John was a marvelous journalist. As a war correspondent he moved closer to shell bursts for a better view. But he did have one weakness. John wasn't son of a bitch enough." I could have pressed Al Rosen in a number of son-of-a-bitching ways, but instead I chose not to make his life more difficult than it already was. Instead, I did a little sidestep and asked if Martin's problems with two ball players, the departed outfielder Ron Blomberg and lefthander Ken Holtzman, proceeded from the fact that both were Jewish. Rosen nodded, now anxious to talk. "First," Rosen said, "we're into the whole area of baseball needling. When I hit a homer against the old Yankees, did I hear 'no-good Jew'? I heard worse. Was Martin one of the needlers? Probably. But Joe DiMaggio hitting a homer would hear 'damn dago' from our bench and whenever Yogi Berra came up, one of our infielders, Johnny Berardino, hung from the top of the dugout and scratched himself like a monkey.

"Second, the individuals. Blomberg, who I thought would be a star, has not become one. Ken Holtzman, for pure baseball reasons that would take an hour, fits poorly with our pitching talent.

"Third, we get to human nature. Scratch deep enough and won't you find some Jews resenting gentiles? Have you looked at the New Testament lately? Scratch deeply and won't you find some gentiles resenting Jews, out of their background, church teaching, whatever? I haven't scratched Billy that deeply, but I know how he runs the club for us. Winning is everything. Losing is nothing. I don't think Billy would have a bit of trouble managing a ball player he thinks is a winner, whatever the guy's religion. Is that an answer?"

When I finished writing what Rosen had made an interesting column I drove to the *Times* and handed it to Joe Vecchione. He read it quickly. Arthur Gelb was sitting next to him. "What do think?" I said to Vecchione. He swallowed a word that sounded like *slurpple* and handed the pages to Gelb. "Fine piece," Gelb told me presently. After that, but only after that, Vecchione said, "Your column is fine." Gelb moved on. "I was sure Rosen would come through," I told Vecchione. "I knew him as a third baseman. You should have seen him in a clutch."

"What's a clutch?" Vecchione said.

"In a car," I said, "you work it to change gears."

"Be serious."

"In baseball, Joe, *clutch* is a term used to describe a tight spot."

"Thanks," he said. I called the column "Keeper of the Zoo." Perhaps to let me know that he not I was sports editor of the *New York Times,* Vecchione changed the title to the inane "Keeper of the Yanks." "Don't despair," Red Smith told me over a drink in Sardi's. "I did a Kentucky Derby column once and the sports editor killed my title and substituted one of his own. It was something like 'Horse Wins Race.'" Amid such characters as Rosenthal and

Vecchione, Smith was not as comfortable at the *Times* as he had been working under the great sports editor Stanley Woodward at the *Herald Tribune,* but he was also deft at hyperbole. To this day I don't know whether he was telling me the truth about his Derby column or if he was echoing the dictum of Jimmy Durante to relax because, "Them's the conditions that prevail."

Long afterward Rosen talked to me with startling candor about the Yankee situation, and how he came to a point where he was no longer willing to remain part of it. But here he was a freshman president and speaking not just to me but to the *New York Times.* His job and the circumstance all but required him to express calm, cheer, and a generally optimistic view, whatever his 3:00 A.M. (or 8:05 P.M.) anxieties. As events were demonstrating, the greatly talented Yankees were, as Rosen said, not choirboys, but neither were they a team. Webster's first definition of that word is applicable: "A group of animals working together." Whatever else the Yankees were doing as the summer of 1978 neared, as a group they were *not* working together.

John McGraw's great 1905 Giant team despised him. I know that because Christy Mathewson told Ring Lardner who told his son, John, who told me. But common antipathy toward a tyrannical (and brilliant) manager united the players in common purpose. *We'll show that miserable McGraw; we're gonna win this ball game, 10 to 0.* The Dodgers began 1947 suffering from acute dyspepsia over the right of a black man, Jackie Robinson, to wear a Brooklyn uniform. The abuse other ball clubs directed against Robinson became so fierce that it created profound sympathy among his teammates. Sympathy, Branch Rickey believed, was "the strongest of emotions"; it made those divided Dodgers into a team. The Stengel-Mantle-Berra Yankees were a team; the Gibson-McCarver Cardinals were a team. The Ted Williams Red Sox, as Ed Linn illustrated in his marvelous Williams biography, *Hitter,* were not. To go beyond Webster and attempt precisely to define a base-ball team is probably fruitless. Too many eddies, cross-currents, and riptides combine in the flow. I'm content to leave the issue with words someone else applied to pornography: "Maybe I can't define it exactly, but I sure as hell know it when I see it." The early 1978 Yankees did not look like a team to me.

AS THE JUNE 15 trading deadline approached, rebellion simmered. "I want to get out of here right away," announced Ed Figueroa, who was emerging as the team's best right-handed starter. "I want to go to Texas or California or Boston. I want to go somewhere where I can pitch every fourth day, not every seven or nine days. I've asked to be traded and they tell me they want me here. Well, I don't feel like playing here anymore." An athlete who talked like that on the record to reporters during baseball's feudal days would have been suspended, fined, dispatched to the minor leagues, or simply released, then blacklisted as a "bolshevik." But by 1978 baseball feudalism was history, like Charlemagne, and in a heady new environment, the players, the agents, the owners, and the rest had not yet discovered how to manage news as they do today.

Mickey Rivers was a crackerjack leadoff man (batting .326 in 1977) and a good enough centerfielder when he wanted to play. But often during 1978 he didn't want to play because he felt un-derpaid by the front office and underappreciated by Martin. He sat out games with minor injuries and loafed on drives he might have flagged. Rivers griped episodically to the press and consistently to his friend Ken Holtzman and to his agent, Nick Buoniconti, for-merly a linebacker for the Miami Dolphins. Buoniconti, a strong and sensitive character out of Springfield, Massachusetts, had fin-ished law school after retiring from football and his counsel to Rivers was direct. "Don't complain to the sportswriters. That won't do any good. Just sit down with Billy Martin and work out your differences man to man." Buoniconti played football for Don Shula, one of the great coaches and an understanding, stable man. Martin, in contrast, was undergoing progressively more severe mood swings, frequently fueled by Scotch. "It got to be very tough to sit down and work out *anything* man to man with Martin," says Gene Michael, then the first-base coach. "You had to catch him just right. Personally I found the best time to talk to Billy was between the fourth and seventh drink." Tall "Stick" Michael's face is straight, but laughter lights his eyes.

Sparky Lyle, the abandoned Cy Young Award winner, continued to fume and added that the handling of Rawly Eastwick was brutal. "He's throwing good when I see him in the bullpen but they just don't use him because they say he used to throw better. Now that don't make no sense. It's not about 'used to.' It's about now." Following a good effort, Andy Messersmith elected to watch the next night's game from the bullpen. Martin said, "You supposed to sit in the dugout. I didn't give you permission to sit in the 'pen."

"What is this?" Messersmith said. "Prison?"

Martin reacted in a patterned way. He resumed referring to Messersmith, Gossage, and Jackson as "George's Boys," and added another phrase. Eastwick became "George's Gamble." Steinbrenner himself had referred to Eastwick as "my gamble," but that was different from Martin's taking up the characterization in a caustic way. Steinbrenner came flying north from Tampa and when Jim Palmer, the Baltimore ace, beat the Yankees, 1 to 0, on June 1 he told Rosen to bring Martin into his office, *right now.* The Yankees' record, 29 and 18, was third best in the majors and the team was second in its division, only three-and-a-half games behind the Red Sox. But Steinbrenner was angered as much by the ambient noises of insurrection as he was by the ball players' not-quite-good-enough performance.

"You're letting too many things get out of control," Steinbrenner said.

"You keep sticking me with players who don't fit," Martin said. "You *think* you know baseball. I'm the guy who really does know baseball."

"Take it easy, Billy," Rosen said.

"I didn't ask you," Martin said.

Presently Steinbrenner and Martin were bellowing. "If you want to fire me," Martin yelled, "go ahead. If I stay, you got to stop telling me how to run my club."

Steinbrenner spoke in forte tones. "Your club? Who's paying the salaries? Who's paying *your* goddamn salary?"

Martin stamped out. The Bronx troika, Steinbrenner, Rosen, and Martin, stood in disarray and, although no one knew it at the time, it was not going to work, ever. Discretion had fled the field. Steinbrenner obviously had the right to reprimand Martin, but was Yankee Stadium, with fifty journalists browsing about, the appropriate site? Whenever Martin was summoned to Steinbrenner's Stadium office, sportswriters would find out about the meeting and ask about a confrontation. This would lead to a small-arms fire of questions at both men and then the bomb, dropped in front of Steinbrenner: "Is Billy Martin through?" It would have been more prudent this simmering night for Steinbrenner to have invited Martin to his own Manhattan base, the Hotel Carlyle, which offers a quiet bar called the Bemmelmans, staffed by an Irish bartender of great discretion. But that would have required a forty-minute trip downtown, and more patience than Steinbrenner possessed under pressure when he was a novice baseball tycoon.

Rosen's role as Yankee president grew ever more blurred and painful. He appreciated the Steinbrenner who hired him and he detested the Steinbrenner who ranted at him. Like most good boxers, across his lifetime Rosen had not been on the receiving end of much abuse. Moss Klein remembers an episode where Steinbrenner loudly berated Rosen by telephone. Rosen held the phone at arm's length and finally said, "Bye, George," and hung up. He would become an outstanding big-league executive and a wealthy man, but in 1978 Al Rosen was a rookie president who needed the job.

Alfred Manuel Martin was no Niccolò Machiavelli, but he had a volume all his own of cunning schemes. He saw Rosen not as a fellow big-league warrior, a great collaborator, but as a rival and, like Reggie Jackson, someone better educated, more elegant, and better paid than he. The interior Martin, so full of sulphurous resentments, didn't know what the hell Rosen was doing there; Rosen was just one more of "George's Boys." It would be better, Martin thought, if Rosen were deposed and he himself became manager–general manager. Rosen brought up a third-string catcher named Mike Heath, essentially to replace Fran Healy, and Martin, overreacting wildly, screamed, "I don't want the guy." Before long he told the sportswriters that he wasn't talking to Rosen anymore. Thus the Yankee manager was now refusing to speak to the Yankee president. Niccolò Machiavelli would have recognized the lunacy and destructiveness (and dark humor) in the situation. Alfred Manuel Martin did not.

THAT NIGHT, JUNE 1, the Yankees flew to Oakland, the first leg of a three-city swing along the Pacific Coast. By this time Charlie Finley had peddled (or let go through free agency) his top-level talent, Jackson, Sal Bando, and Vida Blue, and was fielding the Anonymous Nine, a team with a roster clean of $100,000 salaries, .300 hitters or pitchers with the potential to win fifteen games. (Finley's *Anons* would draw 526,999 fans, a mere 6,500 a game and 1.2 million fewer than the San Francisco Giants, who were attracting customers with such stars as Blue and Willie McCovey shining in Candlestick Park, on the left coast of the bay.) Ron Guidry, seemingly better with every start, struck out eleven *Anons* and the Yankees won, 3 to 1. Guidry's record advanced to 8 and 0 and his earned run average descended to 1.80. Then the Yankees began a nasty skid, losing time after time to mediocre teams. They lost their next games in Oakland, making headlines they didn't like to read.

MESSERSMITH ROCKED

BY THREE HOME RUNS

And

STRUGGLING YANKS FLOP

AGAIN; LYLE HIT HARD

"We'll get better," Martin told the sportswriters. "I'm really not worried." The next day in a gloomy indoor ball field called the Kingdome, the Seattle Mariners, with the worst record in the majors, pounded out seventeen hits and defeated the Yankees, 7 to 3. During the fifth inning John Hale, a Seattle outfielder who was batting .170, stole second base. Martin bolted from the dugout screaming at umpire Steve Palermo, who made the call. Martin looked so wild that another umpire, Don Denkinger, blocked his path. Palermo ejected Martin, who reacted by sticking three fingers into the air. Not one finger but three. Martin never was much at understatement.

As it happened, Lee MacPhail, president of the American League, was watching the game on television. Lee was the son of Larry MacPhail, the so-called Roarin' Redhead who had bought the Yankees from the Ruppert Estate in 1945. As you may recall, Lee was a former Yankee president and the man who signed Thurman Munson. He was a quiet sort, a Swarthmore graduate—one MacPhail who never ever roared. Genuinely disturbed by Martin's gesture, MacPhail issued a bulletin to "all players, coaches and managers," saying that obscene language and obscene gestures "will not be tolerated." In addition, he wrote Rosen, insisting that Martin be reprimanded. When MacPhail's missive leaked to the media, Rosen said, "That letter was tremendously upsetting to me. I believe in the best traditions of baseball. I believe in Yankee tradition. There isn't any excuse for making a gesture like that on the field and it isn't only because children see it. Children are not the only ones involved here. The president of our league, a grown man who's been around, saw that gesture and it bothered him." Rumors of Martin's firing surfaced in every New York sports section; Dick Young wrote, "Martin will be gone from the Bronx in two or three days."

Dick Young, the baseball writer, was a focused feuder, a kind of latter-day Aaron Burr, whose chosen weapons were sheets of yellow Western Union paper and a typewriter. "Poison Pen," the old shortstop, Johnny Logan, would greet him: "Hiya, Poison Pen. Who ya knocking today?" Young would beam. He loved notoriety, confrontation, attention. At his best Young was a very good journalist, but like so many who cover sports (or politics or books or music) his skill fed an arrogance that went unchecked, protected as it was by the First Amendment. I knew Young across four decades; he was a compact, crude, combative man, the product of a broken home (like so many of the '78 Yankees) and a graduate of the CCC, a government work program that felled forests with axes during the Depression. He said he had taken only one writing course in his life, an extension class at NYU. "The professor was a medium-pretty woman who wore eyeglasses," he told me. "I got an A. I didn't write that well then but I took the professor to bed. I think she graded me on my fucking."

Young's press-box strength was weaving clubhouse interviews into his game stories without forgetting to tell how the runs were scored. He believed that the final score belonged in the first sentence of every morning newspaper baseball story. "Sure it's in the headline above the story," he said, "but that isn't my main point. When they don't get the score up top, their stories start wandering. They get mushy. I can't stand wordy stuff. Get the fucking score up top."

He was a bad man to cross. In rough chronological order, he collided with Branch Rickey, Jackie Robinson, Jim Bouton, Tom

Seaver, Norman Mailer, the columnist Jimmy Breslin, the sports-caster Howard Cosell, and Billy Martin. He pounced on Rickey's reputation for underpaying ball players with the nickname "El Cheapo." Robinson was "swelled-headed." Bouton, who tattled on the immoderate behavior of teammates in a diary book, was "a moral leper." Noting Breslin's gut and towering sense of self-importance, Young referred to him as "Fatty the Writer." When Mailer weaved about a press conference while demanding atten-tion from the late heavyweight champion Sonny Liston and finally protested, "I am talking to you as a journalist," Young snapped, "You are not comporting yourself as a journalist." Cosell, Young told me on several occasions, "changed his name from Cohen to Cosell, wears a toupee, and says he tells it like it is." Dick Young was a very bad man to cross, and Martin had crossed him. The specific was the punch, cut back to a shove, in that dispute over closing an area of the Yankee clubhouse. But Young also de-manded special treatment, in the form of exclusive interviews and tips from the people he covered. When he got that, as he did clas-sically from the Brooklyn Dodgers of the 1950s, Ol' Poison Pen turned into Master Lionel Lollipop. The monster in Young could be killed, or anyway anesthetized, by doses of practical kindness in the form of news leaks. But it was not in Billy Martin's nature to cater to a big ego, ball player, club owner, or newspaperman. On the contrary it was his nature to find a way to scrap with big-ego people. As you can tell from the feud list, that was also the nature of Dick Young. So these two complex, gifted, rugged, similar char-acters were bound to pummel one another.

Day after day Young's attacks came like grapeshot... Doesn't Billy look bad?... What's wrong with his health?... I'd like to Scotch some rumors, but I can't... Steinbrenner is furious... The firing can come any time... The team is shot to pieces... Is Stein-brenner flying west?... Who's going to be the new manager?...

Steinbrenner likes Gene Michael... How about Dick Howser?...
Poor Billy. The fella could be out of work TONIGHT!

On Wednesday, June 7, the back page of the *Daily News,* then
the newspaper with the largest circulation in America, announced
in large black capital letters: BILLY NEAR AX AGAIN. Beneath that
headline, writing with studied restraint, even eschewing nasty nicknames, Young made his case against Martin. In this instance he was
able, with genuine skill, mostly to camouflage his personal animus.

> [Martin] is working on getting himself fired. This is one of Billy's
> finest talents, getting the bosses sore at him. It's not that the Yan-
> kees aren't winning games. That's not what makes the bosses
> sore. It's Billy's refusal to recognize that there are such things as
> bosses. To Billy Martin, he's the boss, all the time, of every-
> thing... Martin flies off the handle with the players to prove he's
> the boss, even with the newspapermen. "I know you stayed in
> the clubhouse two minutes after the deadline to leave before the
> game," he'll say as though his authority had been challenged.
>
> The other day after a game he's in the press room having a
> couple of belts and talking baseball. He can be fascinating at
> these times. Suddenly, like Dr. Jekyll drinking the evil potion,
> Billy Martin changes before your eyes. An old Army buddy
> was Billy's guest. "Tell him who was the boss," said Billy Mar-
> tin. "My whole [Army baseball] team was officers, but I was
> the manager. Me. Corporal Martin."
>
> It's a sickness and it is going to destroy him. Martin doesn't
> drink too much. He just talks too much when he drinks. He
> gets the I'm the boss chip on his shoulder. Steinbrenner will
> stay in the background only so long. Then very adroitly he will
> convince Rosen that Rosen has had enough of Billy Martin.
> That's how it will be done when it's done. Steinbrenner will
> make up Rosen's mind for him. That's what being the boss is
> all about, and Al Rosen is smart enough to realize it. That's the
> difference between him and Billy Martin.

I knew Dick Young for thirty-five years, until his death in 1987, and, as Dick would have put it, we had a few belts together. I heard him out on politics, race relations, fornication, and even baseball. I never encountered anyone, including Billy Martin, who so ardently wanted to control every situation—to be "the boss all the time of everything"—as that crackling and never-boring baseball writer, Dick Young.

Young's noisy stuff all but drowned out the case *for* Billy Martin, but Al Rosen made a response. "When things are going bad," he said, "all kinds of people find ways to blame the manager for all kinds of things. I'm convinced the team is going through a slump that won't last. I'm convinced that Billy will pull them out of it. Billy always has been an inspirational guy and he's the one to lead the club out this situation. And he will." Traditionally a vote of confidence in a manager is a prelude to his firing, but Rosen sounded too certain and too sincere to mean anything other than what he said. Steinbrenner, however, was keeping silent.

When Martin was feeling confident, when management had given him reason to feel confident, he ran a ball game in daring and explosive ways. He knew how to use the running game and the bunt; how to rattle an opposing pitcher and how to bully an umpire. He pushed his players toward extraordinary feats. By all accounts Martin was a splendid tactical manager whose weakness lay in what are now called "people skills." (Curiously Joe Torre, managing the Yankees twenty-five years later, is regarded as no better than an ordinary game tactician. But Torre's skills with people, including media people, are superb.)

After the Yankees lost a second time in Seattle, the Mariners winning 4 to 3, the team found itself four-and-a-half games behind the Red Sox. Martin took questions in the visiting manager's office and after most of the reporters left he spoke soberly to Moss Klein. "I really can't believe what's happening," he said. "It's like a nightmare. There shouldn't be this much pressure. Sure we're losing, but its only June. We're not that far behind Boston. I know we're better than them and if everybody just relaxed, we'd be okay. If they keep me on as manager, we're going to beat out the Red Sox by five games. I'm sure of it." At that point Martin's son, thirteen-year-old Billy Joe, walked into the office. "Hey," Martin said, "we had a good time together today, didn't we?"

"He took me fishing down by a wharf," Billy Joe said to Klein. The boy, dark and wiry like his father, lived with his mother in Texas. Martin had flown him to Oakland so they could spend time together, visitation major-league style. "After that," Billy Joe said, "Dad took me to a restaurant on the wharf. We bought French fries and put tabasco sauce on them and fed them to the seagulls. The seagulls liked them. They liked tabasco sauce." Martin beamed. Someone else appeared to take Billy Joe back to the Yankee hotel. "I'm flying him home before we go to Anaheim," Martin said to Klein. "Just in case they fire me in Anaheim, I don't want my boy around for that."

Touched, Klein withdrew to the press box and wrote from the heart: "There is absolutely no reason to fire Billy Martin. Al Rosen insists he won't be, at least for now. George Steinbrenner, though, has the final word. Steinbrenner panics during losing streaks. He fumes and second-guesses every move that Martin makes. He is a super-fan who happens to own the team. Steinbrenner knows how to be successful, but in a business way. He thinks that by making things difficult for Martin, by dropping hints [to Dick Young] of imminent firings, he'll make Billy try harder and make the team do better. What Steinbrenner is actually doing is making the situation worse. He is the one who encourages the nightmare. Steinbrenner won't change his ways. Martin knows that. For the Yankees' good, Steinbrenner shouldn't change his manager, either."

The next day Jackson hit two homers, Guidry struck out ten, and the Yankees defeated the Mariners, 9 to 1. "Now," Graig

Nettles said on the flight to Anaheim, "we're rolling. We've got our streak. One in a row." But the Yankees lost two out of three to the Angels and fell six games behind the Red Sox. They traded Ken Holtzman to the Chicago Cubs for "a minor-league pitcher to be named at a later date." That turned out to be a rangy righthander named Ron Davis, who would win fourteen for the Yankees in 1979. Rosen always had a fine eye for talent. "I wished Kenny luck," he said, "and he wished the same for me. There are too many other things to worry about in this business than to waste time harboring bad feelings." Holtzman still had two-and-a-half seasons to go on the $825,000 contract he signed with the Yankees in 1976. He put in the time with Chicago, but his best years were long gone. Once a twenty-game winner, Holtzman's record with the Cubs was 6 and 12 when he retired. Rawly Eastwick followed Holtzman out of the Bronx, landing in Philadelphia. He was out of baseball by the time he reached the age of thirty-one. Neither Don Gullett nor Andy Messersmith had much left. Shoulder pain was disabling Catfish Hunter. Where was the pitching, the lifeblood of every winning team? Never mind Billy Martin. John McGraw never won without great pitching. The 1927 Yankees of Ruth and Gehrig, the classic muscle team, numbered two Hall of Famers in their starting rotation. Now Ed Figueroa and Rich Gossage were coming around, but mostly this Yankee club's pitching was a tall, thin Louisiana mustache named Ron Guidry, who in one June week threw two shutouts and struck out twenty-nine. Larry Keith, of *Sports Illustrated*, asked Guidry to explain how a 155-pound man could throw a 95-mile-an-hour fast ball. "I'd like to help you, but I can't explain it myself," Guidry said. "I guess it's more a gift than anything else." Keith turned to Billy Martin. "Good as he is, Guidry can't stay unbeaten all season."

"Oh, yeah?" Martin said. "How do *you* know?"

With Holtzman, who had been an idle pitcher but an intensely activist Player Representative, gone, the Yankees' grievance over the discordant welcome-home luncheon disappeared. The Major League Players' Association reports that no record exists of a grievance actually being filed. Marvin Miller, the emeritus union leader, is a man who remembers everything; he insists that he can't recall the episode much less the whimpers of the players who were fined. There is nothing wrong with selective memory if you are protecting your charges from sounding like unalloyed nutcakes.

CHAPTER TWELVE

▼

TEN DAYS THAT SHOOK THE BRONX

LYING A FOUR-ENGINE JET into Tampa, I found myself some-what startled when the pilot began executing a U-turn six hundred feet above a trailer park. A few minutes later he an-nounced, "Sorry, folks. A little plane cut us off. Damned if the same thing didn't happen yesterday." The cabin buzzed with ner-vous chatter as we circled back toward the runway. This time the captain missed the approach. When he (and the rest of us) made it, on the third try, passengers applauded, but not my companion, the late literary lawyer Cy Rembar. "This pilot is one out of three," Rembar said. "I don't applaud captains whose landing average is no better than .333."

"I'll tell you a worse one," Ron Guidry said as we sat in a Florida dugout remembering things and pilots past. "On one of our charter flights in '78, when I was having my best year, an at-tendant came up and said the captain was from Louisiana and he'd like me to go up to the cockpit so he could shake my hand." Presently the captain invited Guidry to sit in the jump seat, be-tween him and the first officer, "so you can see how we handle this thing." As the plane descended, the captain pointed downward and said to the copilot, "Isn't that the runway, right there?"

"No, sir. I believe that's a highway."

"The hell you say. I'm taking this baby down."

"Sir, I wouldn't do that. I believe you're looking at Interstate 95."

The captain shook his head and turned to Guidry. "Ron, you got a map?" After ghastly silence, the two flyers, but not Guidry, broke into raucous laughter. They probably still do when they tell the story, behind closed doors, at the annual beer-and-bourbon bash of the Retired Airline Pilots' Association.

Guidry no longer flies. "If they want old Ronnie for one of those memorabilia shows these days, they have to provide transportation on the ground." But the Guidry of '78 flew high, wide, and handsome. Unlike Munson, he was civil to the press. Unlike Jackson, he avoided the fast lanes of Manhattan. "They tell me there're great restaurants in the city," he said, "but my wife, Bonnie, and I can cook some on our own. You ought to try our crawfish etoufée." Unlike Martin, he kept himself on an even keel. Amid the explosive Yankee personalities, Guidry seemed preternaturally quiet. As Walt Kelly wrote in another context, "The quiet of the man's presence was like the silence of a forest, where the lack of noise does not indicate a lack of life."

When not in an aircraft, Guidry seemed able to cope calmly with whatever came along and he had been that way for years. "When I was ten," he says, "my folks moved to a new part of town [Lafayette, Louisiana] and I was out in the back the first day we lived there and these two older guys came over to me and started pushing me around. I said something to them and they beat me up. Next day the same thing happened. I figured I'd better do something because I didn't want to get beat up every day. My buddy, Bobby, helped me dig this giant hole. We dug for hours. The next day after school I saw those older guys again. I came up to about fifty yards away from them and threw a rock in their direction. They started running after me, like I knew they would. I ran them right in the direction of the giant hole, which I had covered with leaves and brush. I jumped over the spot, but the two of them went right in that giant hole and started hollering. I must have scared them good enough because they never bothered me again." Seventeen years later, in the summer of '78, nobody in the American League could bother Guidry. On June 17, he won his eleventh straight, defeating the California Angels, a team with at least six solid hitters, 4 to 0, and struck out eighteen. The major-league record at the time was nineteen, shared by Steve Carlton and two former Mets, Tom Seaver and Nolan Ryan. Larry Keith wrote exuberantly in *Sports Illustrated*: "As Guidry's strikeouts mounted, the 33,162 fans added to the excitement by booing bad calls and tumultuously clapping, yelling and stomping every time Guidry got two strikes on a batter. Because the Yankees had scored their four runs in the first three innings, the crowd sat passively through New York's other at bats, anxiously waiting for Guidry to start throwing strikes again. When the game ended, the fans gave Guidry a sustained ovation that prompted him to come out of the clubhouse for a curtain call."

In the dressing room, Martin and Jackson vied to praise. "You saw how he pitches," Martin said, "but did you notice how great he *fields* his position?" Jackson said, "He and Jim Palmer are the best athletes I've ever seen among pitchers. The few times I've seen Ron swing the bat makes me think he could be an everyday position player, just the way Bob Gibson could have been." That was a beauteous evening for the Yankees, but with the next afternoon's daylight—it was a Sunday—the endemic ugliness returned. The *Daily News* summed up with another brassy headline:

FIGGY, BILLY FEUD AS FAIRLY

HR WINS FOR ANGELS

Ed Figueroa, the number-two arm behind Guidry, went into the top of the ninth inning against the Angels, tied at 2. He got two out and then, with Ron Fairly coming up, Martin dispatched Art Fowler to the mound with a message: "Pitch around him." This venerable tactic, tracing at least to John McGraw, is distinct from an intentional base on balls. The pitcher is supposed to throw very tough stuff, inducing the hitter to swing at bad balls. Objective: to get the batter out swinging at a bad or at least difficult pitch. Acceptable downside: The batter walks. Fairly, a few weeks shy of his fortieth birthday, was winding down a twenty-one-year career, but he remained a dangerous left-handed hitter, particularly in the Stadium, where the right-field wall was only 310 feet away down the line. "Pitch around him," Fowler repeated. "If you walk him we don't care." Figueroa threw two good outside fast balls, strikes, but very hard to hit. Then he tried to strike out Fairly with a breaking ball low and inside. Fairly straightened out the hook and lined it into the right-field seats. The home run won for the Angels, 3 to 2.

This loss dropped the Yankees seven games behind the Red Sox and led to another of Martin's outbursts. "He [Figueroa] was told to walk the guy who hit the home run," Martin announced to the press. The reporters scuttled over to Figueroa, a tall, sometimes volatile native of Puerto Rico. "Billy told you that?" Figueroa said. "Nobody said I was supposed to walk Fairly." Then adding to the ambient rebellious rumble, "If they don't like the way I pitch, they can just get my butt out of here." In this mood, the Yankees flew to Boston and, starting rookie Ken Clay, soreshouldered Don Gullett, and rookie Jim Beattie, they lost two out of three and fell eight games behind the Red Sox. Why, some wondered in the press, hadn't Martin juggled his pitching rotation so that the ace, Guidry, and the number-two man, Figueroa, got to face the first-place Red Sox? Why was Art Fowler still employed as the pitching coach? Steinbrenner and Rosen were wondering the same things.

TO THE NORTH IN BOSTON, Don Zimmer was thinking pennant because, he said, his luck was finally changing, and, without complaining, he wasn't a complaining sort of fella, he'd had more than his share of rotten breaks. A generation earlier at the age of twenty-two, he was a star prospect in the Dodger organization when a fast ball slammed into the left side of his head, near the speech center of the brain. He had to learn to talk all over again. When he recovered, over many months, he was not quite the player he had been. Still Zimmer persisted and in 1954 he made the Dodgers as a back-up infielder. Then, in 1956, he took a fast ball to the cheekbone which, as he puts it, "stove in the whole side of my face." Again he fought back but in the end Zimmer's twelve-year big-league career (shortstop, second base, third base, outfield, catcher) concluded with disappointment, a lifetime batting average of .235 and more than twice as many strikeouts as walks. "He could have been a good hitter, even with the beanings," said Walter Alston, the longtime Dodger manager, "but he didn't want to be a good hitter. He wanted to be a slugger, like Gil Hodges or Duke Snider. He wasn't big enough so he kept swinging too hard. A stubborn guy, not easy to manage, but also a terrific battler."

In Zimmer's Brooklyn days, he was forever in the face of E. J. "Buzzie" Bavasi, the Dodger general manager, demanding a place in the starting lineup. But Pee Wee Reese was the Dodger shortstop, Jim Gilliam played second, and Jackie Robinson was playing a fine third base. So Zimmer sat on the bench and fumed and said time after time to Bavasi, "Play me or trade me." At length Reese went down with an injury and Zimmer made the starting lineup for two weeks. He hit less than .200. "I played you," Bavasi said to Zimmer. "Now I *can't* trade you."

Baseball was most of Zimmer's life. As his wedding site he chose home plate at Dunn Field in Elmira, New York—*beautiful* Dunn Field, the locals say—where he began his honeymoon by putting in nine innings at shortstop. When his playing days ended, he coached and managed at Key West, Knoxville, Buffalo, Indianapolis, and Salt Lake—truly a road warrior—before returning to the majors in 1971 as a coach for the Montreal Expos. Not one of the clubs that hired him won a pennant, but Zimmer's reputation as a committed and increasingly knowledgeable baseball man grew. He managed San Diego for two years, then came to the Red Sox as a coach and became the manager in 1976. Now in 1978 he was—for the first time in his life—a big-league manager with an eight-game lead. He had grown jowly and bald with the years and *Esquire* magazine needled him as winner of the "Mickey Rooney Look-Alike Contest." The Red Sox pitcher Bill Lee insisted that Zimmer resembled a gerbil and that nickname spread. But as the summer of 1978 came to New England, the hard-luck road warrior soared above the sniping. He had a splendid team and he praised all his key players, except Bill Lee. Dwight Evans in right was even better than the old Dodger, Carl Furillo. Jim Rice was the best hitter around. Carl Yastrzemski was a sure Hall of Famer... George Scott...Carlton Fisk...Fred Lynn. "It's an exceptional ball club," Zimmer said. "Naturally there's pressure on me to win. If I don't I could be in trouble. But any manager would love to have a team like this to manage. I've had some bad breaks in the past. Right now I consider myself a very fortunate guy."

THE YANKEES FLEW TO Detroit, where Guidry won again and the team took three out of four. After that, with Boston coming in for a brief series at the Stadium, the Yankee record stood at 41 and 29, a passable .585 percentage, except that Zimmer's Red Sox had played eight-and-a-half games better. At this point, Steinbrenner and Rosen agreed to fire Art Fowler and replace him with quiet, bespectacled, college-educated Clyde King, once a Dodger righthander, who had previously managed the San Francisco Giants and the Atlanta Braves. Martin erupted. A pitching coach is the manager's chief of staff and as a practical matter front-office people don't fire a pitching coach without the agreement of the manager. "If they get rid of Art, they're gonna lose me, too," Martin said. "Anyways," he told a reporter, "I got bigger things on my mind."

"Such as?"

"Mickey. He may be dying." Suffering from a bleeding ulcer, Mantle had been admitted to Brookhaven Medical Center in Dallas, where doctors described his condition as critical. But he rallied and by this time his condition was "satisfactory." The physicians did warn Mantle that he had better stop drinking. When he said he could not, they pleaded with him to control his consumption. "I told them, all right, I'd switch from straight bourbon to vodka and tonic," he said to me long afterward, "but I couldn't do that, either. I didn't like the taste of quinine."

This was, quite simply, a terrible patch for Billy Martin. When he suggested that drink was killing his old friend Mickey, he was wondering also what all the hard liquor was doing to him. He felt alone. Martin ached to have Steinbrenner as a friend, but Steinbrenner wasn't interested. Martin complained that he sat watching TV by himself in his New Jersey apartment and Steinbrenner never invited him to dinner at "21," or Jimmy Weston's, or any one of those classy action places in New York. He could not bring himself to trust Al Rosen. He had heard rumors somewhere that Rosen was trying to engineer a swap with Bill Veeck. Martin would go to Chicago and manage the White Sox. Bob Lemon would leave the White Sox to manage the Yankees. Martin knew that Lemon and Rosen had been buddies when they played for the Cleveland Indians. They could deny the swap story all they wanted, but you couldn't convince Martin that Rosen wasn't at least trying to make it come true. "That's one sumbitch story," Martin said, "I'd sure as hell like to get confirmed." Someone told Martin that Steinbrenner had put in a call to Walter Alston, the Dodger manager who had stepped down two years before, "to feel him out about the Yankee job." Martin knew Steinbrenner thought Dick Williams, now managing a poor club in Montreal, was a gifted baseball character, tough as nails and a man who had led teams to pennants in Boston and Oakland. It would take plenty to get Williams out of

Quebec, but it could be done. So Bob Lemon, Walt Alston, Dick Williams, and maybe Clyde King were all going to get his job. What a joke. Not a one of them ever played an inning in a Yankee uniform. He was the real Yankee, like Mickey and Whitey, but the creeps in the front office didn't give a damn, and he'd won two pennants in a row and now they were looking to knock him off and what the hell could he do about that? Well, his own gut was okay. He wasn't Mickey. Here's what he could do about that. Hey, where's the Scotch?

THAT WEARISOME TERM "crucial series" riled the sensibilities of the great sports editor Stanley Woodward. "It's a phrase I'd like banished from newspapers," Woodward said, "along with 'spine-tingling game,' 'twin killing' and 'rushing people to the hospital.'" Woodward, a large, myopic, and very strong man, raged at the tendency in sportswriters and deskmen "to call things by names other than their own." He described the results as "The Unholy Jargon." Crucial, which once suggested having the form of a cross, now means, as Webster puts it, an event that marks "the final determination of a doubtful issue. " To go by the books, Webster and baseball, there are seldom crucial series, final determinations, before September; except with all the psychology, mysticism, and madness of a pennant race, there really isn't a "book" that applies. Occasionally one team breaks another's spirit with an early-season sweep, or a pitcher secures his dominance over a major rival—the Giants' Sal Maglie feasted on Brooklyn Dodger bones—starting in April. But most of the time what the newspapers describe as a crucial series is rather an *important* series.

BOSOX IN TOWN FOR CRUCIAL SET, one newspaper announced. (Mr. Woodward didn't care for "Bosox," either. It was almost as bad, he said, as the prose of a renowned afternoon newspaper sportswriter who consistently called the Boston club "the Crimson Hose.") What the headline here meant was that the Red Sox, eight-

and-a-half games out front, were coming to the Stadium to play the Yankees twice. But first, on the afternoon of Monday, June 26, Steinbrenner, Rosen, Martin, and Martin's agent, Doug Newton, met for two-and-a-half hours at the Stadium. Art Fowler, the pitching coach, simply wasn't working out, Rosen said.

"If he goes, I go," Martin said.

"Let's consider what we say carefully," the agent said.

"He isn't getting fired," Rosen said. "We think he'll work out better in another role: roving minor-league pitching instructor." That meant that when Martin wanted to have some drinks with his buddy, he would have to fly to, say, Columbus. A bizarre compromise allowed Fowler to stay with the Yankees and to be joined in a few days by Clyde King. The Yankee pitching coach would then be a committee.

"We want you to win these two from Boston," Steinbrenner said.

"I want that too, George," Martin said.

The meeting drifted toward amiability. Steinbrenner and Rosen seemed to have agreed that an insecure Martin would not manage as well as a secure Martin. When the meeting wound down, Steinbrenner issued a statement that come what may, win or lose, fire, pestilence, or famine, Martin would manage the Yankees for the balance of the season and maybe longer. "This should end the speculation that has been developing of late concerning Billy's job," Steinbrenner said. "We had a solid air-cleaning session. Everything was discussed in considerable detail. Al and Billy got a lot of things ironed out." Sparky Lyle, increasingly cynical and bitter, remembered that in October 1974 Steinbrenner assured a nervous Bobby Murcer, "You'll be here as long as I am." A few days later the Yankees traded Murcer to San Francisco.

Martin's core support remained those white, beer-guzzling fans from New Jersey, but as he struggled to survive, the element of sympathy expanded his base of popularity. Certain sportswriters were depicting Steinbrenner as a tyrant, notably Red Smith, in his repetitive, effective use of "George III." Thus Martin, no stranger to the swagger, became an underdog, like the Continentals at Valley Forge, who kept their blood warm by swigging Old Monongahela, the most popular American "red liquor" of the eighteenth century. When Martin carried his lineup card to the umpires at home plate on the cool, moist evening of June 26, most of the 52,124 fans at the Stadium rose and joined in a prolonged ovation. Martin grinned and merrily waved his Yankee cap. He wasn't alone now; he felt good. He was starting Andy Messersmith, whose right arm seemed stronger and who gave the Red Sox two hits but no runs in the first inning. Roy White led off for the Yankees with a line single. He got a big jump against the Boston ace, Dennis Eckersley, and stole second. Chris Chambliss scored White with another single and Messersmith protected the lead into the fifth inning. Then mighty Jim Rice cracked a two-run homer into the left-field seats. The Sox added a run on two hits in the sixth and went ahead, 4 to 1, in the eighth when Carlton Fisk caught up with a Gossage fast ball and drove it into the lower deck in left. This tough Yankee team then began to rally mostly off Eckersley. Chambliss singled and after Lou Piniella struck out, Jackson singled. The tying run stood in the batter's box. Gary Thomasson, a left-hand-hitting outfielder recently acquired from Oakland, flied to right. Zimmer brought in his best reliever, the righthander Bill Campbell, who walked beefy Jim Spencer, another left-hand hitter, loading the bases. Now the go-ahead run stood in the batter's box. Jay Johnstone, yet a third left-hander, pinch-hit and Campbell's first pitch sank into the dirt. It was drizzling. Nobody got up to leave. Zimmer burst out of the dugout and hurried to the mound. "Calm down," he said.

Campbell nodded.

"Just stay calm and throw the ball over the plate and you'll be fine." Campbell threw a fast strike, then fooled Johnstone with a breaking ball. Johnstone lunged, lost his grip on the bat, and tapped a benign little grounder. The Red Sox held their 4-to-1 edge and increased their first-place lead to a formidable nine-and-a-half games. "There's a lot of time left," Martin said in the clubhouse. "There's the rest of June [three days]. Then July and August and September. We have an awful lot of time." As a matter of fact "we" didn't. Time was running out for Billy Martin.

The next night before an even larger crowd, 55,132, the Yankees played a long, hard, demanding ball game, the kind that over the years Yankee teams win more often than not. Guidry started and retired the first nine Red Sox, while the Yankees chipped away for three runs off one of Boston's lesser starters, Jim Wright. Three runs for Guidry could well have settled things right there, but presently he began to go shaky. The Red Sox reached him for four hits and two runs in the sixth. An inning later George Scott, who had struck out twice, singled and so did Dwight Evans. Guidry walked Butch Hobson, a dangerous right-hand hitter in the midst of a horrific defensive season. (Hobson would make no fewer than forty-three errors at third base that year, a total that contrasted dismally with Nettles' eleven and was more than ten times greater than that of Detroit's Aurelio Rodriguez, the league leader, who made only four. Hobson, as the saying went, fielded with his bat.) Now with bases loaded and a one-run lead, Martin lifted Guidry for Goose Gossage. It was the earliest exit for Guidry all season and the Stadium crowd rose and cheered him as he left the mound. Gossage then tried to overpower shortstop Rick Burleson, but Burleson lined the fast ball into center field and the Red Sox led, 4 to 3. Guidry now stood in danger of becoming a losing pitcher, but the Yankees tied the score with three singles off three Red Sox pitchers in the eighth. After that the game became trench warfare. Gossage pitched five scoreless innings. Lyle relieved him in the twelfth. At eight minutes past midnight, in the fourteenth inning, the Yankees won 6 to 4, on Nettles' two-run homer off Dick

Drago. Next the team would fly through the night to Milwaukee for a doubleheader. "My homer means," Nettles said, cheerfully, "that we can win three games in one day."

They did not. For whatever reasons the Yankees hit feebly and Milwaukee swept the games in County Stadium, 5 to 0 and 7 to 2, before a crowd that included Commissioner Bowie Kuhn and George Steinbrenner, who shared a box with Allan "Bud" Selig, the president of the Brewers. The losses dropped the Yankees into third place, nine-and-a-half games behind the Red Sox, and ended Steinbrenner's brief run as a low-profile owner. During one particularly dolorous Yankee moment, a Nettles pop-up with a man on base, Steinbrenner stood up. Some thought he was trying to jump the box-seat railing and rush onto the field to strangle, slug, or at least dress down his athletes. Kuhn put a hand on Steinbrenner's shoulder, which looked as though the commissioner was restraining one irate Managing Partner. Both men denied that, saying Steinbrenner had simply risen to relieve the tension of the moment. Whatever. No one restrained Steinbrenner after the game.

"First, in defense of my team," he told a mix of New York and Midwestern sportswriters, who surrounded the box where he had been sitting, "they didn't get here until five o'clock in the morning and they have now played ball every day for twenty straight days. The American League leadership responsible for making this schedule should be fired. They make excuses that it's difficult to schedule with fourteen teams, but the truth is that they're incompetents who don't deserve to have their jobs. I'm going to talk to the commissioner and see if he'll take over the schedule making. But aside from that, key players are letting us down. What did Jackson do in the doubleheader? No hits in seven times at bat and he leaves five men on base. Jackson is killing us. I keep close track of his performance. Over the last two weeks, he's hitting .222 with runners on base. That's just plain awful. How can we win when a guy like Reggie, who means so much to the team, is failing us like that?"

He turned to Nettles, who had asked out of the second game, telling Martin that he felt exhausted. "How could Nettles sit in a spot like that when the team really needed him? We're in a bad situation. I predict we'll close the gap between us and the Red Sox but are we gonna catch them? The truth is I don't know. It's hard for me to be optimistic but I want it known that in no way do I feel Billy Martin is responsible for our position. It's injuries and disappointing performances by our key players like Reggie Jackson." The next day, which the Yankees had off, Martin continued to feel rejected because Steinbrenner would not mix with him socially, and Jackson felt wounded because he had been singled out for criticism. "George said he was my friend," Jackson remarked quietly. "If you're my friend, stay my friend. You don't get mad at me for one off day. But I know the score now..."

Steinbrenner told the sportswriters that he realized that he became intense with his ball club, but that was the way he was with everything he did. "I react from the gut," he said Most of the sportswriters accepted this self-appraisal, but I am not sure that it was complete. Steinbrenner told me once: "I'm one damn involved owner and sure I'm a fan, but I'm also a businessman with more than thirty years' experience in running companies, dealing with unions, making up budgets, figuring out corporate taxes, handling hundreds of millions of dollars, and seeing what works and what doesn't." Can one do all those things from the gut alone? I doubt it; the cerebral cortex must be powerfully involved. Steinbrenner's management style has become more sophisticated, but twenty-five years ago, as today, he was emotional but also thoughtful, if not so carefully controlled. He found visceral relief in sounding off, but he also believed that his blares of rage produced positive results. The next time the Yankees played, on June

30, Reggie Jackson, a genuinely offended Reggie Jackson, went 3-for-5 against Detroit, hit a grand-slam homer, knocked in five runs, and led the Yankees in a 10-to-2 rout. Hurt, Reggie took out his pain on the baseball.

Long ago in journalism I worked for strong characters who had been acolytes of William Randolph Hearst and had picked up pieces of the old tyrant's corrosive management style. One, John Denson, ran *Newsweek* when I was the sports editor there and I watched him flare and subside at news conferences, calling one of his deputies "a gnat head" and screaming at another, "I'll bend you till you break!" Denson wore dentures and just before these eruptions his false teeth would grind noisily, leading a decorous research assistant to comment, "When Mr. Denson gets angry, it seems as if he has nuts in his mouth." Gordon Manning, Denson's deputy, quickly said, "Those nuts are mine." For all that, Denson revived a magazine that had been dull as a German medical monograph and after hours he could be both generous and charming. "I inherited a staff that specialized in afternoon naps," he said. "I've had to shout to wake 'em up." Steinbrenner inherited a team that was besmirching the old Yankee tradition. Like John Denson, though with better teeth, he woke up everybody and revived the company.

ON FRIDAY, JUNE 30, a big Chicago story drew comparatively little attention in New York: Bill Veeck fired Bob Lemon as manager of the White Sox and replaced him with Larry Doby, who had been the first black to play in the American League. Veeck had signed him to a Cleveland contract in 1947, three months after Jackie Robinson's debut in Brooklyn, and across thirteen seasons Doby batted .283 and hit 253 home runs. Frank Robinson had become the first African-American manager in the major leagues when he took over Cleveland in 1975. Doby now became the second. Veeck said, "The change is not in any way a commentary on Bob Lemon's ability, but rather is a result of an unusual set of circumstances." Actually, the circumstances were not unusual for Veeck. He was short of cash. He had capitalized his club before free agency and he told me he knew of no way in which he could re-capitalize the White Sox—and thus bid for top-drawer talent—and at the same time keep control of the franchise. Some find a touch of irony there. In a famous baseball litigation Veeck had tes-tified on behalf of freed agency for the late outfielder Curt Flood. Desperate now in a dignified way, he hoped that the fact of a black manager working on Chicago's heavily black South Side would pull in extra fans and with them gate receipts and profits from concession stands; it did not. Lemon had brought a mediocre Chicago team home in third place the year before but currently was stuck, below .500, in fifth. Accepting the job, Doby sounded embarrassed. "When I got the call," he said, "I was surprised and somewhat sad. Bob Lemon and I have been friends for thirty years. We had a long talk before I could agree and Bob said, 'Don't feel upset. We've been friends and we'll still be friends and these things happen in baseball.'" Lemon went back to his home in Long Beach, California, and Veeck said he would become the White Sox chief West Coast scout. All the pieces were in place for a final stroke that would place the Cleveland Connection totally in charge of the New York Yankees. All that was needed was a deto-nator, along the lines of a tactical nuclear explosion. On this Yan-kee team that would follow as the night the day.

Wasteland enveloped the ball club. On July 1 the Tigers beat them, 8 to 4, and in baseball lingo, Andy Messersmith "blew his shoulder." He was finished as a Yankee. After Guidry beat the Tigers, advancing his record to 13 and 0, the Yankees moved to Fenway where the Red Sox defeated them, 9 to 5, on the night of July 3. Carl Yastrzemski and Carlton Fisk each drove in three runs. Ed Figueroa, the Yankee starter, left the game wincing from pain in his right forearm. The Red Sox's consistent Yankee bash-ing—they had beaten the Yankees four times out of six—energized their victim-fans. When the game was done, fireworks boomed and lighted the night above the Charles River, which flows down to Boston harbor. The fireworks were supposed to flare on the next night, July 4, but when you thought of it (as a proper New Englander would think of it) what was more important, anyway, thumping the Bombers from the Bronx or honoring a hoary eighteenth-century declaration written by a redheaded cracker?

It rained on the Fourth. "We can use the breather," Martin said, but his mood was mixed. A group erroneously assigned to his suite at the Sheraton Boston Hotel had awakened him at 7:00 A.M. "That's what happens to you when you fall into third place," he said with a wan smile. He simply could not solve his pitching problems. Maurice Cowen, the team physician, was performing strenuous stretching procedures on Catfish Hunter, designed to loosen and break adhesions in the right shoulder that had been immobilizing the veteran. The stretches were agonizing. Before these unusual ministrations, Cowen used hypnosis to anesthetize his patient. Hunter would not be pitching for a while. Figueroa's pain persisted and the Yankees flew him to Los Angeles to consult orthopedist Frank Jobe. With small success, Gullett was trying to pitch through aches. Ken Holtzman and Rawly Eastwick had been traded. A total of five pitchers from the opening-day roster— about half of the projected staff—was variously injured or gone. Lyle stayed healthy; his affliction was a nasty attitude. Fowler, still hanging on, told Moss Klein, "I have never, never seen anything like this. Injuries happen but our injuries are defying all odds. Except for Ron Guidry we don't have a single good arm." Injuries do happen, of course, but this plague led Steinbrenner to wonder about the physical-conditioning programs in place under Martin and Fowler. The great pitching coach Johnny Sain preached, "An arm will rust out before it wears out." Put simply, regular workouts, including a good deal of supervised throwing between games, keep a staff healthy. Ragged, inconsistent programs do not. Stressed as he was, Martin had been coming to ballparks later and later, and looking so drawn many wondered about his health. He was not supervising conditioning programs, or even batting practice. Almost every Yankee loss started new rumors that he would be fired. Lou Piniella, a solid team player, told reporters, "The truth is there are players here who don't want to be here. More than one. The constant bickering between the guys upstairs and the dugout [Martin] has really hurt us." Steinbrenner had no comment on Piniella's remark but said his office was getting threatening phone calls. *Keep Billy manager, or else...* "Some very rough-sounding people," Steinbrenner said. "They may be Mafia. They say I better keep the Italian guy managing my club or I'll end up wishing that I had. These characters frighten the hell out of my secretaries. They don't want to wake up with a dead horse in their bed."

The Yankees split a pair in Texas and moved on to Milwaukee, where the Brewers swept them and beat Ron Guidry, 6 to 0. With a record of 13 and 1, Guidry remained superb, but he was no longer invincible. "It was an off night," Martin said. "He made bad pitches," Fowler said. Guidry said nothing; he felt upset and he declined to be interviewed.

As the season broke on July 10 for the All-Star game in San Diego, the Yankees were eleven-and-a-half games out of first place. "Do you still honestly believe this team can win the pennant?" a reporter asked Graig Nettles.

"Didn't the Mets have a slogan the year [1969] when they won?"

"Sure," the reporter said. "It was 'Do What Gil Hodges tells you or get your face mashed.'"

"Our slogan," Nettles said, "is, 'All for none and none for all.'" Then, more seriously, "Our only chance is a miracle."

Since Martin was the 1977 pennant winner, he managed the American League All-Stars. Rod Carew's successive triples put the team ahead, but then the National Leaguers rallied and in the eighth inning Martin sent in Gossage to protect a tie. Steve Garvey opened with a triple to right center. Gossage threw a wild pitch. The National League pounded out four runs and won the game, 7 to 3. "When I finished screwing up," Gossage commented some time afterward, "there was more blood and carnage around the mound than you see in a Freddy Krueger [*Nightmare on Elm Street*] movie."

Through the grinding pressure of a close pennant race, it is difficult to retain sanity and impossible to retain civility without the benediction of humor. Such diverse characters as Jackie Robinson, Stan Musial, and Casey Stengel were masters of wit under pressure. When Bobby Thomson's famous "shot heard 'round the world" won a seemingly lost pennant for the 1951 New York Giants, Ralph Branca of the Brooklyn Dodgers, who threw the critical pitch, went on a crying jag. Other Dodgers looked hollow-eyed, as though in shock. Amid the Giants' roaring jubilation, Allen Roth, the Dodger statistician, drily invoked a cliché. As Thomson and the Giants whooped and leaped, celebrating the most exciting pennant victory in the annals, Roth said, deadpan, "Can't win 'em all." For a few moments, anyway, that lightened Dodger gloom. The team survived and won the next two pennants.

Humor is good, but winning is better, and the Yankees had lost the knack. Going into the All-Star exhibition they had been beaten in five out of six. Coming out of it, the team idled in third place, behind Boston and Milwaukee, eleven-and-a-half games off the pace. In this circumstance a new character emerged, settling any and all questions about who was running the Yankees. This character, oddly enough the man who loved the theme from *Patton,* was *Herr* Field Marshal George von Steinbrenner. Brushing aside staff people, Colonel General Rosen and Lance Corporal Martin, the Marshal assumed personal command, called a meeting, and made a speech.

"Will you gather 'round here, please," Billy Martin said, standing at the far end of the main room in the Yankee clubhouse. He was trying to utter a preamble, but von Steinbrenner cut him off, saying twice, very loudly, "Can I have your attention?" The ball players gathered. The Marshal wore a blue blazer, freshly pressed gray slacks, and a button-down shirt with a striped tie. Getting ready for their pregame workouts, the ball players lounged in various states of undress, shirts unbuttoned, socks at half mast. A blazer and necktie looked as formal in that clubhouse as a tuxedo at brunch.

"We've been doing things your way," Steinbrenner began. "For the whole first half of the season, we've done things your way. It hasn't worked. From now on we're going to do things *my* way. We can still win this pennant. I'm not ready to lie down and die. Not by a long shot. I don't expect you men to lie down and die, either. I won't tolerate it. I'm making changes. I don't want anybody griping about the changes, either, running to Billy or complaining to the sportswriters. That will do you no good at all. You're among the best-paid athletes in the world and I'm the man who signs your checks. If you don't want to do things my way, then I'll accommodate you by sending you somewhere else. This is my team. I pay the bills. I'll do what I want. Right up top, I want one thing from every one of you: one-hundred-ten percent effort on the field."

Having demanded the arithmetically impossible, Steinbrenner announced "the new regular batting order":

MICKEY RIVERS, center field
GRAIG NETTLES, third base
THURMAN MUNSON, right field
CHRIS CHAMBLISS, first base
REGGIE JACKSON, designated hitter
GARY THOMASSON, left field
MIKE HEATH, catcher
FRED STANLEY, shortstop
DAMASO GARCIA, second base

Steinbrenner said, "From now on Cedric [Tallis, who bore the title of general manager] will be more prominent in the baseball part of the front office." Al Rosen would concentrate on "business affairs." By selecting the lineup himself, Marshal von Steinbrenner was going a long way toward managing the team and marginalizing Billy Martin. What would be next, phone calls to the dugout ordering bunts and pitching changes? By upgrading Tallis, he was demoting Rosen, the titular president of the Yankees. Steinbrenner did these things quasi publicly since some of the players surely would be talking to the media. After you share matters with twenty-five ball players, a manager, four coaches, and two trainers, the matters you shared cease to be secret. Finally Steinbrenner reminded the players that the Yankee dress code dictated that everybody wear a necktie on travel days and that was one more rule that, dammit, was sure as hell going to be enforced. In short, Steinbrenner would determine who played and who did not, who was traded and who remained, and, finally, how everybody dressed.

When I was a schoolboy, we were required to memorize words spoken by Julius Caesar in 49 B.C.E. when he crossed the river Rubicon, which divided Rome from Gaul, with five thousand legion infantry and three hundred cavalrymen. As a protection for the Roman Republic's civil rulers and senators, tradition forbade a general to ford the Rubicon toward Rome with an army. Caesar considered the stream only briefly before ordering his soldiers to cross. He then said, "*Alea iacta est.*" "The die is cast." Within five years the Roman Republic ceased to exist. On a significantly smaller scale— the democratic borough of the Bronx endures—Steinbrenner cast a fateful die with his extraordinary and unprecedented meeting. Afterwards the Yankee organization would not again be as it had been. No Yankee club owner before, not the baronial Jake Ruppert, the choleric Larry MacPhail, and certainly not mellow Mike Burke, had ever put on such a show of unbridled power.

Steinbrenner's new management style was put to the test that night when the Chicago White Sox played at the Stadium under their new manager, Larry Doby. The White Sox defeated Steinbrenner's Yankees and Steinbrenner's lineup, 6 to 1. Only a ninth-inning homer by the designated hitter averted a shutout.

Injuries were sidelining Buck Dent and Willie Randolph, so the Steinbrenner batting order was at best temporary. Munson's knees were hurting and Steinbrenner thought a switch to the outfield would keep him from breaking down. But putting Munson in right field meant that Reggie Jackson again became the designated hitter. "Everybody's coming to play right field except me," Jackson said to a gaggle of reporters. "I told them all I hit better and I function better when I'm playing right field." He stopped and shrugged. With his World Series heroics forgotten, or anyway discounted, by the man in charge, more than ever Jackson wanted to be traded.

Installing Mike Heath, a rookie of no great distinction, as regular catcher seemed questionable. A catcher has to help the pitching staff stay on course and he has to maintain a commanding position on the field. Uniquely among defensive players, the catcher has the game unfold in *front* of him. He has to call pitches, of course, and call where to throw bunts, and often determine which infielder takes a pop fly. In a pennant race ideally you go with an experienced catcher, as indeed the Red Sox were doing with Carlton Fisk. Gary Thomasson, the left fielder recently acquired from Oakland, was a journeyman. If Steinbrenner's lineup held, Thomasson would play regularly and some very good Yankees, Lou Piniella and Roy White, would not. Finally, Steinbrenner's treatment of Al Rosen was demeaning. Privately he complained that Rosen had let him down by not acquiring a first-class pitcher before the trading deadline. Further, Rod Carew's two triples in the All-Star game underscored Rosen's failure to bring the smooth-swinging veteran home to the Bronx. But Rosen did not have a free hand. Steinbrenner had to approve deals as they developed. In sum, this tumultuous meeting made little sense unless Steinbrenner thought that a bomb, any bomb, exploding in the Yankee clubhouse could only make matters better. No one is a more staunch capitalist than George Steinbrenner. Here he was trying his hand at nihilism.

The meeting, not losing to the White Sox, was the story. Moss Klein's piece in the Sunday *Newark Star-Ledger* ran under a black, boldface six-column headline: YANK REVAMP WILL BE MASSIVE. "By next February or sooner," Klein wrote, invoking a sports-page rarity, the future perfect tense, "several of the following changes, according to Yankee insiders, will have occurred:

"Billy Martin, citing health reasons, will resign as Yankee manager.

"Al Rosen will resign as Yankee president and return to the real world, the world where pitchers' sore arms and Steinbrenner's tantrums don't exist.

"Several prominent players including Thurman Munson, Sparky Lyle, Mickey Rivers, Ed Figueroa and possibly Reggie Jackson figure to be gone from the Yankee scene..."

This was one of many similar reports. All the newspapers grew lively with stories of disorder, even chaos. Security and confidence fled the Yankee scene. The team was moving into a collective anxiety attack. After the White Sox loss, Martin walked into the press room bar and, standing alone, ordered a double Scotch. He wore a black leather jacket; he looked dreadful and combative. As I mentioned earlier, there was a Gatling-gun sense to Martin when he was drinking hard. I approached cautiously, ordered a Scotch for myself, and asked how he was holding up. Martin's right hand wound tight around his old-fashioned glass. "Don't worry about me," he said, sounding as if he had been challenged. "I'm fine." Vertical creases lined his long face. His neck looked stringy. Bags bulged under both eyes. "Listen," he said, "there's some stories going around that I had to go to the hospital for my liver, there was some spot on my liver, and I was maybe dying. Have you heard those stories?"

"Something like that, Billy."

"It was last winter and I was in the hospital, all right, but it wasn't for my liver. I had the flu."

"What hospital?"

"A good one. St. Mary's out in Minneapolis." Martin had told me more than he intended. St. Mary's, which would later be movingly described by Ed Fitzgerald in his book, *That Place in Minnesota,* is not a hospital to which one travels a thousand miles for the treatment of flu. St. Mary's is renowned for its Alcohol Rehabilitation Center. But this brief conversation was winding down. To let me know that he'd had enough of my questions, Martin lifted his glass, sipped, glared, and said through clenched teeth, "Are you still dumb enough to be friends with that prick Dick Young?" I moved on wondering how it was that whiskey, which made Casey Stengel the most genial of companions, turned Billy Martin into a thug. Perhaps they drank different brands of Scotch.

The Yankees salvaged a game from the White Sox, but the strong Kansas City Royals came to the Stadium and swept three, dropping the Yankees into fourth place, behind Boston, Milwaukee, and Baltimore, and leaving them a full fourteen games out of first place on July 17. It seemed sensible for management to begin planning for the season of 1979 and for the players to make certain that their golf-club memberships were current. Losing ball players characteristically find comfort on the links. But then, in a superheated ten-day stretch, Reggie Jackson went jaw to jaw with Steinbrenner and, in emotional freefall, refused to follow a "swing away" sign from Martin. The Yankees suspended Jackson for five days. When he returned, Martin went into his own emotional freefall and savaged both Steinbrenner and Jackson in a short, clever, self-destructive rant. When *that* was done, and Martin's words hit the papers, Steinbrenner fired him. (Technically Martin resigned, but the resignation did not come until after the order to fire him had been issued.) Al Rosen, abruptly restored as a baseball man, convinced Steinbrenner to replace Martin with Bob Lemon, a low-key character who called everybody "Meat." Quite suddenly the long months of group encountering, the ravaging rages and counter-rages, the mouths that moved more briskly than the quickest bat, these things were done. This Yankee team was ready to play baseball. No other team on earth did that as well.

REGGIE JACKSON had been pressing for a meeting. "George," he said on the telephone one day in June, "how much has to happen before you get it through your head that I can't play for Billy Martin?"

"We'll get together soon," Steinbrenner said. But Steinbrenner was in no hurry to hold a session in which his greatest star would likely come out charging and demand, "Get rid of the manager or get rid of me." Such high-ego characters as Babe Ruth, Ty Cobb, and Ted Williams never demanded to be traded. One player who did, the late Fred "Dixie" Walker of the Brooklyn Dodgers, wrote to Branch Rickey that if the Dodgers intended to "keep the Negro, Jackie Robinson," Walker would be unwilling to play another season for Brooklyn. Rickey dealt him to Pittsburgh. (Years afterward, rising up from racism, Walker told me, "Writing that letter was the stupidest thing I've ever done. I'm truly sorry.") Reggie believed, without being able precisely to put his finger on it, that racism, subtle but persistent, went a long way toward explaining his problems with Martin, with some of his teammates, with some of the media, and even, on an almost subliminal level, with Field Marshal von Steinbrenner himself. Jackson and Steinbrenner finally did meet in Steinbrenner's office on the afternoon of Monday, July 17. Larry Keith reported in *Sports Illustrated*: "Steinbrenner listened to

▶
"If I played in New York, they'd name a candy bar after me." He did and they did in 1978.

◀
Stress etches the face of Billy Martin, who lost his managing job in '78.
Baseball Hall of Fame Library, Cooperstown, NY

Manager Bob Lemon, who brought as much calm to the '78 Yankees as that team would ever know. Curious note: The tonic water behind him is zero proof.

Corbis ▼

◄ Leap of Faith: Mickey Rivers, sometimes accused of not hustling, goes airborne in an amazing but futile try to glove a homer at Yankee Stadium in '78.
Corbis

The Pride of New England. Carl Yastrzemski, the Red Sox's great veteran, takes a full-bore swing for a home run in the 1978 playoff game.

▼ *Corbis*

◄

Bucky Dent, the handsome, quiet shortstop who was voted MVP for the 1978 World Series.
Baseball Hall of Fame Library, Cooperstown, NY

►

A road warrior: Don Zimmer, who managed the '78 Red Sox and ended the season in tears.
Baseball Hall of Fame Library, Cooperstown, NY

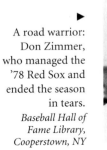

▲ Safe at home: Bucky Dent leaps onto the plate after hitting his famous home run in the 1978 playoff at Fenway Park. Yankee reception committee consists of Roy White (6) and Chris Chambliss.
Corbis

▲ After a Series victory, geniality invades the usually spiky
relationship between Jackson (*left*) and Munson.
Corbis

Why is this man smiling? Martin has just been
rehired to manage the Yankees in '79.
Corbis ▼

▲ The 1978 Boston Red Sox.
Baseball Hall of Fame Library, Cooperstown, NY

The 1978 New York Yankees.
▼ *Baseball Hall of Fame Library, Cooperstown, NY*

Jackson for an hour and a half. He is Jackson's friend, so he gave him sympathy. But he is also Jackson's boss, so he gave him the facts…Steinbrenner agreed with Martin that Jackson should be used primarily as a DH, a job Reggie considers the lot of the aged, inept or infirm." Jackson remembers the meeting differently.

Steinbrenner's Stadium office is a spacious expanse behind his private box. Here to this day he entertains political leaders, industrialists, media stars, and others whose role, like a Manet print, is decorative. "Hi," a model, wearing a filmy blouse and very brief shorts, greeted me once during a close and exciting ball game. "I'm (*breath, breath*) Cheryl." Indeed she was. But now the office would serve as a command post coming under attack. Jackson marched in armed with his agent, Matt Merola, but not much else by way of weaponry. He was first or second among the Yankees in most offensive categories—home runs, RBIs, runs scored, and stolen bases—and he had reduced his errors from a total of seven (at this point the year before) to three. But he had not been hitting *lately*; his batting average for July was .189, with just one home run. Big-league baseball is all about lately. You got a bunch of big hits some time back? Well, so did Rogers Hornsby. How come you didn't belt any big ones last night?

Seated with Steinbrenner as Jackson began to make his case were Al Rosen and Cedric Tallis. Jackson said first that he wanted to play the outfield. Steinbrenner said that Martin was right to use him as a designated hitter because he was "a lousy outfielder." Offended, Jackson said Steinbrenner had once promised to trade him if he asked to be traded. "You're not going anywhere," Steinbrenner said. Voices rose. When everybody needed a distracting presence, Cheryl (*breath, breath*) was nowhere to be found.

Jackson believed that he was being mishandled. Steinbrenner thought Jackson was trying to run the Yankees. There was something to be said for both points of view, but if a Yankee ball player intends to challenge Steinbrenner, he had better be hitting .360. Or .660. At that moment, Jackson's batting average was .260. As Jackson recalls it, Steinbrenner suddenly stood up and shouted, "You better get your head on straight, *boy*!" Rosen and Tallis looked startled. Jackson's jaw tightened. "I mean it. Get your head on straight, boy!"

Jackson shouted back, "Who the hell do you think you're talking to?"

"I'm talking to you."

"Don't talk to me like that again as long as you live." Jackson turned to Rosen. "Al, you're Jewish. How would you interpret that *boy*?" Rosen had been wondering how to restore peace. He had been calculating how best to jump between Steinbrenner and Jackson, should they start swinging. "Reggie," he said, "I'm not sure George meant that the way you're taking it. You both ought to cool down."

"Cool down, hell," Steinbrenner said. "Jackson, get the hell out of my office."

"I kind of like it here," Jackson said. "I'm staying." At that Steinbrenner marched briskly to the door and walked out of his own office at Yankee Stadium. A famous Columbia professor, Irwin Edman, once was so bored at a cocktail party that he, too, walked out. Only while flagging a taxi on Clermont Avenue did Edman realize that he was the host. He had walked out of his own party in his own house. Like Irwin Edman, Steinbrenner had his shining moments in the theater of the absurd.

Billy Martin knew about the meeting. When Jackson walked into the clubhouse glowering, Martin thought, "Something's gone haywire. I'll find out what." But he could not and then the game began, a recovering Catfish Hunter starting against Paul Splittorff, that strong, rangy lefthander. The Yankees knocked out Splittorff in the fourth inning but Hunter tired in the fifth and Martin replaced him with Sparky Lyle. After getting five men out, Lyle said, "That's

it. That's my two innings." He moved on to the clubhouse. Art
Fowler appeared and said, "You've got good stuff. Billy wants you to
go out and pitch the seventh." Lyle said, "I'm not a long-relief man.
You're not going to shove me into that job. Two innings are two
innings. Now the other guy can take over." He then showered,
dressed, and drove home to New Jersey. Later the Royals tied the
game with two ninth-inning runs off Goose (the Other Guy) Gossage. The next two innings were a season unto themselves.

Al Hrabosky, a lefthander with a great villainous mustache,
was pitching for the Royals. He bore the nickname of "the Mad
Hungarian" and he threw hard. Munson would lead off the tenth.
In the on-deck circle, Jackson said, "If you get on, I'm going to
bunt you over." Munson said, "Don't get ahead of yourself. I've
got to get on first." He did, bashing a single up the middle. Reggie
Jackson would hit 563 homers in his career, more than Mantle,
more than Williams, more than Musial. To suggest that he attempted to bunt five times in his twenty-one big-league seasons
would be a reasonable estimate. He had last executed a successful
sacrifice bunt six seasons earlier, in 1972. He had tried to bunt only
once before as a Yankee. That was in September 1977, against the
Red Sox. He failed, after which, Reggie being Reggie, he hit a game-
winning home run on a 3-and-2 count.

If you are almost never required to bunt under pressure, you
may not be much good at actually bunting under pressure, say laying one down against a hopping high fast ball thrown by a mean-
mustached, left-handed Mad Hungarian. But this was one of
Martin's remarkable tactical calls. No one expected Jackson to bunt
and George Brett, at third for the Royals, was playing deep. Reggie
could run. If he managed to tap a bunt toward third, or push the
baseball slowly between Hrabosky and Brett, he would probably
beat the throw to first. The Yankees would have two runners on
base with no one out. Just as remarkable as Martin's call was the
coincidence that Jackson came to the same conclusion, although

his reasoning was different. "I just hadn't been hitting," he says. "That's why a bunt seemed right to me. If I'd been on a tear, no way I'd bunt, no matter where George Brett was playing me."

Martin signaled bunt and Dick Howser, the third-base coach, relayed the sign to Jackson. Hrabosky threw a high inside fast ball, shoving Jackson away from the plate. Jackson took the pitch but first he squared around to bunt. Ball one, and so much for surprise. Brett moved in at third. Martin took off the bunt sign. Martin's reason for bunting, the likely base hit, was gone. Jackson's reason, his current slow hitting stretch, still obtained. Jackson tried to bunt a high fast ball and missed. Howser called Jackson up the third-base line and, in one of those tight, intense on-field conferences, said, "Billy wants you to hit away."

"Listen, Dick, nothing against you, but I'm bunting."

"I hope you know what you're doing," Howser said.

Martin could have called time and joined them. He *should* have called time and joined them. Clearly something was amiss. Jackson had just tried to bunt when the sign ordered him to swing away. But Martin did not call time. In his erupting anger, he lost his perspective and he lost control over the situation.

A fouled bunt with two strikes becomes not merely a foul ball but a strikeout, a rule installed to prevent skilled batters from tapping foul bunts interminably while waiting for a benign pitch. Rare exceptional bunters, Mickey Mantle and Jackie Robinson, sometimes bunted and got a base hit with two strikes. On the record, Jackson was not an exceptional bunter. He tried to bunt a third time and popped the ball into foul territory. Strike three. In the dugout Martin turned to coach Elston Howard and said, "Okay, tell him that's his fucking hit for the day." Howard seemed not to hear. Jackson returned to the bench and took a seat at the far end, distant from Martin. He removed his eyeglasses and laid them carefully, almost delicately, on the bench. If Martin was going to charge, Jackson was ready.

When the inning ended, Martin told Gene Michael, who came trotting in from the first-base coaching box, "Tell Jackson to get the hell out of the dugout and go into the clubhouse." Michael said, "Billy wants you to go inside and take a shower."

"If Billy wants me to go inside," Jackson said, "let him come over and tell me himself." Martin's jaw was firm. His fists were clenched, but he never moved toward Jackson. At that moment, Jackson later told one of his biographers, Mike Lupica, the New York columnist, "I wanted to fight somebody." He didn't mention Martin. He didn't mention Steinbrenner. (Or Lupica didn't report it if he did.) At that moment he just wanted to fight "somebody." Also at that moment, Sparky Lyle, who had ignored Martin just as pointedly as had Jackson, was sitting in front of a television set at home in Demarest, watching the ball game from a sofa and drinking beer. Presently reporters with the *Amsterdam News,* New York's most prominent black newspaper, would wonder why such fierce wrath was directed at Reggie Jackson for defying Martin while a white man who did the same thing was allowed to continue on his way without so much as a harsh look.

Gossage opened the eleventh with a walk to Hal McRae, a tough right-handed hitter, and Whitey Herzog sent U. L. Washington to pinch-run. (Washington had winged heels, but no first name.) John Wathan bunted U. L. to second. Amos Otis hit a long fly to right field. Munson, a sore-legged catcher playing out of position, chugged after the fly, got under it, and dropped the ball. An error for the catcher in the outfield. Washington had tagged up to advance so he could not score, but the Royals now had runners at first and third. Gossage deliberately walked Darrell Porter, got a force at home preserving the tie, and then on a close call walked left fielder Willie Wilson, sending in the tie-breaking run. Wilson was having a docile year, he would bat .217, and Gossage thought the pitch that walked him was a strike. He spun and said to Durwood Merrill, the second-base umpire, "Bad call." Merrill, who should have turned away, said, "It was a ball." Gossage said two words and Merrill ejected him. In essence, Gossage was bounced for complaining to the second-base umpire about a pitch call at home plate. That sort of non sequitur does not happen every evening, or every season. A rookie named Bob Kammeyer replaced Gossage, threw two base hits, and the Royals led, 9 to 5. The Yankees came back with two runs but the game ended when Cliff Johnson flied out. What was Johnson doing in the game? With the next batter representing the tying run, Martin had sent him up to pinch hit for Reggie Jackson, the best clutch hitter on the planet.

Having offered up what may well be the most poorly managed game in Yankee annals, Martin retreated into his windowless office among the catacombs under the Stadium and indulged himself in a tantrum. Yelling at a forte level he threw a clock radio, a Coke bottle, and a few plaques against a wall. The noise carried into the dressing room where reporters were milling about with players. Calming, Martin called Rosen's office and demanded that Jackson be suspended for the balance of the season. "I'm as angry as I've ever been in my life," said the Yankees' resident angry man. Rosen put through a conference call to Steinbrenner in Florida. Alternately screaming and pleading, Martin talked his bosses into suspending Jackson for five days (which worked out to a suspension of four games, as the Yankees would be traveling the next day). When the suspension was announced, a few sportswriters calculated that it would cost Jackson $9,273 in lost salary. Martin said that was great because he intended to donate that money to a fund for indigent old ball players. Laudable, to be sure, except proceeds from the fine would go not to Martin, but to the New York Yankees, Inc., and in the end there wouldn't be any proceeds, anyway. The Yankees could not deduct the fine from Jackson's salary because he had been paid his entire 1978 stipend, $332,000, in advance. Without taking reporters into his confidence, Steinbrenner told Jackson that if he kept quiet, the Yankees would make no effort actually to collect. That bought Jackson's silence. The sum, $9,273, survives as the biggest nonfine in baseball history.

Dick Young, on top of the suspension story, caught up with Jackson, who was walking by himself into the players' parking lot. "How do you feel?" Young said. "Dick, I'm going home. In the morning I'm getting on the first thing smokin' and headin' west." And so Jackson did, dodging a regiment of New York media people camped outside his Fifth Avenue apartment by walking out the back way through a passage ordinarily used by pizza deliverymen and daytime nannies going back to their apartments. At San Francisco International Airport, an American Airlines executive directed the pilot to pause on an access ramp leading from the runway. Reggie alighted there, this time dodging a platoon of media that was deployed in the arrival terminal. A friend drove him to the apartment of an attractive girl in Oakland whom he had been dating. He settled in with her to relax, regroup, and to enjoy his suspension in readily imaginable ways. There was more to life, it seemed, than Billy Martin.

After word of Sparky Lyle's unpunished walkout leaked, the Yankees cooked up a story that Lyle had suffered twinges in his pitching elbow. Few believed that; fewer cared. The story, now reaching its climax—the only Yankee story—was the Reggie and Billy show, with Steinbrenner banging out his bass-drum obbligato. On the chartered jet, when the team flew to Minneapolis for a two-game series, Martin told Jack Lang, a veteran reporter then with the *Daily News,* that he'd have a message waiting when Jackson returned. "If that guy ever disobeys me or ever disregards my signs again," Martin said, "and I want you to print this, I'm going to fine him and suspend him, and he won't ever play for me again." This was a notably parlous example of Dick Young's observation: "To Billy Martin, Billy is the boss, all the time, of *everything.*" The fact is that fines and suspensions may be proposed by a manager but they are decided by the front office. Who determined which athletes would or would not play for the Yankees? Not Martin, as he seemed to assume, nor even Al Rosen. The final responsibility for selecting the Yankee roster twenty-five years ago rested with the Managing Partner, the man who signed the checks, the boss, the field marshal, the old Williams College English major, George M. Steinbrenner III. (Today that responsibility is shared with an imposing group, a sort of general staff that Steinbrenner describes as "my baseball people.")

To a journalist, a tranquil period makes for rotten news days. Torment—the charge of the Light Brigade, Watergate, the Intifada, the 1978 Yankees—is a bonanza. Readers rush to sort out the details in newspapers, and reporters, who enjoy attention as much as anyone else, swell up a bit with a sense of their own importance. The phenomenon runs back hundreds of years. During the eighteenth century, when the three ruling "estates" were believed to be the nobility, the clergy, and the military, Edmund Burke pointed toward the Reporters' Gallery during a debate in the House of Commons. "Yonder [sits] the Fourth Estate," Burke said, "more important far than them all."

Henry Hecht, a short, bespectacled Fourth Estater with the *New York Post*, all but took over the ownership of the Yankees with a column that appeared on July 19. Even the *Post*'s headline was uncompromising:

REGGIE SHOULD
JUST STAY AWAY

Under that *diktat* Hecht wrote:

Enough. Stay home, Reggie. If the Yankees pay you for not playing, great. If they don't, you can afford it. Stay home...
Who needs it? Let's face it, you don't want to play for Billy. You hate him. If Billy gets you fired and you stay, you'll earn

the undying enmity of almost every Yankee, even the ones who can't stand Billy.

You think the situation is intolerable now? Do you know the hell you would have to endure if you were a Yankee next year and and Billy wasn't?

You don't want to be just a DH. But Thurman Munson has already shown in just a few games that he will be a better outfielder than you by next spring at the latest. The Yankee season is lost, just a matter of playing out the string... The atmosphere is so heavy, so laden with hate... The Yankees were lucky to survive without trying to murder the guy in the next locker... Get away, Reggie... Get out of New York... You can't win.

The *Post* is an afternoon paper and Hecht's story stirred up uncounted bubbles in the digestive juices of thousands who sat consuming mealy grilled-cheese sandwiches at hot, crowded New York City lunch counters. I don't doubt Hecht's sincerity or passion, but his story proceeds from a number of mistakes. Munson was not an acceptable major-league outfielder, nor would he become one. In 1979 he caught, played three games at first base and none in right. By then the Yankees had learned to leave outfielding to the outfielders. Jackson played 125 games in right during 1979 and finished with a higher fielding percentage than either Mickey Rivers or Lou Piniella. Second, the Yankees' 1978 season was far from lost in mid-July. But the season would have been lost if Jackson left New York. Besides, before Hecht's article appeared, Jackson had asked to leave New York and been turned down. Finally, in the heat of the moment, Hecht neglected to ask critical questions that would have given his piece less rant and more depth. Why wasn't Billy Martin being fined? Martin lost control of his team by letting Lyle walk out of a game. A pitching staff cannot function as a democracy. On a successful team pitchers work as the managers order them to work. And why wasn't Sparky Lyle suspended for going home? You can't have big-league players walking out in the middle of a game. Then, with Lyle on his couch and the game on the line in the eleventh inning, Martin refused to let Jackson hit because of their dispute in the tenth. Jackson's record argued that adrenal elements such as anger and pressure brought out his slugging best. By benching Jackson for Cliff Johnson, by dissolving in his own bile, Martin missed his last chance to win the game. Other managers have been fired for less. Finally, since we are handing out fines, I'd levy a stiff one on my friend George Steinbrenner for addressing Reggie Jackson as "boy." In calm moments Steinbrenner detests racism. One wishes, and I suspect George still wishes, that his better angels had prevailed. Did his impertinent use of "boy" push Jackson into defying Martin? It certainly may have been a factor. In the middle of the summer of 1978 then, the Yankee scene, the players, the management, the press, did not make a pretty picture. Taking words from another context: "Night owls shriek, where mounting larks should sing."

WITHOUT JACKSON, the Yankees swept the Twins on shutouts by Figueroa and Guidry, whose record advanced to 14 and 1. They were still more than a dozen games behind the Red Sox, still in fourth place. They moved on to Chicago and beat up on the White Sox of Bill Veeck and Larry Doby, sweeping a three-game series. Now, on July 23, they were third, ten games behind Boston and five behind Bud Selig's Brewers. Looking through the Brewers, the Red Sox and their fans began to squirm. The Colossus of the Bronx was gathering strength as the Red Sox were losing it. Rick Burleson, the Boston shortstop, sprained an ankle sliding and couldn't play. Fred Lynn in center could play, but both his ankles were sore. Carl Yastrzemski sprained a wrist and developed backaches, common enough in ball players approaching a thirty-ninth birthday. Yastrzemski's mighty power stroke went on a leave of absence. Butch Hobson at third base suffered from bone chips float-ing inside his right elbow. It hurt every time he threw hard. Key pitchers Mike Torrez and Dennis Eckersley simmered because Don Zimmer had pulled lefty Bill Lee out of the starting rotation and replaced him with a rookie named Bobby Sprowl. Zimmer said it was because Lee's good stuff had disappeared. There was no need to remind New England fans, or the talk-show commentators who popped up around Boston like intensely fertilized dande-lions, that the Red Sox had not won a World Series since Woodrow Wilson left the White House, and that their principal tormentor across all those decades was the Colossus of the Bronx. Some tried to remind Zimmer that Bill Lee was a tough and seasoned com-petitor, even if he was a free-spirited environmentalist. Only two lefthanders in history possessed better lifetime records against the Yankees than Bill Lee. One was a small, stylish craftsman named Dickie Kerr. The other, 17-and-5 against the Yankees before he joined them, was a hard-bitten, hard-throwing character named Ruth. But before Zimmer stopped simmering, Lee had missed three starting assignments. Sprowl worked three of them, won none and lost two. Petulant managing was not the monopoly of Billy Martin.

As the world champion Yankees finally began winning, and winning without Reggie Jackson, Martin's mood brightened like a rainbow. He was showing everybody what a Billy Martin team could do when that broad-backed number 44 was out of the pic-ture. While his team was rolling over the White Sox, he took to vis-iting the Bards' Room at Comiskey Park, that wood-paneled retreat for sportswriters and baseball officials which I'd turned coed for Melissa Ludtke a few seasons back. The place of honor there was at the president's table, where Bill Veeck filled the air with anecdote and opinion on a variety of topics, including baseball, without ever in my presence managing to be dull. "People applaud

Roosevelt for his New Deal," he was saying one night, "but what is the New Deal anyway, but the old Socialist Party platform? Roosevelt stole his ideas from Norman Thomas and applied a little Harvard gloss. That made Roosevelt president of the United States. Norman Thomas [a frequent Socialist presidential candidate] had to go and become a university professor."

Martin stumbled into Veeck's polymathic setting one night and Veeck immediately dropped Roosevelt for some sophisticated baseball trouble-making. Veeck told me that he disliked Steinbrenner because, "I don't care for people who get a head start on everybody else by using their daddy's money. I didn't do that and neither did you." When, speaking of trouble-making, I repeated the remark to Steinbrenner, George came back with a strong response: "I started with some money from my father, sure, but on my own I've made one helluva lot more." I don't believe Veeck would have been all that annoyed by Steinbrenner's inheritance if the Yankees had not been winning pennants. But they *had* been winning pennants and now Veeck softened up Martin with some White Sox Scotch and then flipped him with a hook that would have done Jack Dempsey proud.

"Do you know you could have been working for me, Billy?"

"What do you mean?"

"Your boss is not exactly your number-one fan, Billy. He wanted me to take you off his hands."

"I heard some of that shit," Martin said.

"Foul language," Veeck said, "displays primarily the inadequacy of the speaker's vocabulary." Martin's good mood was wavering now. "Back when Bob Lemon was managing here," Veeck said, "Steinbrenner had [American League President] Lee MacPhail telephone to see if I'd agree to a swap. I'd send Lemon east to manage the Yankees. He's very close with Al Rosen, you know. George wanted to send you here."

"Exactly what happened?" Martin said. "Tell me exactly what the *fuck* happened?"

Veeck winced at the obscenity. "I do like you as a manager, Billy, but I'm afraid I like Bob Lemon as manager a bit more. I told MacPhail that I'd make the deal, but not even up. If I was going to give up Bob Lemon, the Yankees would have to give me you *plus a first-line player.*" Veeck sipped his beer and let silence play its role. Martin knew, everyone knew, that Veeck had since dismissed Lemon. His marvelously Machiavellian comments made powerful points to Martin. The Yankees don't want you; in fact, they're frantic to get rid of you. I wouldn't take you myself on a one-on-one swap even up for a manager I had to fire. Presently and predictably Martin went spinning into the night.

The last act began at O'Hare Airport late on the afternoon of July 23. Jackson rejoined the team that day, not certain that he wanted to rejoin the team. He showed up late and missed the bus to the ballpark. Behind another strong performance by Ed Figueroa, the Yankees defeated the White Sox, 3 to 1, with Jackson, out $7.20 in cab fare, sitting on the bench. Martin expected Jackson to apologize for having failed to hit away, for disobeying an order. Jackson told me he had considered apologizing "to try and keep the peace"—make peace, actually—but concluded that it would accomplish very little. "No matter what I did, it was only a matter of time before Martin found a way to come down on me again." When a reporter asked if his persistent bunting had been an act of defiance, Jackson said, "No. I wasn't defying anybody. I was just playing to win like I always do."

While the Yankees were awaiting their flight to Kansas City, Martin repaired to an airport bar and leaving it encountered Murray Chass of the *New York Times*. Chass asked about the "situation with Reggie," and Martin said in anger, "He still hasn't apologized to me. He has to shut up. We don't need none of his shit. We don't need him coming in and making all of his comments." At about this point Henry Hecht of the *Post* joined them. Martin, still furious that Steinbrenner had tried to trade him, suddenly grouped Steinbrenner and Jackson and volunteered a comment that should have landed him in Bartlett's *Familiar Quotations,* directly between Martin, Abe (1868–1930) and Martin, Edward Sandford (1856–1939).

"The two of them deserve each other," said Martin, Alfred Manuel (1928–1989). "One's a born liar. The other's convicted." Despite Chass's erratic prose he has a good sense of a story. "Can I use that?" he said. "It's on the record," Martin said. He turned toward the boarding gate. Chass walked to a telephone and alerted his newspaper. After Chass checked into the Crown Center Hotel in Kansas City, he telephoned Steinbrenner, who was in Tampa.

Steinbrenner asked if Martin had been drinking and demanded several times, "Did he really say that?" An hour later came a call from Henry Hecht. Steinbrenner seemed more startled than angry, but he was considering his options. Toward midnight he telephoned Rosen in Manhattan, waking him. Rosen was to fly to Kansas City the next morning and fire Martin. At Rosen's direction, Cedric Tallis went to Martin's suite at the Crown Center and asked about the fatal quote. Penitent now and frightened, Martin denied that he had said anything about liars. Rosen: "I found it hard to believe that two reporters had made up the same quote. I took our publicity man Mickey Morabito with me and, nothing against Morabito, I've made happier flights in my time than that one to Kansas City. On top of everything else, the airline lost my suitcase."

After Rosen reached the Crown Center, he telephoned Martin's suite. Martin hung up on him. Rosen sent Morabito to bring Martin to his suite. Morabito encountered Martin walking toward an elevator, carrying a statement scribbled across a half-dozen pages on a tiny message pad. It was the announcement of his resignation. "Let me take this back to my room and write it out for you on a single sheet of paper," Morabito said. "That will be easier for you to read to the writers." Martin acceded. Morabito told Rosen that Martin was quitting. Rosen presented himself at Martin's suite. Martin began to cry. He hugged Rosen. "Tell George I didn't say those things. Tell him I didn't, Al." Keeping his lapels dry, Rosen stepped back. He would not have to fire Martin after all. "If there's anything I can do for you," he said, "give me a call."

Accompanied by Phil Rizzuto, Martin took the elevator to a terrace overlooking the lobby. A local television station had set up its camera there. The New York sportswriters hurried up the escalators. Martin wore dark glasses. More than one reporter thought he was watching a man attending his own funeral. Rizzuto later said, "I was afraid Billy was going to have a heart attack."

Martin began by saying, "There will be no questions and answers with anyone after the statement is made. That means now and forever, because I am a Yankee and Yankees do not talk or throw rocks." He continued:

I don't want to hurt this team's chances . . . with undue publicity. The team has a shot at the pennant and I hope they win it. I owe it to my health and my mental well-being to resign. At this time I'm also sorry about these things that were written about George Steinbrenner. He does not deserve them nor did I say them. I've had my differences with George, but we've been able to resolve them.

Martin thanked Yankee management, the press, his coaches, his players, and when he started to thank "the Yankees' great fans," he broke down and sobbed. The sportswriters studied their shoes. It was a moment of pathos, if not tragedy, and unnerving. "The frightening thing," the late Ed Linn told me, "is that Martin honestly believed every word he said."

▼

CHAPTER THIRTEEN

RESURRECTION

THE MESSIAH ARRIVED quietly in Kansas City a half inch or so behind his sprawling, luminous nose, a moveable monument to the happy hours (and happy months) that brightened the life of Robert Granville Lemon. "After my team wins, I drink to celebrate," Bob Lemon liked to say. "After my team loses, I drink to cheer up." That was not an unusual pattern in the old days of big-league baseball; an all-time all-star team, composed entirely of hard drinkers, would be just about impossible to beat, except in the morning. But then Lemon added his own particular wry chaser. "Aside from that," he would say, "to break up the boredom, I drink after rain-outs." He was a husky, convivial six footer who affected a gruff and bumbling manner, which made many underestimate him. Bob Lemon didn't mind. He knew how good he was.

After traveling across the country in railroad day coaches, sitting up for three or four nights, he began playing what he called "pro ball" as a seventeen-year-old with Oswego (NY) in the Class C Canadian-American League. That was in 1938. He was a rangy California kid who threw right-handed, hit left-handed with power, and was comfortable anywhere a manager put him. Lemon could play outfield, shortstop, or third base. Most of his zipping throws from third base sank—he was gifted with a natural sinker—and reversing the path of Babe Ruth he moved gradually from position player to the mound. After opening the season as the Indians' starting centerfielder, he became a full-time pitcher on Bill Veeck's exciting Cleveland team during 1946. Two seasons later he won twenty games and added two more victories in the World Series when the Indians defeated the Boston Braves, four games to two. Lemon won twenty or more another six times, but during most of his run the Indians chased the Yankees without success. Then in 1954, the American League pennant race reached a memorable climax at the old Cleveland Municipal Stadium on Sunday, September 12, before the largest crowd to see a major-league game up to that time: 84,587 paying customers. The Yankees opened with their left-handed ace, Whitey Ford. A young, healthy Mickey Mantle played center field. The third (and bipolar) musketeer, Billy Martin, was absent. Selective Service, a hangover from the Korean war, persisted after Eisenhower's armistice and Martin had been drafted into the peacetime army the previous April. With the diplomacy that was his hallmark, Martin complained loudly about "having to go into the fucking Army when there's no fucking war." It was a fair point—and better left unsaid.

Sports Illustrated assigned me to cover the doubleheader, which curiously or not so curiously wheeled about men who would be critical to the Yankee season of 1978. I checked in first at the hotel coffee shop, where the Yankees were having breakfast. Mantle, tense, hung over, or both, sat silent. Jerry Coleman, the fine second baseman, said, "You come to bury us?"

"Win and I get to praise you."

"So you've gone to work for some magazine," Casey Stengel said. "Well, you gotta watch them magazine people. They'll make yer stuff look funny, if you let 'em, and I defy anyone to say this team ain't worth a quarter. I don't want to blow up another club, because the race is still going on you can be sure, but Cleveland has played tree-mendous and we been trying to catch 'em. So how can you say our team ain't worth a quarter?"

Around the batting cage the Indians seemed nonchalant. "This is not a rough day," said their second baseman, handsome, high-cheekboned Bobby Avila of Veracruz, Mexico. "All year we play. Now we play. Good team. We play okay."

"When you write your story," said Al Rosen, the Indians' third baseman and best clutch hitter, "can you forget that choke-up stuff? I don't know if you can, but, look, I'm playing out here every day. I know what's going on. Bobby here is gonna lead the league in hitting [at .341]. I'm gonna knock in a hundred RBIs again. We don't beat the Yankees because they choke and we don't lose to the Yankees because we choke. Don't overcomplicate it. The team that wins is simply the better team that day."

Neither club could do much hitting against the starters. Ford went six innings, then told Stengel that his shoulder was tightening. With the teams tied at 1, Stengel sent Superchief Allie Reynolds to relieve in the seventh. Rosen came up with one out and two men on and Reynolds welcomed him with a blazing fast ball at the nose. Rosen ducked and glared. Reynolds glared back. ("The Chief's glare scared *me*," Whitey Ford, "and we were on the same team.") Reynolds now threw a hard slider, low and away. This is textbook pitching, intimidate with a brush back, then work the outside corner. Rosen was not intimidated. He leaned in and lined the slider into the right centerfield gap. Two Indians scored and that was more than Bob Lemon needed. He dominated the Yankees, striking out Mantle three times, and the Indians won the game, 4 to 1. That pretty much settled the pennant race and during the between-games intermission I made my way through the crowded grandstands to the Indians' dressing room. It was a slow process, navigating among whooping Ohio celebrants. By the time I reached the clubhouse, most of the Indians had returned to the field for game two. Lemon sat alone in front of his locker, drinking beer from a paper cup and smiling at the ceiling. "Can you tell me how this feels?" I said. Bob Lemon met my eyes. "Grand," he said. "It feels like a wedding day." Later, in a show of tin-eared arrogance, the managing editor deleted Lemon's comment. "It doesn't sound *appropriate*," he told me. "It even sounds *effeminate*." Lemon went on to start two games in the World Series (which he lost). I began looking for another job.

It was in that World Series of 1954 where Lemon, who had known October triumph, would meet disaster, like Kipling's *beau ideal*. He was on the wrong end of Willie Mays's famous catch in game one and lost on a short home run in the tenth. Then, pitching on three days' rest, he was hit hard in game four. Mays and his team swept the series in the New York Giants' final tune of glory. Lemon finished that Series not only with two losses but with the dreadful earned run average of 6.75. A bad World Series has finished more than one strong pitcher. Lemon recovered and a year later led the American League in victories. Before his playing career ended in 1958 when he was thirty-eight, he had been named to seven consecutive All-Star games. Baseball was Lemon's only trade and next he coached and scouted and managed minor-league teams from Honolulu to Richmond, drinking cheerfully and waiting patiently for the big break. He had a good stint managing at Kansas City and did well with the White Sox, but when he began packing at his home in Long Beach to take over the most contentious of all Yankee teams, Lemon had not participated in a World Series for almost a quarter century. "I knew this finally was my big break," he told me, "provided I wasn't the one that got broken."

Dick Howser, who had been coaching third, managed the Yankees in Kansas City on the night of July 24. The team was winning, 2 to 0, in the seventh inning when Steve Braun of the Royals hit a line drive to right field. Thurman Munson, out of position, froze, ran in, gloved the ball, and dropped it. Then, continuing to play the outfield like a catcher, he stepped on the baseball and kicked it. Two runs scored. Howser brought in Lyle. The Royals won, 5 to 2, leaving the Yankees ten-and-a-half games behind the Red Sox.

The next day Lemon arrived and gathered this taut and be-fuddled team in the visiting clubhouse at the Harry S Truman Sports Complex on Royal Way, hard by the western border of Missouri. Yankee Stadium, like first place, was far away. Lemon put on a Yankee uniform for the first time in his life. Martin had worn number 1. Lemon chose 21. "I wanted to make it clear to everyone," he said, "that I had reached the legal drinking age." Now in the clubhouse he was stone sober and calm. "If I read the papers right," he said, "you fellers won the World Series last year." He rubbed the back of his hand across his mouth. "Do I have that straight?" A few Yankees exchanged looks. Others grinned. Someone said, "Yeah, Skip. We won the World Series last year."

The new manager's strong-jawed face tightened. He looked as though he were about to deliver a philippic. "Well, I guess you know how to play baseball," Robert Granville Lemon said. "I'll try to stay out of your way."

IN WHAT WAS THE most dramatic comeback up to this time, the New York Giants of 1951 came from thirteen-and-a-half games behind the Brooklyn Dodgers on August 11 and caught them in the last few days of the season. The Giants, peopled with Willie Mays, Sal Maglie, and Bobby Thomson, blazed down the stretch, winning sixteen in a row and going 37-and-7, a winning percentage of .841, made all the more remarkable because it was achieved under what Leo Durocher called "a million tons of pressure." That surge forced a three-game playoff, fought brilliantly in now de-molished, well-remembered ballparks, Ebbets Field and the Polo Grounds. The Giants won the deciding game on Thomson's famous ninth-inning home run, called, as I've noted, in a clever lift from Emerson, "the shot heard 'round the world." Then they lost a decidedly anticlimactic World Series to the Yankees. Now under Bob Lemon twenty-seven seasons later, a Yankee squad was to charge, not quite as relentlessly as Durocher's '51 Giants, but close.

There was no lack of hatred around the Yankees of '78. Some was directed at Steinbrenner, some at Martin, some at Jackson, and some at the sportswriters covering the club. An insider close to the team, who does not wanted to be quoted by name, says, "Most of the beat writers were Jews: Henry Hecht, Murray Chass, Moss Klein, and Steve Jacobson [of *Newsday*]. Don't think that was lost on the ball players. As some of them saw it, they were getting slammed in the papers by a gang of New York Jews." Characteristically for ball players who were not playing as well as they should, they were disinclined to blame themselves.

When Bob Lemon took over ninety-six games into what appeared to be a lost season—only sixty-six games remained—he faced Herculean labors. He had to settle down a pitching staff on which critical people were saying things like, "If there is a God, please have Him get me traded." He had to deal with a wounded Reggie Jackson and a disgruntled Thurman Munson. He had to let Steinbrenner know, with tact but force, that he, Bob Lemon, and nobody else would set the lineups and the batting order. In short, he had to become the manager and under him the Yankees had to become a team. You get a sense of how that plays out when it works in a passage from Mark Harris' novel *Bang the Drum Slowly*:

> Nothing in the world could stop us now. Winning makes winning like money makes money, and we had power and pitching and speed, so much of it that if anybody done anything wrong nobody ever noticed. There was too much we were doing right. It was a club, like it should have been all year, but never was but all of a sudden become...

It was important that Lemon had Al Rosen's unquestioning support, notably in keeping Steinbrenner at some distance, but

Lemon, was, as they say in the infantry, point man. He told Rich Gossage, "I know how good you are and I'm just damn glad to have you. You're my closer. Don't start sweating bullets if you give up a couple hits. I gave up more than twenty-five hundred myself." Gossage immediately contrasted these words with Martin's demand back in March that he hit Billy Sample in the head. He smiled and for the first time all season began really to enjoy being a ball player. Lemon told Reggie Jackson, "What I got to say is simple. You hit clean-up every day. Sometimes you'll play right, sometimes you'll DH, but every day you're batting fourth. Meat, do your thing. Just bash a bunch over the wall." Hearing these words made Jackson feel he was being let out of prison. "I could hear the gates clanging shut behind me," he told Mike Lupica of the *Daily News*.

When Lemon called Thurman Munson into his clubhouse office, he said he needed advice. "You know, Meat," Lemon began, "I operate a little different from Billy. I don't like to yell and you won't see me shouting at the umpires all the time, like Billy did. You think that's gonna be a problem?"

"Nah. Billy antagonized umpires and they'd take away the close calls. Catching like I did mostly, I can tell you that they did. *Leave the umpires be* is a good idea, if you can do it."

"Well, now you're catching all the time, unless you're hurting too much. Just let me know if your knees are giving you trouble. You're great at handling pitchers and, you're the captain, so give me some help, will ya? Tell the guys that I want to win just as much as Billy did, but I go about things in a different way. Quieter."

"Sure, Skip," said the captain, all at once a trusted lieutenant.

Lemon offered reassuring comments to Piniella, Nettles, Dent, and Figueroa. There wasn't much he needed to tell Guidry or Hunter. He let the mutinous Sparky Lyle simmer for a bit, then walked past his locker and said, "All right, red ass. I want you in my office. Now!" ("Red ass," or "R. A.," is major-league baseball's venerable term for an angry man. The phrase suggests more than needs to be explained in detail this side of a text on psychosomatic medicine.) Lyle vented complaints for fifteen minutes. He'd won the Cy Young as a closer, then Steinbrenner took his job away and gave it to Gossage. He wasn't getting paid enough. Under Martin he'd be told to warm up, then told to sit down. He wanted to warm up only when it was pretty damn sure he was going into the game. Lemon listened. He could neither bring back 1977 nor set salaries. Besides, he had concluded that right now Gossage was a better closer than Lyle. Lemon was not afraid of confrontation. When Loopin' Lou Piniella indulged his renowned temper by mindlessly throwing his batting helmet close to Lemon's head, the manager called him "a fucking asshole." When Mickey Rivers was late getting to the on-deck circle, Lemon said, "If you don't want to play, that's fine because plenty of guys on the bench are ready. If you're not where you're supposed to be again, Meat, I'll fucking sit you." But in the case of Lyle, Lemon chose diplomacy, mostly in the hope that the pitcher's work would improve. He said he knew he had two fellers who could close and didn't it make sense to work percentages and bring in Gossage against right-hand hitters and Lyle against the left-handers. Lyle said he could go along with that, "but you know damn well you don't have to do it that way. I can get right-hand hitters out. You don't win a Cy Young if you can't." Lemon ignored the comment and said he hoped Lyle would stay with the Yankees for as long as he managed the team. Lyle said that made him feel good, but his Yankee days were dwindling down to a contentious few. With Lyle's constant agitating and complaining Lyle had become, to use another traditional baseball term, a cancer in the clubhouse.

Repairing baseball's most intense, expensive, and badly damaged team was not accomplished overnight. Guidry came up in the rotation for the first game Lemon managed and threw a six-hitter. The Yankees defeated the Royals, 4 to 0. But as the beer drinkers said in countless New York sports bars, "Hey, when

Guidry's goin', my granmudda could manage the team." Back in the Stadium, the Yankees came from behind and beat Cleveland, 3 to 1, on Lou Piniella's clutch homer in the ninth. Gabe Paul, now trying to rebuild the wreck in northern Ohio, arrived in his old Bronx haunt with his new team and said at an impromptu news conference that he had become an "avid newspaper reader." Sitting at a large table in the Stadium press room, Paul said, "Every morning when I get to my office I sit back, put my feet on the desk and start reading a bunch of sports sections. Keeping track of the Yankees from a distance is a very exciting hobby. I relax and enjoy all the situations that keep happening. When I was in the middle, they weren't enjoyable." Paul seemed so genial that somebody asked a loaded question. "When you were running things here, you let [pitcher Mike] Torrez go from the Yankees to the Red Sox [in December 1977]. Then after you got to Cleveland you traded [pitcher Dennis] Eckersley to the Sox [in March 1978]."

"That is so." Paul still was smiling.

"Now Torrez and Eckersley are Boston's best pitchers and people are saying that you sent them there to get even with Steinbrenner for screaming at you and to make sure the Yankees didn't win another pennant."

The smile vanished. "Who is it who is saying that?"

"Uh, people."

"Well, I'm sure George isn't the people you mean." This was Gabe Paul's arcane way of telling the reporters, "So *that's* what Steinbrenner has been saying about me." As always, Paul's public comment was measured. "Torrez simply wanted too much money. Aside from the World Series victories he was no better than a fourteen-and-twelve pitcher last year and I didn't think the Yankees would be needing him. As for Eckersley, I made that deal because it brought me four young players. In time the trade will come out looking great for the Indians." (It never did. Eckersley was very effective in his early Boston years and later, after moving to Oakland, he became an all-star reliever.) Paul said he was sorry about Martin's dismissal "because Billy is a great tactical manager. Lemon? No knock at Bob but I don't see him making a difference. The Red Sox have that big lead and I don't see anybody getting close enough to bother them." In short, this sage baseball man was saying, the pennant race had already been settled.

Lemon kept Jackson on the bench during the Guidry game in Kansas City and again during the Piniella game at the Stadium. The contentious press suggested that Lemon was sitting Reggie at the Stadium to shield him (and Lemon himself) from boos. "Baseball is such a nice, simple children's game," Lemon said. "It's a shame adults have to complicate it and screw things up." He took a breath. "Reggie is rusty. I'm not sending him back out there until he's ready."

On July 27, ten days after the suspension, Jackson returned to the starting lineup. He had not played defense for a month but Lemon sent him out to right field. The old, bizarre Steinbrenner lineup was history. A crowd of 29,255 showed up for a double-header with Cleveland and some greeted Jackson with shouts, "Bunt, Reggie. Bunt." He says he thought, "That's kind of cute. At least they've done some thinking." He heard boos and, Reggie being Reggie, complained about "excess attention" and went five for eight in the two games with a homer and four runs batted in. As Moss Klein put it in the *Newark Star-Ledger,* this was "an un-forgettable return from the Mad Bunting Episode." The teams split the doubleheader and occasionally during a long afternoon fans began to chant, "Bill-eee, Bill-eee." Martin was gone, off fish-ing somewhere, but hardly forgotten.

Across decades, Old Timers' Day at Yankee Stadium had be-come one of baseball's most effective exercises in nostalgia. The Yankees consider the 1939 Lou Gehrig farewell as their first. (Oth-ers find similar promotions as far back as the early 1900s.) Red Patterson organized the second "annual" in 1947. Ever since, they've been held each summer. Even when the Yankees had to play in Shea Stadium, they gained a powerful (and commercial) sense of nostalgia from the annual presence of Joe DiMaggio, who was introduced at his insistence as "the greatest living ball player." On one occasion Casey Stengel, fired in the 1960s, became the hero of the Old Timers' show, dressed in Roman Imperial garb and driven through the outfield gates in a horse-drawn chariot. *Gaius Julius Stengel.*

Old Timers' Day in 1978 was scheduled for Saturday, July 29, at Yankee Stadium, just five days after Martin lost his job. "Is Billy coming back?" Klein asked Al Rosen.

"I've been told that Billy might show up," Rosen said. "I hope he does."

Rosen did not volunteer that Billy had been holding conversations with Steinbrenner. First, at the insistence of his agent, Doug Newton, and his lawyer, a former New Orleans judge named Eddie Sapir, Martin apologized. Then Steinbrenner told Newton, "In my gut I don't think it's right, Billy not being Yankee manager." This led to a meeting, two days after Martin's firing, in Steinbrenner's suite at the Hotel Carlyle on Madison Avenue. A candid discussion grew heated, particularly when Steinbrenner asked Martin to stop drinking. Martin said he would not, but in a kind of counterproposal said that if he ever managed the Yankees again, he'd like a publicity man with him whenever he was exposed to the media, particularly the New York media. Steinbrenner thought that was reasonable and at length told Martin he could come back to manage in '79, "which will give you time to settle down, get your nerves back together. We'll announce it at Old Timers' Day. It will bring down the house. Until then, Billy, don't say a word." But rehiring Martin meant dismissing Lemon and Al Rosen would have none of that. "To get Lemon to relocate from California," he told Steinbrenner, "I promised that he'd manage the rest of this season and for all of 1979 as well."

"Things have changed," Steinbrenner said.

"I don't regard this as being simply my word, George. It's the word of the New York Yankees. If you don't let Lemon manage in 1979, I'm going to resign right now."

On Saturday afternoon Frank Messer, a Yankee broadcaster, introduced the old-timers, Phil Rizzuto, Roger Maris, Ford, Mantle, and DiMaggio. Each drew enthusiastic cheers. "Now," Messer said, "I turn the microphone over to Bob Sheppard for two special announcements.

"May I please have your attention, please, ladies and gentleman," Sheppard began. He already had the attention of an afternoon crowd numbering 46,711. "Bob Lemon will be managing the Yankees for the rest of this season and for 1979. In 1980 he will become General Manager." The rabble in the stands began to boo. "In 1980 and hopefully for many years to come," Sheppard said, "the Yankees will again be managed by Number One..." At that the crowd loosed so loud a roar, you could not hear Sheppard's next words. "Billy Martin."

Martin trotted on to the field and lined up between Whitey Ford and Yogi Berra. He lifted his cap and bowed. As he waved the cap, the cheering grew even louder. The cap became Martin's baton. He conducted this crowd like a maestro and it was a full eight minutes before the cheering subsided. DiMaggio set his jaw. He did not like waiting out an ovation for somebody else.

In the players' lounge Bucky Dent said to Jackson, "They'd better trade me because I ain't playing for him."

"This means I'm gone," Jackson said. "This means they have to get rid of me, doesn't it?" The situation was ludicrous, he felt, and demeaning. Martin had apologized to Steinbrenner. In a way, Steinbrenner had apologized to Martin. But no one, no one at all, had offered Jackson an apology for being publicly branded a liar. After a while Jackson telephoned his father, who still ran a tailor shop in Wyncote, Pennsylvania. "Don't worry about Billy," Martinez

Jackson told his son. "And don't worry about George. Just bow your neck and grit your teeth. And hit. And be a man." The Yankees defeated the Minnesota Twins, 7 to 3. On Sunday the *New York Times* published an eight-column spread under the headline: BILLY MARTIN'S WEEK: MICROCOSM OF A TURBULENT CAREER. This was tabloid stuff, which is not to fault the *Times*. It was becoming a decidedly tabloid year.

ALTHOUGH HE WAS NOT inclined to admit it, Bob Lemon initially had to feel his way, as he came to know his players. Scouting reports and videotapes are helpful but great managing—and Lemon was about to become a great manager, at least for the balance of the season—begins with close-up observation of the players. You want them to succeed, of course, and you accomplish that by meeting their needs and working their strengths, as, say, in calling Jackson "Meat," not "Boy," and telling him, "Do your thing. Just bash a bunch." Try to make Jackson a hit-and-run man, a poke hitter, or a bunter, even in a bunt situation ... well, we saw what happened with Jackson and the bunt. Denigrate him racially and you are well on your way to creating a mutineer.

Facing two or three press conferences a day, managers fall back on the obvious, "I can only play the people the front office gives me." The less obvious key is *how* the manager plays and interplays with those people: his decisions on whom to praise, whom to berate, and whom to leave alone. A manager has to learn the way different batters function with different pitch counts. He needs to study players' defensive skills, which proceed not only from speed, arm, and hands, but also from alertness. Clearly Paul Blair, with a sprinter's speed, was a splendid Yankee outfielder. So was Lou Piniella, who couldn't run much. After watching Piniella for a time, someone described him as "the best slow outfielder in baseball."

Then there is the handling of pitchers, which is a book all by itself. Overall managing guidelines have existed surely since John

McGraw, and probably since the days of Harry Wright, a reformed cricket player who managed Boston to a National League pennant in 1877. Play for a tie at home, where you get the last at bat; on the road always play to win. Never make the third out at third base. You're almost as likely to score that two-out run from second as from third. One can go on for quite a while with textbook tactics, stratagems, and percentage moves. Lots of people, from tweedy academics to sports-bar beer guzzlers, understand percentage baseball, but in the dugout a successful manager runs a game and indeed a season by going *beyond* percentages and texts. He works with and within the abilities, shortcomings, and psyches of his players. As I said, lots of people know the percentages. Precious few can read the existential nature of a major-league team.

By August 2, Lemon's second week as Yankee manager, the ball club had closed to within six-and-a-half games of the Red Sox. The Yankees took two out of three from Cleveland, split a four-game set with Minnesota, and swept Texas, a good, but not spectacular, pace. The big jump was equally the result of a major Red Sox slump—eleven losses in fourteen games during one stretch in July. George Scott, the big first baseman, wasn't hitting; Jim Rice, in the midst of an outstanding season, was going through a quiet time. No fewer than three infielders were walking wounded. Ed Linn, a native New Englander, put it through a wince, "Plague, pestilence and an occasional pulled hamstring were striking down the Red Sox." There was also the matter of history. The Red Sox's traditional play under the pressures of the stretch had been inglorious. In 1974—and twelve members of the '78 squad played on that team—the Red Sox were in first place on August 23 with a seven-game lead. They finished third. In 1977, the Red Sox were in first place with a three-and-a-half-game lead on August 18. They finished tied for second. In the more than three decades that had passed since World War II, the Sox won the pennant only three times despite vast expenditures for talent. Partly this was a result of racism. After giving Jackie Robinson a pro forma tryout in 1945, the Sox turned him down. Four seasons later Robinson became Most Valuable Player in the National League. In 1949 with a clear shot at a teenaged Willie Mays, the Sox passed because "the kid can't handle the curve." Subsequently Mays hit 660 big-league homers, not all off fast balls. With Robinson playing second or third and Mays patrolling center and that portion of left Ted Williams couldn't reach, the Red Sox surely would have dominated baseball for eight or ten years.

Beyond the owner's bigotry, there is also a question of the team's collective character. When Dwight Michael "Dewey" Evans, out of Santa Monica, the Sox's staunch right fielder, emerged from the visitors' dugout at Yankee Stadium on the night of Wednesday, August 2, a fan was waiting. "Hey, Evans," the man shouted from a nearby box, "you guys are doing it again, aren't you? You're choking again, just like you always do. You guys stink." Evans stared straight ahead, neither flinching nor acknowledging the taunt. "We've been hearing that for a few days," he told Moss Klein. "The only thing we can do is keep cool and forget about losing and just play. The way we played early in the year. Even with the injuries we should be winning. We're too good to lose this time." Carlton "Pudge" Fisk, the big catcher from Vermont, chimed in: "Sure 1974 was bad news. I was there. It won't happen this time. This team is too good to fold. This isn't 1974 and it isn't 1977. This is 1978 and we're the best team in the league." Not everyone was convinced. Another fan bellowed: "What has two legs, two arms, and no guts?" The man paused before delivering a forte punch line: "Every guy who's playing for the Red Sox."

But to the surprise and dismay of feral Yankees enthusiasts, the Sox, by this time with African-American Jim Rice established as their best hitter, declined to choke. The Yankees ran up a five-run lead and the Sox came back and caught them with two runs in the fourth, two more in the sixth, and one in the eighth, when Yastrzemski drove in Rice, who had doubled. Rain interrupted play and the game finally was suspended at 1:16 A.M. after Reggie Jackson was called out on strikes in the fourteenth inning. When play resumed the next night, the Red Sox scored two in the seventeenth and won, 7 to 5. In the regularly scheduled game that followed immediately, home runs by Rice, Fred Lynn, and Bob Bailey powered Boston to an 8-to-1 victory. The Yankees came into the series hoping to cut the Red Sox's lead to four-and-a-half games. Now on August 4 they found themselves eight-and-a-half behind, about where they had been when Lemon took over. Making matters worse, on the next night the almost invincible Ron Guidry lost, 2 to 1, to Baltimore's Mike Flanagan. The three-game losing streak dropped the Yankees from third to fourth. They were an interesting ball club, but they seemed stalled, eight-and-a-half games out with fifty-four left to play. Even the inveterately optimistic Lou Piniella said the pennant had slipped out of reach. Panic and resignation hung in the Bronx air and Lemon called another team meeting. "Nothing's been settled," he said. "There are some games that you are not supposed to win, no matter what you do. I believe that. We just played three of those. Put 'em behind you. I'm only asking all of you to play hard. You guys are good. If you play hard, you're gonna win."

"How did the meeting go?" a reporter asked.

"It went like every other clubhouse meeting," Lemon said. "The manager talks. The players don't say a word. At least I wasn't booed." But it was not like any other clubhouse meeting. This cool, shrewd, red-nosed manager, following the hot, impetuous, red-bottomed manager, was building a foundation of trust. After three galling losses, outwardly he remained calm. "I got some pretty good lessons in how to take defeat in the fifteen years I pitched for the Indians," he said. "Hell, I got beat one hundred twenty-eight times. If I'd gone and had one hundred twenty-eight nervous breakdowns, I wouldn't be walking this earth today."

Some of the players, talking among themselves, said, "As long as you play hard, you can lose for this guy and he won't take your head off." Graig Nettles, for one, thought that was particularly important. "You don't *want* to lose," he said, "but you do want to accept losing when it happens. Because it will. It sure as hell will." Reggie Jackson began to say that Lemon was "a welcome father figure." Goose Gossage said, "Pitching for Lem, not Martin, it's like the pressure of the world has come off my shoulders." Hunter, his shoulder stronger, won start after start, feeling comfortable under a manager who knew about winning starts himself.

Second-guessing enraged Martin, but Lemon took it in stride. He appeared to understand that second-guessing intelligently was something a good newspaper sportswriter had to do. Did he consider starting Guidry in that second game against Boston, someone asked, on three days' rest, instead of the customary four? "That's a fair question," Lemon said. "Let me give you my thinking. It isn't worth taking a chance with Guidry, breaking his rhythm. He's been pitching every fifth day and that's what he does best. We have to win all our games, not just rearrange things against Boston."

Lemon made certain that his geniality was not confused with weakness. He had already barked at Piniella and Rivers. When Jackson went into one of his minislumps, Lemon dropped him from the clean-up and posted a lineup with Jackson batting eighth. Jackson said to coach Clyde King, "I'm sick. Tell Lemon I can't play tonight." Was Reggie looking for confrontation? Had he had enough of white men shoving him up and down? Or did he really feel ill? No one is sure. But in a situation where Martin would have streaked his office walls with wild blue language, Lemon took a breath and let Reggie sit. The next day he slotted Jackson seventh. "On a team this good," he said, "hitting seventh is no disgrace." Jackson said he was not so sure about that. But he played.

Things were calm, but only relatively calm—Yankee calm, an

area of underlying disturbance. On August 4, Gabe Paul filed a $3.1 million lawsuit against Steinbrenner. Lawyers said $1.1 million was the value of Yankee stock that Paul owned and had placed in escrow when he took over the Indians. "I have a buyer and that's what he's offered," Paul said. "He's even put the money into an escrow account of his own. The papers are signed and the deal has been approved by the commissioner's office and the president of the league. But George is managing partner and we need his approval to finalize the deal. He's been holding us up for two months."

"I understand the $1.1 million," a reporter said, "but why are you suing Steinbrenner for $3.1 million?"

"I've added the two million," Paul said with an engaging smile, "as punitive damages against George." Presently the litigation did its work. Paul's sale went through and the suit became moot.

On August 9, when the Yankees were halfway through a six-game winning streak, their second-longest of the season, Printing Pressmen's Union No. 2 shut down New York's three principal newspapers, the *Times,* the *Daily News,* and the *Post.* The strike would last for eighty-eight days, into November at the *Times* and the *News.* The *Post* resumed publishing on October 5, amid harsh charges that executives lobbed at one another, but the *Post* still missed the balance of the pennant race. Other unions honored the pressmen's picket lines and about eleven thousand newspaper employees, from editorial writers to truck mechanics, found themselves thrown out of work, forced to subsist on savings, union benefits, and, after seven weeks, New York State unemployment insurance.

The striking union's primary issue was neither wages nor hours but "manning numbers," the size of the force required to run and maintain the gigantic presses on which the newspapers were printed. "The featherbedding is so outrageous," said Rupert Murdoch, who owned the *Post,* "that not one of our pressmen is actually working for more than half the shift for which we pay him." Arthur Ochs Sulzberger, publisher of the *Times,* said, "Manning in our pressrooms is at least 50 percent higher than it is in surrounding suburban newspapers." The publishers hired a firm of efficiency experts, the Technical Service Company of Denver, which confirmed that the presses were overstaffed. The president of the Pressmen's Union, William J. Kennedy, Jr., said the study was rigged and anyway, he wasn't interested in the opinions of cowboys from the Rocky Mountains. His concern was preserving pressmen's jobs. They worked, he said, under terrible conditions, filth, shattering noise, and danger; those giant presses could maul or kill.

Joseph F. Barletto, the general manager at the *News*, proposed a plan in which the papers would hire well-known media authorities to publicize "the featherbedding in our sick industry." (Six long-established New York newspapers had folded in the previous quarter century, seven if you include the *Brooklyn Eagle*.) Walter Mattson, the general manager of the *Times*, opposed the idea on the grounds that it would antagonize William Kennedy. He seemed unaware that Kennedy was telling union associates, "Mattson is the architect of this damn strike." Handling a difficult assignment with imposing neutrality, Jonathan Friendly of the *Times* would later write in a summary of the walkout: "In public, management officers described Mr. Kennedy as intransigent, while in private they said he was too stupid to know how to negotiate and spoke of his pressmen as louts and drunkards." It was many weeks before serious negotiations began. Meanwhile, four tabloids appeared: the *City News*, the *New York Daily Press*, the *New York Daily Metro*, and the *Graphic*. These gave work to some reporters, but none built a significant following.

For the Yankees, players and management, the strike was liberating. The *Newark Star Ledger*, *Newsday*, and other suburban papers continued to publish, but the battle of the back pages, with a *New York Times* tympani obbligato, was over. No more could Dick Young tell millions of readers what was wrong with George Steinbrenner, an inviting target now that Martin had gone. No longer could Henry Hecht demand in large, intimidating type that Reggie Jackson get out of town. For this season at least, Murray Chass' days of shadowing drinking ball players in airports were finished. Asked what this meant later, Bob Lemon spoke openly: "Without those back pages screaming about stuff every day, I was able to keep things quieter. I hated to see the newspaper guys out of work, but the strike, coming when it did, did more for us than if we picked up a twenty-game winner." The Yankees richly enjoyed a freedom ignored in James Madison's Bill of Rights. That was freedom *from* the press.

Some wondered what the absence of high-powered sports sections would do to Yankee attendance. Although space-hungry city editors long complained that sports pages were "mostly free advertising for baseball teams," the evidence suggests that the strike, and the loss of that supposedly free advertising, did nothing at all. Sellouts were rare at Yankee Stadium during the late 1970s, where one saw crowds of about 28,000 (and 27,000 empty seats) per game. This was on a par with attendance for the Red Sox, who of course played in a smaller park, and was significantly lower than the figures posted in Los Angeles, where the Dodgers drew 3,347,845 in '78; almost 42,000 a game, then a major-league record. (The Yankees did not break 3 million until 1999.) With or without New York sports sections, Yankee attendance in 1978 maintained a 2.3-million pace, unimposing by today's standards but at the time fourth best in the majors.

To those sportswriters still employed, the Yankees appeared to spend the balance of August "trying to create a pennant race." To Reggie Jackson, "We already had a pennant race. We were professionals and we had started clicking and everybody knew it and everybody felt it. We'd didn't talk about it. You don't want to let your mind wander. But you know when you're on board the big train and maybe there's a jolt or two but you're gonna have one hell of a ride." Jolts came on a trip to Baltimore and the West Coast, a swing of eleven games in which the team played no better than 6 and 5. The Red Sox also were inconsistent and when the Yankees returned to New York in the small hours of August 25 they found themselves tied for second place, still seven-and-a-half games behind Boston. They were now looking at a stretch of fourteen games, all but two at home, before they were to fly north for a September series with the Red Sox. "We have to get closer," Lou Piniella said. "If we're still this far out when we go to Boston, that's a problem. We should be say, four out or at most five. But no more than that."

In late August, Mickey Rivers and Sparky Lyle found wire-service reporters and said that Steinbrenner ought to be paying them more money. Jackson, who won a game with a grand slam down the right-field line in the Stadium, exploded when an Associated Press sportswriter asked if it was unusual for him to pull a drive that sharply. "Since I've been a Yankee," Jackson said, "I haven't been able to pull the ball, hit the fast ball or do anything— if you listen to everybody around here. 'Reggie can't pull. Reggie can't do this. Reggie can't do that.' All they say is negative things and I'm projected as a bad fellow. What am I supposed to do, tell everybody how I contribute to orphanages and stick up for under-privileged people everywhere? I refuse to do that, but I will tell you this: I'm not a bad fellow. I'm a good guy." With all the newspapers publishing, tabloid types might have called Steinbrenner and read him some comments. *Say, George, Dick Young here. Lyle and Rivers both say that you're a cheap bastard. Any response, Big Guy?* With Martin about, Chass might have caught the manager near a bar and asked if he also thought Jackson was a good guy. But there were no tabloids and there was no Martin. Without a sounding board, the grumbles made little noise and were published quietly in out-of-town papers beside a story about the Olympian decathalete Bruce Jenner and the tennis pro Anand Amritraj winning a charity tennis tournament by defeating another tennis pro, Clark Graebner, who was paired with the blonde heiress-actress Dina Merrill.

Lemon kept his focus on the pennant race. It would be a good thing, he said, if the Yankees could win ten out of the fourteen before the Boston series. We'd have momentum that way, he said, and we can do that, we can win ten out of fourteen. That is not what the Yankees did. They won *twelve* out of fourteen. When they flew to Boston late on September 6, the Boston lead, fourteen games in mid-July, was down to four.

Since Lemon arrived, the Yankees had been playing 30–13 baseball, a .698 pace. After mid-July the Sox played .500 ball and although historically most teams play .500 ball most of the time, that is no way to win a pennant. (Most teams, obviously, are also-rans.) The Boston second baseman, Jerry Remy, was out with a broken wrist. Catcher Carlton Fisk said his cracked rib made him feel as though "someone's sticking a sword into my side." Carl Yastrzemski was playing through injuries to his back, a shoulder, and a wrist. Dwight Evans, beaned on August 29, was suffering from dizzy spells. This may be '78, they were saying in New England pubs from Eastport down to Block Island and clear across to Stockbridge, but our team looks as beat up as those characters in *The Spirit of '76*.

The Boston *Herald American* had been running a front-page box, using very large type to chart the Red Sox's shrinking lead. Radio sports talk shows—Boston led the nation in these—recounted past collapses of the "Crimson Hose" and spun two dozen variations around a theme painfully familiar in the streets around Faneuil Hall—the Fenway Folderoo. In addition, and this is hard precisely to pin down, tinges of racism infested Boston sports talk. Decades earlier a controversial Boston columnist named Dave Egan had taken obscene pleasure in describing Jackie Robinson as "an Afro-American, grown fat in body and in head." That was one Boston sports page in 1952. By the late 1970s the ethnic stuff was subtler, but not gone. George Scott, the big African-American first baseman, had weight problems and some thought it was funny to say on the radio or comment in print, "Hey,

George, give your gut a rest. Lay off those extra helpings of Mamie's southern fried chicken." You may remember Jim Rice's remark to me during spring training when Mike Torrez introduced us: "There are no nice writers." That statement did not come out of nowhere. Both the past and the present whirled about a fine Red Sox team that was four games ahead of the Yankees and, in Don Zimmer's term, "reeling." "But me," Zimmer said, "I refused to lose faith."

Bob Lemon sat in the visitors' dugout taking questions in his loose and laid-back manner. Sweep? Oh, sure, he'd like a sweep, but you don't want to set your goal so high that you put too much pressure on everybody, even including the manager. "On the road," he said, "when you come in to play four against a good team like the Red Sox, you're hoping to win two of them. Two out of four. That would be fine." By the third inning, Lemon was saying to Clyde King, "You know, Meat, we can win *three* out of four." By then the Yankees led, 7 to 0, in a game where Thurman Munson picked up three hits before the Red Sox's number-nine batter, Butch Hobson, had even come to bat. Mike Torrez, a formidable figure who had been slumping—he hadn't won since August 18—started for Boston and began by striking out Mickey Rivers. Most of the Fenway full house, 34,119 paying customers, rose and cheered. But serious Red Sox cheering now was finished. Willie Randolph was safe on an error, Munson singled, Jackson singled, and so it went, creating a base-path carousel. After yielding six hits, Torrez left in the second inning. The Yankees assaulted subsequent relief pitchers impartially.

Striking out Jim Rice in the third, Catfish Hunter strained an abdominal muscle. He still felt pain when he went out to pitch the fourth and after Yastrzemski lined a triple into right center field, Hunter told Lemon that he could go no further. At this point the Yankees were leading, 12 to 0. "When the call for someone to protect a twelve-run lead came down to the bullpen," reliever Ken

Clay later said in high good humor, "there was a fist fight to see who would get the ball." Clay relieved. The Yankees won, 15 to 3. "So many Red Sox fans walked out," Moss Klein recalled, "that we had the earliest-ever jam of cars trying to get away from Fenway Park. All the Boston fans wanted to do was flee the scene."

The next night was just as sour for the town that advertised itself as "the Athens of America" (but that Robert Browning described as "a hole"). A rookie Boston righthander named Jim Wright started against Jim Beattie, a tall, sensitive Yankee freshman out of Dartmouth. Rivers opened the game with a single, stole second, and went to third when Fisk's throw carried into center field. Willie Randolph's grounder scooted under the glove of shortstop "Rooster" Rick Burleson and Rivers scored. In the Yankee dugout someone hollered, "Cock-a-doodle-dooo!" The Yankees settled for two in the first. Piniella led off the second with a triple and scored on Roy White's single. White stole second and went to third as another Fisk throw bounced into center. Dent hit a sacrifice fly, Zimmer changed pitchers, Rivers singled, Munson walked, and Jackson hit a long home run. Before this game was done, the Red Sox had committed seven errors. "I've learned in baseball," Jackson said, "that you should never be surprised by anything you see. But right now I am surprised because I've never seen a team in a crucial series play as badly as the Red Sox did tonight. *Never.*" Beattie went into the ninth inning with a three-hit shutout, but when the Red Sox scored twice, Lemon replaced him. "The kid had thrown one hundred fifty pitches," Lemon said, "and I didn't want to sap his strength. I didn't want that on my conscience. Two days from now he's getting married." The Yankees won, 13 to 2. They were two games behind, sensing a kill and looking directly at two more games with Boston.

On Saturday morning, the Red Sox closed their clubhouse doors and held a meeting. They were going with their best pitcher, Dennis Eckersley, 9-and-0 at Fenway, and they agreed that they should forget the last two nights and take it from here. "Keep your heads high," Don Zimmer said. Eckersley, a sharp-featured native of Oakland, wore a significant black mustache and seemed to many to resemble the King of Spades. The Yankees also led with an ace, Ron Guidry, but he was a lefthander who would have to contend with the left-field wall, officially 315 feet down the line, but actually only 304.7 feet away, according to an aerial survey conducted by the *Boston Globe*. Whatever, the Red Sox had lost only one home game to a lefthander all season and no lefthander had shut them out at Fenway in four years. When they ran out to their defensive positions on a bright, windy afternoon, the Red Sox held their bare fists high in a communal sign that they had come to play. Indeed they had. Rick Burleson began the Boston attack with a first-inning single. Fred Lynn bunted him to second base. Given the gifts of the starting pitchers, Zimmer said, and the wind blowing in toward home, he assumed that this would be a 1-to-0 game. "I wasn't thinking of a big inning off Guidry," he said. "I was just playing so that we'd be the guys with the run." Jim Rice bounced a hard grounder to deep short and when Bucky Dent couldn't make a play, the Red Sox had their second hit. Men on first and third with one out and Yastrzemski and Fisk coming to bat. "I liked those odds," Zimmer says. "I still do." On the mound Guidry kept his focus. He was going to throw hard and keep the ball down. That was how he had pitched in tight spots all season. He was not going to change his style because of the unusual dimensions of Fenway Park. Guidry jammed Yastrzemski, who plunked a grounder directly at first baseman Chris Chambliss. The runners were frozen. Two out. Now, facing "Pudge" Fisk, a 220-pound hulk out of Bellows Falls, Vermont, Guidry threw wicked stuff, low and tight. He was coming inside and if Fisk could pull him over the short wall in left... well, major-league pitching is a high-risk occupation. Fisk could not pull Guidry. Overpowered, he took a third strike. Boston's offense for the day had been concluded.

After Burleson and Rice reached base, Ron Guidry pitched eight-and-two-thirds hitless innings.

The Yankees scored seven times in the fourth, an inning that lives in infamy—at least among the annals of New England sport. Munson opened with a single and Jackson hit a high fly that the wind blew toward the left-field foul line. Running from left center, Yastrzemski made a leaping, twisting catch and fired the ball to second baseman Frank Duffy, whose relay doubled Munson off first base. Superb fielding often goes hand in hand with victory. When the Brooklyn Dodgers defeated the Yankees in the seventh game of the 1955 World Series, a similar double play, left fielder Sandy Amoros to shortstop Pee Wee Reese to first baseman Gil Hodges, proved decisive. But by 1978, Amoros was living on welfare, Reese had retired to the broadcast booth, and Hodges was dead. Besides, the Red Sox were not the Dodgers, although when Reese made his great relay doubling Gil McDougald, a short aggressive character named Don Zimmer sat watching in the Brooklyn dugout.

Now in Boston, Chris Chambliss doubled to right. At Zimmer's direction, Eckersley intentionally walked the lefthand-hitting Nettles to go righthander-righthander against Piniella. Some wind gusts that afternoon were timed at thirty-two miles an hour and this must have been a 32-m.p.h. moment. Piniella sliced a pop fly toward right center field, which he later said, "I hit pretty damn good." Five Red Sox moved toward the ball: centerfielder Lynn, right fielder Rice, shortstop Burleson, first baseman Scott, and second baseman Duffy. They squinted into the bright September sun, trying to read the wind and find the baseball. "I saw it," Eckersley said, "but I couldn't get to it, even though it was coming back toward the infield like a Frisbee." Duffy, closest to the ball, found himself staring straight into the sun. He looked startled when the baseball bounced near his feet. "I can't tell you for sure whose play that was," Zimmer says, "but with five of my guys right near it, and the ball way up in the air, *somebody* is supposed to make the catch." When nobody did, Chambliss scored, Nettles reached third, and Piniella slid safely into second. Eckersley intentionally walked, Roy White, loading the bases and bringing up, speaking of New England infamy, Bucky Dent. Eckersley threw two strikes, then hung a slider that Dent lined safely into left field. Two more hits, a wild pitch, a passed ball, and the Yankees had seven runs. The 7-to-0 victory was the twenty-first game that Guidry had won and the shutout was his seventh. "But I was kinda worried early on," Graig Nettles said. "I mean for a whole hour there we were in a slump." Joe Gergen wrote in *Newsday,* "The Yankees are a game behind and drawing away." On scene the Boston press swarmed about Frank Duffy. How had he managed to flub Lou Piniella's windblown fly? At length Dennis Eckersley, the King of Spades, broke into the interrogation. "Frank didn't lose the ball game," he said. "I did. I lost it when I hung that slider to Bucky Dent."

Before the Sunday game, Dwight Evans, still suffering from dizziness, spoke thoughtfully and sadly. "This isn't the way I imagined the last month of our season," he said. "I thought we'd win maybe 112 games and people would always remember these Red Sox not just as a good team that struggled through a pennant race, but as one of the greatest teams that ever played. I don't buy into the choking talk. We're playing hurt." Indeed, Fisk, Hobson, Yastrzemski, Lynn, Jerry Remy, and Evans himself were suffering from injuries of varying severity. Earlier injuries had plagued the Yankees pitchers and at different times sidelined Dent, Jackson, Munson, Randolph, and Rivers. "If nobody on either of these teams had gotten hurt," Bob Lemon told Boston newspapermen, "it would have been like that 1954 season when the Indians won 111 games and the Yankees won 103. And remember that was when there were only 154 games a season."

Lemon started Ed Figueroa, already a fifteen-game winner, and Zimmer, falling back on his old Dodger connection, went with

Robert John Sprowl, the twenty-two-year-old lefthander recently promoted from the Red Sox farm team in Pawtucket. Sprowl's record there: 7 and 4, with a 4.15 earned run average. Boston is a splendid town for doggerel. Fans once sang to the tune of *O Tannenbaum*, "O Dominic DiMaggio/He's better than his brother, Joe." Now, with a rookie going in the most important game of the year, someone, almost certainly not descended from Emerson, chanted: "Don't throw in the towel—we've got Bobby Sprowl." Why Sprowl instead of the veteran Bill Lee or starting thirty-seven-year-old Luis Tiant on short rest? Zimmer said his former Brooklyn teammate, Johnny Podres, then the Red Sox's minor-league pitching coach, had told him that Sprowl possessed big-league stuff. Zimmer says that his personal dislike of Lee did not influence a decision that even at the time seemed curious. He said he thought Sprowl "would give us five or six good innings." Sprowl opened the game by walking Rivers and Willie Randolph. Munson bounced into a double play, but Jackson singled home Rivers. Sprowl walked Piniella and Chambliss, loading the bases, and as Zimmer walked to the mound to take out Sprowl he heard hoots. Nettles singled off reliever Bob Stanley and the Yankees went on to complete the four-game sweep, 7 to 4. The Red Sox had been alone in first place since May 24. Now on Sunday, September 10, the Yankees had drawn even. Numbers people unsheathed their calculators. In the four games the Yankees outscored the Red Sox 42 to 9. As a team the Yankees batted .396 with an on-base percentage of .508. Loopin' Lou Piniella racked up ten hits, walked twice, reached base on an error, and scored eight runs, one fewer than Boston's collective total. Robert Crane, treasurer of the Commonwealth of Massachusetts, sorrowfully told a *Sports Illustrated* reporter, "This is 1929 all over again." It was a rare sportswriter who called the series anything other than (pause... flourish of hautboys) The Boston Massacre!

One can reasonably argue that Zimmer managed badly. He somehow ended up starting rookies in two of the four games even though baseball history suggests that the mound, in a highly pressurized situation, is no place for a youngster. Having said that, one also has to note that after the humiliating rout, stumpy Don Zimmer stood tall. He rallied his shaken ball players and told them time after time that they were winners and that he was proud to manage them and they sure as hell were still in the pennant race.

The Sox came down to the Stadium five days later. Guidry pitched another two-hit shutout and Catfish Hunter beat Mike Torrez, 3 to 2, dropping Boston three-and-a-half games behind. But the Sox won the next game, 7 to 3, with Eckersley, and after losing in Toronto began an eight-game winning streak that drew them to within a game on the final day of the season. The Yankees were playing well, but two losses in Cleveland hurt. On September 26, Melissa Ludtke and several other woman journalists were allowed into the Yankee dressing room for the first time. A bit of randy horseplay ensued, but only a bit. Everywhere the focus was on the pennant race.

On October 1, the final day of the regular season, Luis Tiant shut out Toronto in Boston. Catfish Hunter started at the Stadium but the Indians hit him hard. Cleveland won, 9 to 2, behind an obscure lefthander named Rick Waits. Gabe Paul's Indians had forced the Yankees into a playoff.

By the morning of October 2 both the Yankees and the Red Sox had won ninety-nine games. That afternoon these rousing ball clubs would meet for a final time at Fenway Park. Only one would win one hundred.

▼

CHAPTER FOURTEEN

THE GAME

A L ROSEN DESCRIBES the Yankee locker room after the disappointing loss to Cleveland as "subdued, but not somber." The team's late-afternoon flight to Boston was much the same. "Remember," Rosen says, "that flight is only about thirty minutes long and remember also that our manager was a professional. And now that Lemon was there, the players were behaving professionally. Jackson, Munson, Guidry, Gossage, and the others, they knew what they had to do the next day. The last thing they needed was one of those Knute Rockne *fight-fight-fight* speeches." Perhaps the next-to-last thing they needed was an agitated Billy Martin, getting smashed very quickly in an airport bar and asking, like a beer-drunk fan, how in hell could a championship team lose a big game to a nothing pitcher, 13-and-15, named Rick Waits? The Martin rant sounds in my mind, as though it truly happened, and I hear the shrill voice, chalk screeching across an endless blackboard. Briefly I shudder. Hysteria in pets, babies, women, and particularly grown men discomfits me. But leaving the perfervid world of my imagination (an exciting place to visit but I wouldn't want to live there) I remember that this is one rant that did not happen. Martin was gone and Bob Lemon, as Rosen said, embodied professionalism.

Rosen himself had sat through a play-off at Fenway Park thirty years earlier when he was a twenty-four-year-old backup infielder on a Cleveland team that finished tied for first place with the Red Sox. "We rode a train for ten hours to get to Boston," he says, "and back then things got a little raucous." In the first sudden-death play-off in American League history, a rookie left-hander named Gene Bearden stilled Boston bats in Fenway and the Indians slugged down Bromo-Seltzer and won a lopsided game, 8 to 3. There was weeping that night on Commonwealth Avenue as there had been before and as there would be again.

With the Yankee players contained and the manager contained and the president contained, only one volcano might rumble. George M. Steinbrenner III had never been around a big-league play-off before, and the Steinbrenner of 1978 was not the brilliant, measured field marshal who commands today. He was an extremely bright executive, but one with less than five years' experience in major-league baseball. One knew that these Yankees could handle pressure. Could their managing partner? That was one question. Another: Who would win the play-off game and then play for the pennant?

THE YANKEES CHECKED INTO the Sheraton Boston, a hotel located in the Prudential Center, a commercial complex dominated by the Prudential Tower, 52 stories and 750 feet high, the second-tallest skyscraper in Boston at the time. The newer 60-story John Hancock Tower was both taller and more provocative. Until engineers made emergency modifications, strong winds repeatedly blew glass panels off the Hancock's slab slides and menaced everyone who dared wander the streets below. Some Bostonians called it "The Killer Building."

Catfish Hunter had dinner with Munson and Piniella. The group was confident without being boisterous. They talked about the four-game sweep at Fenway, 42 runs to 9, and said that if that didn't prove they were a better team than the Red Sox nothing ever would. They swept the Sox then. They ought to win tomorrow. "[Mike] Torrez has been bad-mouthing us all year," Munson said. "We got to stick it to that guy."

Rosen dined quietly with his wife, Rita, and said frankly he was very nervous, more nervous than he'd ever been when playing ball. "I have to admit I'm surprised we're here tonight," he said. "After the four-game sweep, I thought we'd win the pennant by five games."

"Give the Red Sox credit," Rita Rosen said. Al nodded and said mildly, "That's not what I'm paid to do." Tomorrow would be Rosh Hashanah, the Jewish New Year, one of the most sacred holidays in the Jewish calendar. Deeply religious Jews spend Rosh Hashanah in prayer and in contemplation of those who have died during the preceding twelve months. A practical man, Rosen was focused on the present. He was going to Fenway Park, where his job directed him, and unless this nervousness abated he would arm himself not with a Torah, but with a few rolls of antacid pills. He would sit in the Yankee box alongside of George Steinbrenner. Since all the seats there were spoken for, Rita would sit in a neutral area, beside Commissioner Bowie Kuhn. "Antacids and George," Rosen remarked to me, looking bemused. "But I have to tell you, I was very excited."

Ron Guidry retired early. He had beaten Toronto, 3 to 1, on September 28 for his twenty-fourth victory and had been pitching as few ever have. In three of Guidry's last six starts he throttled the opposition with two-hit shutouts. Tomorrow, for the first time all year, he was going to start with three days' rest, not four. "That put a premium on conserving my strength," he said. "Not getting worked up, not getting excited, not getting nothing. I can stay up late as good as anyone, but that night I wanted to get to my room and concentrate on resting and relaxing, if you know what I mean." With only three losses across the six-month season, Guidry possessed the best winning percentage of any twenty-game winner

in history. He felt confident, but had one curious concern. Once
Mike Caldwell of Milwaukee defeated him. Then it was Mike
Flanagan of Baltimore and after that Mike Willis of Toronto. Only
three losses all year and each one to someone called Mike. Who
would be starting for Boston? Michael Augustine Torrez, known as
Mike.

Bob Lemon's strategy was not complicated. He would start
Guidry and then come in with Rich Gossage, back in form now
that Martin was gone and leading American League pitchers in
games saved. Should Guidry falter in the first inning, then Lemon
would relieve with Gossage in the first inning. Lemon intended to
have his best arms work for as long as they could and then fill in, if
he had to, with Sparky Lyle or even with starting pitchers. (He
thought less of Sparky Lyle than Sparky Lyle did.) Go with your
best; if you are going to lose make them beat your best people. This
approach derives at least from Casey Stengel, who employed no
fewer than three outstanding starting pitchers to win the seventh
game of the 1952 World Series. "Sure they're tired," Stengel said,
"but after today they got a long winter to rest up." The 1978 situation was different. If the Yankees won, they would have to fly to
Kansas City for the opening game of the American League Championship Series next day. "But there was no sense in worrying
about that game," Lemon said, "because if we didn't win this
game, we wouldn't even be playing in that game."

Early sleep eluded Rich Gossage. He stretched his very long
frame and tried to think relaxing thoughts. His mind drifted to his
home in Colorado Springs and for a time he could see the presiding majesty of Pike's Peak, the huge red rocks, shaped like gigantic
beer tables, in The Garden of the Gods, and the breathtaking sweep
across the South Plains toward the Ivy peaks, Mount Harvard,
Mount Columbia, and Mount Yale. Abruptly Carl Yastrzemski in-
vaded the travelogue. Gossage found himself imagining that he
was pitching to Yastrzemski in the ninth inning with the champi-

onship on the line. That was not a relaxing thought. He began to perspire. He twisted and rolled. Yastrzemski stayed with him, there was a menacing bat, a baseball version of Macbeth's dagger of the mind. This was no way to fall asleep. Near the Sheraton Boston, a lively bar operated under the name of Daisy Buchanan's, after the captivating heroine of *The Great Gatsby.* Gossage got dressed. He would go down to Daisy's for a few drinks. That would relax him. He would enter quietly and move to a corner of the bar. He didn't expect to be recognized and he did not anticipate seeing anyone he knew. "Then I walked into Daisy's," he says. "I looked around. You could have taken a Yankee team picture."

In the morning Ron Guidry caught an early taxi to Fenway and walked into the Yankee trainer's room. He wanted to be at the ballpark, not have to worry about getting there, and he wanted to be left alone. The trainer's tables were draped with sheets, as doctors' examining tables used to be before crackly paper coverings took hold, and the sheets reached down to the floor. "Gino," Guidry said to Gene Monahan, the head trainer, "I'm just gonna lie down under the table, inside the sheet, and maybe I'll sleep. Make sure you wake me up at 12:15. Until then I don't want to be disturbed by no one. I don't care if the president of the United States calls with an invitation to the White House. If he does, you tell him I said to call back tomorrow."

"I think Mr. Steinbrenner will be coming in," Monahan said. "He'll want to talk to you."

"You're telling me something I already know," Guidry said. "I don't want to be disturbed by no one."

Guidry lay under the table, the sheet blocking glare but not light. "I was semiasleep," he told me. "You know how sometimes you're almost asleep, but not entirely. You're a long way off but you're still aware of what's going on around you." A bit later he heard Steinbrenner enter the room. "Where's Guidry?" Steinbrenner asked in enthusiastic, forte tones.

"I haven't seen him," Monahan said. "Maybe he's gone out to the bullpen."

"If you see him, tell him I want to talk to him."

"I will tell him, Mr. Steinbrenner, if I see him."

Guidry heard every word as he lay silent. At 12:15 Monahan called out the time. Guidry emerged and put on some of his uniform. Herman Schneider, the assistant trainer, gave him a light rub on the left arm and shoulder. The pitcher finished dressing. Someone was playing a portable radio in the clubhouse and a broadcaster named Paul Harvey was speaking portentously about things to come in the next hundred years. "A pill that will raise your IQ," he said. "A door lock that will open at the sound of your voice— and only your voice. The burglars can't get in!" Guidry ignored Paul Harvey and walked out to the bullpen in right center field, arriving at 12:50, precisely fifteen minutes before game time. He would stretch for five minutes and then warm up by throwing thirty pitches. Ten fast balls, ten sliders, then ten more fast balls. Mike Torrez was already throwing in the Red Sox bullpen. He waved to Guidry and mouthed the words, "Good luck." Guidry waved back, and threw his first fast ball.

In an earlier time, pitchers warmed up behind home plate, throwing their stuff over practice plates implanted close to the backstop. As a boy it was exciting to press your face against the screen and watch two big leaguers throw harder, ever harder, and snap off curve balls that, we used to say, dropped off the table. How can you hit that stuff? We also used to say that. How can anybody hit that stuff? The Fenway bleacher fans were close to Torrez and Guidry, but it is not the same thing, having the pitchers prepare way out beyond the outfield, not as rollicking an overture as when they warmed up next to home plate, I mean the real one.

Al Rosen taxied to the ballpark and after guiding his wife toward the commissioner's box proceeded toward his seat. Small, sal-low Roy M. Cohn sat there in an expensive-looking suit. When Rosen told him, "You're in my seat," Cohn turned and sneered, as we have heard. Rosen may have made a fist. He isn't sure. Cohn scooted off.

In October 1977 Mike Torrez, with a little help from Reggie Jackson, had won two World Series games for the Yankees. He became a free agent after that and as Torrez saw matters, the Yankees showed him no respect, none at all, by refusing to make a realistic offer. Remember Gabe Paul's words: "Aside from the World Series, [Torrez] was no better than a 14–12 pitcher. I didn't think the Yankees would be needing him." The Red Sox signed Torrez to a long-term contract for about $540,000 a season, a large baseball salary at the time, and Torrez moved out smartly, posting a record of 15 and 6. But as the Red Sox slumped so did he; across a forty-day stretch he lost six starts in succession. Torrez is, as I've indicated, a profoundly amiable man, a tall native of Topeka with a quick smile and sparkling good looks. On this particular day, the amiability flashed when he wished Guidry luck, but then he had a few things he wanted to prove: that he was a better pitcher than Gabe Paul believed, a better pitcher this day even than Guidry, and that he could win a clutch game for the Red Sox, who traditionally failed to win clutch games. A tempered irony was at play in Fenway this bright October day. The racist Red Sox, the franchise that had spurned both Jackie Robinson and Willie Mays, was now placing its hopes and dreams in the hands of a Mexican-American. Were Robinson alive, he might have smiled.

Before moving to Boston, Torrez had started thirty-one games for the 1977 Yankees; to say he knew the Yankee team is understatement. A disconcerting side effect of free agency is the frequent shift of outstanding players from one contending ball club to another. At the very least this calls for a whole new set of signs and indicators. (The indicator, say a touch to the coach's left earlobe, precedes the signs. Without the indicator, no sign, arm to uniform letters, hands clapped twice, means anything.) The Yankees now could hardly use last year's signs or indicators; Torrez knew them all. Torrez also knew how the Yankees played, which hitters liked which pitches, and he says that before the game he thought Mickey Rivers and Thurman Munson were the keys. Rivers, who liked to be called "Mick the Quick," was a fine base runner and although he weighed no more than 165 pounds, he had some power. He had hit eleven home runs. Grumpo Munson was one ferocious competitor. Considering the Yankee–Red Sox rivalry, most acknowledged that Munson was a fine ball player, "but overall he's not quite up there with Pudge Fisk." Munson thought that he was just as good as Bench and better than Fisk, and he didn't care much for either man.

The plague of injuries was passing but not done. Willie Randolph, the star second baseman Gabe Paul snookered away from Pittsburgh, had strained a hamstring. He couldn't play. Dwight Evans, the Sox's gifted right fielder, still suffered bouts of vertigo. He might pinch hit, but he couldn't play the field. Trying to grab a foul ball in the on-deck circle, Reggie Jackson had bruised a thumb. He could swing his bat as a designated hitter. Lou Piniella would start in right.

Some still talk about the weather. It was an apotheosis, by which I mean an exalted and glorified example, of New England Indian summer. The sunlight dazzled. The shadows looked stark, with knife-edge borders. A quartering wind blew out of right center field. "God, but the air was clear," Rich Gossage says. "One of those days, you know, that makes you glad to be breathing, to be alive."

Torrez began poorly, perhaps nervously, walking jittery Mickey Rivers on four pitches. The crowd, 32,925, sat quiet, silenced by the weight of the suspense, an entire season for two teams coming down to a single game. Munson hit second and Torrez intended to go after his last season's battery mate with low outside sliders, coming up and in with fast balls just enough to keep Munson from leaning over the plate. Torrez struck out Munson, but on the second pitch Rivers stole second, sliding in well ahead of Fisk's throw. Piniella bounced out to third. Torrez got two strikes on Jackson and then tried to throw a high fast ball past him. He must have forgotten either whom he was facing or what month this was. A pitcher trying to overpower Mr. October in the month of October can be acting out a death wish. Reggie drove the ball hard and high into left center field. The baseball soared above the Green Monster and even above the blue-and-white sign beyond the wall, fourteen feet distant, advertising Gilby's Gin. Then the winds of chance interceded. Wind slowed the ball and moved it toward the left-field line. At length it seemed to be tumbling straight down. What would have been a two-run homer on a windless day became an exciting out. Yastrzemski, within a year of his fortieth birthday, ran into the corner and made a splendid catch, digging hard, his back against the wall. Bob Lemon remembered thinking, "Damn, if Ted Williams was still playing left in here, we'd'a had a double for sure."

In the bottom of the first Guidry pitched like Guidry. He retired the Sox in order, striking out Rick Burleson and Jim Rice. Torrez moved strongly through the second and then Yastrzemski led off the Boston half. "Come on," some English majors from Harvard or maybe Tufts liked to shout when Yastrzemski came to bat. "Let's have a locomotive for Yastrzemski. Gimme a Y. Gimme an A. Gimme an S. Gimme a T. Gimme an... oh, the hell with it. We haven't got all day." But this was a quiet crowd and, appropriately for Rosh Hashanah, this was no afternoon for comedy. Guidry's second pitch to Yastrzemski was a fast ball that was supposed to drive into the hitter's thumbs. But Guidry missed. The pitch was up around the letters. Yastrzemski whacked a wicked line drive that hooked around the right-field foul pole. Home run. If Piniella was the best *slow* outfielder in the majors, and he presently would prove that he was, then Yastrzemski surely was the greatest *old* ball player of his time. The drive seemed to unsettle Guidry, or maybe it simply illustrated that his stuff, on short rest, was not the best. Fisk and Fred Lynn both hit hard drives that were caught deep in the outfield before Butch Hobson, the designated hitter, bounced out to end the inning.

The Yankees' first hit came with two out in the third. Mickey Rivers doubled to right. Munson was coming up, a .300 hitter in each of the three previous seasons and now batting .297. Torrez went with hard outside sliders and struck out Munson for a second time. An odd, indeed absurd, incident followed. Leading off the Boston third, George Scott drove a Guidry fast ball high and deep to center field. Rivers started back but couldn't get a vector on the baseball. He backed up with uncertain steps and the ball bounced near the bottom of the wall, a lead-off double for Scott that should have been caught. Rivers jogged in from center field, one hand raised to call time. He had forgotten his sunglasses. I thought of all the splendid baseball people on the Yankee side, Lemon and Berra and Michael and Clyde King, but here on a very bright day, none of the Yankee thinkers had checked out Rivers and said, "Hey! Dummy! You could get blinded out there. Don't go to center without your sunglasses." Was this going to be a saga decided by a mistake? One remembers Benjamin Franklin's musing, "A little neglect may breed great mischief... for want of a nail the shoe was lost; for want of a shoe the horse was lost; and for want of a horse the rider was lost." Now, for want of a pair of sunglasses... But no, this little neglect bred only comic relief, although it did make Guidry throw a few extra pitches. Rivers put on his shades and the Red Sox could not bring big George Scott home. One of the great Yankee traditions is capitalizing on opponents' mistakes, promptly and decisively, sniffing out weakness, as the great heavyweight boxing champions Jack Dempsey and Joe Louis always did. Presented with a gift, Zimmer had infielder Jack Brohamer bunt Scott to third. The runner was frozen there as Burleson bounced to Nettles. One out too late. Jerry Remy lifted a fly ball into medium-deep left center. These were the Red Sox, not Jack Dempsey, Joe Louis, or the Yankees.

Guidry did not have his best stuff and Torrez was at the top of his game. "Which made them about even," someone said. Rick Burleson opened the Boston sixth by lining a double to left. Remy bunted him to third. Being careful not to overswing, Rice slapped a single to center. The Sox led by two runs and they still were charging. Yastrzemski hit a tricky hopper to Chambliss that sent Rice to second. Guidry intentionally walked Fisk to get at the left-handed Fred Lynn and the next play, Don Zimmer insists to this day, decided the game.

"The way Fenway is built," Zimmer says, "you play your outfielders toward center, away from the foul lines. With Guidry pitching, you gave the hitters even more of the lines because he threw so hard. From the Red Sox dugout you can't actually see down the right-field line because a wall comes out and blocks your view. Now the count goes to three and two and Lynn cracks one, I mean a shot, down toward that right-field corner. I jump up and holler. I'm thinking both runners score. I'm thinking now we got 'em four to nothing. But I can't see. I can't actually see, and when the crowd made a sort of groan, I knew something happened that was bad."

Lou Piniella had moved from his usual position in right center and stationed himself some fifty feet closer to the foul line. He saw that Guidry's pitches were not overpowering and reasoned that against a subpar Guidry, Lynn would sharply pull the ball. "That kind of thinking," Zimmer says, "is why Piniella is a fine manager today." Lynn's liner hooked toward the right-field corner and the best slow outfielder in baseball ran down the ball and made an awkward, lunging basket catch. "Nobody plays me where Piniella did," Lynn said later. "What a gambler that guy is."

"Hey," Piniella said, "every time I come up, I guess on every pitch. Gambling is the way I play baseball, but you got to admit that I've done pretty good."

The Sox lead was still only two runs, not a safe margin in Fenway and not a safe margin anywhere against this Yankee team. When was it that the Sox moved ahead in the seventh game, and led 3 to 0 after five innings? Oh yes, in the 1975 World Series. Then Cincinnati came back and beat them in the ninth, 4 to 3. Here in the play-off there were now three runs that Boston might have scored, but did not. George Scott after the misplayed double and then the men on base when Lynn lashed his line drive. But the Yankees turned them back, solidly, brilliantly. The Boston lead was 2 to 0, not 5 to 0, and that would make all the difference.

Mike Torrez says he really had excellent stuff, a fast ball up at ninety-four miles an hour and a slider that snapped sharp and mean, down around the knees. "It was the slider mostly," he said, "when I struck out Munson three straight times. My slider kept him totally confused." With one out in the seventh, Chris Chambliss dumped an opposite-field single to left. Roy White singled to center and Chambliss took second. With the tying runs on base, Lemon sent the left-handed power hitter Jim Spencer to hit for Brian Doyle, who was filling in at second for Randolph. Torrez fired a fast ball and Spencer, swinging late, flied to Yastrzemski. Two out now. The hitter was Bucky Dent, batting .243, with only four home runs for the season. Trim, handsome Bucky Dent, who had spent so many years searching for his father, set his jaw and walked purposefully toward his date with baseball history.

He choked up on a Roy White model bat, light, only thirty-two ounces, and pumped some practice swings. He felt he could hit Torrez. "I got two good swings at him earlier. I got under the ball a bit, but they were good swings. I wasn't thinking home run, but I was thinking this: Hit the damn ball hard."

Pitching out of a stretch, Torrez fired a slider and Dent fouled the baseball into his left instep. He fell to the ground and Gene Monahan burst from the dugout, carrying a tin of ethyl chloride spray, which would freeze the bruise and temporarily stop the pain. While Monahan was working, Roy White wandered off first base and walked into short right field with first-base coach Gene Michael. "What do you think?" Michael said. "Unless he hangs a slider," White said, "I think we're dead."

Mickey Rivers, the Sunglass Kid, crouched on deck. Suddenly he noticed a small crack near the handle of Dent's bat. He went to the rack and handed another Roy White model to an eighteen-year-old batboy named Tony Sarandrea. "Give this to Bucky," Rivers said. "Tell him there are lots of hits in it."

During the delay for Dent's treatment, Torrez stood on the mound and waited. He didn't soft toss back and forth with Carlton Fisk, staying loose. Fisk kept looking into the Yankee dugout as if to see whether Lemon now would pinch hit for Dent. "I might have," Lemon said, "but then I woulda had to activate Michael to play short and Gene was forty years old. I'm kidding. You can't activate anybody in the middle of a game. I couldn't pinch hit for Dent because we were plumb outa infielders."

Dispute persists over the next pitch. Coaching first, Michael saw a hanging slider. Torrez maintains he threw a fast ball. He also says that during the delay, "I lost my rhythm." The pitch came in a little below the letters, near the center of the plate, not blazing fast, and Bucky Dent cracked it hard. As the day warms, the wind at Fenway starts to blow toward the fences, says Zimmer, who managed in Boston for five years. He also says that when Dent swung he thought, "There's a nice little pop to Yaz." Like Frank Duffy during the Boston Massacre, Zimmer had misjudged the ball. It was hit solidly, wind aside, and watching video replays you know from the instant bat meets ball that this will be at least a double and probably more. Yastrzemski retreated to the wall, turned to play the carom, and when the drive carried five feet over the wall and he realized that there would be no carom, his knees buckled. The Red Sox's club professional all but collapsed. Dent circled the bases briskly, poker-faced, but he was thinking, "I've dreamed about doing this since I was a little kid. And now I've done it. Damn. I've done it." Chambliss and White scored ahead of Dent. The homer gave the Yankees a 3-to-2 lead. Torrez walked Rivers for a second time and Zimmer hurried to the mound—the fans were hooting at him—and changed pitchers. "I don't know why he did that," Torrez says. "Munson was coming up and I owned Munson that day. He hadn't even reached me for a hard foul." Zimmer wanted Bob "Bigfoot" Stanley, a 6-foot-4-inch right-hander from Maine, who had won fifteen games and saved ten more that season. On Bigfoot's first pitch, Mickey Rivers stole second base again. This was great Yankee baseball. Press the other guys, pound them, and press them hard again. Munson doubled to left center and the Yankees led, 4 to 2.

Guidry struck out Butch Hobson in the Boston seventh, but George Scott singled to right. Lemon walked to the mound. He had Gossage and Lyle and Clay working in the bullpen. He wanted the Colorado Goose. Guidry hoped to stay in the game. "I can still get 'em," he said. Lemon shook his head. "You've done great, Meat." A touch of emotionalism had entered the manager's thinking. He did not want Ron Guidry to be the losing pitcher. The Red Sox had come back during the season and they well might come back today. The choke-up talk was nonsense. There was no quit in either of these teams. "I'd be damned if I'd let someone having as great a year as Ronnie Guidry end up being the losing pitcher in the most important game of the season," Lemon said. "When I gave the ball to Gossage, he was breathing like a locomotive.

Maybe I was too. These things do get a little intense, don't they?"
A pitch eluded Munson, letting Scott take second, but Gossage,
still breathing hard, struck out a pinch hitter, Bob Bailey, and got
Burleson on a ground ball to Dent.

Jackson led off the eighth inning with a high line-drive home
run, in the general direction of the Prudential Tower, that carried
four rows into the centerfield bleachers, 420 feet from where it first
took flight. "I wasn't thinking about the wind," Jackson says. "I
was determined not to think about the wind. I was just gonna hit
this one so hard that not even a hurricane could stop it. Which I
did." The Yankee lead was 5 to 2.

Gossage looked shaky. The pressure had seized him and he
may have been hyperventilating. Remy opened the Boston eighth
with a double to right. Rice flied out, but Yastrzemski singled to
center, knocking in his second run. Fisk singled and Lynn singled,
scoring Yastrzemski. The Sox were within a run. "My mind began
to drift," Gossage said. "I saw a lake in Colorado and I thought if I
got beat, I'd be out in the Rockies tomorrow. But I stopped that
quick. Very quick. I wasn't supposed to be thinking about fishing.
I was supposed to be saving the biggest game I'd ever pitched."
Gossage retired Hobson on a soft fly and struck out Scott.

The Yanks went quietly in the ninth, but the Sox came rum-
bling. Dwight Evans pinch hit and some Boston fans began to
grumble. Why hadn't Zimmer used Evans earlier, instead of Bob
Bailey? But Evans, still off his game, flied to left. Gossage walked
Burleson and Jerry Remy hit what the players call "a humpbacked
liner" to right. The ball would have been caught, except Piniella
lost it in the glaring late-afternoon sun. "I never saw the damn
thing," he says, "until it bounced about ten feet in front of me."
Piniella guilefully hid his confusion. He patted his glove a few
times and looked up as though he had the baseball all the way.
Then he stretched his arms and spread his legs and made himself

as big as he could be. He couldn't see the ball, but maybe he could block it, the way a hockey goalie blocks a puck. The ball bounced up and slammed into the glove at the end of Piniella's outstretched left arm. Great save! Great save! No goal! Piniella recovered and hurled the baseball toward third, making what he says was "probably the finest throw of my life." Burleson went to second, but no farther. Still, here in the bottom of the ninth, the segment of a game that allows no second chances, the Red Sox had the winning run on base.

Jim Rice cracked a hard drive into right center. The crowd erupted; some thought the ball was gone. Piniella tracked this one perfectly and caught it about twenty feet short of the wall. Burleson advanced to third base and now Yastrzemski, with two hits, two runs scored, and two runs batted in, marched to the plate. The game was on the line and Yaz was up. This was the fantasy that started Gossage perspiring the night before. The crowd was very loud. *Come on, Yaz. Come on, Yaz, baby. Oh, baby, if you ever hit one, hit one now.* This was no fantasy, Gossage thought, this was pretty...damn...terrifyingly *real.* He threw a fast ball. Low. He took two deep breaths. He would stay with the fast ball. That was his best pitch. He was going to live or die with the heater. He threw a beauty, the best he'd thrown all day. Munson later said the pitch "had an extra foot," meaning that it seemed to travel a shorter distance than the others, a testament to the magic of velocity.

Yastrzemski began his stroke up high. He wanted to punch the pitch to left and tie the score. Tie the score at the very least. At best hit a homer longer than the one that Dent had hit. The scorching fast ball bore down on the plate and then veered suddenly toward the handle of Yastrzemski's bat. He swung fiercely and lifted a soft pop fly above third base. A thumb hit.

Nettles looked up. The crowd sat silent. Gossage heard Nettles chirp, "Oh, no. Oh, no. Not me." The wind moved the pop into foul territory and Nettles caught it with apparent ease. "The toughest part of the play," he says, "was not fainting."

Now it was over. "Here are the totals for today's game," the public address announcer said. "New York five runs, eight hits, no errors. The Red Sox four runs, eleven hits, and no errors." That's all there was; there wasn't any more.

Some have called this play-off the greatest of all baseball games. That seems a little sweeping since, after all, none of us has seen every baseball game ever played. Some said this was the greatest pennant race of all time, although actually it was a race not for the pennant but for the right to play for the pennant in the American League Championship Series. But here was such great baseball that excess deserves forgiveness. That game and that season twenty-five years ago call to mind words composed once by Heywood Hale Broun. "Memories so keen," Broun observed, "that those of us old enough can weep, and those who are young can marvel at a world where baseball teams were the center of a love beyond the reach of intellect, and where baseball players were worshipped and hated with a fervor that made bubbles in the blood."

That's how he put it when he typed in his cabin beside the Sawkill Creek in Woodstock, sitting near the ambling water, carefully and uncomfortably perched on an upright stove-length log. (He believed that no one could create well when comfortable.) "The baseball, all of it, was a kind of music," Woodie Broun wrote, "and the singing will never be done."

▼

FINIS CORONET OPUS

J IM TUITE COMPOSED an eloquent, nuanced piece about the game for the *New York Times* News Service. Bucky Dent and the Yankees, he maintained, gave lie to Hemingway's observation [in *The Old Man and the Sea*] "that a man can be destroyed but not beaten. That may apply to the forces that work against old fishermen, but not the Yanks. They defeated the Red Sox *without* destroying them." Tuite himself had been defeated but not destroyed when ousted as sports editor of the *Times* a few years earlier. He remained on staff, an executive without portfolio, and when the strike of 1978 sidelined the regular reporting personnel, Tuite became the best man the *Times* could find to send to Boston. The *Times* took seriously its self-proclaimed role as newspaper of record and during the strike a skeleton staff of nonunion employees covered a few major stories each day and, in addition, abstracted the news. The *Times* couldn't print a daily paper without its pressmen and the other union workers, such as sportswriters, who were required to walk out "in sympathy," but it did continue to transmit wire-service stories and to publish microfilm editions so that records would remain reasonably complete. "The playoff story probably was my best effort," Tuite said, "and I wrote it for a readership of six librarians."

On that bright Yom Kippur afternoon, the Red Sox had played as great a ball game as a losing team can play, reaching a peak of professional accomplishment as they went down. That occurs rarely, but it does occur, playing your best baseball in a shattering defeat. It happened to the Jackie Robinson Dodgers in the World Series of 1952 and the result, according to one of my Brooklyn friends, was "heart-rendering."

Tuite, continuing his poignant prose for the *Times* News Service, mused about the gritty losing manager. "Now Don Zimmer can settle down," he wrote, "without worrying about his line-up against the Royals. Like Robert Browning he will seek 'a privacy, an obscure nook, to be forgotten even by God.'" (That turned out to be more poetry than truth. Zimmer remains a prominent baseball man in the twenty-first century, which I don't believe detracts from the writing of either Tuite or Browning.) After the play-off loss, Zimmer remembers weeping and then, while driving home to Florida, suddenly pulling his car onto the shoulder of an Interstate, stepping outside and howling upward, "Bucky...Fucking... Dent?" The skies, being heedless, made no reply.

Tim McCarver, the reformed catcher who has become a renowned baseball analyst, poses an interesting question. Which was the darker moment in the deeply shadowed history of the Red Sox, the Dent home run or Mookie Wilson's ground ball dribbling slowly between the legs of first baseman Bill Buckner and costing the Sox the 1986 World Series to a scrappy but not overwhelming team of New York Mets? Answering his own question with brio, McCarver says, "Dent's homer because Dent was a Yankee and losing a big game to the Yankees is the most terrible fate that can befall the Boston Red Sox on a ball field."

The Yankees moved on to Kansas City for the American League Championship Series and there, in the flat prairie country where Billy Martin had ranted, resigned, and wept, they split a pair with the Royals. (1978 was one vintage year for major-league managers' tears.) The Yankees then swept two at the Stadium, the second a 2-to-1 victory behind Guidry, that won the set, 3 games to 1, and with it the Yankees' third consecutive pennant. In the clubhouse, Reggie Jackson, wearing only a white towel and glittery gold chains, approached Lemon and said, "I want to tell you to your face that you are one hell of a manager."

"Thanks," Bob Lemon said, and for the first time in anyone's memory he blushed. Next Jackson vigorously shook hands with Munson. "I'm taking you to Abe's [a Manhattan restaurant Jackson favored] and you and I are really going to party. I want you to pick up the tab, Thurm, but if you don't, I will and if neither one of us can pay it, George will. How the hell is that?" Champagne flowed. The two broke into bubbly laughter. "Whee," wrote Dick Young. "The Thurman-Jax United." On the field against Kansas City, Jackson's results had been typical Mr. October: a .462 batting average with two homers and six runs batted in across four games. Baseball has not had another post-season performer who equals the Reggie Jackson of 1977 and '78. "He was," said Earl Weaver of Baltimore, "simply the best late-season hitter who ever lived."

During the Kansas City play-off, a contentious letter arrived in Al Rosen's office. The writer said that he was a Yankee fan and "a religious Jew," and felt seriously distressed to have observed Rosen sitting in that box at Fenway Park on Rosh Hashanah. He knew Rosen had gone to Fenway, the fan wrote, because he himself had seen him sitting there, seen him "clear as day" on television. Rosen's brief response was to the point. "I respect religion myself, but if you are as religious as you claim to be, what were you doing watching television on Rosh Hashanah?"

THE 1978 WORLD SERIES, matching the Yankees and the Dodgers, recalls a phrase cited by one of my predecessors at the *New York Herald*, Henry Morton Stanley, on finding Dr. David Livingstone. "Finis coronat opus," Stanley wrote in the *Herald* of August 10,

1872. *The end crowns the work.* As Reggie Jackson put it 106 years later, "We were good and we were confident. We really never had any doubt that we were going to win it all. That was how it just had to end up." The Dodgers were coming off their own rousing League Championship Series victory over the Philadelphia Phillies and Tommy Lasorda, a repeat pennant winner himself, was making confident, self-promoting noises. "When I nick myself shaving," he said more than once, "I bleed Dodger blue." He signed autographs to strangers, "You and the Dodgers are both great!" Some found him a dynamo. To others Lasorda was something else. Insufferable.

Steve Garvey had hit four homers in the four games against the Phils, prompting some California sportswriters to call him "The New Mr. October." But by the time the 1978 World Series ended, only one Mr. October was standing. Garvey hit .208 in the Series, with no home runs. He struck out seven times. All that prompted Ron Fimrite of *Sports Illustrated* to rename the Dodgers' amiable, square-jawed first baseman. In Fimrite's amusing prose, Garvey became "Mr. Late September." As Jackson himself might put it, there is only one Mr. October. Accept no substitutes.

Confident or not, the Yankees were never really in the first game, which Tommy John won for the Dodgers, 11 to 5. Jackson had batted in all the Yankee runs in the next game when he came up in the ninth inning with two out and runners on first and second. A twenty-one-year-old right-handed power pitcher, Bob Welch, was relieving for the Dodgers, who led, 4 to 3. The count went full and as Welch wound up, the runners broke. With two out and a full count it was an automatic hit and run. Trying to concentrate on Welch, Jackson suddenly, unwillingly, picked up Bucky Dent, sprinting from second. The distraction cost Jackson a tiny fraction of a second, but with a 95-mile-an-hour fast ball hurtling at you, even the blink of an eye can be terminal. Here on October 11 at Dodger Stadium, with the tying and winning runs on base, Mr.

October fell into an atypical imitation of Casey at the Bat. He swung and missed. Mighty Reggie had struck out. Furious, he stomped off the field and hurled his bat, which sailed close to Bob Lemon's head. Lemon chased Jackson down the corridor leading from the dugout, bumped him against the wall, and said, "I'm sick of bats coming close to my head. Cool down, dammit. You're not *that* good." Jackson's eyes welled with tears, and he cooled down. "It was as though I had offended my own father," Jackson says.

Guidry pitched game three back in the Bronx and the Yankees won, 5 to 1. This would be Guidry's final appearance of the year and it moved his record for all phases of the season to 27 and 3, a winning percentage of .900. The Yankees won thirty-two of the thirty-seven games Guidry started. One can certainly argue that the quiet Cajun, who played rhythm-and-blues drums to keep his wrists strong, had put together the best single year of any pitcher in the annals of the modern major leagues. (Charles "Ol Hoss" Radbourn won fifty-nine for the Providence Grays in 1884, but the rules were very different back then. Ol Hoss pitched, so to speak, in another country.)

The fourth game, the Dodgers' last dance, turned on an unusual play in the sixth inning that became known as "Reggie Jackson's Sacrifice Thigh." Reggie Smith had put the Dodgers ahead with a three-run homer in the fifth. When Jackson singled home Roy White with one out an inning later, the Dodger lead was trimmed to 3 to 1. Lou Piniella nubbed a soft line drive to Bill Russell, the Dodger shortstop, which Russell caught, then dropped. Russell ran to second base, forcing Jackson, who was standing halfway between first base and second, where he had stalled when it appeared Russell would make the catch. Jackson did not want to be doubled off first and end a promising inning. But now that the ball had bounced out of Russell's glove, he forced Jackson and threw on towards first to double Piniella, a slow runner. Jackson held his ground and Russell's throw glanced off his right hip.

Piniella was safe, Thurman Munson scored from second base, and the Yankees went on to win in ten innings, 4 to 3.

Lasorda led a caterwauling Dodger protest. The rule is clear and simple. A batter is out when a base runner deliberately moves into a throw. If runners were allowed to block throws with flailing arms or bumping hips or grinding thighs, the game would go chaotic. Just as a runner needs an unimpeded path, so does a throw. The Dodgers maintained that Jackson had moved into Bill Russell's throw. Not only Lasorda but such essentially courteous people as Tommy John and Steve Garvey raised their voices in screams and curses.

"Here's what happened," a shrill Bill Russell told the first-base umpire, one Frank Victor Pulli. "Piniella's line drive sank. That's why it bounced off my glove. I wasn't trying to drop it. When I picked it up, I instinctively stepped on second and threw on to first. Jackson moved into my throw. It was an illegal, cheating play on Jackson's part."

Pulli consulted with Joe Brinkman, the second-base umpire, but got no help. Brinkman said he had been staring at second to make sure Russell touched the base. Wouldn't his eyes have then followed Russell's throw? Brinkman insists that they did not. Pulli's final words sounded uncertain, but they were conclusive. "From my angle, I couldn't tell whether Reggie moved into the throw, but I saw the play as not intentional interference." Long afterwards sportswriters, noting the Bronx crowd of 56,445, wondered about intimidation. Would the play have been called *against* the Yankees if the teams had been meeting at Dodger Stadium? And, of course, no one knows. This may be a good time to recall three mordant lines from T. S. Eliot:

> *What might have been is an abstraction*
> *Remaining a perpetual possibility*
> *Only in a world of speculation.*

And one of Reggie Jackson's sentences as well: "I was just walking down the street and this baseball came up and bit me on the leg."

PRACTICALLY, THE 1978 World Series was done. After losing game
four, the Dodgers vented their anger on the media, most refusing
to be inteviewed by New York broadcasters and the area sportswriters who were not on strike. (Although the *Times* and the *Daily
News* still were out, the *New York Post* had resumed publishing.)
The Dodger players who said anything complained about the
quality of the Yankee Stadium playing surface, the presence of a
woman reporter in their dressing room, and the hostility of the
Yankees' home crowd. "I know this makes us seem like a bunch of
assholes," Bill Russell said, "but that's what playing in New York
does. It makes you an asshole." So much for Jackie Robinson, Lou
Gehrig, Christy Mathewson, and all the others who achieved nobility playing baseball in New York City.

Russell's remark infuriated the Yankees. He had attacked their
home field and their home fans and he had implicitly attacked
them. The next day they beat the Dodgers, 12 to 2, and they
clinched their second straight Series victory by winning the sixth
game in Los Angeles, 7 to 2. The stirring last act was a rematch between young Bob Welch and Jackson, who came to bat in the seventh inning with one man on base. Jackson was excited at getting
another chance at Welch. So were his teammates. "Time to pay
back the kid, Reggie," Nettles said. "Get him, Buck," Catfish
Hunter said.

Jackson loosened up, walked into the batter's box, and took
one swing. "What's the name of those mountains behind center
field at Dodger Stadium?" he asked me.

"The San Gabriel range," I said.

"That's where I hit Bob Welch's fast ball," Jackson said, and his
smile was a sunburst.

———

A SELECT MEDIA GROUP voted Bucky Dent Most Valuable Player of the 1978 World Series. Dent batted .417, 170 points above what would eventually be his career average, and batted in seven runs. Jackson hit .391, 129 points above what would be his career average, but representative of his standard of excellence during Yankee Octobers. Since Jackson hit two home runs and knocked in eight runs, the MVP competition should have been close. It wasn't. Dent became the unanimous choice of the nine people who voted. All were white.

Sorrow and disorder followed. On October 31, 1978, Bob Lemon's youngest son, Jerry, died of injuries suffered four days earlier when his Jeep overturned on Interstate 10, near Phoenix. The tragedy devastated Lemon and for the rest of his days, grief haunted this once ebullient man. After sixty-four games in 1979, he stepped down as Yankee manager. The team was in fourth place. "You could just tell," says Ron Guidry, a compassionate man, "that his heart wasn't in it any more." Lemon died in California on January 11, 2000, when he was seventy-nine.

On August 2, 1979, Thurman Munson, practice-landing his new twin-engine jet, undershot a runway at the Akron–Canton airport. The ensuing fiery crash took his life. Munson was thirty-two.

To continue the necrology, Dick Young, the godfather of in-your-face sportswriting, died at the age of sixty-nine on August 31, 1987. "My favorite kind of letter from a reader," Young told me once, "begins, 'Dear Sir, You cur.' But that doesn't even slow me," he continued with a broad grin. "I shoot off a telegram back to the reader that goes like this: 'Fuck you. Rude letter follows.'"

When Lemon stepped down in 1979, Billy Martin, of all curious characters, replaced him. Economic realities being what they were, neither Reggie Jackson nor Bucky Dent quit the team. But the Yankees stayed in fourth place, finishing thirteen-and-a-half games out, and that forced another Martin exit. In the years from 1975 through 1988 he would serve five separate stints as Yankee manager, and he got better and better at farewell scenes. But except for the 1977 team, no Yankee club managed by Martin won a World Series. Billy Martin died at sixty-one, when his pickup truck veered off an icy road near Fenton, New York, on Christmas Day, 1989. Not all the details have been clarified but alcohol played a role in the accident. Martin was not wearing a seatbelt. Metaphorically he never did.

Gabe Paul did not realize his final dream of building a championship team in Cleveland, but he remained cheerful and optimistic throughout a long, rich life. Paul died at the age of eighty-eight on April 26, 1998. "Baseball has lost a treasure," someone then wrote. Catfish Hunter contracted amyotrophic lateral sclerosis—Lou Gehrig's disease—in his late forties, and gradually lost control of his body. Before long he was unable to button his shirt. He died on September 9, 1999, a month after he had fallen and struck his head on a stone terrace. Hunter was fifty-three.

AS FOR THE YANKEE TEAM itself, the years following the great 1978 season were troubled. Rosen resigned in 1979 after telling me, "I'm afraid that if George shouts at me one more time, I'm going to flatten him. Then I'd be finished in baseball. You're simply not allowed to punch out your boss."

Rosen moved on to build a playoff team in Houston and a pennant-winner in San Francisco. He is now part of a baseball brain trust that Steinbrenner annually gathers in spring training. Mellowed a bit, this splendid warrior says, "The salient thing today is that I am grateful and always will be grateful to George for bringing me back into baseball."

After Jackson had an off year in 1981, Steinbrenner let him go to the California Angels. Playing in Anaheim during 1982, Jackson led the American League in home runs. Steinbrenner has since conceded, "Losing Reggie was a mistake." Steinbrenner thought he was acquiring a second Jackson when he signed the powerful free agent Dave Winfield in 1981. But during the World Series that fall, which the Yankees lost to the Dodgers, Winfield batted twenty-two times and collected one hit, a single. His World Series batting average came in at .045. "We've had Mr. October," Steinbrenner told more than one reporter. "Now I seem to have acquired Mr. May." Many laughed. Winfield did not. When at length he was elected to the Hall of Fame, Winfield chose to enter not as a Yankee but as a San Diego Padre.

FOR MOST OF THE 1980s and early 1990s, Yankee teams staggered about, finishing fifth four times and once as low as seventh. To their fans this sounded a disquieting echo of the dreary CBS days. Rescue came with certain front-office moves and the hiring of Buck Showalter, who managed the Yankees to the top of the American League East in 1994 when a strike stopped baseball. It was the closest the team had come to a pennant in thirteen years. When Steinbrenner replaced Showalter with Joe Torre after the 1995 season, media people fired volleys of derision. Someone called Torre "Clueless Joe." Ian O'Connor's words in the sports section of the *Daily News* were particularly harsh. Commenting on Torre's first press conference, in which the new arrival spoke respectfully of Steinbrenner, O'Connor wrote, "It is always a sad occasion when a man becomes a muppet." Torre then managed the Yankees to a World Championship in his first season, and to three more in the next four years. He is without question the most successful Yankee manager since Casey Stengel won those five consecutive World Series in the middle of the twentieth century.

THE NEWSPAPER STRIKE, so significant to the '78 Yankee season, ran for eighty-eight days. Rupert Murdoch's *Post* broke ranks with the *Times,* and the *News* and resumed printing on October 5.

The other papers did not settle with the unions for another month. In all the *News* was said to have lost $75 million, the *Times* $65 million, and the *Post* $10 million, making up most of its early losses during the month when it published, and sold advertising space, without major competition. Under a new contract, the publishers were allowed to reduce the number of pressmen they employed, but only through death, retirement, resignation, or discharge with cause. The union, which had not sought to gain sweeping change, mostly succeeded in achieving job security for its members.

THE ISSUE OF WOMEN in major-league clubhouses has essentially become moot. When I was asked to speak at an American Press Institute Forum on sports journalism five years ago, I was pleased to note that the attendees included no fewer than five women sports editors. I've always regarded the question of women interviewing naked athletes as a catchy sideshow. Do male reporters enter locker rooms used in the Women's National Basketball Association or by the Cornell women's field hockey team? Those are not questions on which the future of the republic depends. Melissa Ludtke deserves recognition for her pioneering suit, which in practice went beyond the issue of nudity and brought an overdue focus on widespread policies that had barred women from working in sports sections. Ludtke's own career as a baseball writer turned out to be a brevity. In its April 9, 1979 issue, *The New Yorker* published an article called "The Sporting Scene (Women Reporters)" which tried to summarize the dressing-room situation. The writer, Roger Angell, interviewed a number of sportswriters, and had Ludtke uttering this self-destructive quote: "I think I was a symbol for Time, Inc. More than fifty percent of the employees there are women and some of them filed a complaint against discrimination with the New York Division of Human Rights. It was settled by agreement and my suit was the most convenient way for Time, Inc. to show its support for women. But the basic workings of my magazine haven't changed very much." As Billy Martin lost his job for citing his employer as a felon, Melissa Ludtke lost hers for suggesting that her employers were chauvinist. She was yanked from her showy spot at *Sports Illustrated* and exiled into the obscurity of one of *Time* magazine's bureaus. When last I heard, she had become a free lance, which she always was at heart, and had begun writing a book about single motherhood.

I WOULD BE REMISS not to point out differences between the 1978 Yankees and the Yankees of today. I undertook some research for this book during spring training 2000, basing myself in the Radisson Bay Harbor Hotel in Tampa, a short drive from Legends Field, where the team plays its home exhibition games. "But don't think it's like it used to be," said Arthur Richman, Steinbrenner's "senior advisor on media relations."

"What do you mean, Artie?"

"There's nobody at the hotel."

In the 1970s, when player salaries were a small fraction of what they have become, the spring training hotel was a ball club's headquarters. The athletes, the manager, the coaches, and most media people lived in one hotel, The Galt Ocean Mile, when the Yankees trained at Fort Lauderdale. You then would see players in the lobby, in the dining room, in the bars, and sometimes with their families at poolside. It was easy for reporters to strike up casual conversations. No longer. Today's ball players earn millions of dollars and they rent houses or condominiums, often near golf courses. They don't come together at a common residence, the sort of superdormitory that was the old baseball hotel. Now they come together at the ball park, where media people find much of the space off limits.

The room where Yankee coaches dress is closed to reporters. Joe Torre spends forty-five minutes a day sitting in the dugout with sportswriters. Journalists wanting further talk in Torre's office are directed to make an appointment through the publicity staff. In spring training, as during the regular season, clubhouses now include a series of lounges from which media people are barred. The trainer's room, so vital to a reporter's ascertaining the extent of an injury, is off limits. Steinbrenner, once the most open of club owners, now walls himself off from the media behind a prominent New York public relations company.

The players, at least when I was there, seemed to look through the sportswriters unless a specific interview was scheduled. The old open bantering that made a clubhouse fun to cover was nonexistent. "Most of them just don't care about us," one bright reporter said, asking that I not mention her name. "I don't know whether it's the money or what, but they feel they're above us. There's only one Yankee who when I sit down and talk with him cares anything at all about me or about my life. That's Bernie Williams. With the rest, it's 'I gotta play golf. How long will this take? Good-bye.'"

The media pretty much overwhelmed the Yankees in 1978 and today the Yankees have established systems to prevent that from happening again. This approach, managing the news, is old stuff in Hollywood and politics, but it is relatively new in baseball. "We *have* to do these things," a veteran baseball executive told me (another person asking that I not use his name). "The way today's press looks for scandal and sex, even when there isn't any there, we're forced to close a lot of doors. I don't personally like it, but media today gives us no choice."

Happily, there were no closed doors for me when I went about talking with the great Yankee characters of the 1970s, Gossage and Guidry, Bucky and Reggie, Willie Randolph, Nettles, peerless Al Rosen, and the rest. I came away appreciating what they'd been through: blood, toil, tears, and sweat and, to amend the famous Churchill phrase ... joy.

Here's to you, Bucky and Goose, Gator and Graig, Louie P. and Reggie Jax. Rest in peace, Woodie, Gabe, Catfish, and "Lem." And you, too, Thurman the Grump and Billy the Batty Battler. It was something, really something, having you fellers around.

—ROGER KAHN
Stone Ridge, N.Y.
Christmas, 2002

AN INFORMAL BIBLIOGRAPHY

▼

S OME LIKE TO DETAIL the various neuroses that afflicted the October Men. One neurosis that did not affect them was writer's
block. No fewer than seven of these extraordinary Yankees
have lent their name to collaborative books. Baseball ghosts have
never seen better times, before or since.

Balls by Graig Nettles and Peter Golenbock, G. P. Putnam's
Sons: 1984. The focus here is on a later season (1983), when the
Yankees finished third. Nettles is a witty fellow and that pretty
much carries the book.

The Bronx Zoo by Sparky Lyle and Peter Golenbock, Crown:
1979. An often funny, sometimes whiny, so-called diary. I say so-
called because two people composing a diary confuses me. Does
the principal sit at his night table after a stressful day, clutch his
beloved Waterman and then in the intimacy of his bedroom begin,
"Dear Diary and, uh, collaborator?"

Guidry by Ron Guidry and Peter Golenbock, Prentice-Hall:
1980. Pleasant and quiet, like the pitcher, and poignant in the pas-
sages about Guidry's retarded brother Travis.

Number One by Billy Martin and Peter Golenbock, Dell: 1980.
Unfiltered Martin, and thus strong stuff. As a chaser I'd recommend

a *Virgin* Mary or possibly one Prozac with half a glass of water. Don't look for Martin to list his blunders. Almost always—surprise!—the other feller was wrong.

The most commercially successful of the Golenbock–Yankee books was *The Bronx Zoo,* and after Lyle went to Philadelphia in 1980, the energetic writer and his agent, Jay Acton, proposed a second "diary," this time a view of life with the Phillies. A publisher was talking about a significant advance payment but before signing the check asked to meet Lyle, Golenbock, and the agent. "Everything is going good," Lyle told the publisher, "except the Phillies know about the other book, so none of the guys will talk to me." Acton said he never saw a publisher's six-figure-advance offer disappear so quickly.

Before his shocking early death, the Yankees' star catcher found time to work on *Thurman Munson* with Martin Appel (Coward, McCann, and Goeghegan: 1978). In it, Munson says that he wrote poetry while in high school. "I don't mean 'Casey at the Bat,' either. I'd write about children or God or things that required some sensitivity. I'm rather proud of my efforts." Appel adds a touching epilogue.

Appel is also listed as "editorial assistant" in Bowie Kuhn's *Hardball: The Education of a Baseball Commissioner* (Times Books: 1987), a strong and straightforward account of the game as Kuhn perceived it, covering characters as diverse as George Steinbrenner and Melissa Ludtke. Kuhn was, as he himself puts it, "stiff-necked" and "often starchy." In these pages he seems perfectly candid and so becomes sympathetic, if not quite cuddly.

Reggie Jackson broke into the hardcover world with *Reggie,* an autobiography written with Mike Lupica, the columnist for the *Daily News* (Villard: 1984.). Lupica writes nicely and the book is consistently entertaining, if not profound. Now in his fifties, Jackson feels he is ready to compose a book of greater depth. I hope he does.

Two solid newspapermen, Bill Madden and Moss Klein, collaborated on *Damned Yankees* (Warner Books: 1990), an accurate
and irreverent overview of the Yankees from 1977 through 1989,
concluding with some interesting lists. "All the Man's [Steinbren-
ner] PR Men"—there were ten during the relevant period. "Ron
Guidry's Catchers (1975–88)"—there were 25. "Billy Martin's
Ring Record"—the authors list eighteen fist fights between 1952
and 1988. Martin won all but four.

Madden returned to what Ring Lardner called "the lit'ry life"
when he collaborated with Don Zimmer on *Zim: A Baseball Life*
(Total Sports Publishing: 2000). Here you find Zimmer's view of
how and why the Red Sox lost the 1978 division championship.
(He still doesn't like Bill Lee.) One nice note: Some years afterward, when he became a Yankee coach, Zimmer rented a home
Bucky Dent owned in New Jersey. "Just what I needed," Zimmer
comments. "Everywhere in the place, on every wall, was all this
memorabilia, different pictures of that damn home run. I turned
every one around and left 'em that way for the rest of my stay."

Rich "Goose" Gossage was an intimidating pitcher but a thor-
oughly amiable man. Both aspects come through in *The Goose Is
Loose,* an autobiography with Russ Pate (Ballantine: 2000). A very
nice memoir.

I have saved for last the two most ambitious and complicated
books on the 1970s Yankees, both by Ed Linn: *Inside the Yankees:
The Championship Year* [1977] (Ballantine: 1978) and *Steinbrenner's Yankees: An Inside Account* (Holt, Rinehart and Winston:
1982). I admired Linn's work for many years, dating from his articles in *Sport* magazine during the 1950s. For both these books,
Linn developed valuable sources within the Yankee organization,
and his own insights, like his writing, are splendid. His distaste for
Steinbrenner dominates, but in the end of *Steinbrenner's Yankees*
there is a bit of mellowing, and some musing about the conclusion
of the great Reggie Jackson era. "You are now building a good, gray

Yankees," Linn writes to Steinbrenner, "filled with all those nice guys you could meet any Sunday morning in church. Is it possible that we are going to end up with a good, gray George Steinbrenner III?"

Not exactly, but we now have a calmer and more subdued Steinbrenner than most would have imagined possible. Linn realized as well as anyone that tranquility takes some of the fun out of baseball writing. "Say it ain't so, Boss," he concludes.

ACKNOWLEDGMENTS

WRITING A BOOK, as opposed to writing a screenplay, is an individual act, by which I mean you don't have actors, directors and producers, and their brothers-in-law, changing your words and massaging your points of view. It is also a solitary activity, best undertaken, at least for me, alone, in the quiet, behind closed doors. But that is not to say one works without help.

This my third book for Harcourt in about five years and I have been constantly buoyed by the support of two professional associates who have become friends: Robert N. Solomon, my attorney and agent, suffers writers, or anyway *this* writer, gladly. Under pressure he can quote from the Aeneid by rote, not a prerequisite for passing the bar examination. Dan Farley, the president of Harcourt, is a gentleman of culture who could have as easily excelled in academia as in publishing.

John Mattis provided speedy, accurate research help throughout my several years of labor, bringing to the job splendid baseball knowledge and many sharply focused insights. Quite simply, he is a treasure. David Rolston researched the 1978 New York newspaper strike and the wanderings of Melissa Ludtke after she was forced to leave *Sports Illustrated*. Moss Klein, of the *Newark-Star Ledger*, shared his old Yankee yearbooks and the clips of his Yankee stories across two years. I covered a little baseball with Moss' dad, the late Willie Klein, and I think Willie would be very proud of his son.

Linda Puskar, the Library/Media specialist for the Pelham, New York, school district, was field marshal for library services. Helping out were Susan Thaler and Nancy Testa of the Field Library in Peekskill, New York. From her eyrie in New Hampshire, Anne Lunt copy-edited the manuscript. From his bunker at the National Baseball Library in Cooperstown, Bill Francis checked the facts.

Two editors at Harcourt made significant contributions to the planning and execution of *October Men*. Walter Bode was on hand early and his successor, Andrea L. Schulz, later provided important, thoughtful, and intelligent suggestions and an intangible but essential element: enthusiasm.

Arthur Richman of George Steinbrenner's staff arranged interviews with Rich Gossage, Ron Guidry, Graig Nettles, Willie Randolph, and Don Zimmer. Clyde King, Gene Michael, Yogi Berra, and Al Rosen gave generously of their time. Clete Boyer and former Governor Brendan Byrne provided comments and support. Johnny Oates, a gracious man, was another valuable source. The two noble Romans in the Yankee Media Relations office, Rick Cerrone and Jason Zillo, were most helpful. I hope Reggie Jackson's great contribution to *October Men* is evident in the pages of the manuscript.

Bucky (Long Ball) Dent, then coaching for the Texas Rangers, shared his memories. When I asked what happened to the bat with which he smote the famous homer, Dent said, "Oh, a couple of weeks later a friend asked me if he could have it and I gave it to him." Dent paused and made a little sigh. "The other day a collector paid $64,000 for it." *Res ipsa loquitur,* to increase by one third the number of Latin words in the book. The thing speaks for itself.

My thanks to all.

That's all there is. There isn't any more.

INDEX

▼

Aaron, Hank, 131, 208
Alexander, Doyle, 119
Allen, Maury, 97
Alston, Walter, 269, 271–72
Amoros, Sandy, 329
Anderson, Dave, 180, 232
Anderson, George "Sparky," 119, 121
Angell, Roger, 139, 360
Appel, Marty, 88, 91, 142–43, 179–80
Astor, William Waldorf, 47
Autry, Gene, 87, 208
Avila, Bobby, 212, 306

Bailey, Bob, 319, 347
Baker, Frank, 5
Bando, Sal, 123, 131, 133, 219, 256
Barletto, Joseph F., 322
Barrow, Edward Grant, 44, 49, 52, 53, 65, 226–27
Barry, Jack, 5
Bartlome, Robert E., 75

Baseball Hall of Fame, 115, 142, 201, 217
Bauer, Hank, 105–6
Bavasi, E. J. "Buzzie," 269
Bavasi, Peter, 87
Beard, Gordon, 222
Bearden, Gene, 334
Beattie, Jim, 268, 327
Bench, Johnny, 118–22, 145, 158, 209, 340
Bender, Chief, 5
Berardino, Johnny, 250
Berra, Yogi, 6, 9, 11–12, 64, 65, 101, 102–3, 106, 114–17, 142, 143, 153, 174, 250, 315, 342
Beutel, Bill, 90
Bird, Doug, 163
Black, Joe, 100–101
Blair, Paul, 152, 242, 246, 316
Blomberg, Ron, 250–51
Blue, Vida, 131, 178–81, 256
Bonds, Barry, 116
Bonds, Bobby, 116, 222, 268
Bonham, Bill, 209

Boudreau, Lou, 13
Bouton, Jim, 258–59
Branca, Ralph, 13, 15–16, 282
Braun, Steve, 307
Brener, Steve, 188
Breslin, Jimmy, 258–59
Bressler, Raymond "Rube," 5
Brett, George, 291–92
Brinkman, Joe, 227–28, 355
Brohamer, Jack, 343
Broun, Heywood Hale "Woodie,"
    8–9, 145, 349
Brown, Joe David, 57–58
Brush, John, 42
Buckner, Bill, 351
Buoniconti, Nick, 253–54
Burke, Edmund, 296
Burke, Michael, 35, 62–69, 143,
    198, 228, 238–39, 284
Burleson, Rick, 275, 298, 327–29,
    341, 343, 347
Busch, August, 79
Bush, Joe, 7–8
Bush, George W., 87

Cady, Steve, 214
Caldwell, Mike, 336
Calley, Rusty, 89
Campanella, Roy, 14
Campanis, Al, 87
Campbell, Bill, 274–75
Campbell, Jim, 110
Campos, Jenny, 129–30
Cannon, Jimmy, 6, 249
Carbo, Bernie, 151
Carew, Rod, 109, 208, 214,
    281–82, 285
Carlton, Steve, 267
Carpenter, Ruly, 87
Carpentier, Georges, 47–48

Carter, Jimmy, 27, 169–70,
    222–23, 228
Cater, Danny, 198
Cerone, Rick, 231
Cey, Ron, 164–65
Chambliss, Chris, 123, 150, 163,
    167, 244, 246, 274, 283,
    328–31, 343, 344, 346
Chapman, Ray, 37–38
Chase, Hal, 36–37
Chass, Murray, 206, 214, 217–18,
    227, 301–2, 309, 323
Cherry, J. Carlton, 83, 86–88
Chesbro, Jack, 41–42
Chilcott, Steve, 129
Chiles, Eddie, 87
Christian, Linda, 111
Clark, Al, 243
Clark, Matthew E., Jr., 75
Clay, Ken, 243–44, 268, 326–27,
    346
Clemente, Roberto, 171
Clymer, Adam, 237
Cobb, Ty, 6–7, 142, 161, 162, 233,
    288
Coggins, Rich, 93
Cohn, Roy M., 30, 338–39
Coleman, Jerry, 100, 305
Collins, Eddie, 5
Collins, Joe, 102
Considine, Bob, 200
Contie, Leroy, Jr., 79
Cooke, Robert Barbour, 58
Corbett, Brad, 87, 110
Cosell, Howard, 218–19, 258–59
Cowen, Maurice, 158, 203, 280
Cox, Billy, 234
Cox, Bobby, 4, 207
Crane, Robert, 331
Creamer, Robert, 40–41
Criger, Lou, 42

Cronin, Joe, 110
Cronkite, Walter, 218
Crosley, Powell, 177
Crowley, Bill, 154
Crown, Lester, 68
Cunningham, Pat, 80, 81
Cy Young Award, 26, 182, 193,
    196–200, 202, 254, 311

Daley, Arthur, 249
Dark, Al, 14
Davis, Eric, 190
Davis, Ron, 263
Dean, Dizzy, 123
DeBusschere, Dave, 232
Deegan, Bill, 121
Dempsey, Rick, 227
Denkinger, Don, 257
Denson, John, 278
Dent, Bucky, 1, 31, 146–47, 151,
    153–55, 177, 184, 231, 246,
    285, 315, 328, 330, 344–48,
    350–51, 353, 357, 362
Devery, William S., 39, 41, 43
Dewey, Thomas E., 10
Dickey, Bill, 142
Dickey, Glenn, 130–31
DiMaggio, Joe, 6, 9, 11–12, 36,
    50–51, 53, 54, 59, 62, 65, 90,
    93, 99–100, 143, 164, 166–67,
    199–201, 208, 249–50, 314,
    315
Doby, Larry, 22, 212–13, 278,
    284–85, 298
Dooley, Lib, 46
Downey, Jack, 97–98
Doyle, Brian, 344
Drago, Dick, 275–76
Drebinger, John, 53–54, 59, 101
Dressen, Charlie, 15, 99–101

Duffy, Frank, 329–30, 345
Dugan, Joe, 45, 46
Duncan, Dave, 131
Duren, Ryne, 106–7
Durocher, Leo, 14, 99–100, 150,
    214, 235, 308–9
Durso, Joseph, 96, 115

Early, George M., 93
Eastwick, Rawley, 181–82, 193,
    201, 202, 210, 233, 243, 254,
    263, 280
Eckersley, Dennis, 210–11, 274,
    299, 312–13, 327–30, 332
Eckert, William D., 196–97
Edwards, Bruce, 54
Effrat, Louis, 174–75
Egan, David, 325
Ehrlichman, John Daniel, 76
Eisenhower, Dwight, 305
Elberfeld, Norman "Tabasco Kid,"
    41
Ellis, Doc, 116, 204–5, 219
Ellis, Joseph J., 144
Epstein, Ben, 19–20, 104
Epstein, Mike, 132, 133
Estrada, Augustin, 175–76
Evans, Dwight Michael "Dewey,"
    270, 275, 318, 325, 330, 340,
    347

Fairly, Ron, 267–68
Farrell, Frank, 39, 41, 43
Feeney, Chub, 96
Feller, Bob, 212–13
Figueroa, Ed, 116, 192–93, 202–3,
    211–12, 219, 224, 242, 253,
    263, 267–68, 280, 286, 298,
    301, 330–31

Fimrite, Ron, 160, 353
Fingers, Rollie, 123, 194
Finley, Charles O. "Charlie," 33, 77,
    83–86, 90, 91, 123–24, 129,
    131–32, 178–80, 185–86, 256
Fishel, Robert O., 88
Fisk, Carlton, 145, 270, 274, 279,
    285, 318, 325, 330, 340–42, 345
Fitzgerald, Ed, 287
Flanagan, Mike, 319, 336
Flood, Curt, 279
Ford, Betty, 232
Ford, Gerald, 169
Ford, Whitey, 34, 64, 65, 90, 95,
    104–6, 135, 144, 305–6, 315
Fosse, Ray, 132
Foster, George, 121
Fowler, Art, 159–60, 267–68, 270,
    273, 280–81, 291
Frazee, Harry, 44–46
Freedman, Andrew, 38, 69
Frick, Ford C., 10, 196, 216
Friedrich, Otto, 183
Froemming, Bruce, 121
Fugazy, William "Bill," 21, 224
Furillo, Carl, 9, 100–101, 270

Galloway, Randy, 110
Gamble, Oscar, 145–46
Garcia, Mike, 212–13
Garr, Ralph, 208
Garvey, Steve, 164–65, 282, 353,
    355
Gehrig, Lou, 36, 37, 50, 62, 65, 90,
    131, 143, 145, 173, 249, 263,
    313, 356
Gelb, Arthur, 248, 251
Gergen, Joe, 330
Gibson, Bob, 64, 267

Gilliam, Jim, 269
Goldin, Harrison, 228–30, 239
Goldwater, Barry, 58
Goldwater, Robert, 58
Golenbock, Peter, 182, 197–98
Goodman, Irv, 111–12
Gordon, Joe "Flash," 226–27
Gossage, Goose, 24, 25–27, 70,
    169, 178–79, 182, 184,
    192–95, 198–99, 201, 205–7,
    209–10, 214, 217, 219, 227–28,
    231–32, 236, 242, 243, 254,
    263, 274–75, 281–82, 291,
    293–94, 309–11, 320, 336–37,
    340, 346–49, 362
Graham, Frank, Jr., 59, 98
Graham, Frank, Sr., 3–4
Grant, M. Donald, 114–15,
    216–17
Greenberg, Hank, 44, 131
Grich, Bobby, 124–25
Griffey, Ken, Sr., 120, 121
Griffith, Cal, 109
Griffith, Clark, 41
Grote, Jerry, 217
Guidry, Ron, 23–25, 27–28, 70,
    138, 163, 165, 192–93, 202,
    216, 217, 222, 240–41, 256–57,
    262–63, 265–68, 275, 279,
    280, 281, 298, 311–13, 319,
    320, 328–29, 330, 333,
    335–39, 341–44, 346, 352,
    354, 357, 362
Gullett, Don, 177, 202, 233, 263,
    268, 280

Haas, Moose, 219
Haldeman, Harry Robins "Bob,"
    76

Hale, John, 257
Hall of Fame, 115, 142, 201, 217
Harrelson, Bud, 217
Harris, Mark, 309
Harris, Bucky, 58
Healy, Fran, 137, 144, 154, 163,
    241, 256
Hearst, William Randolph, 278
Heath, Mike, 256, 283, 285
Hecht, Henry, 296–97, 302, 309,
    322–23
Heilmann, Harry, 6–7
Herzog, Whitey, 161, 163, 185, 293
Hisle, Larry, 219
Hobson, Butch, 275, 299, 326,
    330, 342
Hodges, Gil, 14, 100–101, 114, 161,
    162, 269, 281, 291, 329
Holleran, Joseph, 52
Holmes, Larry, 175, 176
Holtzman, Ken, 116–17, 120, 138,
    192–93, 202–3, 214, 219,
    230–31, 233, 250–51, 253,
    263–64, 280
Hooton, Burt, 166, 167–68
Hornsby, Rogers, 289
Hough, Charlie, 168
Houk, Ralph, 93, 151
Howard, Elston, 116, 142, 153,
    163, 189, 292
Howsam, Robert, 179
Howser, Dick, 292, 307–8
Hoyt, LaMarr, 145
Hoyt, Waite, 45
Hrabosky, Al, 291–92
Huggins, Miller, 44, 45
Hunter, Bunker, 68
Hunter, Catfish, 23, 77–78, 82–92,
    120, 124, 133, 136, 138, 149,
    164, 177, 203–4, 209, 224, 227,
    231, 233, 234, 263, 280, 290,
    320, 326–27, 332, 334–35,
    356, 358
Hurdle, Clint, 244–45
Huston, Tillinghast L'Hommedieu
    "Cap," 43–45, 47

Iacocca, Lee, 21–22
Iorg, Garth, 231
Irvin, Monte, 14

Jackson, Martinez Clarence,
    127–28, 315–16
Jackson, Phil, 232
Jackson, Reggie, 16, 31, 36, 70, 83,
    89–90, 123–40, 201–4, 209,
    211, 213–14, 347, 352–58, 362
  background of, 1, 127–30
  joins the Yankees, 36, 123–27
  Lemon and, 320
  Martin and, 127, 152–60, 223–24,
    288–90, 293–301, 315–16
  on Oakland A's, 129–34, 179
  and the Reggie! Bar, 191, 214,
    220–22
  and Sport magazine, 133–39,
    144–45, 149–50, 171
  and Yankees' 1977 season,
    150–55, 157, 160–61, 163–68,
    221
  and Yankees' 1978 season, 24,
    171–73, 177, 179, 191, 219–22,
    226, 228, 231, 241–44, 246,
    254, 256, 267, 274–78, 283,
    285–91, 293, 294, 295,
    297–99, 301, 309–10, 313,
    316, 319, 320, 322–24, 327,
    329, 333, 339–40

Jacobson, Steve, 309
James, Arthur, 3–4
James, Bill, 5, 12
Jankowski, Gene, 218
Jaworski, Leon, 78
Jeter, Derek, 39
Jobe, Frank, 280
John, Tommy, 188, 353, 355
Johnson, Arnold, 60
Johnson, Byron Bancroft "Ban,"
    41–44
Johnson, Cliff, 26, 203, 224–25,
    231, 244, 294, 298
Johnstone, Jay, 274–75
Jones, Cleon, 113–15
Jordan, Michael, 232

Kaat, Jim, 109
Kahn, Roger, 187–88, 219–20
Kammayer, Bob, 294
Kapstein, Jerry, 27
Keeler, "Wee" Willie, 41
Keith, Larry, 148, 149, 263, 267,
    288–89
Kelley, Ray, 48–49
Kelly, Walt, 266
Kennedy, William J., Jr., 322
Kerr, Dickie, 299
Killebrew, Harmon, 109
King, Clyde, 270, 271–73, 320,
    326, 342
King, Martin Luther, Jr., 11,
    196–97
Kingman, Dave, 178, 181, 217
Kinsella, W. P., 18, 245
Kirshbaum, Larry, 190
Klein, Moss, 22–23, 141, 191–92,
    202, 207, 209, 234, 255,
    261–62, 280, 286, 309, 313,
    314, 318, 327

Kleinow, John "Red," 42
Klutts, Mickey, 209, 224–25
Kluttz, Clyde, 85, 87
Koch, Edward, 237–40
Koppett, Leonard, 176
Koufax, Sandy, 64, 82, 177, 196,
    240
Kroc, Ray, 87
Kucks, Johnny, 105–6
Kuhn, Bowie, 70, 79–81, 83–84,
    86, 119, 142, 179–80, 187,
    188–89, 196–97, 235, 276, 335
Kunkel, Bill, 243
Kush, Frank, 129
Kuzava, Bob, 101–2

Laird, Tom, 50
Lang, Jack, 295
Lansky, Meyer, 58
Lardner, John, 172, 250
Lasorda, Tommy, 168, 187–88,
    353, 355
Latham, Arlie, 12–13
Lee, Bill, 157, 210–11, 270, 299,
    331
Lemon, Chet, 221–22, 225,
    345–47
Lemon, Jerry, 357
Lemon, Bob, 22–26, 212–13, 221,
    271–72, 278–79, 288,
    300–301, 304, 306–23,
    325–26, 330–31, 333, 336,
    341, 342, 346, 352–54, 357
Lepkowski, Stanley, 75
Lieb, Fred, 48
Lindsay, John V., 66–67, 228,
    239–40
Linn, Ed, 20–21, 45, 46, 71, 80,
    252–53, 303, 317
Lockman, Whitey, 14–15

Logan, Johnny, 258
Lombardi, Vince, 129
Lopat, Eddie, 34
Lopes, Davey, 164–65
Luce, Claire Booth, 183–84
Luce, Henry, 182–83
Ludtke, Melissa, 169, 182–90, 299, 332, 360
Lupica, Mike, 126, 293, 310
Lyle, Sparky, 25–27, 70, 138, 153, 163, 182, 192–95, 197–202, 205, 210, 214, 220, 224, 230, 243, 254, 273, 280, 286, 290–91, 293, 295, 297–98, 310–11, 324, 336, 346
Lynn, Fred, 270, 298–99, 319, 328, 330, 342–44

Mack, Connie, 3, 4–5, 33, 179
MacPhail, Lee, 52, 143, 257, 300–301
MacPhail, Leland Stanford "Larry," 52–57, 71, 224, 257, 284
Maglie, Sal, 14, 272, 308
Manning, Gordon, 278
Mantle, Mickey, 17, 36, 64, 65, 70, 90, 93, 95, 103–6, 108, 132, 135, 139–40, 143–44, 164, 174, 208, 214, 219–20, 234, 271, 292, 305, 306, 315
Maris, Roger, 64, 164, 208, 219–20, 315
Marshall, Mike, 197
Martin, Billy, 16, 23, 29–30, 36, 59–60, 70, 94–113, 115–27, 129–30, 135, 138, 140–44, 176–77, 180–82, 226–28, 305, 309, 310, 312–16, 320, 351–52, 360

background of, 1, 97–98
as baseball player, 4, 19, 29, 95, 99–109, 191–92, 233–34
becomes Yankee manager, 94–97, 110–12
Berra and, 115–17
death of, 357
drinking problems, 19–20, 246, 271, 286–87, 302, 314, 333, 357
early manager positions, 110
Jackson and, 127, 152–60, 223–24, 288–90, 293–301, 315–16
management style of, 94–95, 148–49, 204–7, 213–14, 233–35, 268
press relations and, 117–18, 120, 153–54, 159–60
resignation from the Yankees, 22, 302–3
as scout, 109
Steinbrenner and, 95–97, 110–12, 113, 121–23, 154–57, 164, 176–77, 209–10, 236, 255–56, 259, 270–71, 273–75, 277, 282–86
and Yankees' 1977 season, 148–60, 163–64, 166, 170–71
and Yankees' 1978 season, 239–44, 246, 253–63, 268, 270–71, 273–75, 277, 280–84, 286–93, 301–2
Martin, Billy Joe, 262
Martin, Joan Salvini, 97
Mathewson, Christy, 3, 12–13, 38, 194, 252, 356
Matlack, Jon, 216–17
Mattson, Walter, 322
May, Carlos, 63
Mayberry, John, 231

Mayor's Trophy, 234
Mays, Carl, 37–38, 45
Mays, Willie, 13–14, 96, 131–32,
    208, 238, 242, 307, 308, 318,
    339
McCarthy, Joe, 49–50, 143
McCarver, Tim, 351
McCovey, Willie, 256
McDaniel, Lindy, 63, 177, 197
McDonald, John, 54–55
McDougald, Gil, 102, 329
McGarigle, Bob, 37–38
McGovern, George, 76
McGraw, John Joseph, 3–4, 7–9,
    38–39, 42–43, 46, 47, 60,
    99–100, 149, 160–61, 199, 224,
    235, 252, 263, 267–68, 316–17
McGuire, J. Basil, 52
McKay, Dave, 231
McNamara, John, 139
Meany, Tom, 56–57
Medich, Doc, 116, 177
Merola, Matt, 289
Merrill, Durwood, 293–94
Messer, Frank, 315
Messersmith, Andy, 78, 181–82,
    202–3, 208–10, 233, 254, 263,
    274, 279
Michael, Gene, 19, 167–68, 254,
    259–60, 293, 342, 345
Miller, Bob, 109
Miller, Frank, 194
Miller, Marvin, 230, 235, 264
Millones, Peter, 248
Mingori, Steve, 186
Minoso, Minnie, 185–87
Molitor, Paul, 219
Monahan, Gene, 337–38, 345
Monroe, Earl, 232
Morabito, Mickey, 302–3
Morgan, Joe, 118–20, 209

Moss, Dick, 83
Most Valuable Player, 131, 148, 318
Motley, Constance Baker, 189
Mueller, Don, 15
Munson, Thurman, 31, 63, 70, 82,
    87, 93, 121, 136–38, 141–46,
    173, 201–3, 224, 225, 226,
    230–31, 236, 243, 246, 257,
    266, 283, 285, 286, 291, 297,
    307–10, 326–29, 331, 333,
    334–35, 340–44, 346, 352,
    354–55, 357
  background of, 1, 143
  in Yankees' 1977 season,
    148–50, 152, 154–55, 163, 165
Murcer, Bobby, 273
Murdoch, Rupert, 6, 359
Murrow, Edward R., 218
Musial, Stan, 139–40, 161, 162,
    203, 208, 282
Mutrie, "Truthful Jim," 162

Narron, Jerry, 209
Nettles, Graig, 25, 31, 70, 81–82,
    92–93, 123, 124, 135–36, 155,
    163–64, 180, 209, 224–27,
    230–32, 262–63, 275–77, 281,
    283, 320, 330, 343, 348–49,
    362
Newcombe, Don, 15, 196
Newton, Doug, 200, 273, 314
New York Highlanders, 40–43
Nixon, Richard, 21, 39, 69–70,
    74–76, 78
North, Billy, 132
Norton, Ken, 175–76

Oates, Johnny, 165
O'Connor, Ian, 359

O'Connor, Richard, 146
Olderman, Murray, 133–34
Oliva, Tony, 109
O'Malley, Walter Francis, 61, 72, 77–78, 86, 96, 236, 248
O'Neill, Thomas "Tip," 75–76
Orr, Dave, 161, 162
Otis, Amos, 242–44, 293

Pafko, Andy, 100–101
Page, Joe, 54–56
Paige, Satchel, 240
Palermo, Steve, 257
Paley, William, 65–68
Palmer, Jim, 124, 193, 197, 267
Parent, Freddie, 42
Patek, Fred, 243
Patterson, Arthur "Red," 34, 58–59, 313–14
Paul, Gabe, 68–69, 80–82, 86–87, 94, 95, 110–11, 115, 123–25, 138–39, 145–46, 173, 180–82, 193–95, 212, 249, 312–13, 332, 339, 340, 357–58
    resignation from Yankees, 176–78
    sues Steinbrenner, 321
    and Yankees' 1977 season, 154–60, 164, 166
    and Yankees' 1978 season, 170–71
Pennock, Herb, 5, 45
Pepe, Phil, 225, 242
Perez, Tony, 120
Perry, Gaylord, 110
Peterson, Fritz, 63
Piniella, Lou, 4, 27, 31, 149, 155, 159, 160, 163, 177, 190–91, 231, 274, 281, 285, 297, 311–13, 316, 319–20, 324, 329, 330, 331, 334–35, 340–44, 347–48, 354–55
Plank, "Gettysburg Eddie," 5
Podres, Johnny, 331
Pope, Alexander, 139–40
Porter, Darrell, 242, 293
Power, Vic, 16–17
Prager, Joshua Harris, 12
Price, Jackie, 53
Proxmire, William, 237–39
Pulli, Frank Victor, 355
Putnam, Pat, 176

Quarry, Jerry, 175

Radbourn, Charles "Ol' Hoss," 3, 354
Randolph, Willie, 116, 138, 151, 155, 158, 163, 167, 177, 231, 285, 326, 327, 331, 340, 362
Raschi, Vic, 33–34
Rau, Doug, 203
Reed, Willis, 232
Reese, Harold "Pee Wee," 9, 10–11, 14, 15, 103, 173, 238, 269, 329
Rembar, Cy, 265
Remy, Jerry, 330, 343, 347
Rennie, Rud, 33–34
Revering, Dave, 179
Reynolds, Allie, 19, 33–34, 100, 226, 306
Rice, Grantland, 41–44
Rice, Jim, 151–52, 210, 211, 270, 274, 317–19, 326, 328–29, 341, 348
Richardson, Bobby, 64, 107
Richman, Arthur, 361

Rickey, Branch, 9–10, 54, 71, 150, 224, 252, 258–59, 288
Ritchie, Anne, 187–88
Ritter, Lawrence, 5, 36
Rivers, Mickey, 24, 116, 123, 136, 147, 224–25, 230, 242, 244, 253, 283, 286, 297, 311, 320, 324, 326, 331, 340–42, 345, 346
Rizzuto, Phil, 9, 53, 154, 241, 303, 315
Robinson, Brooks, 124
Robinson, Frank, 278
Robinson, Jackie, 9–12, 14–15, 90, 102–3, 118, 133, 171–72, 189, 203–4, 252, 258–59, 269, 278–79, 282, 292, 318, 339, 351, 356
Rodriguez, Alex, 39
Rodriguez, Aurelio, 275
Rollo, Pat, 19–20
Rose, Pete, 57, 86, 118–19, 121, 209
Rosen, Al, 22–23, 25, 28–30, 141–42, 221, 268, 270–71, 273, 283–90, 296, 300, 306, 309–10, 314, 333–35, 338–39, 352, 358, 362
    as baseball player, 13, 22, 173–75, 212–13, 227, 334
    fines Yankee players, 223–30
    joins Yankees, 175–76, 182
    Martin's resignation and, 302–3
    and Yankees' 1978 season, 178–81, 189–90, 199–201, 212–13, 246, 249–58, 261, 262
Rosenthal, Abe, 248, 251–52
Roth, Allen, 282
Roth, Mark, 49
Rudi, Joe, 123–25, 177
Rudolph, Dick "Lefty," 5, 6

Ruppert, Jacob "Jake," 32, 43–44, 47, 49–52, 199, 236, 284
Russell, Bill, 164–65, 354–56
Ruth, Babe, 7–9, 16, 35–36, 40–42, 45–49, 51, 62, 70, 90, 93, 96, 161, 162, 196, 208, 219–20, 222, 249, 263, 288, 305
Ryan, Frank, 71
Ryan, Nolan, 82, 193, 197, 217, 267
Ryan, Patricia, 183–84

Saigh, Fred, 79
Sain, Johnny, 102, 280
Sample, Billy, 205–7, 310
Samuel, Marsh, 74
Sapir, Eddie, 314
Sarandrea, Tony, 345
Schaap, Dick, 71
Schang, Wally, 45, 46
Schneider, Herman, 338
Schneider, Russell, 176
Scott, Everett, 45, 46
Scott, George, 151, 270, 275, 317, 325–26, 342–44, 346
Seaver, Tom, 209, 217, 258–59, 267
Seitz, Peter, 84
Selig, Allan "Bud," 87, 276, 298
Sheehy, Pete, 90, 94
Sheppard, Bob, 221, 315
Shore, Ernie, 46
Showalter, Buck, 359
Shula, Don, 253–54
Singleton, Ken, 217
Smith, Walter "Red," 16, 57, 80, 101–2, 115–16, 122, 139, 157, 216, 221–22, 248–49, 251–52, 273–74
Snider, Duke, 14, 101–2, 238, 269
Sosa, Elias, 167–68

Spahn, Warren, 85
Spencer, Jim, 181, 186, 224, 274, 344
Splittorff, Paul, 163, 290
Sports Illustrated, 182–84, 220, 263, 267, 305, 360
Sprowl, Bobby, 299, 330–31
Stallings, George, 4–5
Stanky, Eddie, 204
Stanley, Bob, 331, 346
Stanley, Fred "Chicken," 120, 148, 283
Staub, Rusty, 217
Stearns, John, 216
Steinbrenner, George Michael III, 1–2, 30, 36, 62, 115, 118, 133, 154–57, 176–82, 201–2, 205–7, 212, 237–38, 262, 309–10, 313–16, 321–23, 324, 337, 358–59, 361
  background of, 72–74
  federal grand jury indictment, 69–70, 74–76, 78–81
  as football coach, 73, 236
  Hunter and, 92–93
  Jackson and, 123–27, 148, 150–51
  management style of, 20–23, 27–28, 32–33, 58, 70–72, 81, 121–23, 146, 166, 179–82, 193–95, 198, 209, 213, 236, 254–56, 276–78, 282–86, 293–96, 311–12, 334–35
  Martin and, 95–97, 110–12, 113, 121–23, 154–57, 164, 176–77, 209–10, 236, 255–56, 259, 270–71, 273–75, 277, 286–88
  and Martin's resignation, 302–3
  Paul lawsuit and, 321
  purchase of Yankees, 35, 68–75
  and Yankees' 1978 season, 170–71, 217–20, 223–24, 229, 234, 236, 268, 270, 271, 273, 276, 277, 281, 283–86, 288–90, 293–96, 298–300, 302–3
Steinbrenner, Henry, 72
Stengel, Casey, 4, 7–9, 17, 19, 34, 35, 58–60, 64, 93, 96, 99–102, 106–7, 115, 122, 129, 149, 160, 191–92, 204, 249, 282, 305–6, 314, 336, 359
Stevenson, Alexandra, 233
Stevenson, Samantha, 232–33
Stoneham, Charles H., 47
Stoneham, Horace, 61
Stonsifer, Howard, 220
Stouffer, Vernon, 74
Sullivan, Neil, J., 66
Sulzberger, Arthur Ochs, 321–22
Sutter, Bruce, 194
Sutton, Don, 86–87, 165–66

Tallis, Cedric, 29, 180–82, 283–84, 289–90, 302
Tenace, Gene, 91
Thomas, Charles, 9–10
Thomasson, Gary, 274, 283, 285
Thomson, Bobby, 13–16, 282, 308
Tiant, Luis, 210–11, 331, 332
Tidrow, Dick, 23, 202, 243
Tilden, Bill, 8
Topping, Daniel R., 34–35, 52–53, 55–60, 64–65, 104–6
Toropov, Brandon, 70
Torre, Joseph Paul, 4, 157, 216, 234, 261, 359, 361
Torrez, Michael Augustine, 151–53, 163, 165, 166, 178, 211–12, 214, 299, 312, 326, 332, 335–36, 338–46
Tuite, Jim, 247–48, 350–51

Turner, Ted, 157
Tyler, George, 5
Tyson, Mike, 176

van Doorn, John, 248
Vaughn, Mo, 39
Vecchione, Joe, 248–49, 251–52
Veeck, Bill, 20–22, 44, 65, 71, 145,
    177, 182, 184–87, 208–9, 271,
    278–79, 298–301, 305
Vernon, Mickey, 29
Virdon, Bill, 93–94, 113, 151

Waits, Rick, 23, 332, 333
Walker, Dixie, 199, 288
Walker, Gary, 126
Walker, Fleet, 9
Ward, Robert, 134–37, 139,
    144–45
Washington, U. L., 293
Wathan, John, 293
Weaver, Earl, 82, 227–28, 233, 352
Webb, Del E., 34–35, 52–53,
    57–58, 60, 61, 64–65
Weiss, George, 52, 54–55, 58–60,
    65, 105, 106, 108–9
Weiss, Hazel, 55–56
Welch, Bob, 353, 356
Wendler, Harold, 240
Wertz, Vic, 212–13
Weyant, Helen, 52
White, Bill, 241
White, Frank, 243
White, Roy, 158, 224, 274, 285,
    327, 330, 344–46, 354
Wilhelm, Hoyt, 194, 201
Wilkins, Roger, 171–72
Williams, Bernie, 362
Williams, Dick, 93, 132, 271–72

Williams, Edward Bennett, 70,
    79–81
Williams, Ted, 139–40, 142, 161,
    208, 215–16, 252–53, 288, 318,
    341
Willis, Mike, 336
Wilson, Mookie, 351
Wilson, Willie, 293–94
Winfield, Dave, 358
Winkles, Bobby, 129
Wirz, Robert, 188–89
Wood, Wilbur, 220–21
Woodward, Stanley, 252, 272
World Series, 45, 49, 51, 53, 56, 57,
    64, 86, 92, 100, 104, 114–15,
    118, 121–22, 131, 140, 161–64,
    166, 171, 188, 357
Wright, Jim, 275, 327
Wynn, Early, 174, 212–13
Wynn, Jimmy, 153

Yankee Stadium, 47–49, 60–61,
    65, 66–67, 90, 116, 189,
    228–30, 237–38, 323
Yastrzemski, Carl, 151, 158, 270,
    279, 298–99, 325, 326, 328–30,
    336–37, 341–43, 346–48
Yeager, Steve, 165
Young, Cy, 196
Young, Dick, 117–18, 258–62, 287,
    295–96, 322–24, 352, 357
Young, Jimmy, 175

Zanon, Lorenz, 175
Zerilli, Joe, 58
Zimmer, Don, 31, 268–70,
    274–75, 299, 326–32, 343,
    345–47, 351
Zisk, Richie, 217